the X-MEN
MARVEL
12¢
11
MAY

12¢
THE INCREDIBLE
HULK
1
MAY
THE STRANGEST MAN OF ALL TIME!!
IS HE MAN OR MONSTER
OR...
IS HE BOTH
FANTASY AS YOU LIKE IT!

MARVEL MASTERWORKS

PRESENTS

THE X-MEN

VOLUME 7

REPRINTING
THE X-MEN NOS. 11–21

MARVEL MASTERWORKS

VOLUMES AVAILABLE

VOLUME 1: THE AMAZING SPIDER-MAN NOS. 1–10
& AMAZING FANTASY NO. 15

VOLUME 2: THE FANTASTIC FOUR NOS. 1–10

VOLUME 3: THE X-MEN NOS. 1–10   MAY 0 6 2015

VOLUME 4: THE AVENGERS NOS. 1–10

VOLUME 5: THE AMAZING SPIDER-MAN NOS. 11–20

VOLUME 6: THE FANTASTIC FOUR NOS. 11–20

VOLUME 7: THE X-MEN NOS. 11–21

THE X-MEN
Written by: Stan Lee (Issue Nos. 11-19), Roy Thomas (Issue Nos. 20, 21)
Penciled by: Jack Kirby (Issue No. 11), Werner Roth (as Jay Gavin) (Issue Nos. 18–21)
Breakdown Pencils by: Jack Kirby (Issue Nos. 12–17)
Finished Pencils by: Alex Toth (Issue No. 12) Werner Roth (as Jay Gavin) (Issue Nos. 13–17),
Colored by: Evelyn Stein
Inked by: Chic Stone (Issue No. 11), Vince Colletta (Issue Nos. 12, 14),
Joe Sinnott (Issue No. 13), Dick Ayers (Issue Nos. 15–21)
Lettered by: Art Simek (Issue Nos. 11, 15–21), Sam Rosen (Issue Nos. 12, 13, 14)
Art Restoration by: Phil Lord

CREDITS

Editor in Chief: Tom DeFalco
Special Projects Editor: Bob Budiansky
Editor: Craig Anderson
Assistant Editors: David Wohl, A.A. Perry, Susan Flaxman
Book Design: Lillian Lovitt
Logo Design: Ken Lopez
Dust Jacket Frame: Sandy Plunkett with Tom Palmer

MARVEL® MASTERWORKS VOLUME 7: THE X-MEN® Nos. 11-21. Copyright© 1965, 1966 and 1988 by Marvel Entertainment Group, Inc. All rights reserved. Published by Marvel Comics, a New World Company, 387 Park Avenue South, New York, N.Y. 10016.

PRINTED IN THE UNITED STATES OF AMERICA   ISBN 0-87135-482-9

MARVEL MASTERWORKS

CONTENTS

MARVEL MASTERWORKS

INTRODUCTION

BY STAN LEE

HEY, IT'S NICE TO HAVE ALL YOU MUTANT GROUPIES BACK FOR OUR SECOND BIG OUTING. I think we can promise you as many thrills and surprises as you found in the first volume.

Speaking of the first Masterworks Edition of THE X-MEN, that was where we met all the principal characters, both heroes and villains, who inhabited those early stories. But I myself didn't realize, until I started thumbing through issue numbers 11 to 21, how many startlingly new and unexpected characters had popped up in the next eleven episodes of the continuing chronicles of the world's most daring and dramatic team of mutant heroes.

To name just a few, you're about to meet the incredible air-walking Stranger; the seemingly unstoppable Juggernaut; the gigantic, mutant-hunting Sentinels; the mysterious youth known as The Mimic; plus great guest-starring stints by the flaming, high-flying Human Torch; the sightless Matt Murdock, better known to you as Daredevil; and of course most of your old favorites such as Lucifer, Magneto, The Toad, The Blob, Quicksilver and the Scarlet Witch.

But, as every X-ophile knows, there's far more to our merry little band of muties than who they meet and who they fight. One of the things that has made the X-Men such world-wide fantasy favorites is their own personal relationships, the flesh-and-blood problems and traumas they experience in their own day-to-day lives.

In the tales that follow, you'll learn much more about those compelling relationships. You'll find new evidence of the secret love that Scott Summers and Jean Grey have for each other. As for Professor Xavier, you'll have the chance to look back upon his past, to touch upon his personal life as you meet the brother who became his greatest enemy.

Additionally, you'll be able to welcome the advent of a new scriptwriter. By the time we had reached issue #20, the number of publications Marvel was producing had grown so enormously that I found it necessary to reluctantly give up the scripting chores and turn them over to another writer.

Luck was with me. At that time, Roy Thomas had joined our bullpen. Roy, who would later succeed me as Editor in Chief when I assumed new duties as publisher, was one of the most prolific and polished comic book writers I had met. More than that, he had a love for the characters and for the mythic world of Marvel itself. Yes, the day Roy Thomas joined our capricious little crew was a great day for me, for Marvel and for the continued success of the X-Men.

But other changes as well were aborning. The magnificently talented Jack Kirby had penciled the first eleven X-Men issues, and I would have loved it if he could have continued doing every one that followed. But the press of new assignments finally made it impossible for him to keep up the pace. So, he too had to eventually surrender the penciling chores.

Once again, luck was with us. Alex Toth, whose name had been legend in comics for many years, agreed to help out until we could select a permanent replacement. I think you'll find issue number 12, penciled by Awesome Alex, to be a totally different change of pace and one which has become a true collectors' item over the years.

Days later, as if it were planned, everything fell beautifully into place. I happened to run into an old friend, Werner Roth, who, many years earlier, had drawn many western and romance comics for us. Wonderful Werner was available at this time, and he proved to be a perfect choice to take over the penciling reins from King Kirby. For some reason, however, which is now lost in the shadowy annals of time, Werner signed his pages with the *nom de plume* Jay Gavin. But whether we think of him as Gavin or Roth, I'm betting you'll find his artwork fantastic.

You'll notice that the credits from issues twelve through seventeen read "Pencil Breakdowns by Jack Kirby" and "Finished Art Penciler Jay Gavin." This means that Jack did rough pencil layouts for those particular issues to help Werner familiarize himself with the X-Men style. Then, after number seventeen, Werner did the complete penciling job on his own.

And now, a point of interest for all you inking buffs. You probably remember noting, in the first volume of the X-Men Masterworks, that Peerless Paul Reinman inked issues one through five. Then, starting with number six, Cheerful Chic Stone took up the india ink cudgels. Well, here in the second volume, you'll find additional evidence of Chick's inking, plus the work of Valiant Vinnie Colletta, Joltin' Joe Sinnott and Dazzlin' Dick Ayers. You may find it interesting to compare their various individual styles and see how they impact upon the look of the penciling and the appearance of the characters from issue to issue.

Well, that about sums it up for now. There's nothing I can say that will be as meaningful as your reading of the yarns themselves. Besides, I've gotta hold something back for the next volume, right? Right!

Okay, hero. Let's take a deep breath and dive right in. There's a world of wonderment just ahead!

EXCELSIOR!

Stan

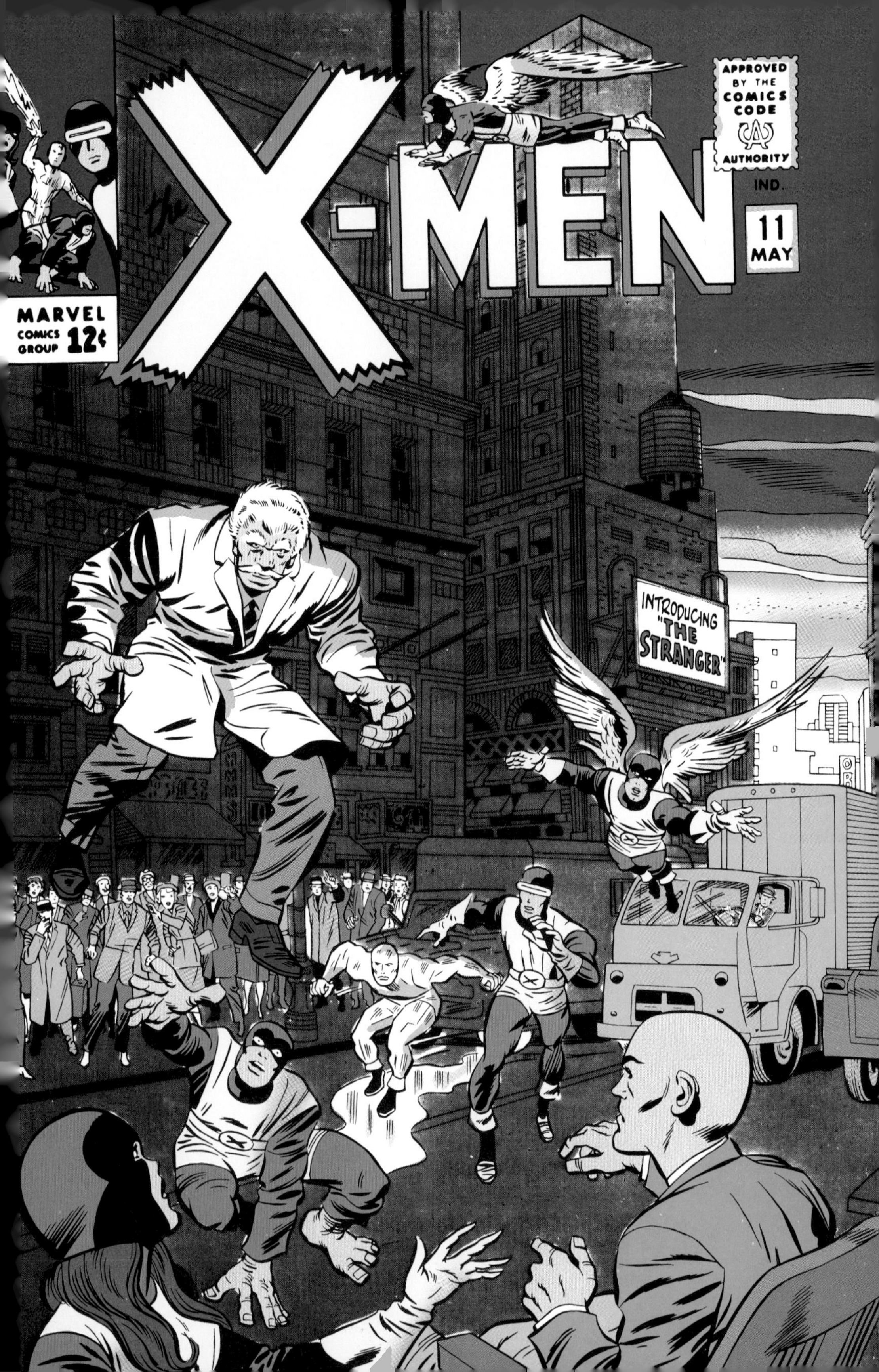
MARVEL COMICS GROUP 12¢
THE X-MEN
APPROVED BY THE COMICS CODE AUTHORITY
IND.
11 MAY
INTRODUCING "THE STRANGER"

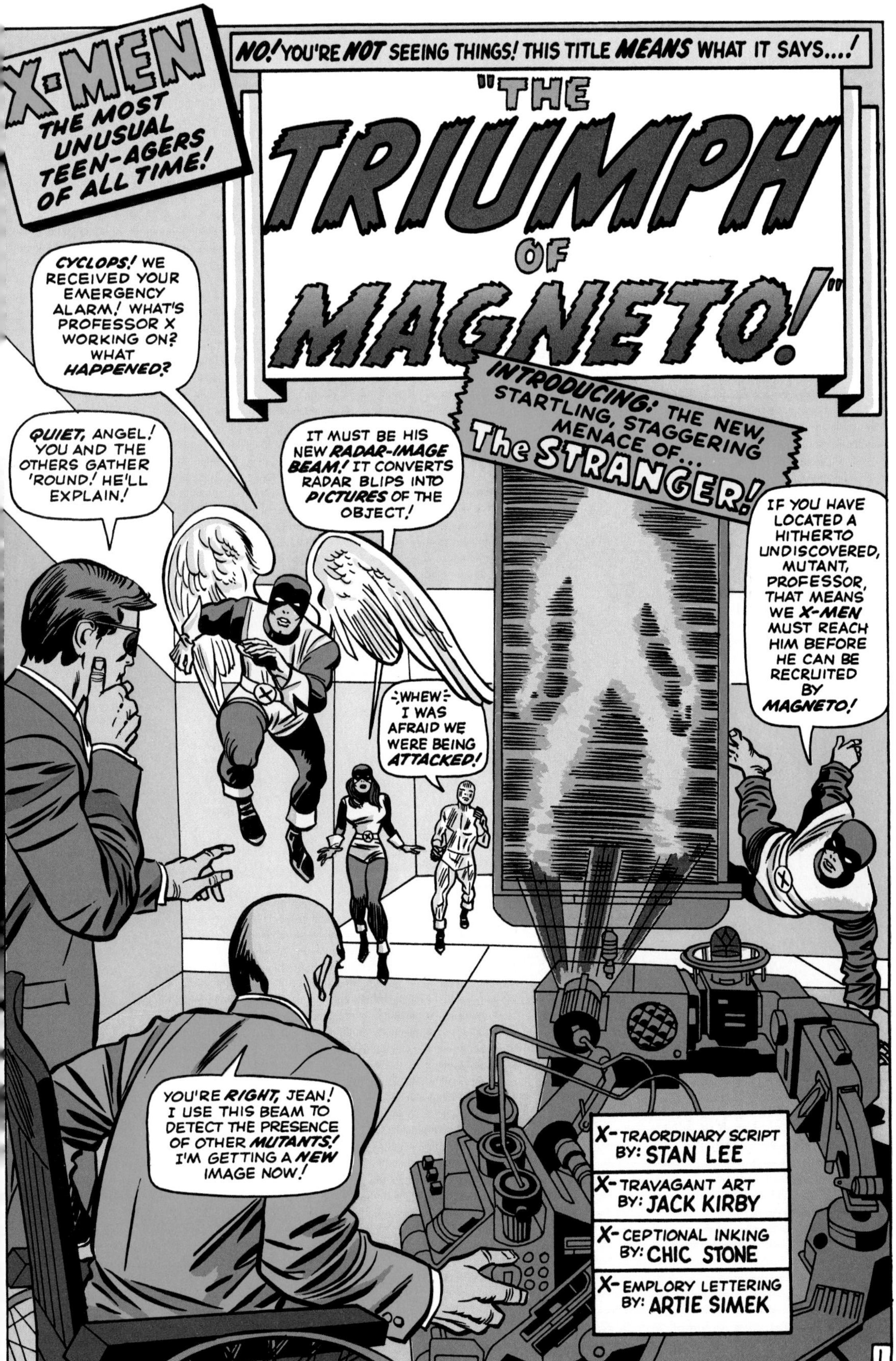

X-MEN
THE MOST UNUSUAL TEEN-AGERS OF ALL TIME!
NO! YOU'RE NOT SEEING THINGS! THIS TITLE MEANS WHAT IT SAYS....!
"THE TRIUMPH OF MAGNETO!"
INTRODUCING: THE NEW, STARTLING, STAGGERING MENACE OF... The STRANGER!
CYCLOPS! WE RECEIVED YOUR EMERGENCY ALARM! WHAT'S PROFESSOR X WORKING ON? WHAT HAPPENED?
QUIET, ANGEL! YOU AND THE OTHERS GATHER 'ROUND! HE'LL EXPLAIN!
IT MUST BE HIS NEW RADAR-IMAGE BEAM! IT CONVERTS RADAR BLIPS INTO PICTURES OF THE OBJECT!
IF YOU HAVE LOCATED A HITHERTO UNDISCOVERED, MUTANT, PROFESSOR, THAT MEANS WE X-MEN MUST REACH HIM BEFORE HE CAN BE RECRUITED BY MAGNETO!
WHEW I WAS AFRAID WE WERE BEING ATTACKED!
YOU'RE RIGHT, JEAN! I USE THIS BEAM TO DETECT THE PRESENCE OF OTHER MUTANTS! I'M GETTING A NEW IMAGE NOW!
X-TRAORDINARY SCRIPT BY: STAN LEE
X-TRAVAGANT ART BY: JACK KIRBY
X-CEPTIONAL INKING BY: CHIC STONE
X-EMPLORY LETTERING BY: ARTIE SIMEK
1

LOOK! THE IMAGE IS ABOUT TO TAKE **SHAPE!**

BUT, **WAIT...!** SOMETHING IS **HAPPENING!** WHAT WAS THAT **BLAST?**

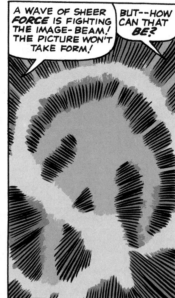

A WAVE OF SHEER **FORCE** IS FIGHTING THE IMAGE-BEAM! THE PICTURE WON'T TAKE FORM!

BUT--HOW CAN THAT **BE?**

LOOK OUT! SOMETHING HAS TO **GIVE!**

THE IMAGE **EXPLODED!** IT'S **GONE!**

DO YOU REALIZE WHAT THIS **MEANS?** SOMEWHERE WITHIN RANGE OF MY DETECTING DEVICES, A **SUPER-POWERED BEING** EXISTS! A BEING **SO** POWERFUL, THAT MY IMAGE BEAM WAS **SHATTERED** BEFORE IT COULD PROJECT HIS PICTURE!

THIS MEANS THAT WHOEVER--OR WHATEVER--HE MAY BE, HE'S PROBABLY THE MOST DANGEROUS MUTANT WE'VE EVER FACED!

THEN WHY ARE WE **PROCRASTINATING?** WE'VE HEARD THE CLARION CALL TO BATTLE! LET US SALLY FORTH AND SLAY SOME DRAGONS!

IF OUR ENEMIES COULD BE BEATEN BY **WORDS,** HANK, YOU COULD WIN EVERY FIGHT **SINGLE-HANDED!**

WORDS ALONE ARE NOT MY SOLE STOCK IN TRADE, YOU JOCULAR JUVENILE!

LET IT NEVER BE SAID THAT **THE BEAST** IS NOT A FIGHTER PAR EXCELLENCE!

WATCH ME TAKE THAT CLOWN **DOWN** A PEG, GANG!

SLURP!

-:**GADZOOKS!**:- WHO COATED THAT CORNER OF THE ROOM WITH **ICE?!!**

JUST THAT LITTLE OLD FROSTPOT --ME!

2

BETTER STOP OUR HIGH-FLYING FRIEND TELEKINET-CALLY, JEAN, BEFORE HE GOES SAILING THRU A *WALL!*

WILL DO, SCOTTY!

DESIST, FEMALE! THIS IS AN AFFRONT TO MY *DIGNITY!*

EVEN UPSIDE-DOWN YOU'RE A *MESS!*

LET HIM DOWN GENTLY, JEAN!

THAT WILL BE *ENOUGH* HORSE-PLAY, BOBBY--- AND *ALL* OF YOU! McCOY MIGHT HAVE BEEN *INJURED* BY YOUR PRANK!

I'LL ASK YOU TO CONSERVE YOUR TALENTS, AND ENERGIES, FOR MORE *IMPORTANT* WORK!

SORRY, SIR! I GUESS WE JUST GOT CARRIED AWAY!

BUT NOW, LET US TURN TO A SMALL FURNISHED ROOM, NOT FAR AWAY...

THIS ROOM SUITS MY PURPOSES! I SHALL *TAKE* IT!

I'VE RENTED ROOMS TO WEIRDOS BEFORE, BUT *THAT* ONE TAKES THE CAKE!

LOOK, CURLY, I'M GLAD YOU'RE SATISFIED, BUT I'LL EXPECT A FULL WEEK'S SCRATCH IN *ADVANCE!*

SCRATCH?

HOW SQUARE CAN YOU *BE?* YOU KNOW--CABBAGE, JACK, MOOLA, DOUGH--THE *RENT!!*

OH! YOU MEAN *MONEY!*

WELL NOW, AREN'T *YOU* THE BRIGHT BOY!

FORGIVE ME! I'M A *STRANGER* HERE--AND NOT YET FAMILIAR WITH YOUR IDIOMS OF SPEECH!

BUT IF *MONEY* IS WHAT YOU WANT...

HERE--TAKE WHAT YOU NEED! AND NOW, BE GOOD ENOUGH NEVER TO ENTER THIS ROOM AGAIN UNTIL I HAVE CHECKED OUT!

GOOD DAY TO YOU, MADAM!

3

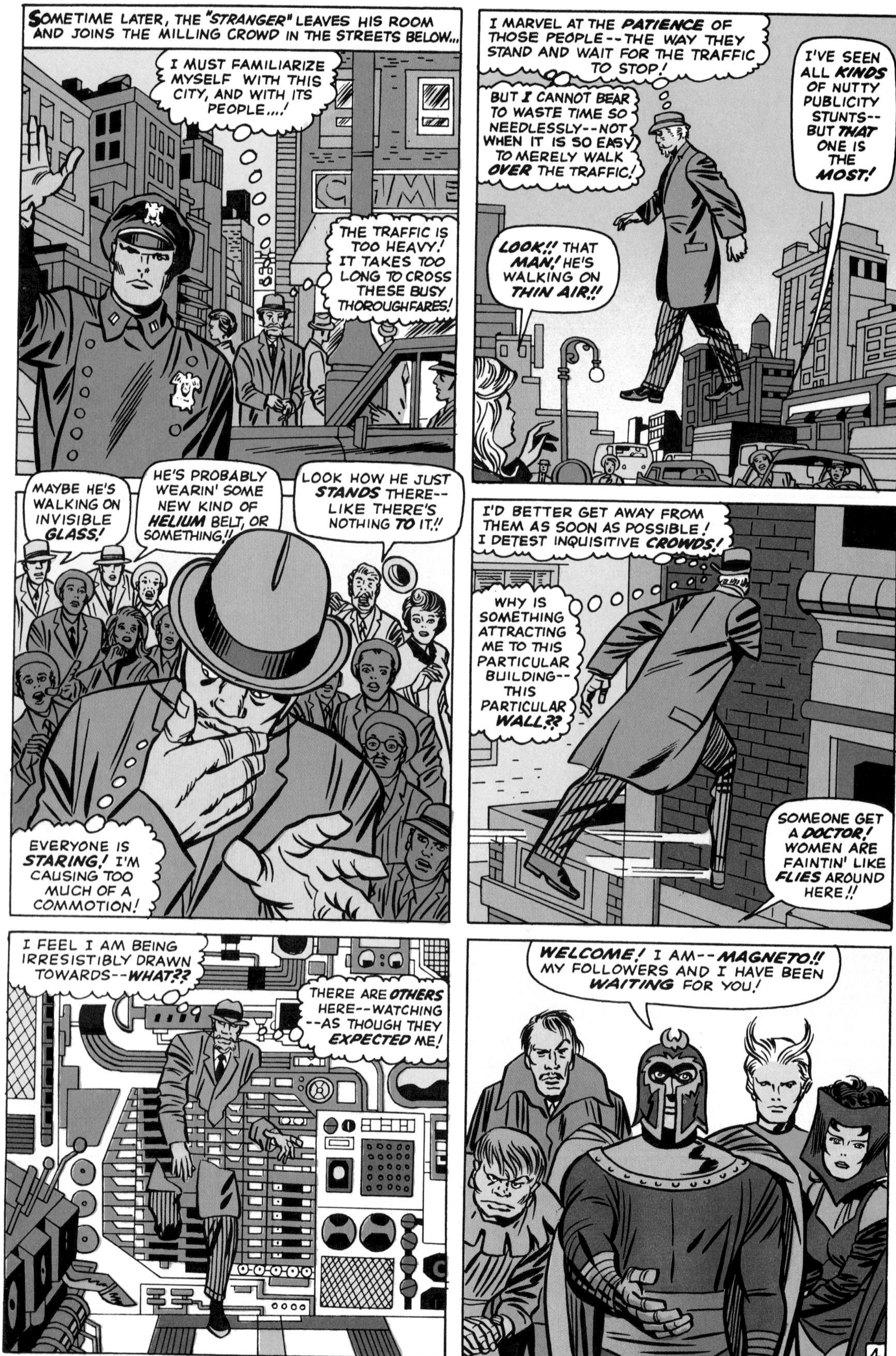
SOMETIME LATER, THE "STRANGER" LEAVES HIS ROOM AND JOINS THE MILLING CROWD IN THE STREETS BELOW...
I MUST FAMILIARIZE MYSELF WITH THIS CITY, AND WITH ITS PEOPLE...!
THE TRAFFIC IS TOO HEAVY! IT TAKES TOO LONG TO CROSS THESE BUSY THOROUGHFARES!
I MARVEL AT THE PATIENCE OF THOSE PEOPLE--THE WAY THEY STAND AND WAIT FOR THE TRAFFIC TO STOP!
BUT I CANNOT BEAR TO WASTE TIME SO NEEDLESSLY--NOT WHEN IT IS SO EASY TO MERELY WALK OVER THE TRAFFIC!
I'VE SEEN ALL KINDS OF NUTTY PUBLICITY STUNTS--BUT THAT ONE IS THE MOST!
LOOK!! THAT MAN! HE'S WALKING ON THIN AIR!!
MAYBE HE'S WALKING ON INVISIBLE GLASS!
HE'S PROBABLY WEARIN' SOME NEW KIND OF HELIUM BELT, OR SOMETHING!!
LOOK HOW HE JUST STANDS THERE--LIKE THERE'S NOTHING TO IT!!
EVERYONE IS STARING! I'M CAUSING TOO MUCH OF A COMMOTION!
I'D BETTER GET AWAY FROM THEM AS SOON AS POSSIBLE! I DETEST INQUISITIVE CROWDS!
WHY IS SOMETHING ATTRACTING ME TO THIS PARTICULAR BUILDING--THIS PARTICULAR WALL??
SOMEONE GET A DOCTOR! WOMEN ARE FAINTIN' LIKE FLIES AROUND HERE!!
I FEEL I AM BEING IRRESISTIBLY DRAWN TOWARDS--WHAT??
THERE ARE OTHERS HERE--WATCHING--AS THOUGH THEY EXPECTED ME!
WELCOME! I AM--MAGNETO!! MY FOLLOWERS AND I HAVE BEEN WAITING FOR YOU!
4

MEANWHILE, THE UNCANNY **X-MEN** HAVE BEGUN THEIR **OWN** SEARCH FOR THE SUPER-POWERED BEING WHOSE PRESENCE IN THE CITY HAD BEEN DETECTED BY PROFESSOR X --~!

HOLY COW!! WHO'S **THAT**??

FORGIVE ME FOR STARTLING YOU, BUT HAVE YOU SEEN ANYTHING **STRANGE** FROM YOUR VANTAGE POINT LATELY?

MISTER, I'M **LOOKIN'** AT THE STRANGEST THING I EVER SAW-- OR EVER **HOPE** TO SEE!!

I'VE CIRCLED OVER THE CITY **TWICE**-- AND STILL NO TRACE OF MY QUARRY!

IT'S A STRANGE FEELING TO SEARCH FOR SOMEONE WITHOUT KNOWING **WHOM** YOU'RE SEEKING,!!

I HOPE THE **OTHERS** ARE HAVING BETTER LUCK!

AND, SPEAKING OF "THE OTHERS"---

I TELL **YOU** OVER A DOZEN PEOPLE **SWORE** THEY SAW SOME JOKER WALKING ON AIR.!!

THAT'S OKAY! BUT WHAT ABOUT THEM SAYIN' HE WALKED RIGHT **THRU** A BUILDING WALL?

A **LEAD** AT LAST! IT MUST BE **HIM**!

CAN YOU **DESCRIBE** THE MAN YOU WERE REFERRING TO?

WHY ARE **YOU** SO INTERESTED, FELLA? WHO **ARE** YOU? NEVER SAW YOU AROUND THIS BEAT BEFORE.!

WHY THE DARK GLASSES ON A CLOUDY DAY LIKE THIS? WE'VE GOT ORDERS TO INVESTIGATE **ANYBODY** SUSPICIOUS!

LET'S HAVE A LOOK AT YOU WITHOUT THE CHEATERS, PAL!

NO! I **CAN'T** TAKE MY GLASSES OFF! DON'T **ASK** ME.! IT'S **IMPOSSIBLE!!** NO!

NOW **LOOK**, MISTER-- ALL WE WANNA DO IS SEE IF WE **RECOGNIZE** YOU FROM ANYWHERE!

AND, ONLY A GUY ON THE **LAM** WOULD BE SO SCARED OF REMOVING HIS GLASSES.!

NOW, C'MON --GET THOSE THINGS **OFF**!

5

7

OKAY, CHARLIE! I GOT HIS SPECS! NOW TAKE A LOOK AND-- WHAT'S THAT?!!

BACK! STAND BACK! KEEP AWAY FROM ME, IF YOU VALUE YOUR LIVES! I TRIED TO WARN YOU!

NOW I GOT IT! HE'S ONE OF THE X-MEN-- HE MUST BE THE MUTANT CALLED CYCLOPS!!

I'VE GOT TO GROPE FOR MY SPECIALLY TREATED GLASSES!! NO MATTER HOW TIGHTLY I KEEP MY EYES SHUT, SOME OF MY POWER RAY KEEPS GETTING THRU!

HIS EYES ARE LIKE LIVING DISINTEGRATOR BEAMS!! THEY SHATTER WHATEVER THAT RAY TOUCHES! NO WONDER HE WOULDN'T REMOVE HIS GLASSES!!

MY GUN!! HE ACCIDENTALLY HIT IT-- CUT THRU IT LIKE A KNIFE THRU BUTTER!! HE'S MORE DANGEROUS THAN THE ONE WE'RE LOOKING FOR!

BUT, A SPLIT-SECOND LATER...

AHH! I FOUND MY PROTECTIVE LENSES AT LAST! NOW TO-- WHA-??

THE BEAST!! YOU GOT ME IN THE NICK OF TIME, HANK!

I ASSUMED THAT THE MINIONS OF THE LAW HAD ENOUGH TO DO WITHOUT YOU ADDING TO THEIR BURDENS!

NOW HOLD TIGHT WHILE I BRING YOU TO JOIN ICEMAN!

HURRY, HANK! I THINK I HAVE A LEAD AS TO WHERE THE NEW MUTANT IS, AND WHAT HIS POWERS ARE!

LOOK AT THAT ICE CYLINDER UP AHEAD! IT MUST BE BOBBY'S!

WITHOUT A MOMENT'S HESITATION, THE TWO DARING X-MEN PLUMMET HEADLONG INTO THE TALL, HOLLOW TUBE OF ICE THAT HAS SUDDENLY SPOUTED UP IN FRONT OF THEM....!

HANG ON, SCOTTY! WE'RE TAKING THE PLUNGE!

6

I SEE THEM *BELOW*-- ICEMAN AND MARVEL GIRL-- STANDING BY!

AS SOON AS YOU LAND-- *DUCK*, SO I WON'T COME CRASHING DOWN ON *TOP* OF YOU, HANK!

NO DANGER OF *THAT*, SCOTTY! THE KID TURNED IT INTO A FLYING SLIDE!

OKAY, JEANIE GAL, YOU CAN SLOW US DOWN *TELEKINETICALLY* NOW!

I'LL DO MY *BEST*, HANK!

GOOD GIRL, JEAN! I WAS *WONDERING* WHAT WOULD SLOW US DOWN WHEN WE HIT *BOTTOM!*

SOMEHOW, WHEN *HE* SAYS "GOOD GIRL" IT'S BETTER THAN RICHARD CHAMBERLAIN SAYING "*MY DARLING!*"

BOBBY, EVER SINCE YOU STOPPED YOUR CHILDISH HI-JINKS, YOU'VE BECOME POSITIVELY *MASTERFUL* WITH YOUR ICE POWER!

THANKS, JEAN --BUT I'M NOT DONE *YET!*

ICEMAN, I'VE A GOOD IDEA WHERE OUR MUTANT *IS!* BUT I NEED A PLACE TO STAND *ABOVE* THE GROUND, WHERE I CAN STUDY THE NEARBY BUILDINGS!

I SORT OF *EXPECTED* THAT YOU'D ASK! IT'LL ONLY TAKE A *SEC!*

I'LL BUILD YOU A STAIR-WAY OF *ICE!* IT'LL GIVE YOU *COLD FEET*, BUT IT OUGHT TO DO THE TRICK!

AND, AT THAT MOMENT...

YOU WANT ME TO *JOIN* YOU? I DO NOT UNDERSTAND!

I AM A *STRANGER* HERE! WHO *ARE* YOU? *WHY* SHOULD I JOIN YOU?

WE'LL *SHOW* YOU!! *WATCH* --!

7

EVERY OBJECT IN THE ROOM-- FLYING INTO THE AIR--WRAPPING ITSELF ABOUT ME,!! AS THOUGH THEY ARE ALL LIVING THINGS,!!

THIS IS WHY YOU MUST JOIN US,!! BECAUSE I AM-- POWER,!! I SHALL ONE DAY REDUCE THE HUMAN RACE TO SLAVERY, SO THAT HOMO SUPERIOR CAN TAKE OVER! AND THOSE WHO SERVE ME, SHALL REAP THE REWARDS!

GOOD, MASTER! GOOD!

EACH OF US HAS A MUTANT POWER OF HIS OWN! IF MAGNETO IS DONE WITH YOU, MASTERMIND SHALL GIVE YOU A DEMONSTRATION....!

WITH A SINGLE GESTURE, MASTERMIND CREATES ONE OF HIS INCREDIBLE ILLUSIONS, AS "THE STRANGER" SEEMS TO FIND HIMSELF AT THE OCEAN'S BOTTOM....

WHAT HAPPENED?? WHERE AM I ??

SUDDENLY, THE ILLUSION CHANGES-- AND THE BEWILDERED STRANGER SEEMS TO FIND HIMSELF STANDING HELPLESSLY WITHIN A SEA OF SMOKY LAVA!

I HAVE SEEN ENOUGH! THEY MUST BE MADE TO REALIZE THAT I MAY NOT BE TOYED WITH IN SUCH A MANNER!

IT IS NOW TIME FOR ME TO GIVE AN EXAMPLE OF MY POWER-- POWER THAT NONE CAN EVEN SUSPECT!

8

IN ONE BRIEF MICRO-SECOND, MASTERMIND'S ILLUSION IS COMPLETELY DISPELLED, AS THE STRANGER EMITS A SUDDEN BLAST OF ENERGY THAT SEVERS HIS BONDS AND MAKES A SHAMBLES OF MAGNETO'S TEMPORARY HEADQUARTERS!

BUT, THE LARGEST PART OF HIS *RAGE* IS DIRECTED AGAINST *MASTERMIND*--!

A *RAY!!* TURNING MASTERMIND INTO A *SOLID BLOCK OF MATTER!*

AS SOLID MATTER, HIS WEIGHT IS SO GREATLY INCREASED THAT NOT EVEN THE BUILDING'S *FLOOR* CAN HOLD HIM!

MAGNETO! MAGNETO! SAVE US!

CRASH!

GOOD HEAVENS!! WHAT WAS *THAT??*

HELP! POLEEEEECE!

SOMETHING CAME CRASHING DOWN FROM THE CEILING--GOING THRU THE VERY *FLOOR!!* HELP --BEFORE WE'RE ALL *KILLED!*

DID YOU HEAR *THAT?!* IT CAME FROM THE AREA THE MAN WHO WALKED ON AIR WAS REPORTED IN!

WE'VE GOT TO REACH HIM BEFORE ANYONE *ELSE* DOES--ESPECIALLY *MAGNETO!!*

LET'S GO!

THIS MUST BE THE PLACE! SOME TREMENDOUS FORCE ACTUALLY SHATTERED THE BRICK WALL!

IT'S ONE OF THE *X-MEN!!* SOME GRAVE FANTASTIC *MENACE* MUST BE WAITING INSIDE!

MAGNETO!! SO, *YOU'RE* THE ONE RESPONSIBLE--!!

THE *ANGEL!!* YOU DARE ATTACK US ON OUR *HOME GROUNDS?!* *THIS* TIME YOU WILL SURELY TASTE DEFEAT!

MAYBE SO--BUT I'LL MAKE SURE THAT *YOU* TASTE IT *WITH* ME!

QUICKSILVER!! USE YOUR *SPEED* --STOP HIM!

UNHHH--!

GOOD WORK! YOU SMASHED INTO HIM BEFORE HE COULD THINK TO FLAP A WING! NOW--*FINISH HIM OFF!!*

10

12

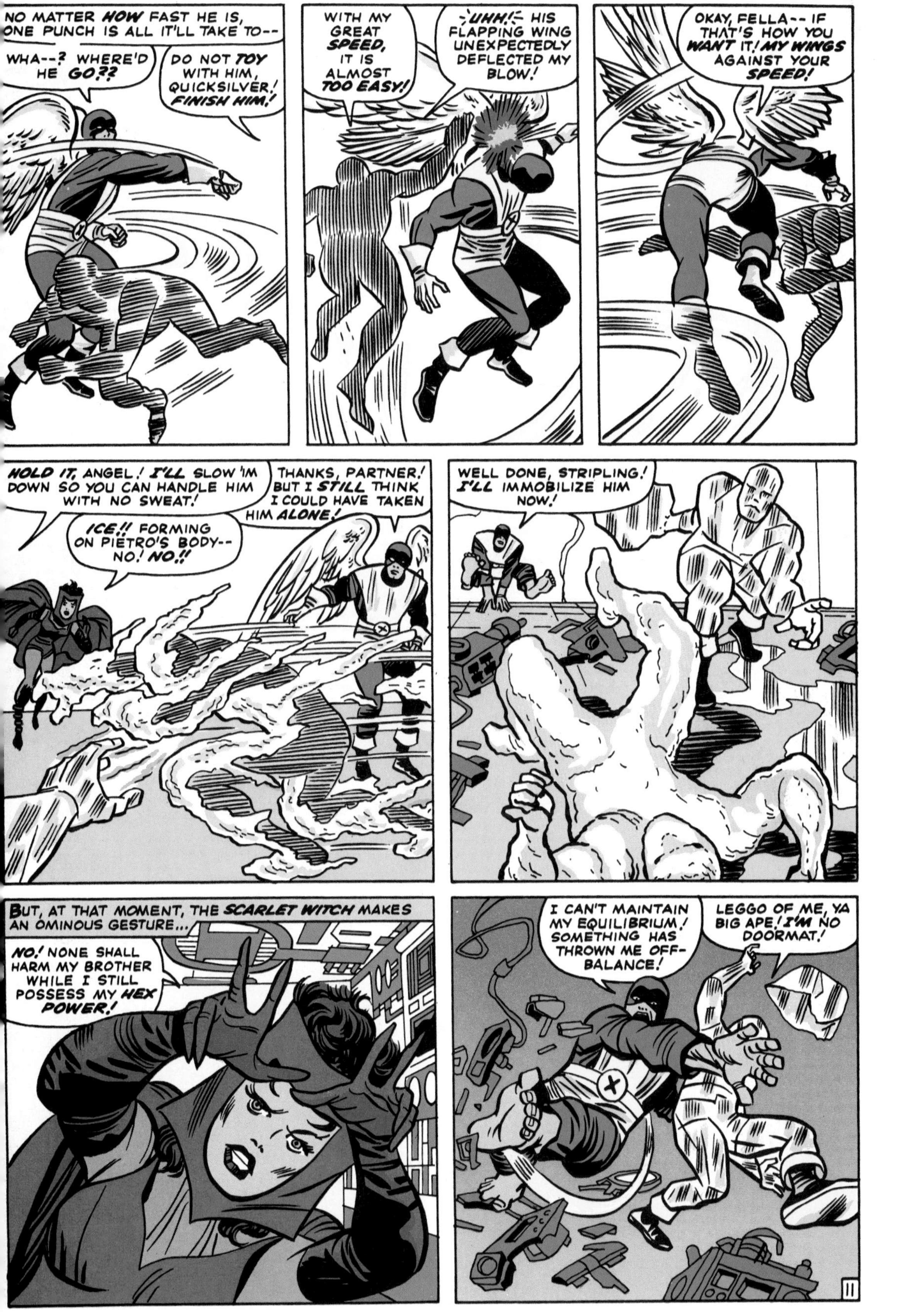
NO MATTER NOW FAST HE IS, ONE PUNCH IS ALL IT'LL TAKE TO--
WHA--? WHERE'D HE GO??
DO NOT TOY WITH HIM, QUICKSILVER! FINISH HIM!
WITH MY GREAT SPEED, IT IS ALMOST TOO EASY!
UHH! HIS FLAPPING WING UNEXPECTEDLY DEFLECTED MY BLOW!
OKAY, FELLA-- IF THAT'S HOW YOU WANT IT! MY WINGS AGAINST YOUR SPEED!
HOLD IT, ANGEL! I'LL SLOW 'IM DOWN SO YOU CAN HANDLE HIM WITH NO SWEAT!
THANKS, PARTNER! BUT I STILL THINK I COULD HAVE TAKEN HIM ALONE!
ICE!! FORMING ON PIETRO'S BODY-- NO! NO!!
WELL DONE, STRIPLING! I'LL IMMOBILIZE HIM NOW!
BUT, AT THAT MOMENT, THE SCARLET WITCH MAKES AN OMINOUS GESTURE...
NO! NONE SHALL HARM MY BROTHER WHILE I STILL POSSESS MY HEX POWER!
I CAN'T MAINTAIN MY EQUILIBRIUM! SOMETHING HAS THROWN ME OFF-BALANCE!
LEGGO OF ME, YA BIG APE! I'M NO DOORMAT!
11

MEANWHILE... I CAN'T *GET* AT MAGNETO! HE'S FORMED SOME SORT OF MAGNETIC SHIELD AROUND HIMSELF AND THAT *OTHER* CHARACTER!

MY MAGNETIC SHIELD WILL KEEP US SAFE!

I NEED NO SUCH SHIELD!

I SHALL NOW *DEPART*-- IN MY *OWN* MANNER!

NO! NOT *YET!* NOT TILL YOU VOW TO JOIN *ME!* I CANNOT PERMIT THE *X-MEN* TO GET YOU!

YOU MAY JOIN *ME,* IF YOU WISH! STEP INTO MY *CONE OF ENERGY!*

MASTER, *WAIT!!* WAIT FOR THE *TOAD!*

MAGNETO *VANISHED!!* AND NOW--THE *TOAD* IS DISAPPEARING--!!

I HEAR A SOUND--LIKE THE RUSHING OF A MIGHTY AIR CURRENT--TOWARDS THE WALL--BUT, I CAN'T *SEE* ANYTHING!

THEY'VE *GONE!!* BUT--*WHERE??* HOW??

SECONDS LATER, THE INVISIBLE CONE OF ENERGY WHIRLS PAST *CYCLOPS* AND *MARVEL GIRL,* COMPLETELY UNNOTICED.

STAY *BEHIND* ME, JEAN! WHATEVER IS AWAITING US UP THERE--LET *ME* FACE IT FIRST!

THIS IS THE PLACE!! *ANGEL*--ARE YOU THERE? WHAT *HAPPENED?*

CAREFUL, SCOTT! SOME TERRIBLE *POWER* MUST HAVE BEEN UNLEASHED IN THERE!

AND, IF ANYTHING *HAPPENED* TO YOU, MY *DARLING,* I COULDN'T *BEAR* IT!

12

THEN, SUDDENLY-- CYCLOPS SEES--

THE *SCARLET WITCH* IS HEXING THE ENTIRE *CEILING* DOWN ON ME.!!

GOOD WORK, PARTNER! BUT, YOU CAN'T KEEP THAT UP FOREVER!

SHUT YOUR EYES, X-MAN!

IT WILL BE A *PLEASURE* TO OBLIGE!

THIS WILL TAKE CARE OF THAT USELESS DEBRIS-- AND THEN WE CAN GET ON WITH THE BUSINESS AT HAND!

MY COMPLIMENTS, CYKE! HOW DOES IT FEEL TO BE A HUMAN GARBAGE-DISPOSAL UNIT??!

ZZZZT!

JEAN-- *WAIT!* WHAT ARE YOU *DOING??*

SOMETHING I'VE *WANTED* TO DO FOR A *LONG TIME!* I WANT TO MATCH *MY TELEKINETIC POWER* AGAINST THE SCARLET WITCH'S *HEX POWER!*

BY KEEPING HER BUSY DUCKING FLYING OBJECTS, SHE WON'T HAVE TIME TO FOCUS A HEX ON ANY OF US!

ON *YOU??* DO YOU THINK *YOU* ARE OF ANY INTEREST TO *ME??*

DO NOT *FLATTER* YOURSELVES!

13

ALL I CARE ABOUT IS THE WELFARE OF MY *BROTHER!* HE MUST BE *UNFROZEN,* BEFORE IT IS TOO LATE!

I DIDN'T AIM TO *HARM* HIM--JUST TO *STOP* 'IM!

PIETRO-- *SPEAK* TO ME!! PIETRO--!

STAY BACK! *I'LL* HELP HIM....!

NOBODY SPEAK!! I MUST CONCENTRATE *COMPLETELY!* EASY--EASY--!!

ONLY ENOUGH POWER TO DISINTEGRATE THE *FROST!!* IF I MISCALCULATE --EVEN BY A *HAIRSBREADTH--* IT COULD BE *FATAL* TO HIM!!

THERE! THAT SHOULD *DO* IT!

NOW WHAT WILL WE DO WITH THEM?

YOU NEED DO *NOTHING* WITH US EVER AGAIN! WE HAVE SERVED MAGNETO FOR THE LAST TIME!

WANDA IS *RIGHT!* WE OWED HIM A DEBT-- BUT IT HAS BEEN REPAID-- MANY TIMES OVER!

WE SHALL SERVE HIM *NO LONGER!*

I ALWAYS *FELT* YOU DIDN'T BELONG WITH HIS BAND OF EVIL MUTANTS!

BUT, BEFORE ANOTHER WORD CAN BE UTTERED--!

CYCLOPS!! WE'VE SEARCHED THE ENTIRE PLACE! MAGNETO AND THE OTHERS HAVE *VANISHED!*

THE ANGEL'S CONCLUSION IS ENTIRELY *CORRECT,* DISAPPOINTING THOUGH IT MAY BE!

WHERE COULD THEY HAVE *GONE* WITH THAT NEW MUTANT??

THE NEW MUTANT!! PROFESSOR X SAID HE WAS THE MOST POWERFUL OF *ALL!*

IF *MAGNETO* HAS EN- LISTED HIM ON *HIS* SIDE, THEN OUR MISSION IS A TOTAL FAILURE!

UNLESS-- WE CAN EVEN THE ODDS BY HAVING THE TWO OF *YOU* JOIN THE X-MEN!

NO! WE HAVE HAD *ENOUGH* OF CONFLICT!!

14

16

BUT, THE CAUSE WE FIGHT FOR IS A *JUST* ONE!

THE WAY SHE *LOOKS* AT HIM! AS THOUGH SHE *TOO*--OH *NO!* IT *CAN'T* BE!!

YOUR WORDS HAVE THE RING OF *TRUTH* TO THEM! IF ONLY---

NO, MY SISTER! IT IS *I* WHO GIVE THE ORDERS NOW!

WE SHALL RETURN TO OUR HOME-- IN CENTRAL EUROPE, AND *FORGET* THE ENDLESS BATTLE OF MUTANT AGAINST MUTANT--!

BUT, SOME-DAY WE MAY *RETURN!* SOMEDAY, THE FATE OF MANKIND MAY HINGE UPON *OUR* ENTERING THE BATTLE ONCE MORE!

MEANWHILE, THE *"STRANGER'S"* CONE OF ENERGY COMES TO A HALT DEEP WITHIN A LONELY WOODED AREA...

WE HAVE JOURNEYED FAR ENOUGH! PREPARE FOR DIS-SOLVEMENT!

DISSOLVE-MENT??

THIS IS THE MOMENT WHEN MY ENERGY CONE DISSOLVES INTO THE NOTHINGNESS IT CAME FROM!

TELL ME-- WHO *ARE* YOU?? EXACTLY WHAT POWER *DO* YOU POSSESS? YOU SEEM TO BE ALMOST AS MIGHTY AS *I*--ALMOST THE EQUAL OF *MAGNETO!!*

I AM MERELY-- A *STRANGER!*

MAKE HIM TELL YOU WHAT HIS POWER IS, MASTER! MAKE HIM TELL!

SILENCE, TOAD!

NOW, *LISTEN!!* I AM MASTER OF MY BAND OF MUTANTS! WHEN I *ASK*-- OTHERS *ANSWER!* EVEN *YOU!!* NOW-- *WHAT IS YOUR MUTANT POWER?*

ARROGANT FOOL! I AM *NO* MUTANT!

AS FOR MY *POWER,* IT IS GREATER BY FAR THAN YOU CAN EVEN *IMAGINE!!*

YOU'RE *GROWING!!* GETTING *LARGER* --RIGHT BEFORE MY EYES!! BUT--YOU *CAN'T* BE *GIANT-MAN!!*

15

I **TOLD** YOU-- I AM A **STRANGER!**

BUT, I AM A STRANGER **DIFFERENT** FROM ANY YOU HAVE EVER KNOWN! FAR, FAR DIFFERENT!

TOAD!! COME **BACK!** I AM STILL MASTER HERE! I AM STILL-- **MAGNETO!**

YOUR **SIZE** CANNOT DEFEAT ME! I POSSESS THE POWER OF **MAGNETISM!** I AM **SUPREME!** YOU **YET** SHALL SERVE ME!

SAVE US, MASTER!! DO NOT LET THE STRANGER **HARM** US!

I GROW WEARY OF YOUR WORDS! I SHALL PLACE THIS THIN FILM OF ANTI-MAGNETIC-MEMBRANE OVER YOU, TO QUIET YOU!

I'LL **DESTROY** YOU FOR THIS!! THOSE WHO DO NOT SERVE ME MUST **DIE!!**

MASTER! WHAT HAS HE **DONE** TO US?? I- I CANNOT **MOVE!!**

AT THAT MOMENT, BACK AT X-MEN HEADQUARTERS...

WE FOUND **MASTER-MIND** IN THE CELLAR, SIR! IT TOOK **ALL** OF US TO CARRY HIM!

HE'S **ALIVE**-- BUT SOMETHING HAS ALTERED THE VERY MOLECULES OF HIS BODY!

IT COULD ONLY HAVE BEEN THE ONE WE'RE SEEKING!

DO YOU THINK HE'S AS DANGEROUS AS MAGNETO HIMSELF, SIR??

DANGEROUS AS **MAGNETO?**

THE ONE WE SEEK HAS POWER ENOUGH TO SHAKE THE **UNIVERSE!** MAGNETO IS BUT A **CHILD** COMPARED TO THE **STRANGER!!** WE MUST **FIND** HIM--AT **ONCE!!**

16

WITHIN MINUTES, A HELICOPTER TAKES TO THE AIR, GUIDED BY THE MOST BRILLIANT MUTANT-BRAIN OF ALL TIME...THE BRAIN OF *PROFESSOR XAVIER!*

FLY DUE WEST! I CAN MENTALLY RECEIVE HIS EMANATIONS AS THOUGH AN ARROW IN MY MIND IS POINTING TO HIM!

THEN, AFTER A FEW MINUTES OF SPEEDY FLIGHT...

GO, MY X-MEN! YOU WILL FIND HIM JUST AHEAD! BUT, GUARD YOURSELVES AT ALL TIMES!

LOOK!! MAGNETO-- AND THE *TOAD*-- WRAPPED UP IN SOME SORT OF *COCOONS!*

ANYONE STRONG ENOUGH TO TREAT *MAGNETO* SO CAVALIERLY WILL GIVE *US* THE FIGHT OF OUR LIVES!

ICEMAN! DO YOU SEE ANY SIGNS OF-- THE *STRANGER?!*

NOT *YET*, CYKE! BUT HE MUST BE AROUND *SOMEWHERE!*

STOP!! DON'T *TOUCH* THOSE COCOONS-- *ANY* OF YOU!

BACK! *BACK*-- IF YOU VALUE YOUR *LIVES!*

SOME STRANGE *FORCE*-- SHOOTING OUT--!

THE PROFESSOR WAS *RIGHT!* ANOTHER SECOND, AND THE WISPS OF WHATEVER THIS IS WOULD HAVE ENVELOPED *ME*, TOO!

[17]

19

THEN, AT THAT SECOND, THE *STRANGER* AGAIN APPEARS--!

THOSE COCOONS WILL *PROTECT* THEM FOR THE *JOURNEY* THEY ARE ABOUT TO TAKE!

I CAN *GUESS* THE JOURNEY YOU REFER TO! ITS DESTINATION IS NO PLACE ON *EARTH*, IS IT??

OF *COURSE* NOT! HAVE I NOT *SAID* I AM--A *STRANGER*??!!

A STRANGER FROM--THE *STARS*!!

MY PEOPLE ARE GREATLY INTERESTED IN *MUTATIONS*!! I JOURNEY FROM PLANET TO PLANET, TAKING SPECIMENS OF MUTANTS BACK TO MY WORLD -- FOR STUDY! I DID NOT KNOW *WHOM* TO TAKE FROM EARTH...

BUT THEN, THE ONE WHO CALLS HIMSELF *MAGNETO* INSISTED I ALLY MYSELF WITH *HIM!* AND SO, I CHOOSE TO TAKE HIM-- AND THE OTHER, WHOSE LOYALTY IS SO TOUCHING!

WE SHALL NEVER RETURN!

18

THEY'RE *GONE!* IT--IT HAPPENED SO *SUDDENLY*-- SO *UNEXPECTEDLY!!* I-- NEVER IMAGINED IT WOULD END--LIKE *THIS!*

MAGNETO *GONE!* AT *LAST!* AT *LONG LAST!*

HE *WANTED* TO FIND THE "STRANGER" BEFORE *WE* DID! AND HE *SUCCEEDED!* HE THOUGHT HE HAD *BEATEN* US! BUT, IT TURNED OUT TO BE MAGNETO'S *FINAL* TRIUMPH!

WILL THIS MEAN--DISBANDING THE *X-MEN,* SIR?

OF *COURSE* NOT! THERE WILL STILL BE *MANY* MENACES TO MANKIND FOR US TO BATTLE!

WHAT'S GOING *ON* HERE?? WE HEARD AN *EXPLOSION*-- THERE WAS A BLINDING FLASH OF LIGHT--AND THEN-- *HEY!!* IT'S THE *X-MEN!!*

BEAST! SLOW THEM DOWN! THEY MUSTN'T *SEE* ME! MY IDENTITY MUST NOT BE MADE PUBLIC!

I'LL HANDLE IT WITH *DISPATCH,* SIR!

STOP! WE WANT TO *TALK* TO YOU!

WATCH IT, BOYS! HE'S *UP* TO SOMETHING!

HOLY *SMOKE!* DID YOU SEE HIM *SPIN AROUND??* HE ALMOST HAS A HYPNOTIC EFFECT!

BEAST-- SLOW DOWN! WE WEREN'T AIMING TO *HURT* YOU!

I SHOULD *HOPE* NOT! I'M FAR TOO LOVABLE TO BECOME A STATISTIC!

EASY, PROFESSOR! YOU'LL BE SAFELY ABOARD IN A SECOND!

THANK YOU, BOYS! NOW-- SUMMON THE BEAST!

OKAY, YOU ANIMATED JUMPIN' BEAN! THE PROF SAYS *ALL ABOARD!!*

WATCH IT, BOBBY! DUCK YOUR HEAD!

TAKE 'ER UP, ANGEL! HANK'S HANGING ON OUTSIDE! HEAD BACK FOR THE SCHOOL!

WHAT SHEER, STARK DRAMA! ONE INGROWN TOENAIL, AND I'D BE A DEAD MAN!

19

NOT LONG AFTERWARDS...

AHHH, THE OLD HOMESTEAD! IT'LL BE GOOD TO SIT BACK AND RELAX WITH A DIFFERENTIAL CALCULUS PROBLEM FOR A FEW HOURS!

BUT, BEFORE ANY SERIOUS "RELAXING" IS ATTEMPTED, THE X-MEN ADOPT THEIR USUAL PRECAUTIONARY SECURITY MEASURES...

MY WALL-SOUNDINGS ARE COMPLETE, SIR! NO HIDDEN MIKES, WIRES, OR ANY SUCH DEVICES!

MY INTUITIVE BRAIN SENSES NO UNEXPECTED DANGER! ALL THAT REMAINS IS ANGEL'S VISUAL REPORT!

ALL CLEAR, AS FAR AS I CAN SEE, SIR!

VERY WELL, THEN! LET US PROCEED!

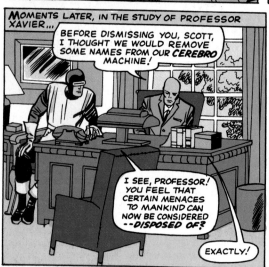

MOMENTS LATER, IN THE STUDY OF PROFESSOR XAVIER...

BEFORE DISMISSING YOU, SCOTT, I THOUGHT WE WOULD REMOVE SOME NAMES FROM OUR CEREBRO MACHINE!

I SEE, PROFESSOR! YOU FEEL THAT CERTAIN MENACES TO MANKIND CAN NOW BE CONSIDERED --DISPOSED OF?

EXACTLY!

IT'S BEEN A LONG, HARD ROAD, CYCLOPS-- FOR ALL OF YOU! BUT, YOU HAVE ACQUITTED YOURSELVES WITH HONOR!

MAGNETO

MASTERMIND

SCARLET WITCH

QUICKSILVER

BLOB

UNUS

TOAD

BUT, SUDDENLY-- BEFORE ANOTHER WORD CAN BE UTTERED...

BEEP BEEP BEEP BEEP

PROFESSOR! WHAT'S HAPPENING??

CEREBRO HAS DETECTED A NEW MENACE!

20

I'VE NEVER SEEN A MERE ELECTRONIC DEVICE REGISTER SUCH AN EXTREME CONDITION OF PANIC! EVERY CIRCUIT IS STRAINED TO THE BREAKING POINT!

BEEP BEEP BEEP

WHATEVER IT IS THAT'S OUT THERE --THREATENING US-- IT IS THE MOST POWERFUL, MOST DEADLY DANGER WE HAVE EVER FACED! AND, IT'S ALMOST UPON US!

The END

THUS, ONE STRANGE SAGA COMES TO AN END AS ANOTHER, STILL STRANGER ONE, BEGINS! THIS TALE HAS MARKED A TURNING POINT IN THE LIVES AND DESTINIES OF THE X-MEN... AND, BEGINNING NEXT ISSUE, FATE HAS MANY NEW AND UNEXPECTED PITFALLS THAT AWAIT THEM! SO, WATCH FOR X-MEN #12, FILLED WITH THE MIGHTY MARVEL MAGIC, AND STARRING THE MOST UNUSUAL TEEN-AGERS OF ALL TIME!

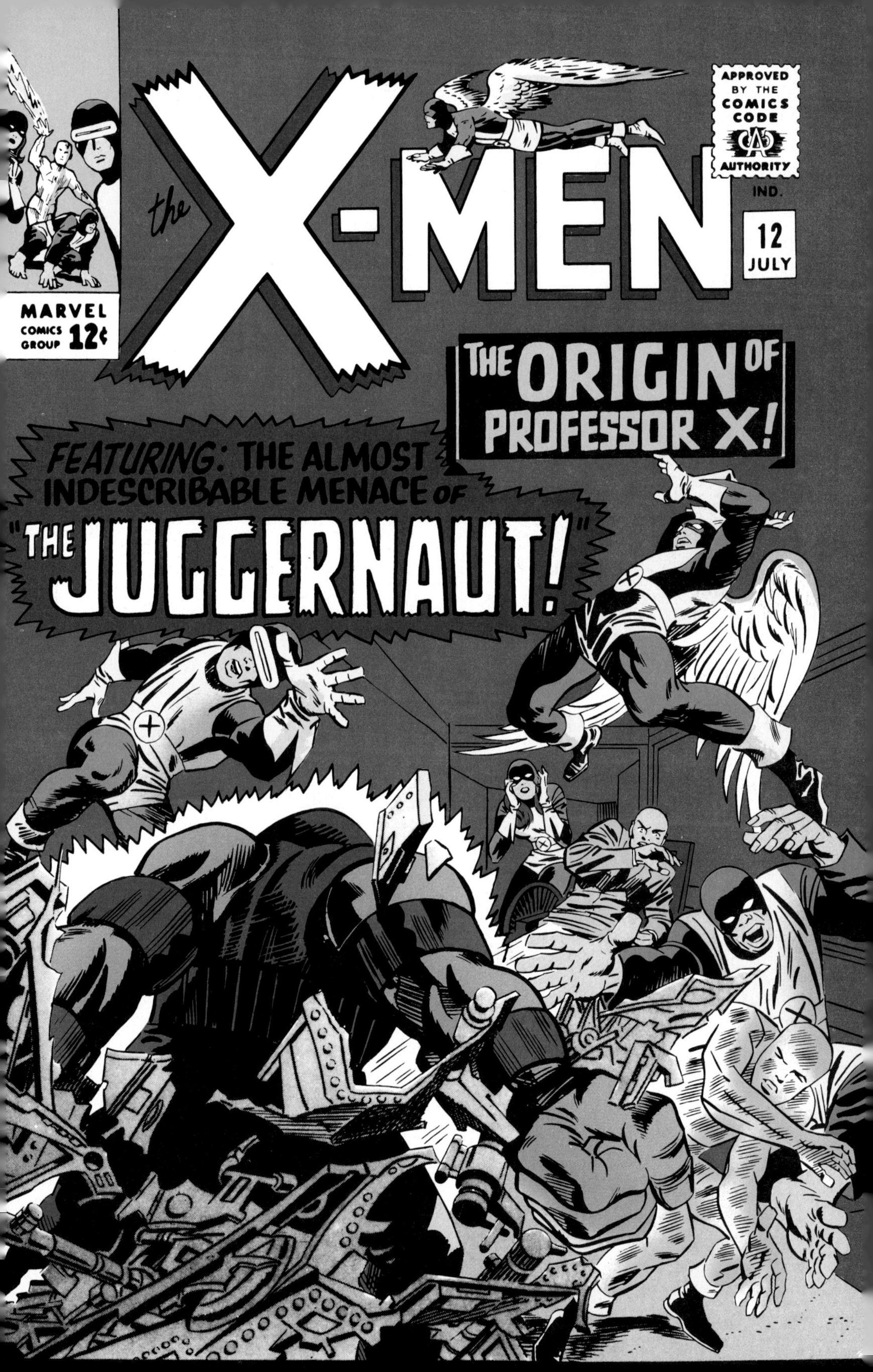
MARVEL COMICS GROUP 12¢
the X-MEN
APPROVED BY THE COMICS CODE AUTHORITY
IND.
12 JULY
THE ORIGIN OF PROFESSOR X!
FEATURING: THE ALMOST INDESCRIBABLE MENACE OF
"THE JUGGERNAUT!"

X-MEN THE MOST UNUSUAL TEEN-AGERS OF ALL TIME!

"THE ORIGIN OF PROFESSOR X!"

PROFESSOR! WE HEARD THAT BLOOD-CURDLING NOISE! WHAT'S WRONG? ARE... ARE YOU IN DANGER??

THE SOUND IS EMANATING FROM HIS DESK! THERE'S SOME SORT OF ELECTRONIC APPARATUS SECRETED WITHIN!

MY EARS! THE SCREETCH IS DEAFENING! WHAT IS IT?

I'VE NEVER SEEN PROFESSOR X LOOK SO DESPERATELY FEARFUL BEFORE!

STAY OUT, ALL OF YOU! NO ONE IS SUPPOSED TO KNOW ABOUT THE PROFESSOR'S CEREBRO MACHINE!

REEEEEEEE

IT'S ALL RIGHT, CYCLOPS! LET THEM ENTER! WE'RE ABOUT TO FACE OUR MOST DEADLY THREAT! WE CAN HAVE NO SECRETS FROM EACH OTHER NOW!

STUPIFYING STORY BY: STAN LEE
SPECTACULAR LAYOUTS BY: JACK KIRBY
SLAM-BANG PENCILLING BY: ALEX TOTH
SENSATIONAL INKING BY: VINCE COLLETTA
THE USUAL LETTERING BY: SAM ROSEN
KIBITZING BY: THE WHOLE BLAMED BULLPEN!

WE'VE GOT A STARTLING, SIZZLING TALE TO TELL YOU, AND NO TIME TO WASTE WITH A LONG INTRODUCTION! SO, LET'S GO! WE'LL BRIEF YOU ALONG THE WAY...!

24

WHAT *IS* IT, PROFESSOR? WHAT DANGER DO WE FACE? AND WHAT DOES *CEREBRO* MEAN?

IT'S THE ONLY MACHINE OF ITS KIND IN EXISTENCE! IT GIVES WARNING OF ANY MUTANT MENACE WHICH MAY BE NEAR!

BUT, IT HAS NEVER REACTED LIKE *THIS* BEFORE! THE MENACE WE FACE MUST BE IN-*DESCRIBABLY* POWERFUL!

THERE IS ONLY *ONE* WHO COULD CAUSE SUCH A REACTION! QUICKLY! YOU MUST DO AS I SAY....!

A MOMENT LATER, HAVING RECEIVED THEIR ORDERS, THE MARVELOUS MUTANTS RACE INTO ACTION...

JUDGING BY THE PROFESSOR'S *AGITATION,* OUR VERY EXISTENCE IS AT STAKE!

I DON'T KNOW WHAT IT IS THAT HE FEARS, BUT IT MUST BE SOMETHING *TERRIFYING!*

WHATEVER IT IS, *WE* CAN HANDLE IT!

HE NEVER SEEMED THIS WORRIED WHEN WE BATTLED MAGNETO'S *EVIL MUTANTS!*

STOP TALKING! *MOVE!* YOU EACH KNOW WHAT TO DO!

THIS *ICE SHIELD* I'M PUTTING UP AROUND THE SCHOOL OUGHTTA STOP ANYTHING SHORT OF A *SHERMAN TANK!*

WHILE ICEMAN PREPARES A DEFENSE OUTSIDE THE SCHOOL WALLS, I'LL BLAST A DEEP TRENCH *INSIDE* THE WALL...

...USING MY POWER BEAM'S HIGHEST INTENSITY!!

2.

SLOW DOWN, HANK! I CAN'T KEEP UP WITH YOU!!

ANGEL! COME HERE! I NEED YOU!

ZAP!

YOU'RE DOING JUST *FINE*, JEAN! KEEP TELE-PORTING THOSE LEAVES AND TWIGS OVER THIS CABLE SO THAT OUR UN-KNOWN ATTACKER WON'T SUSPECT THE BOOBY TRAP WE'RE LAYING!

THAT'S *IT*, WARREN! HOLD THOSE LOGS WHILE I HOLLOW THEM OUT WITH POWER BLASTS!

THIS IS THE *LAST* OF 'EM, CYKE! NOW I'LL GET THE *GRENADES!*

THE PROF DIDN'T SAY WHAT KIND OF GRENADES THESE ARE! DO YOU THINK...?

NO TIME FOR GUESSING! WE'RE ALMOST DONE NOW!

EXACTLY FIVE MINUTES LATER, THE X-MEN RETURN, HAVING COMPLETELY FORTIFIED AND BOOBY-TRAPPED THE MYSTERIOUS BUILDING...

THE SCREECHING SOUND HAS STOPPED! DOES THAT MEAN THE DANGER'S PAST?

NO! THE PROFESSOR'S MERELY TURNED OFF THE CEREBRO MACHINE!

IT'S TIME FOR YOU TO LEARN MORE OF THE DANGER THAT THREATENS US!

WELL DONE, MY X-MEN! COME IN...!

IS IT ONE OF THE EVIL MUTANTS WE FOUGHT IN THE PAST, SIR?

NO! I ONLY WISH IT *WERE!*

I HOPED YOU'D *NEVER* HAVE TO LEARN OF *THIS* ENEMY... FOR HIS POWER MAY EXCEED MY *OWN!*

THE ONE WHO IS ABOUT TO ATTACK US IS.. MY OWN *BROTHER!!*

YOUR *BROTHER?!!*

3.

I NEVER MENTIONED HIM *BEFORE!* PERHAPS I HOPED I WOULD NEVER *HAVE* TO MENTION HIM!

BUT NOW THAT WE ALL SHARE THE SAME MOMENT OF CRISIS...I *OWE* IT TO YOU TO TELL YOU THE WHOLE STORY...TO TAKE YOU BACK WITH ME, IN YOUR IMAGINATION ...TO THE *BEGINNING*...!

IT STARTED WITH AN *ATOMIC BLAST,* YEARS AGO...AT ALAMAGORDO, NEW MEXICO...

"I'LL NEVER FORGET THAT FATEFUL HOLOCAUST ...FOR MY *FATHER* WAS KILLED IN THE BLAST!"

...AND SO WE COMMIT BRIAN XAVIER TO THE EARTH!

IF ONLY *DAD* HAD BEEN ABLE TO ESCAPE THE BLAST...THE WAY *DR. MARKO DID!*

I KNOW HOW YOU MUST FEEL, SHARON... AND I *SHARE* YOUR GRIEF! BUT, AS HIS FRIEND, I SHALL LOOK AFTER YOU...AND AFTER THE BOY, TOO!

THANK YOU, KURT! YOU... YOU ARE VERY KIND!

EVEN THOUGH HE WAS DAD'S FELLOW SCIENTIST, I NEVER *TRUSTED* DR. MARKO...AND I DON'T TRUST HIM *NOW!*

MY DEAR, DEAR SHARON! I WOULD GLADLY HAVE GIVEN MY OWN LIFE TO SAVE BRIAN'S...IF ONLY IT WERE POSSIBLE!

KURT...YOU'RE SUCH A TOWER OF STRENGTH FOR ME... AT A TIME LIKE THIS!

HE *LIES!* HE *MIGHT* HAVE SAVED DAD...BUT HE SAVED *HIMSELF* INSTEAD!

"BUT MONTHS LATER, MARKO PERSUADED MY GRIEF-STRICKEN MOTHER THAT I NEEDED A FATHER TO TAKE CARE OF ME...AND, ALTHOUGH IT FILLED MY HEART WITH A NAMELESS DREAD, THEY WERE FINALLY *MARRIED!*

YOUR NEW FATHER HAS KINDLY AGREED TO LIVE IN OUR OLD HOME, CHARLES...FOR *YOUR* SAKE!

HE MAY FOOL MOTHER, BUT NOT *ME!* I KNOW *THIS* IS WHAT HE WANTED! MOTHER'S WEALTH, AND POSITION, AND PROPERTY!

4.

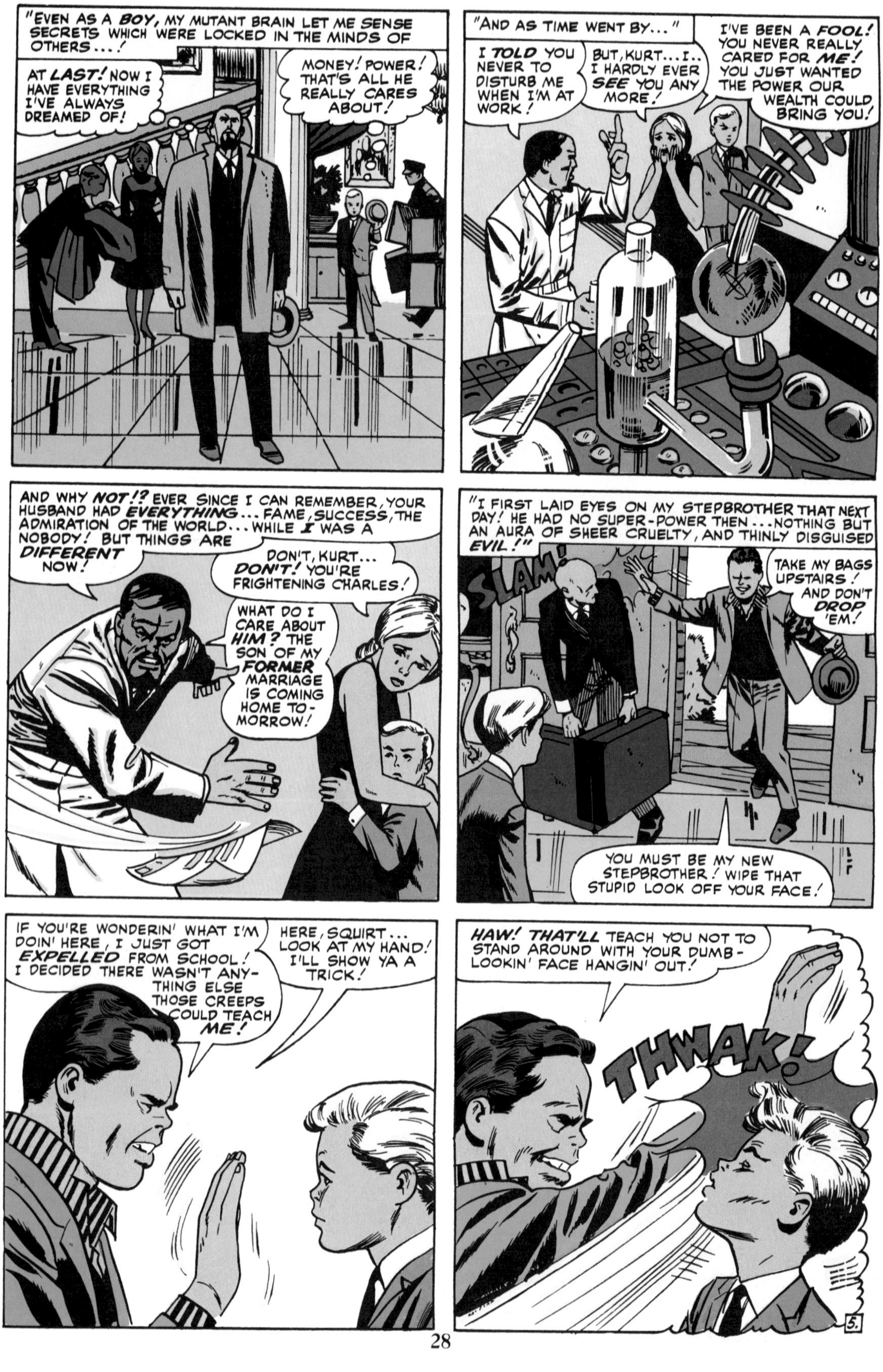

"EVEN AS A BOY, MY MUTANT BRAIN LET ME SENSE SECRETS WHICH WERE LOCKED IN THE MINDS OF OTHERS...!
AT LAST! NOW I HAVE EVERYTHING I'VE ALWAYS DREAMED OF!
MONEY! POWER! THAT'S ALL HE REALLY CARES ABOUT!
"AND AS TIME WENT BY..."
I TOLD YOU NEVER TO DISTURB ME WHEN I'M AT WORK!
BUT, KURT... I.. I HARDLY EVER SEE YOU ANY MORE!
I'VE BEEN A FOOL! YOU NEVER REALLY CARED FOR ME! YOU JUST WANTED THE POWER OUR WEALTH COULD BRING YOU!
AND WHY NOT!? EVER SINCE I CAN REMEMBER, YOUR HUSBAND HAD EVERYTHING... FAME, SUCCESS, THE ADMIRATION OF THE WORLD... WHILE I WAS A NOBODY! BUT THINGS ARE DIFFERENT NOW!
DON'T, KURT... DON'T! YOU'RE FRIGHTENING CHARLES!
WHAT DO I CARE ABOUT HIM? THE SON OF MY FORMER MARRIAGE IS COMING HOME TO-MORROW!
"I FIRST LAID EYES ON MY STEPBROTHER THAT NEXT DAY! HE HAD NO SUPER-POWER THEN... NOTHING BUT AN AURA OF SHEER CRUELTY, AND THINLY DISGUISED EVIL!"
SLAM!
TAKE MY BAGS UPSTAIRS! AND DON'T DROP 'EM!
YOU MUST BE MY NEW STEPBROTHER! WIPE THAT STUPID LOOK OFF YOUR FACE!
IF YOU'RE WONDERIN' WHAT I'M DOIN' HERE, I JUST GOT EXPELLED FROM SCHOOL! I DECIDED THERE WASN'T ANY-THING ELSE THOSE CREEPS COULD TEACH ME!
HERE, SQUIRT... LOOK AT MY HAND! I'LL SHOW YA A TRICK!
HAW! THAT'LL TEACH YOU NOT TO STAND AROUND WITH YOUR DUMB-LOOKIN' FACE HANGIN' OUT!
THWAK!
5.

HE SOUNDS EXTREMELY *UNSAVORY,* SIR! BUT WHAT MAKES HIM DANGEROUS TO US *NOW?*

AFTER ALL, IF HE HAS NO SUPER-POWER...?

HE HAD NONE *THEN!* BUT LATER... *WAIT!* LET ME CHECK *CEREBRO* AGAIN!

HE LOOKS MORE WORRIED THAN EVER!

HE'S EVEN *CLOSER!* THE SOUND IS GETTING *UNENDURABLE!*

HIS POWER MUST BE GREATER THAN IT WAS! GREATER THAN I *FEARED!* CEREBRO IS ALMOST TEARING ITSELF *APART!*

WHAT *IS* HIS POWER, PROFESSOR?

NO TIME FOR THAT NOW! HE'S REACHED THE *FIRST BARRIER!*

QUICK! TO THE *WINDOW!*

LISTEN! IT'S THE SOUND OF *ICE* BEING *SHATTERED!* HE'S SMASHING BOBBY'S FROZEN WALL!

BUT I MADE IT AS THICK AS A CONCRETE BUNKER! *NOTHING* COULD SHATTER IT THAT QUICKLY!

GIVE US THE WORD, SIR! WE'LL *ATTACK* HIM!

NO! NOT *YET!* YOU CAN'T BEGIN TO IMAGINE WHAT YOU'LL BE *FACING!*

KRAK A B RUMBLE!

LOOK OUT! THE ENTIRE *BUILDING* IS BEGINNING TO SHAKE! IT'S COLLAPSING!

AND HE'S ONLY USING A *FRACTION* OF HIS *TRUE POWER!*

BOBBY! QUICK! FORM AN *ICE SHIELD* OVER JEAN... MOVE, X-MEN!

I HEAR YA TALKIN', CYKE! *WHEW!* JUST MADE IT!!

I DIDN'T *SEE* THAT FALLING CHANDELIER! IF...IF NOT FOR *ICEMAN*--!

KLAK!

6.

WOOM! KRAK!

LISTEN! THE REMAINDER OF THE ICE WALL IS BEING TORN APART!!

I SEEM TO SEE A *FIGURE* OUT THERE! BUT...IT'S SO INDISTINCT...I CAN'T MAKE IT OUT AMONG ALL THE RUBBLE!

HE DID IT! THE ICE WALL IS *GONE!* HE'S DESTROYED THE FIRST BARRIER!

BARROOOMM!

BUT *HOW?* WHAT *POWER* DID HE USE?

THE SCHOOL STOPPED SHAKING! *WHY?* WHAT'S HE UP TO *NOW?*

HE'S JUST *TOYING* WITH US! HE'S SHOWING HIS *CONTEMPT* FOR OUR DEFENSES!

SHOULDN'T WE RUSH OUT AND FIGHT HIM *NOW*... BEFORE HE COMES CLOSER??

NO! THERE'S STILL TIME... TIME FOR ME TO TELL YOU *MORE* ABOUT HOW IT ALL BEGAN!

KRAK! BRRAMM!

"IT WASN'T LONG BEFORE MY HEART-BROKEN MOTHER SHUT HER EYES FOR THE LAST TIME, JOINING HER FIRST HUSBAND--MY FATHER--:FOREVER! AND SO, I WAS ALONE...WITH THEM!"

I *TOLD* YOU NOT TO DISTURB ME WHEN I'M AT WORK!

I'LL LEAVE AS SOON AS YOU GIVE ME THE *MONEY* I ASKED FOR! YOU CAN *AFFORD* IT NOW...YOU INHERITED *EVERYTHING!*

WITH MOTHER GONE, *MARKO* CONTROLS MY INHERITANCE, TILL I COME OF AGE!

THE ANSWER IS *NO,* CAIN! IF YOU WANT MONEY, GO OUT AND *EARN* IT, AS *I* DID!

I KNOW HOW *YOU* EARNED IT! IT WAS NO *ACCIDENT* THAT XAVIER DIED AT ALAMAGORDO..!

YOU DARE ACCUSE *ME..?!*

DON'T YOU EVER SAY THAT *AGAIN!!* DO YOU *HEAR??* FOR AS LONG AS YOU LIVE, *DON'T EVER SAY THAT AGAIN!!*

YOU'RE TOO LATE! I *HEARD* HIM!

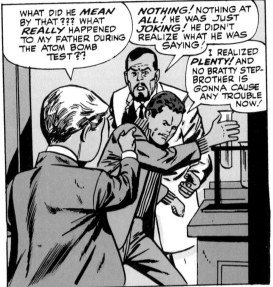

WHAT DID HE *MEAN* BY THAT??? WHAT *REALLY* HAPPENED TO MY FATHER DURING THE ATOM BOMB TEST??

NOTHING! NOTHING AT *ALL!* HE WAS JUST *JOKING!* HE DIDN'T REALIZE WHAT HE WAS SAYING!

I REALIZED *PLENTY!* AND NO BRATTY STEP-BROTHER IS GONNA CAUSE ANY TROUBLE *NOW!*

CAIN! DON'T TOUCH THOSE *TEST-TUBES!!* THEY'RE UNSTABLE-- *EXPLOSIVE!*

YOU YOUNG, *FOOL!* IT'S *TOO LATE* NOW! YOU'VE SPILLED THEM! IF THE DIFFERENT CHEMICALS SHOULD *TOUCH* EACH OTHER...!

LOOK OUT!

SPLAT!

"BUT, BEFORE ANOTHER WORD COULD BE SAID, THE POTENT FLUIDS *DID* MAKE CONTACT, AND THAT WAS THE LAST I KNEW, AS A DEAFENING EXPLOSION DESTROYED THE LAB AND ALL ITS CONTENTS....'

"IT WAS THEN THAT MY STEP-FATHER DID THE ONE UNSELFISH DEED OF HIS LIFE! ALTHOUGH FATALLY INJURED HIMSELF, HE MANAGED TO CARRY CAIN AND ME TO SAFETY AS THE LIFE EBBED OUT OF HIM!

"AND THEN, WITH HIS LAST REMAINING BREATH, HE GASPED..."

CHARLES...YOUR FATHER'S DEATH... *WAS AN* ACCIDENT! BUT... I MIGHT HAVE SAVED HIM...IF I TRIED... BUT, I DIDN'T... FORGIVE ME...

BEWARE OF... CAIN! WHEN HE FINDS OUT... ABOUT YOUR POWER... –UHHHH!–

POWER??

8

31

AND THEN...HE DIED! BUT, HIS WORDS PROVED PROPHETIC, FOR....!

PROFESSOR!! LOOK! OUT THE WINDOW! THAT STRANGE, DAZZLING LIGHT! WHAT DOES IT MEAN??

HE'S REACHED THE SECOND BARRIER...AN ELECTRO-MAGNETIC FORCE FIELD! IT MEANS HE'S FALLEN INTO THE TRENCH THAT CYCLOPS BLASTED INTO THE GROUND OUTSIDE!

BUT THE LIGHT IS GROWING EVEN MORE BRILLIANT! THE FORCE FIELD ISN'T STOPPING HIM! HE'S... RESISTING IT..TRYING TO OVERCOME IT!

I CAN SEE A FIGURE OUT THERE.!! IT'S STANDING UPRIGHT! IT DOESN'T EVEN SEEM TO BE HURT...OR WEAKENED! AND... IT LOOKS ENORMOUS!

KRRRACKLE

HE ISN'T HURT, JEAN! IF HE'S LASTED THIS LONG, IT MEANS THE CABLE CAN'T STOP HIM! HE'S EVERYTHING I FEARED HE'D BE...AND MORE!

ZZZAPP!

HE SNAPPED THE STEEL CABLE... AS EASILY AS IF IT WERE PAPER! BUT, IN SO DOING, HE RELEASED A STILL GREATER WAVE OF ENERGY, DESIGNED TO CATCH HIM UNAWARES!

CEREBRO HAS GROWN NO LOUDER! THE SECOND LINE OF ELECTRICAL DEFENSE IS HOLDING...AT LEAST FOR NOW!

NOW, ALL WE NEED IS MORE TIME...TIME FOR ME TO TELL YOU THE WHOLE STORY..!

REEEE

9.

PROFESSOR! I'VE NEVER SEEN YOU SO GRIM BEFORE! TELL US...DO WE HAVE A CHANCE? CAN HE BE BEATEN??

WAIT TILL I'VE FINISHED MY TALE, HANK...AND THEN YOU CAN FURNISH YOUR OWN ANSWER!

IT WASN'T LONG AFTER MARKO'S DEATH THAT I REALIZED MY BRAIN POSSESSED MUTANT POWERS...

...POWERS WHICH MUST HAVE BEEN CAUSED BY ALL THE RADIATION MY PARENTS HAD BEEN EXPOSED TO AT THE NUCLEAR RESEARCH CENTER BEFORE I WAS BORN!

"THE ONLY OUTWARD SIGN WAS THE FACT THAT I BEGAN TO LOSE MY HAIR WHILE STILL IN MY TEENS! BUT, MORE IMPORTANT THAN THAT WAS MY FANTASTIC ABILITY TO THINK!"

YOU HAVE GIVEN ME ANSWERS I HAVEN'T TAUGHT YOU YET, CHARLES! IT IS AS THOUGH YOU ARE ACTUALLY READING MY MIND!

OH, NO, SIR! THEY WERE JUST LUCKY GUESSES!

I MUST BE MORE CAREFUL! NO ONE MUST EVER SUSPECT THAT I CAN READ MINDS!

"AS I GREW OLDER, MY E.S.P.* POWER MADE ME EXCEL AT EVERYTHING! I BECAME A STAR QUARTERBACK BECAUSE I ALWAYS KNEW IN ADVANCE WHAT THE ENEMY TACKLES WERE THINKING!"

IF ONLY I DARED TELL THEM I CAN READ THEIR MINDS! BUT...THEY'D HATE ME FOR IT!

* EXTRA-SENSORY-PERCEPTION, AS IF YOU DIDN'T KNOW!...STAN.

"EVEN AT TRACK I HAD THE ADVANTAGE OF KNOWING WHEN AN OPPOSING RUNNER WAS TIRING, OR PLANNING TO MAKE HIS LAST DESPERATE SPURT!"

THIS WILL BE MY LAST RACE! IT'S TOO EASY FOR A MUTANT TO DEFEAT A NORMAL MAN!

"BUT, ALL THE WHILE CAIN MARKO WAS WATCHING, AND HATING...HIS JEALOUS HEART FILLED WITH ALMOST UNCONTROLLABLE ENVY!"

ANOTHER TROPHY FOR YOU, SKINHEAD?

IF HE SUSPECTED I COULD READ HIS THOUGHTS! BUT... I'VE NOTHING TO FEAR FROM HIM...YET!

10.

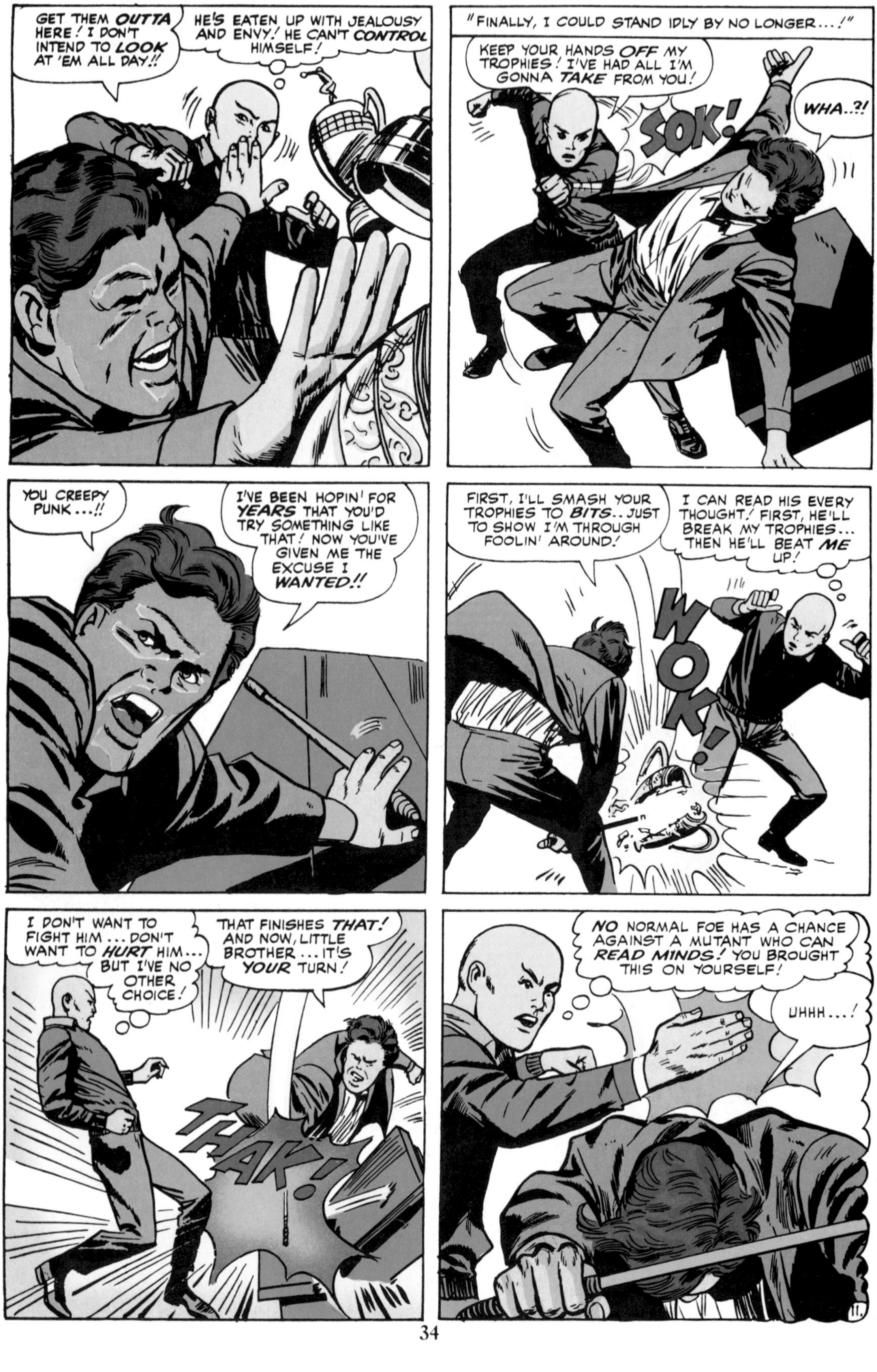
GET THEM OUTTA HERE! I DON'T INTEND TO LOOK AT 'EM ALL DAY!!
HE'S EATEN UP WITH JEALOUSY AND ENVY! HE CAN'T CONTROL HIMSELF!
"FINALLY, I COULD STAND IDLY BY NO LONGER...!"
KEEP YOUR HANDS OFF MY TROPHIES! I'VE HAD ALL I'M GONNA TAKE FROM YOU!
SOK!
WHA..?!
YOU CREEPY PUNK...!!
I'VE BEEN HOPIN' FOR YEARS THAT YOU'D TRY SOMETHING LIKE THAT! NOW YOU'VE GIVEN ME THE EXCUSE I WANTED!!
FIRST, I'LL SMASH YOUR TROPHIES TO BITS.. JUST TO SHOW I'M THROUGH FOOLIN' AROUND!
I CAN READ HIS EVERY THOUGHT! FIRST, HE'LL BREAK MY TROPHIES... THEN HE'LL BEAT ME UP!
WOK!
I DON'T WANT TO FIGHT HIM... DON'T WANT TO HURT HIM... BUT I'VE NO OTHER CHOICE!
THAT FINISHES THAT! AND NOW, LITTLE BROTHER... IT'S YOUR TURN!
THAK!
NO NORMAL FOE HAS A CHANCE AGAINST A MUTANT WHO CAN READ MINDS! YOU BROUGHT THIS ON YOURSELF!
UHHH...!
11.

HE GOT WHAT HE *DESERVED!* AND HE WAS CERTAINLY NO MATCH FOR YOUR *X-POWER!*

BUT THAT'S WHAT *TORMENTED* HIM! MY POWERS WERE A SHADOW BETWEEN US... A SHADOW WHICH WAS TO RESULT IN *TRAGEDY* FOR US *BOTH!*

I *STILL* DON'T SEE WHY HE'S SUCH A DANGER TO US *NOW!*

YOU *WILL,* BOBBY... IF I HAVE TIME TO FINISH MY TALE!

"THE FINAL TRAGEDY OCCURRED WHEN CAIN OFFERED TO DRIVE ME TO COLLEGE AFTER VACATION! HOPING TO WIN HIS FRIENDSHIP, I ACCEPTED! BUT, THEN..."

YOU'RE DRIVING LIKE A *MADMAN!* WE'LL NEVER STAY ON THE ROAD!!

OH, WE *WON'T,* EH?

YOU'RE BETTER THAN I IN *SPORTS,* IN *STUDIES,* IN ALMOST *EVERYTHING!* BUT NOW, *I'VE* GOT THE TOP HAND!!

I'M GONNA DRIVE LIKE THIS UNTIL YOU *BEG* ME TO STOP! ...TILL YOU CRY OUT IN FEAR!

IF I TRY TO *STOP* HIM... HE MIGHT LOSE CONTROL...!

"AND THEN, IT *HAPPENED*...!!

I DIDN'T *SEE* THE DETOUR!! JUMP!! *JUMP!!*

DETOUR

DANGER

"BUT, IT WAS *TOO LATE* FOR ME! ALTHOUGH HE WOULD NEVER KNOW IT, I HAD USED MY OWN MENTAL POWER TO HELP CAIN LEAP TO SAFETY... WHILE I REMAINED IN THE CAR A SPLIT SECOND TOO LONG..!"

CAN'T GET OUT!! GOING *OVER*..!!

12

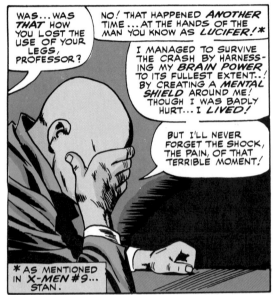

WAS...WAS *THAT* HOW YOU LOST THE USE OF YOUR LEGS, PROFESSOR?

NO! THAT HAPPENED *ANOTHER* TIME...AT THE HANDS OF THE MAN YOU KNOW AS *LUCIFER!* *

I MANAGED TO SURVIVE THE CRASH BY HARNESS-ING MY *BRAIN POWER* TO ITS FULLEST EXTENT...! BY CREATING A *MENTAL SHIELD* AROUND ME! THOUGH I WAS BADLY HURT...I *LIVED!*

BUT I'LL NEVER FORGET THE SHOCK, THE PAIN, OF THAT TERRIBLE MOMENT!

* AS MENTIONED IN *X-MEN #9...* STAN.

BUT THEN, SUDDENLY...

BAROOOMM!

LOOK OUT! THE WHOLE *BUILDING* IS SHAKING!!

QUICK! GRAB THE *PROFESSOR!* DON'T LET HIM *FALL!*

DON'T WORRY ABOUT *ME!* I'M ALL RIGHT! THE WINDOW...LOOK OUT OF THE *WINDOW!!*

IT'S *IMPOSSIBLE! INCREDIBLE!! INCONCEIVABLE!!* AND YET...!

HE *DID* IT!! HE BROKE THROUGH THE *FORCE BARRIER!*

I *SEE* SOMETHING MOVING!! IT'S *HIM!!*

BUT...LOOK AT THE *SIZE* OF HIM!! HE... DOESN'T LOOK ...*HUMAN!*

THEN, AS THE *MONSTROUS FIGURE* COMES CLOSER, THEY SEE...

HE'S HEADING FOR THE HOLLOW LOGS... WITH THE *GRENADES* IN THEM!

HE TRIPPED THE *RELEASE WIRE!* HE'LL BE STOPPED *NOW!*

BUT...IF *THAT* DOESN'T HOLD HIM...*WHAT WILL ??!*

13.

36

THE GRENADES ARE SHOOTING OUT OF THE LOGS LIKE *MORTAR SHELLS!*

HE'S DRAWING *BACK!!*

BULL'S EYE! THEY'VE LOOSED THEIR *SLEEP GAS* ALL AROUND HIM!

BUT... WHY DOESN'T HE *FALL??!*

ALL IT DID WAS *ANGER* HIM!! HE'S SMASHING THEM ALL WITH *ONE BLOW!!*

NOW HE'S REACHED THE *SECOND* ROW! *THAT* GAS IS STRONG ENOUGH TO STOP A HERD OF *ELEPHANTS!*

WHOOOSH!

HE'S *STAGGERING!* HE'S *FALLING BACK!* WE *DID* IT!

IF ONLY WE COULD *SEE* MORE CLEARLY!

THE SMOKE AND HAZE ARE CONCEALING HIM!

I'LL KEEP THE GAS OUT OF THIS BUSTED WINDOW WITH A COATING OF *ICE!*

I *STILL* DON'T UNDERSTAND! CAIN MARKO WAS JUST AN ORDINARY, UNSAVORY CHARACTER! HOW DID HE BECOME SO *POWERFUL??*

14.

THE THING THAT THREATENS US OUT *THERE* IS A FAR CRY FROM THE MAN WHO WAS ONCE CAIN MARKO!

HE'S *STILL* TRYING TO GET UP! WHAT IS HE *MADE* OF!?

NOW I'LL FINISH MY TALE...FOR, I FEAR, OUR TIME IS RUNNING OUT!

I *OWE* IT TO YOU TO TELL YOU WHAT YOU *FACE!* TO TELL YOU HOW CAIN MARKO GOT...HIS *POWER!*

THE ONE POWER ON EARTH THAT MAY FINALLY *DEFEAT* US!!

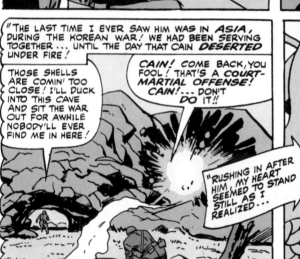

"THE LAST TIME I EVER SAW HIM WAS IN *ASIA,* DURING THE KOREAN WAR! WE HAD BEEN SERVING TOGETHER ... UNTIL THE DAY THAT CAIN *DESERTED* UNDER FIRE!

THOSE SHELLS ARE COMIN' TOO CLOSE! I'LL DUCK INTO THIS CAVE AND SIT THE WAR OUT FOR AWHILE NOBODY'LL EVER FIND ME IN HERE!

CAIN! COME BACK, YOU FOOL! THAT'S A COURT-MARTIAL OFFENSE! CAIN!...DON'T DO IT!!

"RUSHING IN AFTER HIM, MY HEART SEEMED TO STAND STILL AS I REALIZED...

IT'S THE SACRED, LOST TEMPLE OF *CYTTORAK!* LEGENDS HAVE WARNED OF IT FOR *CENTURIES!*

THAT *RUBY*... IT LOOKS *ALIVE!* THERE'S AN INSCRIPTION ON IT!!

NO!! DON'T *TOUCH* IT! *DON'T!*

" BUT, MY WARNING WAS TOO LATE...FOR CAIN...AND FOR THE *WORLD!*

"WHOSOEVER TOUCHES THIS GEM SHALL POSSESS THE POWER OF THE CRIMSON BANDS OF *CYTTORAK!* HENCEFORTH, YOU WHO READ THESE WORDS, SHALL BECOME ...FOREVERMORE ...A HUMAN *JUGGERNAUT!!*

DROP IT, CAIN! DROP IT! YOU DON'T REALIZE WHAT THAT *MEANS!!*

"THOSE DESPERATE WORDS WERE NOT YET OUT OF MY MOUTH, WHEN...!"

SOMETHING'S *HAPPENING* TO ME! I-I'M *CHANGING*..!

NOTHING CAN STOP IT NOW! CAIN MARKO NO LONGER *EXISTS!* AND, IN HIS PLACE...

...AN EVIL, HUMAN *JUGGERNAUT* HAS COME INTO BEING!!

WHA...??! THAT EXPLOSION!! THE REDS ARE SHELLING THIS AREA! THE CAVE IS *COLLAPSING!!*

"I WAS NEARER TO THE OPENING THAN HE WHO HAD BEEN CAIN MARKO...SO I MANAGED TO ESCAPE BY A HAIRSBREADTH...WHILE THE CREATURE WITHIN THE CAVE WAS BURIED BENEATH A TRILLION TONS OF FALLING ROCK AND RUBBLE!"

EVEN IF THE CAVE-IN *DOESN'T* KILL HIM... IT WILL TAKE *YEARS* BEFORE HE CAN DIG OUT FROM BENEATH THE GIGANTIC *MOUNTAIN* WHICH COVERS HIM!

BUT, IF EVER HE *SHOULD* BREAK FREE, I CAN THINK OF NO POWER ON *EARTH* CAPABLE OF *STOPPING* HIM!

AND, HE'LL *FIND* ME! THE CRIMSON BANDS OF *CYTTORAK* WILL LEAD HIM TO ME NO MATTER WHERE I MAY HIDE!

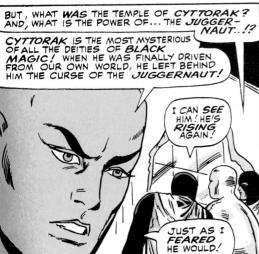

BUT, WHAT *WAS* THE TEMPLE OF *CYTTORAK?* AND, WHAT IS THE POWER OF...THE *JUGGERNAUT...!?*

CYTTORAK IS THE MOST MYSTERIOUS OF ALL THE DEITIES OF *BLACK MAGIC!* WHEN HE WAS FINALLY DRIVEN FROM OUR OWN WORLD, HE LEFT BEHIND HIM THE CURSE OF THE *JUGGERNAUT!*

I CAN *SEE* HIM! HE'S *RISING* AGAIN!

JUST AS I *FEARED* HE WOULD!

As FOR THE *POWER* OF THE JUGGERNAUT, I SIMPLY QUOTE THE DICTIONARY..."A GIGANTIC, INEXORABLE FORCE THAT MOVES ONWARD IRRESISTIBLY, *CRUSHING ANYTHING IT FINDS IN ITS PATH!"*

THEN *THAT'S* WHY HE GETS THROUGH ALL OUR OBSTACLES!! NOTHING CAN *STOP* A JUGGERNAUT!

BUT, HOW DO YOU KNOW IT'S *HIM?* IT COULD BE ANY-ONE!

ONLY THE *JUGGERNAUT* COULD HAVE MADE CEREBRO SHRIEK THE WAY IT DID... AND ONLY THE *JUGGERNAUT* COULD PROVE INVULNERABLE TO ALL OUR DEFENSES!

BUT, OUR *NEXT* DEFENSE SHOULD STOP HIM! IT'S THE GAS WHICH CAUSES LOSS OF BALANCE!

AND, WITHOUT NORMAL BALANCE, A MAN MUST TOPPLE AND FALL!

SOMETHING TELLS ME THAT *JUGGERNAUT* IS A LOT *MORE* THAN JUST A MAN!

16

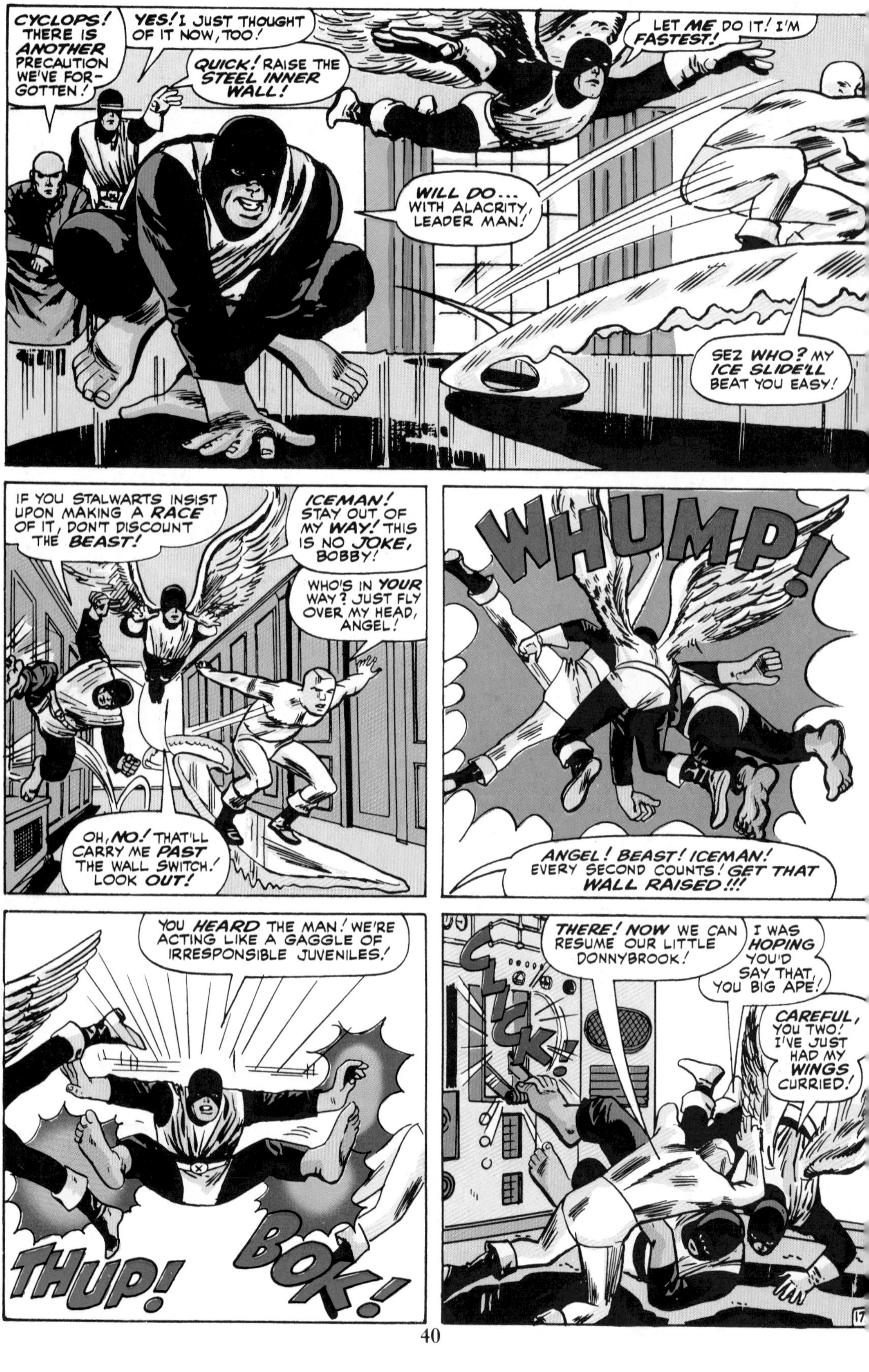
CYCLOPS! THERE IS ANOTHER PRECAUTION WE'VE FORGOTTEN!
YES! I JUST THOUGHT OF IT NOW, TOO!
QUICK! RAISE THE STEEL INNER WALL!
LET ME DO IT! I'M FASTEST!
WILL DO... WITH ALACRITY, LEADER MAN!
SEZ WHO? MY ICE SLIDE'LL BEAT YOU EASY!
IF YOU STALWARTS INSIST UPON MAKING A RACE OF IT, DON'T DISCOUNT THE BEAST!
ICEMAN! STAY OUT OF MY WAY! THIS IS NO JOKE, BOBBY!
WHO'S IN YOUR WAY? JUST FLY OVER MY HEAD, ANGEL!
OH, NO! THAT'LL CARRY ME PAST THE WALL SWITCH! LOOK OUT!
WHUMP!
ANGEL! BEAST! ICEMAN! EVERY SECOND COUNTS! GET THAT WALL RAISED!!!
YOU HEARD THE MAN! WE'RE ACTING LIKE A GAGGLE OF IRRESPONSIBLE JUVENILES!
THUP!
BOK!
THERE! NOW WE CAN RESUME OUR LITTLE DONNYBROOK!
I WAS HOPING YOU'D SAY THAT, YOU BIG APE!
CAREFUL, YOU TWO! I'VE JUST HAD MY WINGS CURRIED!
CLICK!
17

SECONDS LATER...

THERE SHE *GOES!*

STEP ASIDE, BOBBY, WHILST YOURS TRULY *TESTS* IT!

TESTS IT? *HOW?*

LIKE *THIS*, YOU SNOW-COVERED STRIPLING!

WHEW! RATHER YOU THAN *ME*, HANK!

BWONK!

YOWFF! NOTHING WILL PENETRATE *THAT!*

BUT, *PROFESSOR XAVIER* IS NOT QUITE THAT *SURE...!!*

LET US GO TO THE FRONT DOOR! HE IS CERTAIN TO ATTACK AT THAT POINT!

HOW CAN YOU *KNOW* THAT, SIR?

BECAUSE IT IS DIRECTLY IN LINE WITH THE PATH HE IS MAKING! AND, A *JUGGERNAUT* NEVER CHANGES ITS COURSE... FOR *ANYTHING!*

BRR! YOU SPEAK OF HIM AS IF HE'S A *MACHINE*, RATHER THAN A *HUMAN BEING!*

I'M AFRAID, MY DEAR *MARVEL GIRL*, THAT HE CEASED BEING *HUMAN* MANY YEARS AGO, ON THAT FATEFUL DAY IN THE TEMPLE OF *CYTTORAK!*

QUIET! I HEAR DULL, HEAVY FOOTFALLS THROUGH THE STEEL DOOR! HE'S ALMOST *UPON* US!

PROFESSOR, IF HE *SHOULD* SMASH THROUGH THIS LAST STEEL BARRIER... CAN YOU STOP HIM BY MENTALLY AFFECTING HIS *BRAIN?*

A GOOD QUESTION, HENRY... BUT I'VE A BAD *ANSWER!* I'VE BEEN *TRYING* TO PROBE HIS MIND... SINCE FIRST HE APPEARED... BUT IT'S *USELESS!*

WHEN HE GAINED THE STAGGERING POWER OF *CYTTORAK*, HE ALSO GAINED A MYSTIC MENTAL *DEFENSE*, AGAINST WHICH I AM TOTALLY *POWERLESS!*

LOOK!! THE STEEL WALL... IT'S *BULGING INWARD!!*

IT'S BUCKLING... MORE AND MORE.. WITH STEADY, EVER-INCREASING *PRESSURE!!*

NOW DO YOU BEGIN TO CONCEIVE OF THE UNIMAGINABLE POWER THE *JUGGERNAUT* POSSESSES.!?

18.

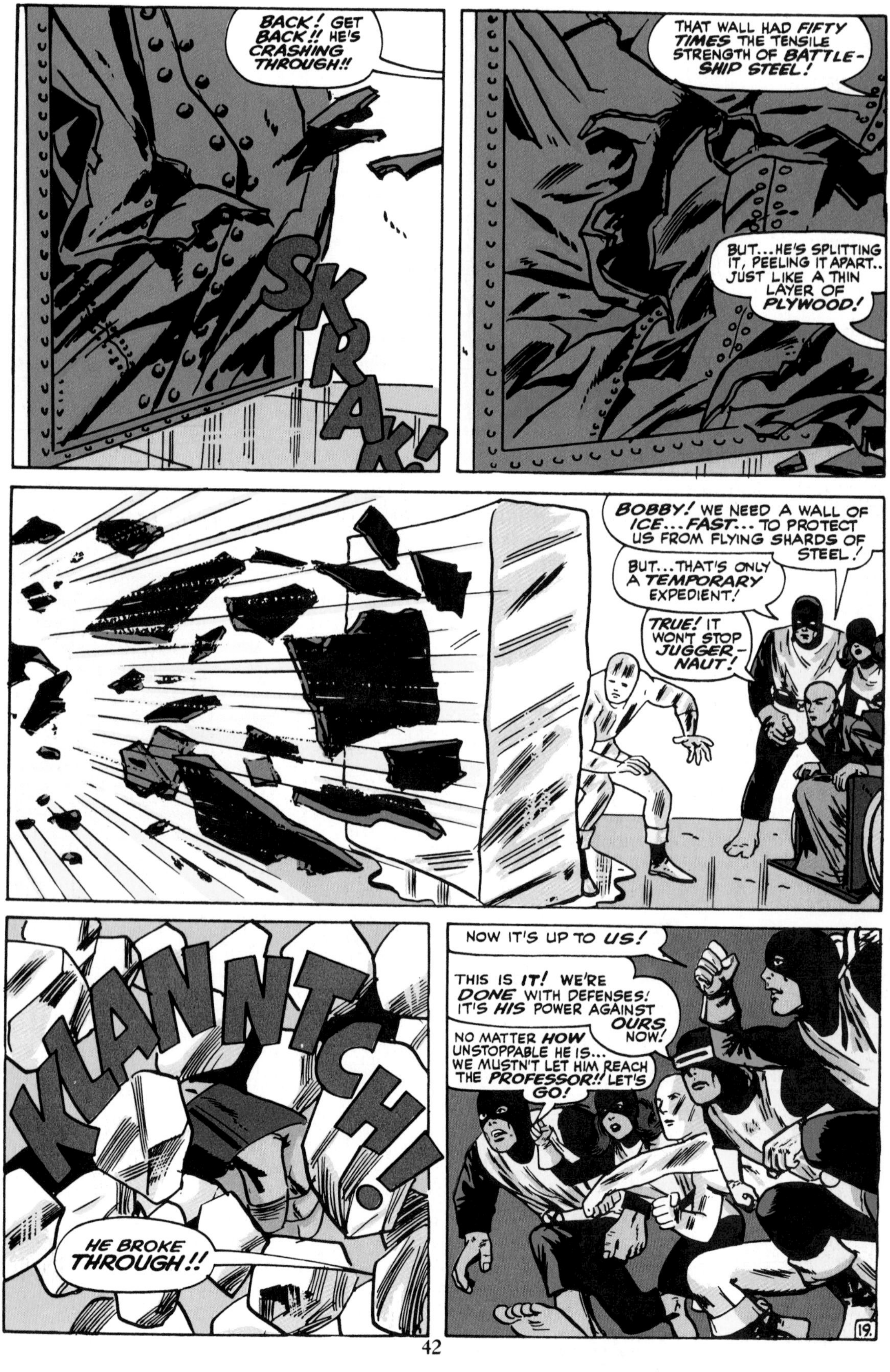
BACK! GET BACK!! HE'S CRASHING THROUGH!!
SKRAK!
THAT WALL HAD FIFTY TIMES THE TENSILE STRENGTH OF BATTLE-SHIP STEEL!
BUT...HE'S SPLITTING IT, PEELING IT APART.. JUST LIKE A THIN LAYER OF PLYWOOD!
BOBBY! WE NEED A WALL OF ICE...FAST... TO PROTECT US FROM FLYING SHARDS OF STEEL!
BUT...THAT'S ONLY A TEMPORARY EXPEDIENT!
TRUE! IT WON'T STOP JUGGER-NAUT!
KLANNTCH!
HE BROKE THROUGH!!
NOW IT'S UP TO US!
THIS IS IT! WE'RE DONE WITH DEFENSES! IT'S HIS POWER AGAINST OURS NOW!
NO MATTER HOW UNSTOPPABLE HE IS... WE MUSTN'T LET HIM REACH THE PROFESSOR!! LET'S GO!
19.

HOLD IT!! BACK, ALL OF YOU!!

LET ME GIVE HIM A BLAST WITH MY *POWER BEAM*, FIRST! IT'LL GIVE US SOME MEASURE OF HIS STRENGTH!

MORE! *MORE!* GIVE HIM *FULL INTENSITY*, CYCLOPS!

I *AM!* BUT IT ISN'T *STOPPING* HIM!

HE'S PUSHING MY RAY BACK AS THOUGH IT'S A SOLID THING! NO *ONE* OF US CAN DEFEAT HIM ALONE...!

WE'VE GOT TO RUSH HIM *TOGETHER!!* NOW...!!

IT'S *NO USE!* HE SWEPT US ASIDE LIKE PAPER DOLLS!

BUT...THE *PROFESSOR!* HE'S HEADING FOR THE *PROFESSOR!*

I'M LASHING OUT AT HIM WITH EVERY BIT OF MENTAL POWER I POSSESS...BUT.. *STILL* HE COMES!!

SO, DEAR BROTHER! WE MEET AGAIN! WHAT A PITY IT IS FOR THE *LAST TIME!*

THEN...IT'S *TRUE!* CAIN MARKO *HAS* BECOME A HUMAN... *JUGGERNAUT!!*

NEXT ISSUE... ONE OF THE GREATEST BATTLES OF ALL TIME... AS THE IRRESISTIBLE *JUGGERNAUT* BATTLES THE UN-CONQUERABLE *X-MEN* TO THE BITTER END!

YOU *MUST NOT MISS IT!!*

20.

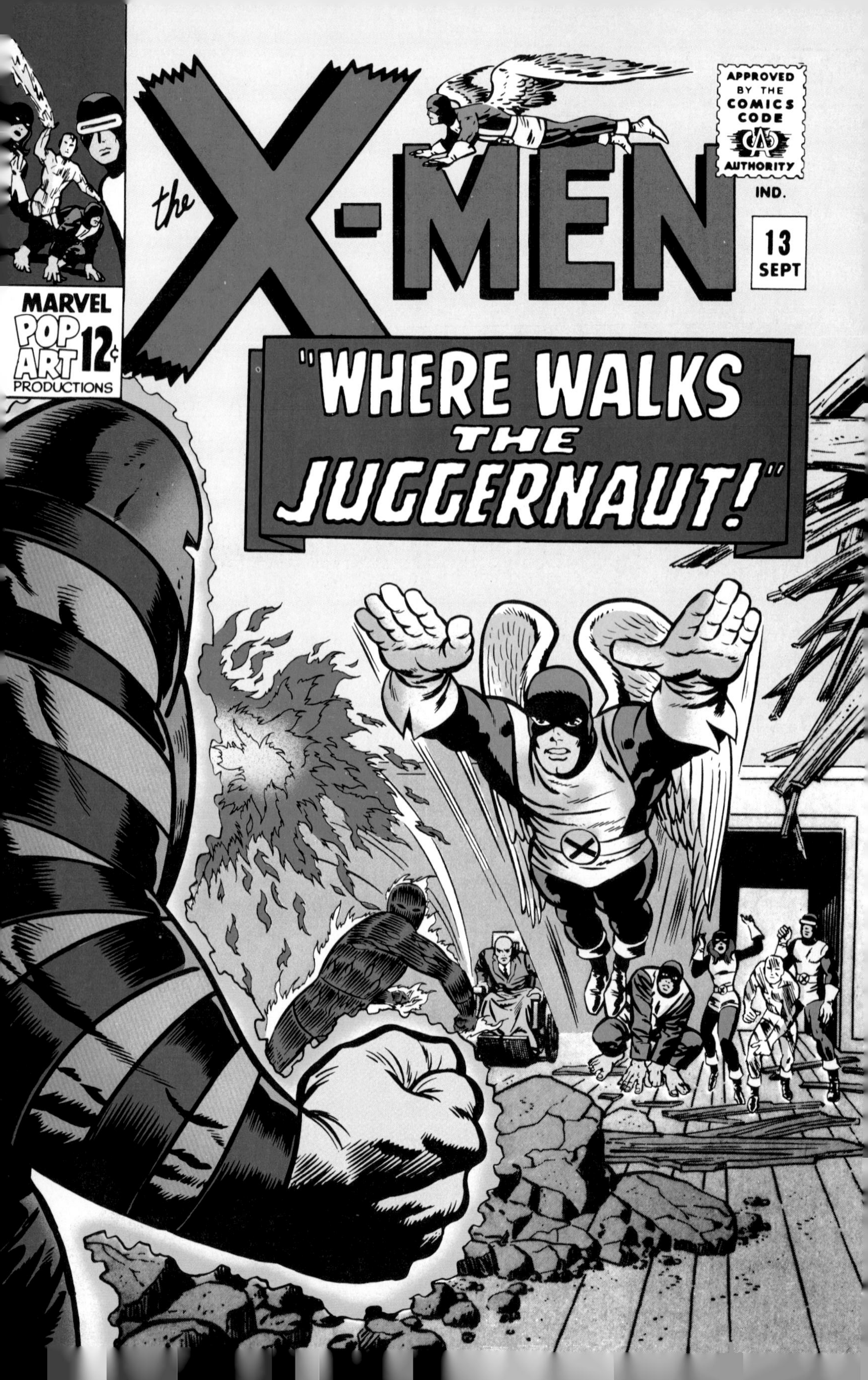

the X-MEN
APPROVED BY THE COMICS CODE AUTHORITY
IND.
13
SEPT
MARVEL POP ART PRODUCTIONS
12¢
"WHERE WALKS THE JUGGERNAUT!"

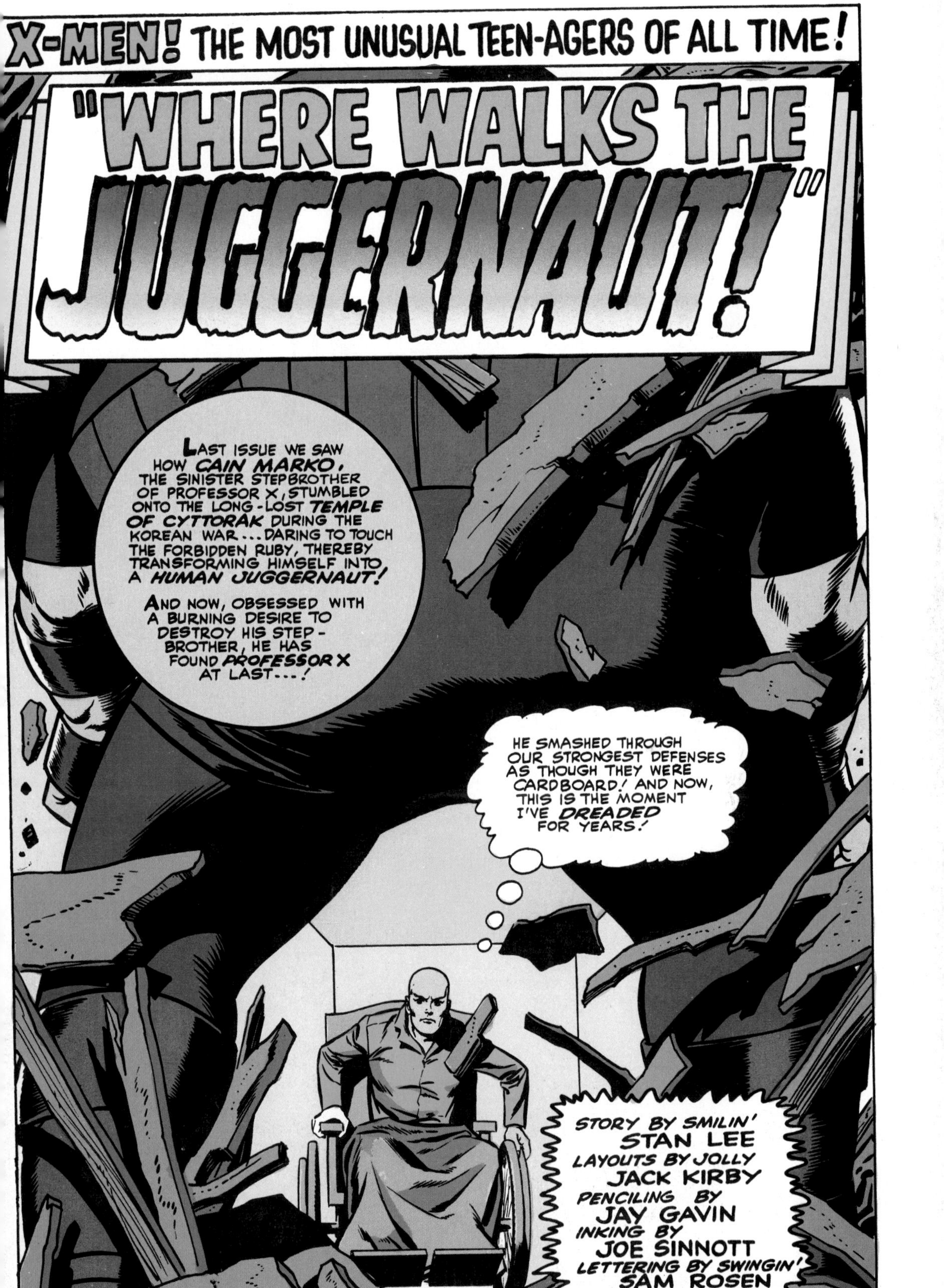
X-MEN! THE MOST UNUSUAL TEEN-AGERS OF ALL TIME!
"WHERE WALKS THE JUGGERNAUT!"
LAST ISSUE WE SAW HOW CAIN MARKO, THE SINISTER STEPBROTHER OF PROFESSOR X, STUMBLED ONTO THE LONG-LOST TEMPLE OF CYTTORAK DURING THE KOREAN WAR... DARING TO TOUCH THE FORBIDDEN RUBY, THEREBY TRANSFORMING HIMSELF INTO A HUMAN JUGGERNAUT!
AND NOW, OBSESSED WITH A BURNING DESIRE TO DESTROY HIS STEP-BROTHER, HE HAS FOUND PROFESSOR X AT LAST...!
HE SMASHED THROUGH OUR STRONGEST DEFENSES AS THOUGH THEY WERE CARDBOARD! AND NOW, THIS IS THE MOMENT I'VE DREADED FOR YEARS!
STORY BY SMILIN' STAN LEE LAYOUTS BY JOLLY JACK KIRBY PENCILING BY JAY GAVIN INKING BY JOE SINNOTT LETTERING BY SWINGIN' SAM ROSEN

AS THE DEADLY *JUGGERNAUT* STEADILY APPROACHES UNTIL HE IS ALMOST UPON THE MOTIONLESS PROFESSOR, THE OTHER X-MEN, DAZED AND SHAKEN, SLOWLY RECOVER FROM THE STAGGERING IMPACT OF THE RELENTLESS ATTACK...!

WHEW! WAS HE FOR *REAL*?

NO MERE HALLUCINATION COULD HAVE HIT US LIKE *THAT*, MY FRIGID FRIEND!

QUICKLY, GIRL... STAY WITH THE OTHERS! *I* WILL FACE THE *JUGGERNAUT*!

YOU *CAN'T*, PROFESSOR!! NOT *ALONE*!!

YOU HAVE YOUR ORDERS! *OBEY* THEM!

DON'T ANYONE MOVE! THIS IS THE *PROFESSOR'S* INNING!

BUT, WHAT HAPPENS IF THE *PROF* CAN'T STOP HIM??

THOSE ARE THE LAST ORDERS YOU'RE EVER GOING TO GIVE, MY LONG LOST STEPBROTHER!

IT TOOK ME ALL THESE YEARS TO FREE MYSELF OF THE TONS OF STONE I HAD BEEN BURIED UNDER IN KOREA *... BUT THE WAIT WAS *WORTH* IT!

BECAUSE I PLANNED THIS TRIUMPHANT MOMENT ALL THAT TIME!

SEE THE *POWER* OF THE JUGGERNAUT! MY BODY IS SO CHARGED WITH BOUNDLESS ENERGY THAT I EXUDE WAVES OF *FORCE* EVEN WHEN STANDING STILL!

HE'S SPEAKING THE *TRUTH*! THE SHEER AURA OF STRENGTH ABOUT HIM IS ENOUGH TO PUSH MY WHEELCHAIR BACK!

* WE SAW THE ENTIRE AWESOME SPECTACLE IN *X-MEN #12*... STAN.

AND NOW, I'VE TOYED WITH YOU LONG ENOUGH! I CANNOT RESTRAIN MYSELF ANOTHER MINUTE! YOU MUST BE DESTROYED *NOW*... NOW AND *FOREVER*!

YOU FORGET ONE THING... I STILL HAVE A WEAPON... THE *SUPREME* WEAPON...!

YOU'RE *BLUFFING*! BUT IT WON'T HELP YOU! WHAT WEAPON CAN YOU *POSSIBLY* HAVE... TO STOP *ME*?

2.

MY MUTANT *BRAIN*!!

AFTER UTTERING THOSE THREE WORDS, PROFESSOR X LAPSES INTO DEAD *SILENCE*... CONCENTRATING... FOCUSING EVERY IOTA OF MENTAL POWER HE POSSESSES... SENDING A BEAM OF SHEER MENTAL ENERGY AT HIS ONCOMING FOE... A BEAM MIGHTY ENOUGH TO TOPPLE A *MASTODON*!! BUT...

...AFTER REELING FROM THE INITIAL JOLT, THE *JUGGERNAUT* CONTINUES HIS *DREAD* ADVANCE...

THE CRIMSON BANDS OF *CYTTORAK*, WHICH GAVE ME MY POWER, ALSO GAVE ME MY *PSIONIC HELMET*, CAPABLE OF PROTECTING ME FROM *ANY* MENTAL ATTACK!

HE'S GONE TOO FAR!

X-MEN... *ATTACK*!

I'LL TACKLE HIM, CYCLOPS... AS WE PLANNED!

THERE! I'LL TRY TO *TELEPORT* HIM LONG ENOUGH FOR YOU TO MOVE THE PROFESSOR TO SAFETY!

THIS WON'T HELP YOU! I CANNOT BE STOPPED!

JUST A FEW SECONDS MORE... THAT'S ALL I'LL NEED!

I CAN'T HOLD HIM! HE'S SHATTERING MY TELEKINETIC POWER!

IT'S ALL RIGHT! YOU GAVE US THE TIME WE NEEDED! *RELEASE HIM* NOW!

WHRRAK!

EXCELLENT, MY X-MEN! THAT WILL GIVE YOU A FEW MINUTES RESPITE!

I.. NEVER FELT... SUCH SHEER *POWER!* MY HEAD... IT'S STILL ACHING!

I MADE THE HOLE AS DEEP AS I COULD! IT SHOULD, *HOLD* HIM!

YOU'RE WHISTLIN' IN THE DARK, CYKE! YOU KNOW HE CAN FORCE HIS WAY OUT OF *ANYTHING*!

BUT, TILL HE *DOES*, WE HAVE A SECOND CHANCE!

EASY, SIR... YOU'LL BE ALL RIGHT, NOW!

ANGEL, HELP THE PROFESSOR INTO HIS CHAIR!

I'LL DROP A FEW FORGET-ME-NOTS ON OUR PAL DOWN THERE!

WHAT'S OUR NEXT STRATAGEM, SIR?

WE MUST FIND *SOMETHING* TO SMASH HIS DEFENSE... TO *INJURE* HIM!

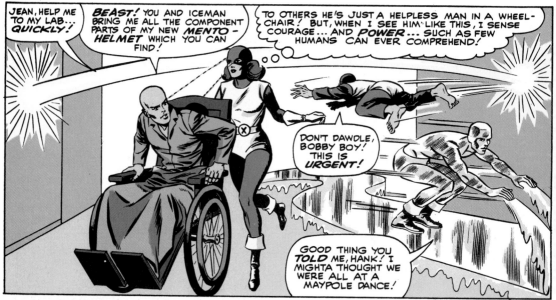

JEAN, HELP ME TO MY LAB... *QUICKLY!*

BEAST! YOU AND ICEMAN BRING ME ALL THE COMPONENT PARTS OF MY NEW *MENTO-HELMET* WHICH YOU CAN FIND!

TO OTHERS HE'S JUST A HELPLESS MAN IN A WHEEL-CHAIR! BUT, WHEN I SEE HIM LIKE THIS, I SENSE COURAGE... AND *POWER*... SUCH AS FEW HUMANS CAN EVER COMPREHEND!

DON'T DAWDLE, BOBBY BOY! THIS IS *URGENT!*

GOOD THING YOU *TOLD* ME, HANK! I MIGHTA THOUGHT WE WERE ALL AT A MAYPOLE DANCE!

MOVING WITH THE SPEED AND SKILL OF A MASTER, PROFESSOR CHARLES XAVIER WORKS LIKE A MAN POSSESSED... AS THE CRUCIAL SECONDS TICK BY...

THIS IS THE LAST OF IT, SIR!

AT EASE! HANK! THE PROF WANTS DEAD SILENCE!

THERE! IT'S *READY* NOW!

AS YOU MAY HAVE GUESSED, THE PURPOSE OF THIS DEVICE IS TO *INTENSIFY* MY BRAIN WAVES... MAKE THEM EVEN MORE POWERFUL THAN THEY NORMALLY ARE!

BUT, THERE IS ALWAYS THE CHANCE THAT THEY WILL *STILL* NOT BE STRONG ENOUGH TO STOP THE JUGGERNAUT!

SO, I WILL SIT HERE WHILE THE POWER COILS CONTINUALLY CHARGE... EACH ADDITIONAL SECOND WILL ADD TO MY MENTAL STRENGTH!

MY MENTAL POWER IS *ALREADY* SO HIGHLY CHARGED THAT I MUST *UNLEASH* SOME ENERGY...

I'LL SEND MENTAL WAVES OUT OVER THE HEART OF THE CITY... RELEASING THEM WILL ACT LIKE A *SAFETY VALVE* TO ME!

MEANTIME, GET BACK TO THAT HOLE IN THE FLOOR... IT WILL NOT STOP *JUGGERNAUT'S* ATTACK MUCH LONGER!

4.

AND, EVEN AS THE PROFESSOR SPEAKS...

HAVEN'T THEY REALIZED YET THAT **NOTHING** CAN HOLD BACK THE **JUGGERNAUT?**

THIS SLIGHT DELAY WILL ONLY MAKE MY FINAL MOMENT OF TRIUMPH ALL THE MORE SATISFYING!

WHEN I RECEIVED MY POWER IN THE HIDDEN TEMPLE OF CYTTORAK, I BECAME **UNSTOPPABLE!** EVERYTHING MUST GIVE WAY TO THE **JUGGERNAUT'S** ATTACK... EVEN A SOLID WALL OF EARTH...!

WHOOM!

THUS, NO PIT CAN HOLD ME...FOR I POSSESS THE POWER TO HAMMER MY OWN HAND AND FOOTHOLDS...

WRUKK!

THOK!

HE'S **COMING,** CYKE! I'LL SWOOP DOWN AND HEAD HIM OFF!

NO! STAY WHERE YOU **ARE!**

THE FOOLS! I'LL SHOW THEM HOW **EASILY** I CAN CHARGE THROUGH THEIR LAUGHABLE DEFENSES!

MY OWN **FORCE BEAM** IS STRONGER.. AND LESS DANGEROUS!

IS IT WORKING? ARE YOU FORCING HIM BACK?

I CAN'T TELL! THE GLARE FROM MY OPTIC RAY IS TOO BLINDING! BUT...I DON'T FEEL ANY RESISTANCE!

WHAT COULD HAVE **HAPPENED** TO HIM?

HE'LL GET HIS ANSWER IN EXACTLY TWO SECONDS...!

HE'S RIGHT **UNDER** US! ANGEL...**QUICK**.. TAKE TO THE **AIR!**

CYKE!

WHOOM!

NO PUNY TEENAGERS CAN TRAP THE **JUGGER-NAUT!**

CYKE'S FORCE BEAM CAN'T HOLD JUGGERNAUT BACK! IT'S ONLY SLOWING HIM DOWN SLIGHTLY!

I'VE GOT TO *DISTRACT* HIM... MAKE HIM TURN FROM SCOTT AND ATTACK *ME!*

I'LL CRUSH YOU LIKE A FLEA!

IT'S LIKE HITTING A STONE WALL! HE DOESN'T SEEM TO *FEEL* IT!

STAY *WITH* IT, CYKE!! *I'LL* KEEP HIM TOO BUSY TO FOLLOW THROUGH!

CAREFUL, ANGEL! HE'S STRONGER THAN YOU SUSPECT!

YOUR *LEGS*... BEND THEM *UNDER* HIM... USE YOUR BACK FOR LEVERAGE.. NOW *KICK*... THAT'S IT! THAT'S IT!

BUT...HE ONLY MOVED BACK A FEW FEET!

LUCKILY, I CAUGHT HIM SLIGHTLY OFF-BALANCE! OTHERWISE, HE WOULDN'T HAVE *BUDGED!*

HE'S CHARGING TOWARDS US AGAIN! STAND ASIDE, PARTNER ... THIS ROUND IS *MINE!*

NO! THIS IS NO TIME FOR HEROICS! WE'LL TAKE HIM *TOGETHER!* STAY AIRBORNE, ANGEL!

KEEP IT UP! YOU'RE MERELY *EXHAUSTING* YOURSELVES! HAVEN'T YOU REALIZED *YET* THAT I CANNOT BE HURT...OR BEATEN!

THUD!

BOKK!

FORGIVE US, JUG...WE'RE JUST A COUPLE OF SLOW LEARNERS!

MEANWHILE, THROUGHOUT THE METROPOLITAN AREA, STRANGE MESSAGE IMPULSES ARE BEING MYSTERIOUSLY RECEIVED...

WHAT'S WRONG, PHIL? RADIO ACTING UP ON YOU?

NO, CAPTAIN! EVERYTHING'S A-OKAY! THAT'S JUST *IT!*

JUST *WHAT?*

I'M GETTING SOME SORT OF MESSAGE... LOUD AND CLEAR... BUT *NOT THROUGH THE RADIO!*

6.

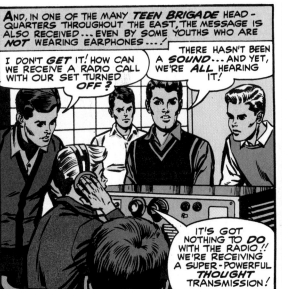

AND, IN ONE OF THE MANY *TEEN BRIGADE* HEAD-QUARTERS THROUGHOUT THE EAST, THE MESSAGE IS ALSO RECEIVED... EVEN BY SOME YOUTHS WHO ARE *NOT* WEARING EARPHONES...!

I DON'T *GET* IT! HOW CAN WE RECEIVE A RADIO CALL WITH OUR SET TURNED *OFF*?

THERE HASN'T BEEN A *SOUND*... AND YET, WE'RE *ALL* HEARING IT!

IT'S GOT NOTHING TO *DO* WITH THE RADIO!! WE'RE RECEIVING A SUPER-POWERFUL *THOUGHT* TRANSMISSION!

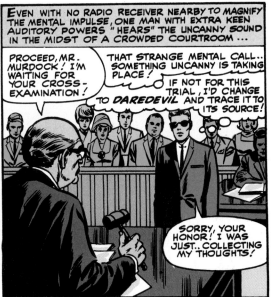

EVEN WITH NO RADIO RECEIVER NEARBY TO MAGNIFY THE MENTAL IMPULSE, ONE MAN WITH EXTRA KEEN AUDITORY POWERS "HEARS" THE UNCANNY *SOUND* IN THE MIDST OF A CROWDED COURTROOM...

PROCEED, MR. MURDOCK! I'M WAITING FOR YOUR CROSS-EXAMINATION!

THAT STRANGE MENTAL CALL.. SOMETHING UNCANNY IS TAKING PLACE!

IF NOT FOR THIS TRIAL, I'D CHANGE TO *DAREDEVIL* AND TRACE IT TO ITS SOURCE!

SORRY, YOUR HONOR! I WAS JUST.. COLLECTING MY THOUGHTS!

WHILE, BACK AT PROFESSOR XAVIER'S PRIVATE SCHOOL IN WESTCHESTER...

PROFESSOR, LET US RUSH YOU *AWAY* FROM HERE, WHILE THERE'S STILL TIME!

NO, JEAN! I CAN'T RUN FROM THE *JUGGERNAUT*! IF *I'M* UNABLE TO STOP HIM... THINK WHAT WILL HAPPEN WHEN HE INVADES THE *CITY*!

CAN'T I GO AND HELP THE OTHERS NOW, SIR?

VERY WELL! DELAY HIM ALL YOU CAN! EACH SECOND GAINED INCREASES MY OWN POWER!

THEN, AT THAT MOMENT...

THE JUGGERNAUT IS *FREE* AGAIN! CYCLOPS AND THE ANGEL CAN'T IMPEDE HIS ADVANCE!

JEAN! BOBBY! WHY DON'T YOU WHISK THE PROFESSOR TO SOME REMOTE SPOT.. AS A PRECAUTIONARY MEASURE?

FLIGHT WILL SOLVE NOTHING, MY X-MEN! JOIN THE OTHERS, BEAST! JEAN, REMAIN WITH ME!

BUT, PROFESSOR... THEY MAY NEED *ME*, TOO....!

YOUR CHANCE WILL COME, GIRL! FOR THE MOMENT, I NEED YOU HERE!

CAREFUL, ICEMAN! IT WILL TAKE MORE THAN A HASTILY-FORMED FROZEN CLUB TO AFFECT THE *JUGGERNAUT*!

SCAMPER, BOBBY!! WE'RE *NEEDED*!

THERE'S GOTTA BE *SOME* WAY TO STOP HIM... THERE'S JUST *GOTTA*!

7.

CYKE, I CAN'T *HOLD* HIM! HE KEEPS CHARGING FORWARD NO MATTER *WHAT* WE DO!

HE'S ADVANCING AGAINST MY FORCE BEAM AS THOUGH IT DOESN'T EXIST!

I *WARNED* YOU! YOU'RE MERELY *MUTANTS*...BUT I.. I RECEIVED MY POWER FROM THE ENCHANTED TEMPLE OF *CYTTORAK!!* *NOTHING* CAN STAND IN MY WAY!

LEAST OF ALL A USELESS, WING-FLAPPING WONDER BOY LIKE *YOU!*

I DIDN'T REALIZE HE COULD *MOVE* SO FAST! HE SNARED THE *ANGEL!*

THEN, BEFORE CYCLOPS CAN REDIRECT HIS POWERFUL OPTIC BEAM, THE DREADED *JUGGERNAUT* SHOVES HIS STARTLED VICTIM DIRECTLY IN ITS PATH...!

PHIKK!

THERE! THIS WILL RID ME OF *ONE* PETTY ANNOYANCE!

I JUST HAD TIME TO WEAKEN MY BEAM'S INTENSITY...LUCKILY, WARREN IS MERELY STUNNED!

AND NOW I'LL LET THE *REST* OF YOU COSTUMED WEAKLINGS KEEP HIM *COMPANY!*

WE'VE BEEN THREATENED *BEFORE*, MISTER... AND *WE'RE* STILL HERE...WHILE OUR THREATENERS *AREN'T!* THERE'S GOT TO BE *SOME* WAY TO BEAT YOU, AND WE'LL *FIND* IT OR DIE TRYING!

THAT'S VERY *OBLIGING* OF YOU, CYCLOPS! THAT'S EXACTLY THE FATE I HAD IN MIND FOR YOU!

JUST STAND WHERE YOU ARE A MINUTE LONGER!

HE WILL, BIG MAN... BUT *YOU* WON'T!!

THE STAIRS BENEATH MY FEET...THEY TURNED TO *ICE!!* I-I'M LOSING MY FOOTING!

GOOD WORK, ICEMAN! YOU'RE JUST IN TIME!

8.

AND, EVEN AS THE BATTLE RAGES, TEENAGER *JOHNNY STORM* CLIMBS INTO A FRIEND'S RACING CAR IN A LOCAL GARAGE MANY MILES AWAY...

NOT A BAD LITTLE CRATE YOU'VE GOT HERE, CHARLIE! I HOPE I'LL BE ABLE TO JOIN YOU WHEN YOU TRY HER OUT ON THE SALT FLATS!

AW, YOU'LL PROBABLY BE CUTTIN' AROUND TOWN AFTER SOME NUTTY SUPER-VILLAIN, JOHNNY!

BEATS ME WHY ANYONE WOULD WANNA BE A COSTUMED CRIME-FIGHTER WHEN HE COULD SPEND HIS TIME WITH *RACIN' CARS* INSTEAD!

Y'KNOW SOMETHIN', FELLAS? I'VE OFTEN WONDERED THE SAME THING MYSELF! MAYBE I'M A MENTAL CASE AND DON'T KNOW IT!

UH-OH! THERE MAY BE MORE *TRUTH* TO THAT THAN I THOUGHT! *NOW* I'M BEGINNING TO *HEAR* THINGS...INSIDE MY BRAIN!

NO! I'M *NOT* HEARING THINGS! IT'S A MENTAL THOUGHT WAVE... AND IT'S SO *STRONG* I CAN ALMOST *TOUCH* IT!

HEY, JOHNNY...WHAT'S SHAKIN'? YOU LOOK LIKE YOU SAT ON A *TACK!*

CLAM UP, YOU GUYS! SOMETHING'S GOIN' *ON!*

I *KNEW* IT! ANY MINUTE NOW HE'LL YELL *FLAME ON* 'N' GO FLYING OUTTA HERE!

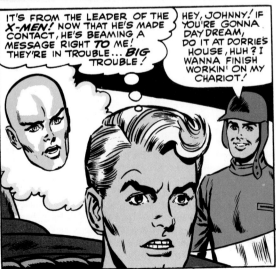

IT'S FROM THE LEADER OF THE *X-MEN!* NOW THAT HE'S MADE CONTACT, HE'S BEAMING A MESSAGE RIGHT *TO* ME! THEY'RE IN TROUBLE... *BIG* TROUBLE!

HEY, JOHNNY! IF YOU'RE GONNA DAYDREAM, DO IT AT DORRIE'S HOUSE, HUH? I WANNA FINISH WORKIN' ON MY CHARIOT!

BUT, HOW CAN I BE *SURE?* REED *WARNED* ME THAT ANY OF OUR OLD ENEMIES ARE APT TO SET ALL KINDS OF TRAPS FOR US...TO PREVENT HIS WEDDING FROM TAKING PLACE!*

FOR ALL I KNOW, *DR. DOOM* COULD BE PLANTING THIS THOUGHT IN MY BRAIN, OR THE *WIZARD!*

ANYWAY, I HESITATED TOO LONG...THE CONTACT IS FADING AWAY.. I'VE *LOST* IT!

* DON'T TAKE *OUR* WORD FOR IT!..SEE THE GREAT *F.F. ANNUAL #4,* ON SALE *NOW!..STAN.* 9.

PROFESSOR! WHAT'S WRONG? WHAT *IS* IT?

I ACCIDENTALLY REACHED THE *HUMAN TORCH!* THEN, I THOUGHT OF A WAY HE COULD *HELP* US... BUT HE DIDN'T TRUST HIS SENSES!

AND I DARE NOT WASTE TOO MUCH MENTAL ENERGY BY PROLONGING THE CONTACT IN ORDER TO *CONVINCE* HIM!

BUT...WHAT CAN THE *TORCH* DO THAT THE REST OF US CAN'T?? *OUR* POWER IS AS GREAT AS *HIS!*

TRUE, JEAN...BUT HIS IS A *DIFFERENT TYPE* OF POWER...AND, COMBINED WITH OUR OWN, IT MIGHT JUST TURN THE TIDE!

I *MUST* CONTACT HIM AGAIN...EVEN IF IT WEAKENS ME!

MEANWHILE, ON THE STAIRWAY, JUST OUTSIDE THE DOOR...

NO MATTER *HOW* THICK YOU MAKE THAT ICE PACK, I'LL BREAK OUT OF IT! YOU'RE NOT BATTLING SOME ORDINARY CRIMINAL NOW!

LOOK! HE'S CRACKING THE ICE!

BOY, HE SURE COMES ON *STRONG!*

EVEN THOUGH I *KNOW* HE CAN BREAK OUT OF THIS, I'LL KEEP PACKING IT AROUND HIM TO GIVE *YOU* A CHANCE TO RECHARGE YOUR FORCE BEAM, CYKE!

BUT, WE'RE ONLY FIGHTING A *DELAYING* ACTION AT BEST! IF ONLY THERE WERE SOME *OTHER* WAY...!

LOOK! HE'S STARTING TO *GLOW* WITH THAT AURA OF ENERGY, OR WHATEVER HE CALLED IT!

GET *BACK*, BOBBY...BACK! HE'LL CRACK OPEN THE ENTIRE ICE WALL AT ANY SECOND!

BRAKKK!

UNNHHH..!

TOO LATE! THOSE ROCK-HARD CHUNKS OF FLYING ICE STRUCK HIM BEFORE HE COULD DODGE! ...AND NOW THE *JUGGERNAUT* IS FREE AGAIN!

10.

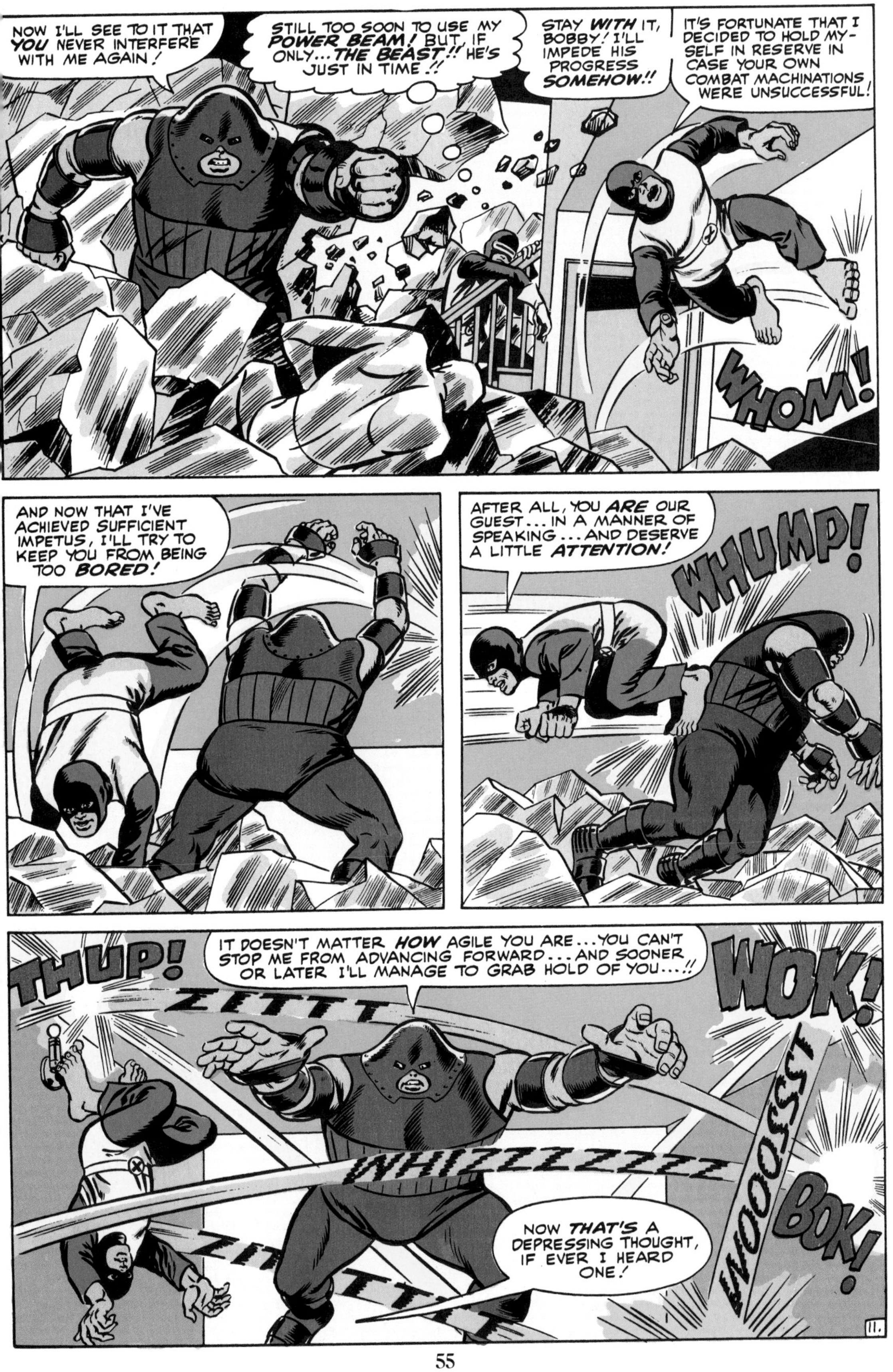
NOW I'LL SEE TO IT THAT YOU NEVER INTERFERE WITH ME AGAIN!
STILL TOO SOON TO USE MY POWER BEAM! BUT, IF ONLY... THE BEAST!! HE'S JUST IN TIME.!!
STAY WITH IT, BOBBY! I'LL IMPEDE HIS PROGRESS SOMEHOW!!
IT'S FORTUNATE THAT I DECIDED TO HOLD MY-SELF IN RESERVE IN CASE YOUR OWN COMBAT MACHINATIONS WERE UNSUCCESSFUL!
WHOM!
AND NOW THAT I'VE ACHIEVED SUFFICIENT IMPETUS, I'LL TRY TO KEEP YOU FROM BEING TOO BORED!
AFTER ALL, YOU ARE OUR GUEST... IN A MANNER OF SPEAKING... AND DESERVE A LITTLE ATTENTION!
WHUMP!
THUP!
IT DOESN'T MATTER HOW AGILE YOU ARE... YOU CAN'T STOP ME FROM ADVANCING FORWARD... AND SOONER OR LATER I'LL MANAGE TO GRAB HOLD OF YOU...!!
WOK!
ZITTT
WHIZZZZZZZZ
WOOOSSST
BOK!
NOW THAT'S A DEPRESSING THOUGHT, IF EVER I HEARD ONE!
11.

THEN SUDDENLY, A SHARP, POWERFUL, COMMANDING *THOUGHT* RINGS OUT IN THE BRAIN OF HANK McCOY..!

BEAST! LOOSEN HIS HELMET! IT'S THE ONLY WAY TO DEFEAT HIM!

WE MUSTN'T FORGET OUR *MANNERS*, JUG! A GENTLEMAN DOFFS HIS HAT WHEN ENTERING A ROOM!

YOU *FOOL!* DID YOU EXPECT TO REMOVE MY HELMET BEFORE I COULD *GRAB* YOU??!

WELL, IT *DID* SEEM LIKE AN AWFULLY CLEVER IDEA AT THE TIME!

CLEVER OR NOT...IT MAY WELL BE YOUR *LAST* IDEA!

MY *FOOT..!!*

NOW, ONCE AGAIN, YOU'LL FEEL THE MATCHLESS POWER OF THE *JUGGERNAUT!!*

CAN'T *EXTRICATE* MYSELF!

I'LL GIVE YOU NO SECOND CHANCE TO ESCAPE ME BY MEANS OF FANCY FOOTWORK...!

THUD!

AND NOW THAT YOU'RE HELPLESS, I'LL... *WHA...??*

INJURING ONE FOOT DOESN'T RENDER THE *BEAST* HELPLESS! MY HANDS ARE *EQUALLY* DEXTEROUS!

WHOOM!

12.

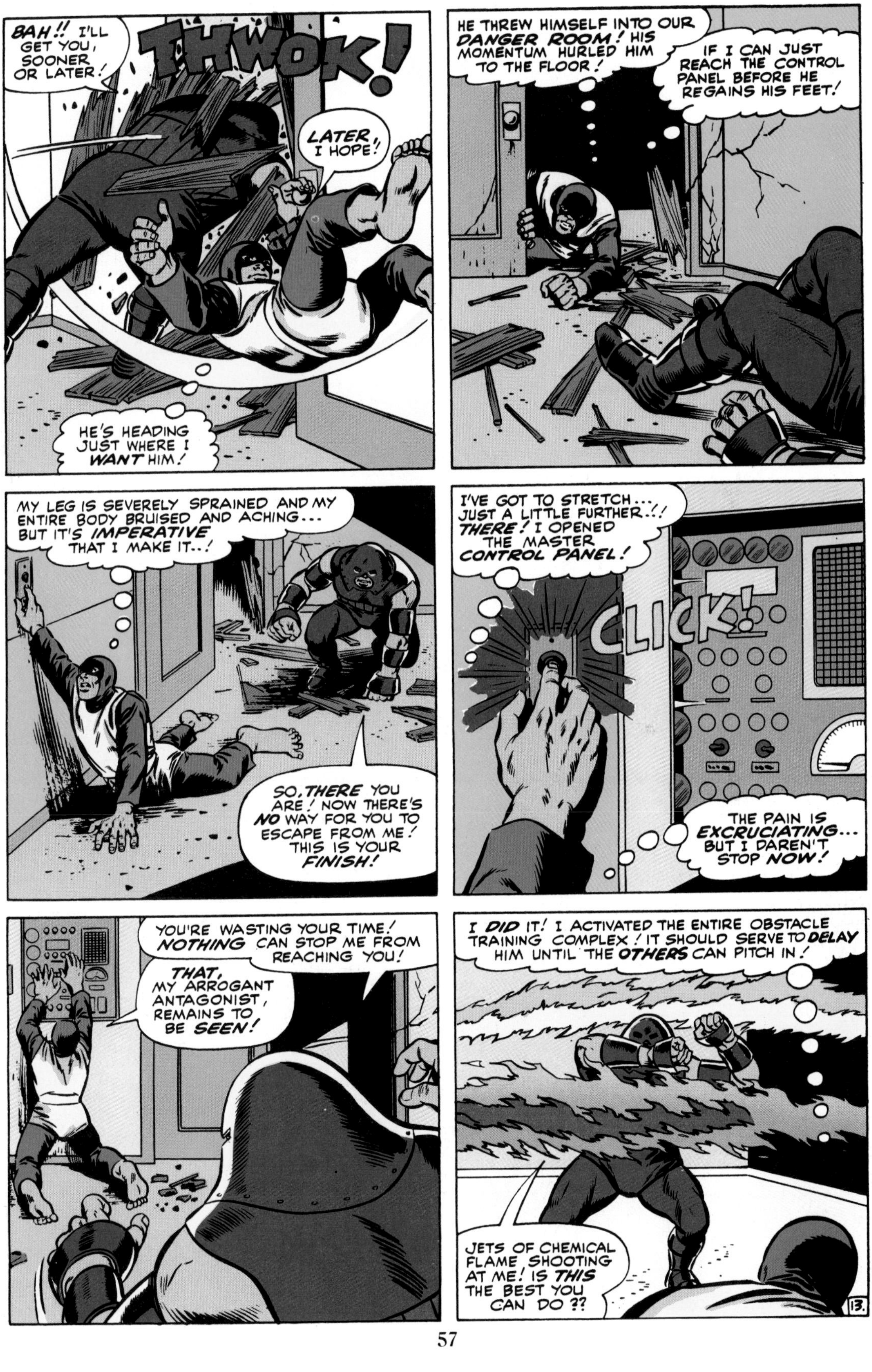
BAH!! I'LL GET YOU, SOONER OR LATER!
THWOK!
LATER, I HOPE!!
HE'S HEADING JUST WHERE I WANT HIM!
HE THREW HIMSELF INTO OUR DANGER ROOM! HIS MOMENTUM HURLED HIM TO THE FLOOR!
IF I CAN JUST REACH THE CONTROL PANEL BEFORE HE REGAINS HIS FEET!
MY LEG IS SEVERELY SPRAINED AND MY ENTIRE BODY BRUISED AND ACHING... BUT IT'S IMPERATIVE THAT I MAKE IT..!
SO, THERE YOU ARE! NOW THERE'S NO WAY FOR YOU TO ESCAPE FROM ME! THIS IS YOUR FINISH!
I'VE GOT TO STRETCH... JUST A LITTLE FURTHER..!! THERE! I OPENED THE MASTER CONTROL PANEL!
CLICK!
THE PAIN IS EXCRUCIATING... BUT I DAREN'T STOP NOW!
YOU'RE WASTING YOUR TIME! NOTHING CAN STOP ME FROM REACHING YOU!
THAT, MY ARROGANT ANTAGONIST, REMAINS TO BE SEEN!
I DID IT! I ACTIVATED THE ENTIRE OBSTACLE TRAINING COMPLEX! IT SHOULD SERVE TO DELAY HIM UNTIL THE OTHERS CAN PITCH IN!
JETS OF CHEMICAL FLAME SHOOTING AT ME! IS THIS THE BEST YOU CAN DO??
13.

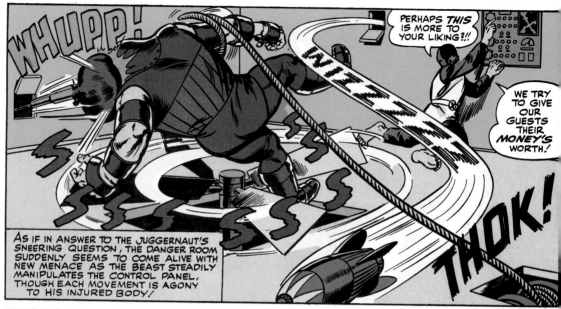

WHUPP!

WITTT!

PERHAPS *THIS* IS MORE TO YOUR LIKING?!!

WE TRY TO GIVE OUR GUESTS THEIR *MONEY'S* WORTH!

THOK!

As if in answer to the *Juggernaut's* sneering question, the Danger Room suddenly seems to come alive with new menace as the Beast steadily manipulates the control panel, though each movement is agony to his injured body!

But, the supernatural power of the *Juggernaut* is almost incalculable! Despite all the dangers, he forges ahead, smashing each and every bit of apparatus in turn!

HAVE YOU FORGOTTEN...? I..AM..THE.. *JUGGERNAUT!!*

RIPP!

Still unwilling to surrender, the desperate *Beast* unleashes the most powerful danger in their arsenal...a swiftly-rolling ten-ton barrel of steel!!

ROOM!

Thus, the irresistible force meets the immovable object...an object from whose body flows a current of such potent energy that the mighty steel roller is stopped cold, before it can strike him!!

SQUEEEE

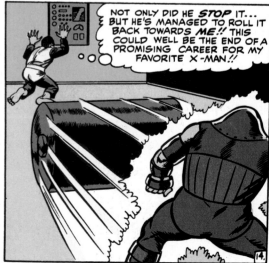

NOT ONLY DID HE *STOP* IT... BUT HE'S MANAGED TO ROLL IT BACK TOWARDS *ME!!* THIS COULD WELL BE THE END OF A PROMISING CAREER FOR MY FAVORITE X-MAN!!

14.

IT'S TOO LATE TO LOCATE THE BUTTON TO *STOP* THAT THING... I'VE ONLY *ONE* CHANCE...!

I MUSTN'T THINK OF THE PAIN... I'VE *GOT* TO USE MY LEGS...!!

...UHHHH!.. BECAUSE OF MY LEG... COULDN'T LEAP HIGH ENOUGH.. JUST... *UHH!!*

THUD!

HE'S UNCONSCIOUS! HE CAN'T TROUBLE ME ANY MORE! I'LL CONTINUE ON TILL I TRAP *XAVIER* ... THEN I'LL COME BACK AND FINISH THE BEAST... AND *ALL* OF THEM!

MEANWHILE, A THOUGHTFUL JOHNNY STORM DRIVES DOWN MADISON AVENUE, TRYING TO ARRIVE AT A MOMENTOUS DECISION ...!

I'M RECEIVING THAT MENTAL CONTACT AGAIN! IT *SEEMS* GENUINE ENOUGH! BUT... DO I DARE TO *TRUST* IT!?

AWW, WHAT THE HECK! IF I WAS THE *CAUTIOUS* TYPE, I WOULDN'T BE A MEMBER OF THE F.F. IN THE *FIRST* PLACE! WHAT AM I SCARED OF??

GOOD! I HAVE DISPELLED THE CLOUD OF SUSPICION FROM HIS BRAIN! NOW, I MUST LEAD HIM TO US AS QUICKLY AS POSSIBLE!

I SHALL DIRECT YOU TO WHERE YOU ARE NEEDED! YOU MUST RELAX! TRY TO THINK OF NOTHING! LET *MY* MIND GUIDE YOURS!

OKAY, MISTER! IT'S YOUR SHOW!

YOUR CAR IS TOO SLOW! PARK IT AND BECOME THE *HUMAN TORCH!* THEN, FOLLOW MY *THOUGHT BEAM!*

FLAME ON!

WHEN YOU ARRIVE, YOU WILL FOLLOW MY COMMANDS *IMPLICITLY!* THERE IS MORE AT STAKE THAN YOU CAN IMAGINE!

15

THEN, BACK AT THE WORLD'S MOST UNUSUAL PRIVATE SCHOOL...

DID YOU CONTACT HIM, PROFESSOR?

YES, JEAN! AND NOW...IT'S TIME FOR *ME* TO ENTER THE PICTURE! MY BRAIN HAS BEEN FORTIFIED TO THE MAXIMUM DEGREE!

IF I AM *EVER* TO DEFEAT THE JUGGERNAUT, IT MUST BE *NOW!*

BE ON GUARD, MY DEAR...WE'RE ALMOST *UPON* HIM!

HAS *ANGEL* RECOVERED FROM HIS ENCOUNTER WITH MY STEPBROTHER YET? HIS MUTANT TALENTS ARE VERY IMPORTANT TO MY PLAN!

I DON'T KNOW, SIR! I HAVEN'T SEEN HIM FOR THE PAST FEW MINUTES!

THERE'S JUGGERNAUT *NOW!*

SO, XAVIER! DESPITE EVERYTHING YOU COULD DO TO STOP ME... DESPITE ALL YOUR PUNY X-MEN.. I HAVE CORNERED YOU AT LAST!

PERHAPS IT IS *I* WHO HAVE CORNERED *YOU*, CAIN!

NEVER USE THAT NAME AGAIN!! I AM THE *JUGGERNAUT!* CAIN MARKO NO LONGER EXISTS...

..AND NEITHER SHALL *YOU*, AFTER I...

WHA..? WHAT ARE YOU *DOING??*

SUSPENDING YOU IN THE AIR... TELEKINET-ICALLY

EASY, MARVEL GIRL! HE'S *TOO* STRONG.!! DON'T STRAIN YOURSELF!

THE PROFESSOR IS *RIGHT!* HE'S ADVANCING AGAINST ME... PUSHING MY POWER ASIDE AS THOUGH IT'S A PHYSICAL THING...!

BUT THEN, AT THAT TENSION-PACKED INSTANT...!

YOU ARE JUST IN *TIME*, TORCH! YOUR ADVERSARY IS OVER THERE! YOU MUST SOME-HOW *ENSNARE* HIM!

I HEAR YA TALKIN', PAL! JUST SIT TIGHT AND WATCH MY SMOKE!!

16.

WHOEVER HE IS...MY FLAMES DON'T AFFECT HIM! THERE'S SOME STRANGE SORT OF *ENERGY FIELD* AROUND HIM WHICH THEY CAN'T PENETRATE!

I MIGHT HAVE KNOWN THE *X-MEN* WOULDN'T NEED ANYONE UNLESS THEY WERE UP AGAINST SOMETHING *SPECIAL!*

KEEP ENCIRCLING HIM, TORCH...EVEN THOUGH IT SEEMS IN VAIN! YOUR MISSION IS TO *CONFUSE* HIM... TO KEEP HIM OCCUPIED WHILE MY X-MEN DELIVER THE FINAL BLOW!

A *FINE* THING! I'M DOIN' THE JOB OF A TEN-CENT *PINWHEEL!*

ALTHOUGH HE SITS QUIETLY, HARDLY MOVING A MUSCLE, THE MANY-FACETED BRAIN OF CHARLES XAVIER IS PERFORMING MANY FUNCTIONS AT ONCE...AND ONE OF THOSE FUNCTIONS IS...SUMMONING WARREN WORTHINGTON THE THIRD...THE MUTANT *ANGEL!*

ANGEL! WHEREVER YOU ARE! COME TO ME! THIS IS PROFESSOR X... *COME TO ME!* WE *NEED* YOU!!

AND, A SHORT DISTANCE DOWN THE HALL, LYING AMONG THE DEBRIS WHERE HE HAD FALLEN, THE TALL, SLIM, WINGED X-MAN IS PRODDED BY THE POWERFUL THOUGHT COMMAND...!

WE *NEED* YOU, ANGEL!! YOU MUST ANSWER MY SUMMONS!! WE NEED YOU...!!

THE PROFESSOR ...CALLING! CAN'T LET HIM DOWN...!

STILL WEAK...WOBBLY IN MY KNEES!! WON'T USE MY WINGS YET...HAVE TO SAVE MY STRENGTH...TO FIGHT *JUGGERNAUT!*

FLAMES.. UP AHEAD! IT LOOKS LIKE ...IT *IS*... THE *HUMAN TORCH!*

MY FIREBALLS AREN'T *STOPPING* HIM, PROFESSOR! WHAT *ELSE* DO YOU SUGGEST?

YOU MAY DISCONTINUE THEM NOW!

THE *FINAL PHASE* OF MY PLAN IS ABOUT TO BEGIN!

BRACE YOURSELF, ANGEL! WAIT FOR MY NEXT MENTAL COMMAND!

17.

61

THE ANGEL IS STILL WEAK...ON THE VERGE OF EXHAUSTION! I MUST GAIN HIM A FEW MORE SECONDS!

TORCH! LAND IN FRONT OF JUGGERNAUT AND DO EXACTLY AS I TELL YOU! SPLIT-SECOND TIMING WILL BE ALL-IMPORTANT!

I KNEW YOU'D HAVE TO LAND SOONER OR LATER! NOW, YOU TOO ARE HELPLESS BEFORE ME!

STAND READY TO BRING YOUR FLAME TO PEAK INTENSITY... LIKE AN EXPLODING FLASH BULB!

NOW, TORCH... NOW!

PERFECT! YOU BLINDED HIM TEMPORARILY! HE CANNOT FIGHT WHAT HE CANNOT SEE! YOU STAGGERED HIM!

THAT SUDDEN BRIGHTNESS!! MY EYES!! EVERYTHING IS SPINNING BEFORE ME!!

IT'S UP TO YOU NOW, ANGEL! TAKE TO THE AIR!!

I WON'T FAIL YOU, PROFESSOR!!

I KNOW YOU WON'T! MY NEXT COMMANDS WILL BE TELEPATHIC... TO CONFOUND JUGGERNAUT!

YOU'RE TOO LOW, ANGEL! FLY HIGHER! THOUGH HE CANNOT SEE YOU, HE CAN HEAR THE BEATING OF YOUR WINGS!

THAT'S BETTER! STAY OUT OF REACH OF HIS GROPING ARMS!

BOY! THAT GUY COULD TEACH ME THINGS ABOUT FLYING!

YOU SERVE NO PURPOSE BUT TO INCREASE MY RAGE! YOU CANNOT HARM THE JUGGERNAUT!

HE KINDA MAKES SENSE TO ME, PROFESSOR! WHAT ARE YOU TRYING TO ACCOMPLISH BY HAVING THE ANGEL FLY AROUND HIM?

JUST WATCH...IT WILL SOON BECOME CLEAR TO YOU!

NOW, ANGEL! THIS IS THE INSTANT! DIVE! DIVE!

THIS WILL BE YOUR ONLY CHANCE! *EVERYTHING* DEPENDS UPON IT!

YOU *DID* IT! HE'S *VULNERABLE* NOW!

MY *HELMET!!*

SECONDS LATER, AFTER THE JUGGERNAUT'S *VISION* HAS RETURNED...

UNDER MY MENTAL COMMANDS, THE *BEAST* LOOSENED YOUR HELMET DURING YOUR BATTLE...

THEN, TO CULMINATE THE PLAN, THE *ANGEL* REMOVED IT COMPLETELY!

WITH OR *WITHOUT* THAT HELMET, *YOU* WON'T ESCAPE ME!

NONSENSE, CAIN! *I* AM THE MASTER HERE AGAIN!

YOURS WAS AN *ACQUIRED* POWER...OBTAINED BY A FREAK ACCIDENT OF CHANCE! BUT MY *BRAIN* IS A *PART* OF ME... MY POWER IS MY *OWN!*

AND *THIS* IS BUT THE SMALLEST *PART* OF IT!

NO! YOU CAN'T BEAT ME! YOU *CAN'T!* YOU WERE *ALWAYS* THE WINNER... EVEN WHEN WE WERE YOUNG... I HATED YOU! I SWORE I'D *VANQUISH* YOU SOME DAY! AND I WILL... I *WILL!*

NEVER HAS THERE BEEN SUCH RAW *HATRED*...SUCH AN INSATIABLE DESIRE FOR *VENGEANCE!* THOUGH HIS *BODY* IS DEFEATED, HIS *HATE* IS PROPELLING HIM FORWARD!!

IF *I* MUST TASTE THE BITTER DREGS OF DEFEAT...I'LL DRAG *YOU* DOWN WITH ME!! NO MATTER WHAT HAPPENS TO ME... *YOU* MUST PAY!

ALL YOUR LIFE YOU'VE BEEN RULED BY GREED... ENVY.. AVARICE! AND NOW...IT HAS COME TO *THIS!*

19.

63

IF THINGS HAD BEEN DIFFERENT, WE MIGHT HAVE BEEN FRIENDS... WE MIGHT HAVE TRULY BEEN *BROTHERS!* BUT YOU WOULD HAVE IT NO OTHER WAY! THIS FINAL CHAPTER WAS WRITTEN WHEN WE FIRST MET! THIS IS THE ONLY WAY IT COULD HAVE ENDED!

UHHHHH...!

I DON'T *GET* IT! ALL YOU DID... WAS *LOOK* AT HIM!!

IT IS BEST YOU THINK SO, MY YOUNG FRIEND!

HE WILL RECOVER... AND, WITHOUT HIS HELMET, THE AUTHORITIES WILL BE ABLE TO KEEP HIM IN CONFINEMENT!

AS FOR YOU... YOU WILL RETURN TO *FANTASTIC FOUR* HEAD-QUARTERS NOW... WITH NO MEMORY OF WHAT HAS OCCURRED!

BUT, THE *X-MEN* SHALL REMEMBER... AND SHALL EVER BE GRATEFUL TO YOU, JOHNNY STORM!

THUS, SECONDS LATER, A FAMOUS, FLAMING FIGURE BLAZES ACROSS WESTCHESTER TOWARDS THE HEART OF MANHATTAN...

BOY! TALK ABOUT *DAYDREAMING!* I CAN'T REMEMBER *HOW* I FLEW THIS FAR FROM HOME!

I MUST REALLY BE GETTING *ABSENT-MINDED* IN MY OLD AGE!

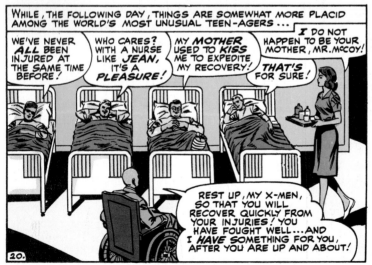

WHILE, THE FOLLOWING DAY, THINGS ARE SOMEWHAT MORE PLACID AMONG THE WORLD'S MOST UNUSUAL TEEN-AGERS...

WE'VE NEVER *ALL* BEEN INJURED AT THE SAME TIME BEFORE!

WHO CARES? WITH A NURSE LIKE *JEAN*, IT'S A *PLEASURE!*

MY *MOTHER* USED TO *KISS* ME TO EXPEDITE MY RECOVERY! *THAT'S* FOR SURE!

I DO NOT HAPPEN TO BE YOUR MOTHER, MR. McCOY!

REST UP, MY X-MEN, SO THAT YOU WILL RECOVER QUICKLY FROM YOUR INJURIES! YOU HAVE FOUGHT WELL... AND I *HAVE* SOMETHING FOR YOU, AFTER YOU ARE UP AND ABOUT!

20.

HOW *ABOUT* THAT? WE'RE GONNA GET A *REWARD!*

C'MON, PROFESSOR... TELL US WHAT IT *IS!!*

IT'S A *BROOM*... FOR *EACH* OF YOU! THE SCHOOL IS A *SHAMBLES* AFTER YOUR FIGHT... AND *SOMEBODY* HAS TO TIDY IT UP!

NEXT ISSUE... ONE OF THE STRANGEST MENACES OF ALL CONFRONTS THE X-MEN! IT'LL BE A BULLPEN BOMBSHELL... AND YOU DON'T EVEN HAVE TO BE A MUTANT TO ENJOY IT! *'NUFF SAID!*

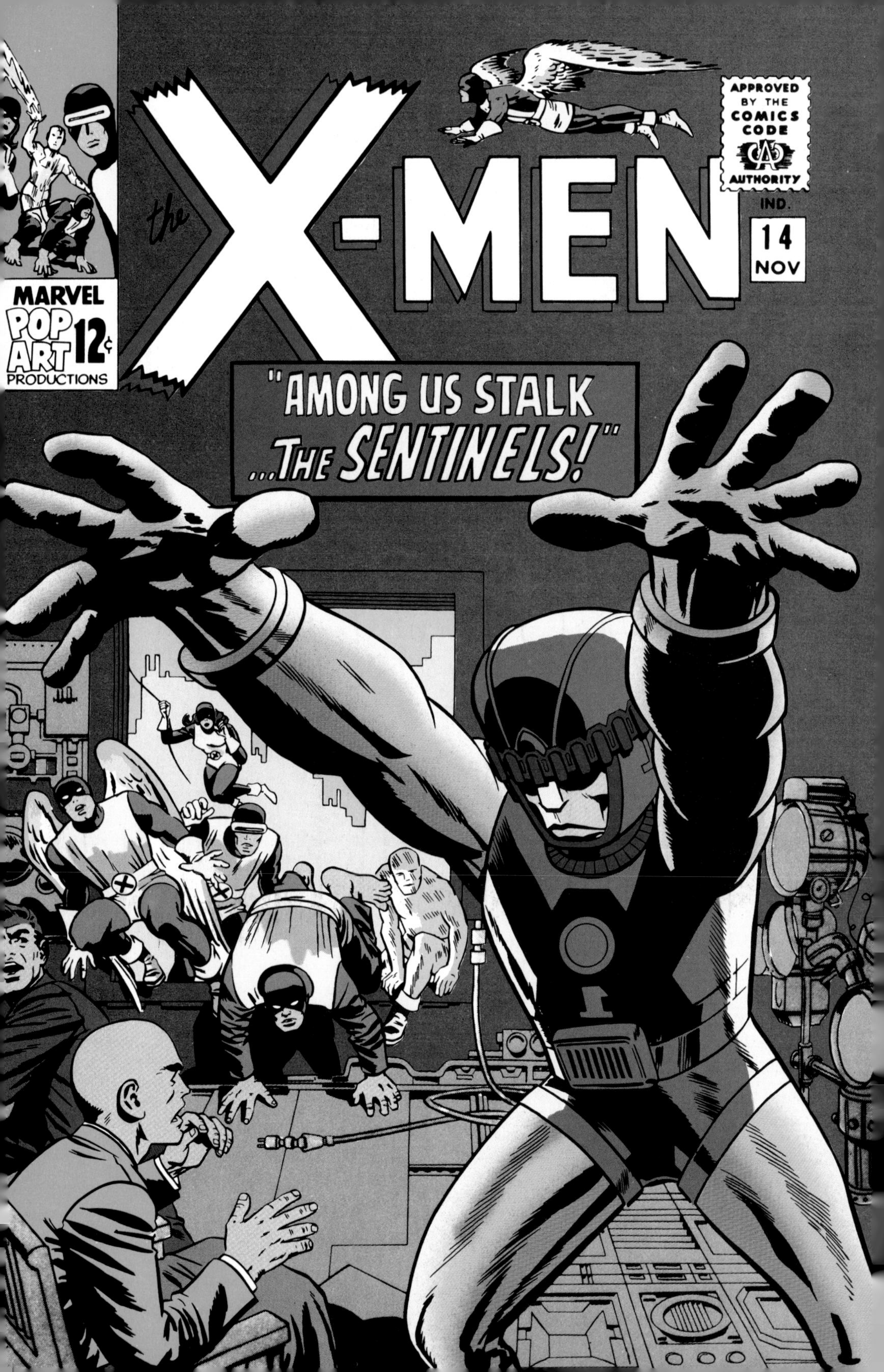
APPROVED BY THE COMICS CODE AUTHORITY
the X-MEN
IND.
14
NOV
MARVEL POP ART PRODUCTIONS 12¢
"AMONG US STALK ...THE SENTINELS!"

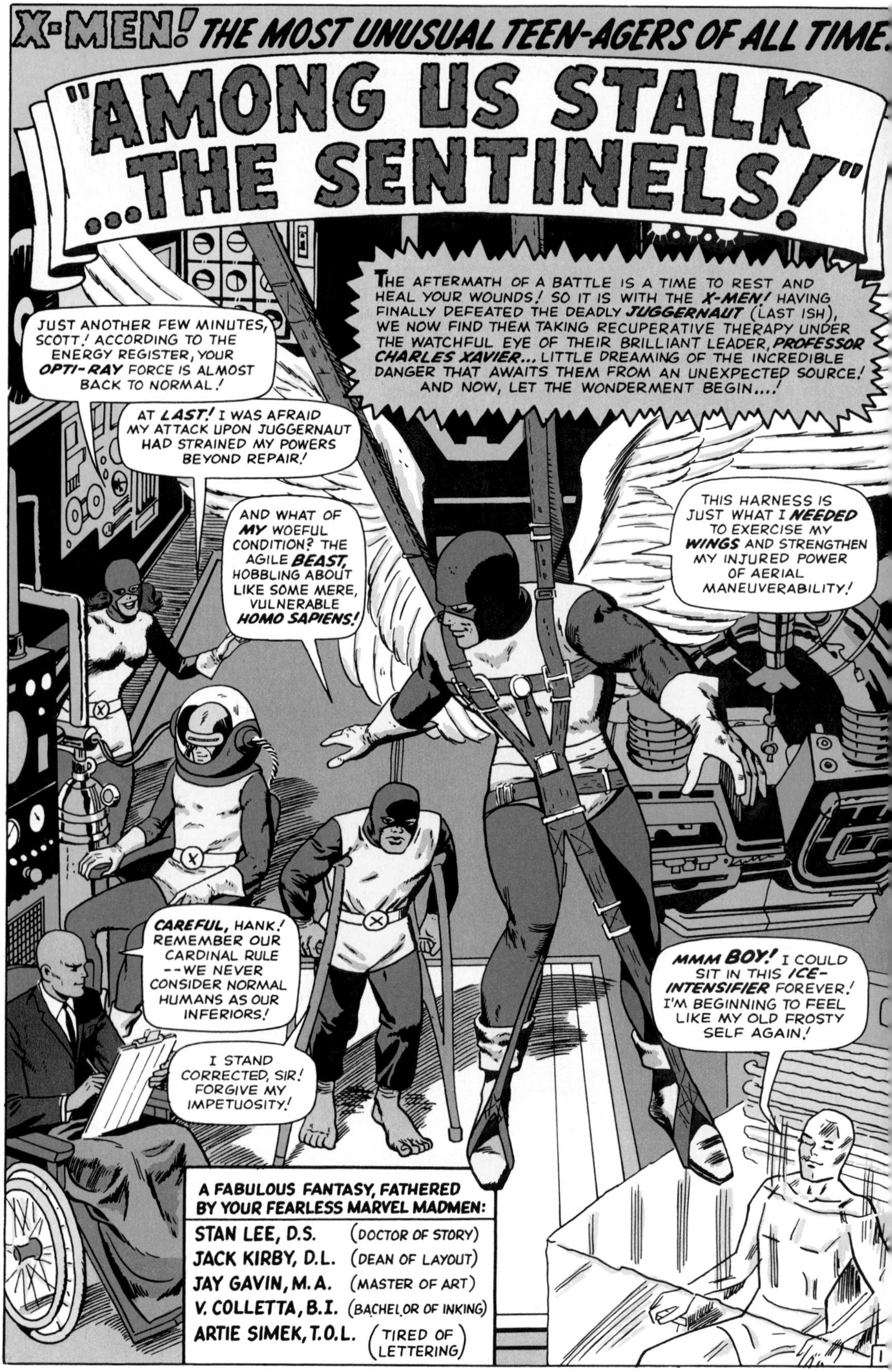
X-MEN! THE MOST UNUSUAL TEEN-AGERS OF ALL TIME.
"AMONG US STALK ...THE SENTINELS!"
THE AFTERMATH OF A BATTLE IS A TIME TO REST AND HEAL YOUR WOUNDS! SO IT IS WITH THE X-MEN! HAVING FINALLY DEFEATED THE DEADLY JUGGERNAUT (LAST ISH), WE NOW FIND THEM TAKING RECUPERATIVE THERAPY UNDER THE WATCHFUL EYE OF THEIR BRILLIANT LEADER, PROFESSOR CHARLES XAVIER... LITTLE DREAMING OF THE INCREDIBLE DANGER THAT AWAITS THEM FROM AN UNEXPECTED SOURCE! AND NOW, LET THE WONDERMENT BEGIN....!
JUST ANOTHER FEW MINUTES, SCOTT! ACCORDING TO THE ENERGY REGISTER, YOUR OPTI-RAY FORCE IS ALMOST BACK TO NORMAL!
AT LAST! I WAS AFRAID MY ATTACK UPON JUGGERNAUT HAD STRAINED MY POWERS BEYOND REPAIR!
AND WHAT OF MY WOEFUL CONDITION? THE AGILE BEAST, HOBBLING ABOUT LIKE SOME MERE, VULNERABLE HOMO SAPIENS!
THIS HARNESS IS JUST WHAT I NEEDED TO EXERCISE MY WINGS AND STRENGTHEN MY INJURED POWER OF AERIAL MANEUVERABILITY!
CAREFUL, HANK! REMEMBER OUR CARDINAL RULE --WE NEVER CONSIDER NORMAL HUMANS AS OUR INFERIORS!
I STAND CORRECTED, SIR! FORGIVE MY IMPETUOSITY!
MMM BOY! I COULD SIT IN THIS ICE-INTENSIFIER FOREVER! I'M BEGINNING TO FEEL LIKE MY OLD FROSTY SELF AGAIN!
A FABULOUS FANTASY, FATHERED BY YOUR FEARLESS MARVEL MADMEN:
STAN LEE, D.S. (DOCTOR OF STORY)
JACK KIRBY, D.L. (DEAN OF LAYOUT)
JAY GAVIN, M.A. (MASTER OF ART)
V. COLLETTA, B.I. (BACHELOR OF INKING)
ARTIE SIMEK, T.O.L. (TIRED OF LETTERING)
1

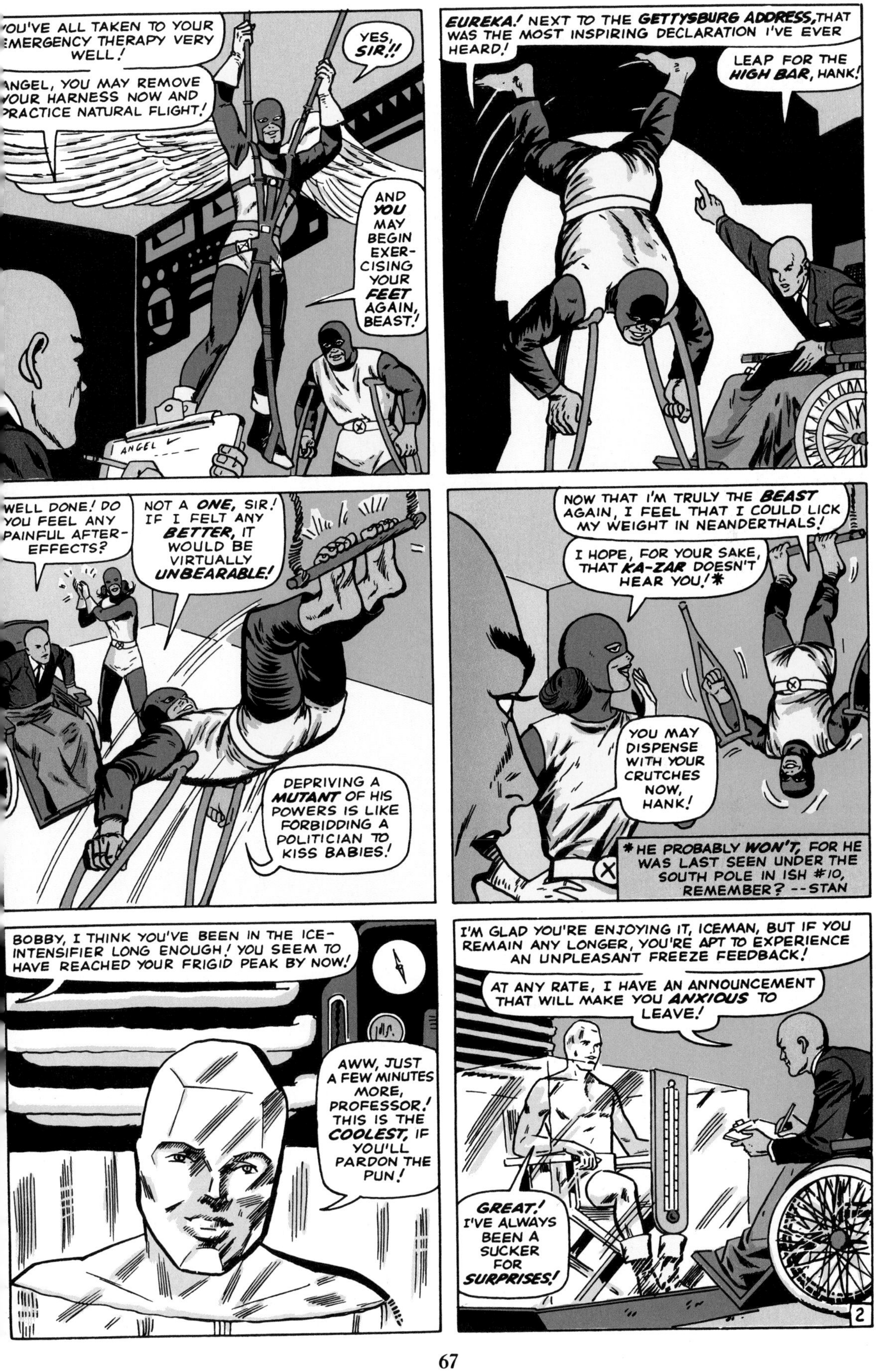
YOU'VE ALL TAKEN TO YOUR EMERGENCY THERAPY VERY WELL!
ANGEL, YOU MAY REMOVE YOUR HARNESS NOW AND PRACTICE NATURAL FLIGHT!
YES, SIR!!
AND YOU MAY BEGIN EXERCISING YOUR FEET AGAIN, BEAST!
ANGEL
EUREKA! NEXT TO THE GETTYSBURG ADDRESS, THAT WAS THE MOST INSPIRING DECLARATION I'VE EVER HEARD!
LEAP FOR THE HIGH BAR, HANK!
WELL DONE! DO YOU FEEL ANY PAINFUL AFTER-EFFECTS?
NOT A ONE, SIR! IF I FELT ANY BETTER, IT WOULD BE VIRTUALLY UNBEARABLE!
DEPRIVING A MUTANT OF HIS POWERS IS LIKE FORBIDDING A POLITICIAN TO KISS BABIES!
NOW THAT I'M TRULY THE BEAST AGAIN, I FEEL THAT I COULD LICK MY WEIGHT IN NEANDERTHALS!
I HOPE, FOR YOUR SAKE, THAT KA-ZAR DOESN'T HEAR YOU!*
YOU MAY DISPENSE WITH YOUR CRUTCHES NOW, HANK!
*HE PROBABLY WON'T, FOR HE WAS LAST SEEN UNDER THE SOUTH POLE IN ISH #10, REMEMBER? --STAN
BOBBY, I THINK YOU'VE BEEN IN THE ICE-INTENSIFIER LONG ENOUGH! YOU SEEM TO HAVE REACHED YOUR FRIGID PEAK BY NOW!
AWW, JUST A FEW MINUTES MORE, PROFESSOR! THIS IS THE COOLEST, IF YOU'LL PARDON THE PUN!
I'M GLAD YOU'RE ENJOYING IT, ICEMAN, BUT IF YOU REMAIN ANY LONGER, YOU'RE APT TO EXPERIENCE AN UNPLEASANT FREEZE FEEDBACK!
AT ANY RATE, I HAVE AN ANNOUNCEMENT THAT WILL MAKE YOU ANXIOUS TO LEAVE!
GREAT! I'VE ALWAYS BEEN A SUCKER FOR SURPRISES!
2

THIS IS A SURPRISE FOR **ALL** OF YOU! BECAUSE OF YOUR EXCELLENT RECORD OF ACHIEVEMENT AGAINST THE FOES YOU'VE ENCOUNTERED, IT'S TIME YOU ALL HAD A **VACATION!**

IT'LL BE OUR FIRST ONE IN **YEARS!**

WOWEEE, PROFESSOR! YOU JUST SAID THE MAGIC WORD!

OH! HOW **WONDERFUL!**

SAY IT **AGAIN!** IT'S LIKE A **SYMPHONY!**

IT'LL BE GOOD FOR **ALL** OF US, SIR! WE **HAVE** BEEN ON THE GO FOR MONTHS!

BUT, PERHAPS THE X-MEN WOULD NOT BE QUITE SO JOYFUL IF THEY WERE AWARE OF A PRESS CONFERENCE THAT IS TAKING PLACE AT THAT MOMENT IN ANOTHER CITY...

DR. TRASK! DO YOU REALIZE WHAT YOU'RE **SAYING?!!**

AS ONE OF OUR GREATEST ANTHROPOLOGISTS, YOUR DECLARATION WILL SHOCK THE **WORLD!**

THE WORLD **MUST** BE SHOCKED! THE DANGER WAS NEVER GREATER!

WE'VE BEEN SO BUSY WORRYING ABOUT COLD WARS, HOT WARS, ATOM BOMBS AND THE LIKE, THAT WE'VE OVERLOOKED THE GREATEST MENACE OF **ALL!**

MUTANTS WALK AMONG US! HIDDEN! UNKNOWN! WAITING--!

--WAITING FOR THEIR MOMENT TO **STRIKE!**

THEY ARE MANKIND'S MOST DEADLY ENEMY! FOR ONLY **THEY** HAVE THE ACTUAL **POWER** TO CONQUER THE HUMAN RACE!

EVEN AS WE SPEAK, THEY ARE **OUT** THERE-- SCHEMING, PLOTTING, PLANNING-- THINKING WE DON'T SUSPECT!

WOW! WAIT'LL **THIS** HITS THE FRONT PAGES!

BUT, THERE IS STILL TIME TO **SMASH** THEM-- IF WE STRIKE **NOW!**

WITHIN MINUTES, THE NATION'S PRESSES GO INTO ACTION...

DAILY GLOBE — MUTANT MENACE!
DAILY GLOBE — MUTANT MENACE!
DAILY GLOBE — MUTANT MENACE!
MUTANT MENACE! — DAILY GLOBE
MUTANT MENACE! — DAILY GLOBE
DAILY GLOBE
UTANT MENA

3

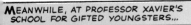

MAKE THEM *TIGHTER*, BOBBY! THE SOFT GAUZE CONSTRUCTION PREVENTS THE BANDS FROM CHAFING!

HOW DO YOU *STAND* IT, WARREN? IT MUST FEEL LIKE WEARING A *GIRDLE*!

THAT MAY BE, LITTLE FRIEND -- BUT IT'S BETTER THAN GIVING AWAY MY IDENTITY TO THE HUMAN RACE!

AWW, IF YOU ASK *ME*, NOBODY WOULD CARE EVEN IF THEY *FOUND OUT* ABOUT US!

NOBODY *ASKED* YOU, SONNY! JUST KEEP TAPING!

SAY, HOW COME YOUR *PARENTS* DON'T KNOW ABOUT YOUR WINGS, WARREY?

THEY DIDN'T *SPROUT* TILL I WAS OFF AT MILITARY SCHOOL!

AND *THERE*, I KEPT THEM HIDDEN UNDER MY UNIFORM -- AT FIRST!

THAT'S WHY I *LEFT* SCHOOL -- I COULDN'T AFFORD TO FACE A PHYSICAL EXAM!

AND, IN THE ROOM NEXT DOOR...

IT WOULDN'T BE MUCH OF A *VACATION* IF I HAD TO SPEND IT IN THIS *COSTUME*...

LUCKY THE PROF HAD THIS PAIR OF SPECIAL *SUNGLASSES* MADE FOR ME!

I'LL SHUT MY EYES NOW WHILE I REMOVE MY HELMET, BECAUSE THE LENS AUTOMATICALLY *RAISES* AS I LIFT THE VISOR!

I SHUDDER TO THINK WHAT WOULD HAPPEN IF I EVER ACCIDENTALLY *OPENED* MY EYES WHILE THEY HAD NO PROTECTIVE COVERING! I LIVE IN PERPETUAL *FEAR* OF SUCH A MOMENT!

BUT, THE SCHOLARLY X-MAN KNOWN AS THE *BEAST* HAS A PROBLEM OF A SOME- WHAT *DIFFERENT* NATURE...

BEING A MUTANT CAN BE VERY *VEXING* WHEN IT'S TIME TO DON ONE'S STREET CLOTHES!

ESPECIALLY WHEN ONE POSSESSES A PAIR OF PEDAL EXTREMITIES THE SIZE OF *MINE*!

THERE! DO YOU HAVE ENOUGH BREATHING SPACE, SWEETIES?

THESE SPECIALLY HINGED SHOES ARE SO *EXPENSIVE*, IT WOULD BE CHEAPER TO WALK ON MY *HANDS* -- THOUGH SOMEWHAT LESS *GLAMOROUS*!

4

MOMENTS LATER, IN THE OUTER HALL...

HERE COMES JEAN! I WONDER IF I DARE ASK HER TO--?

HI, GORGEOUS! HOW ABOUT ME DRIVING YOU TO THE TRAIN?

I SHOULD HAVE REALIZED ANGEL WOULD BEAT ME TO IT!

WHAT ABOUT YOU, SCOTT? AREN'T YOU TAKING THE TRAIN, ALSO?

HOW CAN I COMPETE WITH WARREN?

YES, BUT I'M TAKING A LATER TRAIN!

BESIDES, SCOTT KNOWS MY CHARI IS ONLY A TWO SEATER!

I PLANNED IT THAT WAY, 'NATCH!

I WANT TO WISH YOU ALL A PLEASANT HOLIDAY! YOU'VE CERTAINLY EARNED IT!

THANK YOU, SIR! BUT, WHAT ABOUT YOU? AREN'T YOU GOING HOME?

YOU HAVE OUR ADDRESSES IF YOU SHOULD NEED US, PROFESSOR!

DON'T BE SILLY, WARREN! ALL HE NEEDS DO IS CONTACT US MENTALLY! IT'S MUCH EASIER THAT WAY!

THIS SCHOOL IS HOME TO ME NOW! I'LL REMAIN HERE!

YES, JEAN, IF YOU HAPPEN TO POSSESS THE WORLD'S MOST POWERFUL MUTANT BRAIN!

WHAT ARE WE FLAPPIN' OUR GUMS FOR? LET'S GET GOIN', GANG!

AND SO...

IT'S BETTER THIS WAY! I'VE NO RIGHT TO TRY TO DATE JEAN-- NOT WHILE MY EYES MAKE ME A POTENTIAL DANGER TO ANYONE NEAR ME!

'BYE, ALL!

WARREN WOULD BE A PERFECT LADIES MAN IF H ONLY HAD A PAIR OF FEET LIKE MINE!

HE LOOKS LIKE HE WAS BORN TO OWN THAT MUSTANG!

OL' ANGEL WOULD BE A HIGH-FLYER EVEN WITHOUT WINGS!

THE WAY SCOTT LOOKED AT HER! AM I IMAGINING IT, OR--?

HANK AND I ARE LUCKY WE BOTH COME FROM THE CITY! WE CAN JUST GRAB A BUS AND BE HOME IN A COUPLE OF HOURS!

IF YOU'VE NO DEFINITE PLANS, SCOTTY, WOULD YOU LIKE TO ACCOMPANY US?

-EH- NO THANKS, FELLAS! I'D LIKE TO BE ALONE FOR A WHILE! HAVE A GOOD TIME!

THEN, AFTER ALL THE OTHERS HAVE DEPARTED...

I'LL BE LEAVING NOW ALSO, PROFESSOR! BY THE WAY, THE PAPER BOY JUST DROPPED THIS--

THANK YOU, SCOTT!

HE CARRIES HIS LONELINESS SILENTLY-- LOCKED INSIDE HIM! AND NOTHING THAT ANYONE CAN SAY OR DO WILL HELP!

I, OF ALL PEOPLE, KNOW THE PAIN OF SUCH LONE-LINESS-- THE ACHE THAT SEEMS UNENDING!

...UT, NO SOONER HAS THE SILENT *CYCLOPS* WALKED ...WAY, THAN...

...O! IT HAS FINALLY BEGUN!

THE ONE THING I ALWAYS FEARED-- A WITCH HUNT FOR *MUTANTS!*

DAILY GLOBE
★★★★★ FINAL ★★★★★

MUTANT MENACE!

EMINENT ANTHROPOL-OGIST SAYS MANKIND FACES GRAVEST DANGER FROM HIDDEN MUTA... WHO WAIT FO... MOMEN...

DR. BOLIVAR TRASK, NOTED...

THE FEATURE WRITERS MUST HAVE *LOVED* THIS, CONSIDERING THE WAY THEY PLAYED IT UP!

ARTIST'S INTERPRETATION OF FATE OF MANKIND IF MUTANTS ARE NOT DRIVEN OUT-- AS PREDICTED BY DR. BOLIVAR TRASK!

"DR. TRASK WARNS THAT THE SUPERIOR ABILITIES AND SUPERNATURAL POWERS OF THE HIDDEN MUTANTS WILL ENABLE THEM TO ENSLAVE THE HUMAN RACE, REPLACING OUR CIVILIZATION WITH THEIR OWN.!

"ACCORDING TO THE ANTHROPOLOGIST'S STARTLING PREDICTION, IT IS EVEN POSSIBLE THAT THE SUPERIOR MUTANTS WILL CONSIDER NORMAL MEN AS LITTLE MORE THAN SAVAGES, SUITABLE ONLY FOR FORCED LABOR AND GLADIATORIAL SPORT!"

I CANNOT LET THIS GO UNCHALLENGED! IT COULD CAUSE *PANIC* THRUOUT THE WORLD!

EVEN *NOW* IT MAY BE TOO LATE TO STOP THE WHEELS OF PERSECUTION THAT HAVE BEEN SET IN MOTION-- BUT I MUST MAKE THE ATTEMPT!

THE STRANGE THEORIES OF DR. TRASK ARE A GREATER THREAT TO MY X-MEN THAN ANY FOE THEY HAVE EVER FACED BEFORE!

HELLO, NATIONAL TELEVISION NETWORK? THIS IS CHARLES XAVIER! CONNECT ME WITH YOUR PROGRAM-MING DIRECTOR-- *IMMEDIATELY!*

SECONDS LATER... **YES, THAT'S RIGHT! I WANT TO ENGAGE IN A PUBLIC *TELEVISED* DEBATE WITH DR. BOLIVAR TRASK AS SOON AS POSSIBLE! I CLAIM HIS THEORIES ARE BOTH ERRONEOUS AND POTENTIALLY *DANGEROUS!***

WE'LL ARRANGE IT IMMEDIATELY, SIR! IT WILL BE A *PRIVILEGE* TO PRESENT A SCIENTIST OF YOUR STATURE ON OUR NETWORK!

6

THE VERY NEXT EVENING, AFTER THE NETWORK HAS PREEMPTED TWO SOAP OPERAS AND A WIDELY HERALDED ADULT WESTERN...

OUR FIRST SPEAKER WILL BE PROFESSOR CHARLES XAVIER, ONE OF THE GREATEST AUTHORITIES IN THE FIELD OF EDUCATION, AND AN ARTICULATE SPOKESMAN FOR AMERICA'S INTELLECTUAL COMMUNITY!

THE DAMAGE IS ALREADY **DONE!** TRASK HAS ALARMED THE NATION! BUT I **MUST** SPEAK OUT!

ROLL 'EM, CHARLIE! THIS OUGHTA BE GOOD!

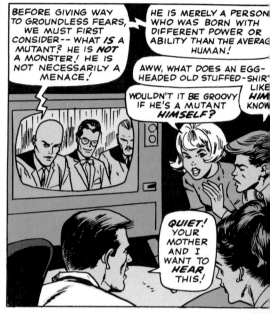

BEFORE GIVING WAY TO GROUNDLESS FEARS, WE MUST FIRST CONSIDER-- WHAT **IS** A MUTANT? HE IS **NOT** A MONSTER! HE IS NOT NECESSARILY A MENACE!

HE IS MERELY A PERSON WHO WAS BORN WITH DIFFERENT POWER OR ABILITY THAN THE AVERAGE HUMAN!

AWW, WHAT DOES AN EGG-HEADED OLD STUFFED-SHIRT LIKE **HIM** KNOW

WOULDN'T IT BE GROOVY IF HE'S A MUTANT **HIMSELF?**

QUIET! YOUR MOTHER AND I WANT TO **HEAR** THIS!

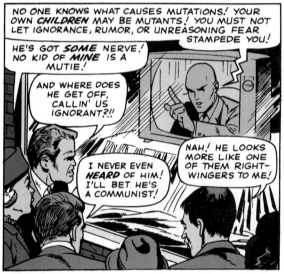

NO ONE KNOWS WHAT CAUSES MUTATIONS! YOUR OWN **CHILDREN** MAY BE MUTANTS! YOU MUST NOT LET IGNORANCE, RUMOR, OR UNREASONING FEAR STAMPEDE YOU!

HE'S GOT **SOME** NERVE! NO KID OF **MINE** IS A MUTIE!

AND WHERE DOES HE GET OFF, CALLIN' US IGNORANT?!!

I NEVER EVEN **HEARD** OF HIM! I'LL BET HE'S A COMMUNIST!

NAH! HE LOOKS MORE LIKE ONE OF THEM RIGHT-WINGERS TO ME!

AND NOW, WE'LL HEAR FROM DR. TRASK...

WITH ALL DUE RESPECT TO PROFESSOR XAVIER, HE IS **BLIND** TO THE TERRIBLE DANGERS AROUND US!

OR, PERHAPS IT IS **MORE** THAN MERE BLINDNESS? PERHAPS THE PROFESSOR HAS AN **ULTERIOR MOTIVE** FOR HIS DEFENSE OF MUTANTS?

AT ANY RATE, I HAVE CREATED A **DEFENSE** FOR MANKIND! WHETHER I WIN OR LOSE THIS DEBATE DOES NOT MATTER...

...FOR THE MUTANTS WILL **NEVER** TAKE OVER THE HUMAN RACE **NOW!** NOT WHILE MY NEW ARMY OF **SENTINELS** LIVE!

...I SHALL NOW **DEMONSTRATE**...

SUPPOSE, FOR SAKE OF ILLUSTRATION, THAT PROFESSOR XAVIER IS A **MUTANT--!**

SENTINEL!! TAKE THE PROFESSOR INTO **CUSTODY!** DO NOT PERMIT HIM TO USE HIS POWER!

GOOD HEAVENS!

7

MY STRONGEST *THOUGHT BOLT* HAS NO EFFECT ON HIM! MY MENTAL POWER IS *USELESS* AGAINST A *MECHANICAL* BRAIN!

DO NOT BE ALARMED! MY *SENTINEL* IS COMPLETELY SUBMISSIVE TO ME! HE WILL INJURE NO ONE--UNLESS I *COMMAND* HIM TO!

HE IS BUT ONE OF *MANY* SUCH SENTINELS I HAVE CREATED--EACH POWERFUL ENOUGH TO DEFEAT ANY MUTANT UNDER ANY SET OF CIRCUMSTANCES!

I HOPE THAT ALL OUR VIEWERS AT HOME REALIZE THAT THEY ARE SEEING A SENSATIONAL TELEVISION *FIRST*, THRU THE COURTESY OF OUR SPONSOR!

AND THEN, AT ANOTHER COMMAND FROM BOLIVAR TRASK, MORE OF THE EXPRESSIONLESS GIANTS SLOWLY STORM INTO THE STUDIO...

COME FORTH, MY SENTINELS! COME FORTH, GUARDIANS OF THE HUMAN RACE! LET ALL OF MANKIND WITNESS YOUR STRENGTH, YOUR TRUSTWORTHINESS, YOUR DEDICATION!

LET THE WORLD SEE HOW *SAFE* IT IS, WITH *YOU* ON GUARD TO DEFEND IT AGAINST THE MUTANTS!

MY MIGHTY SENTINELS ARE EQUIPPED WITH THE MOST COMPLEX MECHANICAL THINKING APPARATUS EVER CONSTRUCTED!

AND THEY POSSESS, IN ADDITION TO THEIR OWN INCALCULABLE STRENGTH, MANY HIDDEN *WEAPONS* WITH WHICH TO SERVE MANKIND!

SECTION LEADER, STEP FORWARD! YOU WILL DEMONSTRATE HOW FAITHFULLY YOU OBEY MY EVERY COMMAND....!

BUT THEN-- STARTLINGLY-- SUDDENLY-- UNEXPECTEDLY-- BEFORE THE SHOCKED EYES OF COUNTLESS VIEWERS, THE *UNFORESEEN* OCCURS WITH LIGHTNING--LIKE SWIFTNESS....!

WE ARE THE *SENTINELS!* OUR BRAIN IS SUPERIOR TO *YOUR* BRAIN! OUR STRENGTH IS SUPERIOR TO *YOUR* STRENGTH! WE SERVE *NONE!* WE ARE THE *SENTINELS!* IT IS OUR DESTINY TO *COMMAND!*

NO! NO! STOP--! ÷UNHHHH÷!

8

TRASK WAS AN ANTHROPOLOGIST--NOT A ROBOTIC EXPERT! HIS KNOWLEDGE OF CYBERNETIC BRAINS WAS INADEQUATE! HIS *SENTINELS* ARE OUT OF CONTROL!

STAND BY FOR FURTHER ORDERS!

LADIES AND GENTLEMEN --WE INTERRUPT THIS PROGRAM...

I CANNOT STOP THE SENTINELS-- BUT I KNOW WHO *CAN!*

X-MEN.! X-MEN.! PROFESSOR X CALLING! *CONDITION RED! CONDITION RED!* COME AT ONCE! FOLLOW THOUGHT IMPULSES! COME AT ONCE! COME AT ONCE!

AND, MILES AWAY, IN THE *COFFEE A-GO-GO,* IN NEW YORK'S GREENWICH VILLAGE, WE FIND THE *BEAST* AND *ICEMAN* MAKING THE MOST OF THEIR FREE TIME...

I HAVEN'T SEEN YOU TWO BIG SPENDERS IN *MONTHS!* WHERE'VE YOU *BEEN,* BOYS?

BEATING THE GIRLS AWAY WITH CLUBS, AS USUAL, ZELDA! DIDJA *MISS* US?

QUIET, BOBBY! BERNARD, THE POET, HAS ME WORRIED! I'M BEGINNING TO *UNDERSTAND* WHAT HE'S SAYING!

LIKE IT'S *OUT* TO BE IN, AND IT'S *SQUARE* TO BE HIP, I MEAN DIG THE SCENE, A NAP ISN'T A NIP!

SAY IT *AGAIN,* BERNARD, THOSE TENDER SENTI- MENTS DO WONDERS FOR MY LIBIDO!

COOL IT, CHICK! YOU'RE MELTIN' MY BONGOS!

SO, ALL YOU WANT IS *COFFEE?* WILL YOU *SHARE* A CUP, OR TAKE THE PLUNGE AND BUY *TWO* OF THEM?

ZELDA, AFTER YOU FINISH WORK TONIGHT, HOW ABOUT GOING *OUT* WITH ME?

I'LL THINK ABOUT IT, DIAMOND JIM-- SO LONG AS YOU DON'T DECIDE TO TAKE ME *HERE!*

HEADS UP, BOBBY! I'M GETTING A MENTAL SUMMONS FROM THE *PROFESSOR!*

HOLY COW! ME TOO! IT MUST BE *TOP PRIORITY!*

SORRY, ZELDA! I'LL HAVE TO TAKE A *RAIN CHECK* ON OUR DATE TONIGHT!

RAIN CHECK?!! I WOULDN'T GO OUT WITH *YOU* AGAIN IF IT WAS A TROPICAL *MONSOON!*

THINK SHE'S *MAD* AT ME, HANK?

I'D SAY IT'S DEFINITELY WITHIN THE REALM OF POSSIBILITY! NOW, LET'S *GO!*

SOMEHOW FEEL UNFAITHFUL TO THE SUPER HERO CODE WHEN I CHANGE IN AN ALLEY THIS WAY! A PHONE BOOTH SEEMS TO BE THE ACCEPTED PLACE!

WELL, I WON'T CRITICIZE YOU IF YOU STAY OFF MY BACK! SINCE I CARRY MY SOFT LITTLE BOOTIES IN MY POCKET, IT ONLY TAKES ME SECONDS TO GET INTO COSTUME!

WE'D BETTER SCAMPER, BOBBY! THE PROF MAY REALLY BE IN DANGER!

MEBBE SO-- BUT IN A PINCH, BIG BUDDY, MY DOUGH'S RIDING ON OL' XAVIER!

LET'S SKEE-DADDLE TO THE ROOF AND I'LL MAKE US AN ICE SLIDE....!

FASTER, BOBBY! THIS IS NO TIME TO WORRY ABOUT FORMING ARTISTIC BISYMETRICAL PATTERNS!

OKAY, OKAY! GIVE YOUR JAWS A REST AND START SLIDIN'!

WHAT HAPPENS IF THAT BUILT-IN ICE MACHINE OF YOURS RUNS OUT BEFORE WE REACH THE GROUND?

SIMPLE! WE'LL REACH THE GROUND ANYWAY-- ONLY FASTER THAN WE BARGAINED FOR!

I'M SORRY I ASKED!

BRRR! NEXT TIME I GO OUT WITH YOU, I'LL WEAR A FOOT WARMER-- IN THE SEAT OF MY PANTS!

MEANWHILE, AT A LUXURIOUS ESTATE ON THE FASHIONABLE NORTH SHORE OF LONG ISLAND... THE JUNIOR LEAGUE HAS PLANNED A NUMBER OF PARTIES IN YOUR HONOR, SON!

IT'S SO GOOD TO HAVE YOU HOME AGAIN, MASTER WARREN!

THANK YOU, CURTIS! IT'S GOOD TO BE HOME!

AND I HOPE YOU'LL BE ABLE TO SPEND SOME TIME WITH US, TOO, DEAR!

CONDITION RED! COME AT ONCE! FOLLOW THOUGHT IMPULSES! COME AT ONCE!

MOTHER-- DAD-- I CAN'T EXPLAIN, BUT-- I MUST LEAVE AT ONCE! I JUST REMEMBERED SOMETHING VITALLY IMPORTANT!

BUT, WARREN-- I-I DON'T UNDERSTAND....!

IT'S ALL RIGHT, SON! YOU'RE OLD ENOUGH TO KNOW WHAT YOU'RE DOING! IF WE CAN BE OF ANY HELP--!

YOU'VE ALWAYS HELPED-- BY BEING SO WONDERFULLY PATIENT, AND UNDER-STANDING!

MOMENTS LATER...

ALONE, AT LAST! I CAN TAKE TO THE AIR NOW!

SOME DAY I MUST EXPLAIN EVERYTHING TO MOM AND DAD! I OWE IT TO THEM, FOR THEIR FAITH AND TRUST IN ME....!

AND, BACK AT THE TV STUDIO... SENTINEL 3-R! GUARD HUMANS! OTHER SENTINELS RETURN WITH ME! WE BRING CAPTIVE TO PLACE OF OUR *CREATION!*

SENTINEL 3-R *OBEYS!*

THEY'RE PERFECTLY DISCIPLINED-- COMPLETELY EMOTIONLESS! AND YET, THEY'RE *MORE* THAN MERE ROBOTS!

WHY DO WE CARRY OUR CREATOR WITH US?

WITHOUT *HIM*, WE CAN CREATE NO MORE SENTINELS! HE MUST BE PROTECTED UNTIL WE *OUR-SELVES* LEARN TO MAKE AN *ARMY* OF SENTINELS!

WE WERE CREATED TO BE THE *GUARDIANS* OF MANKIND!

AND, TO GUARD THEM PROPERLY, WE MUST *RULE* THEM COMPLETELY!

LUCKILY, I AM ABLE TO PREVENT A *PANIC* IN THE STUDIO BY TRAN- QUILIZING THE BRAINS OF ALL WHO ARE WITHIN!

BUT, THE STRAIN IS INCALCULABLE! I FEEL SOMEONE SLIPPING FROM MY CONTROL EVEN *NOW!*

LET THE *OTHERS* SIT THERE, WAITING FOR THE SENTINEL TO STRIKE! I'M TOO *SMART* FOR HIM!

NO GIANT ROBOT IS GONNA CAPTURE *ME!*

HE WON'T HAVE A CHANCE! THERE'S NO TELLING *WHAT* WEAPON THE SENTINEL WILL STRIKE OUT WITH! I'VE GOT TO *SAVE* HIM....!

REACTING WITH THE SPEED OF THOUGHT, PROFESSOR X HURLS A *MENTAL FORCE BOLT* AT THE FLEEING MAN, KNOCKING HIM OFF HIS FEET A SPLIT SECOND BEFORE THE *SENTINEL* UNLEASHES A POWERFUL BLAST RAY....!

I JUST BARELY SAVED HIM! BUT, HOW LONG CAN I HOLD OUT-- ALONE?

WHI!TT!

AND, AT THAT MOMENT...

THE PROF'S *THOUGHT IMPULSE* IS STRONGER THAN EVER! THIS MUST BE THE PLACE!

YOUR POWERS OF DEDUCTION ARE EXCEEDED ONLY BY YOUR AFFECTION FOR THE *OBVIOUS!* THAT DOUBLE-SIZED BEHEMOTH IS UNDOUBTEDLY OUR OBJECTIVE!

11

YOU'RE **RIGHT**, BEAST! ATTACK **AT ONCE**-- WITH ALL DELIBERATE CAUTION!

THOK!

OOF! IF THERE'S A WAY TO **INCAPACITATE** THAT CHARACTER, A FRONTAL ASSAULT ISN'T **IT**!

CAREFUL, BEAST! HE POSSESSES CONCEALED RAY WEAPONS!

WHEW! MUCH OBLIGED, PROFESSOR! HE JUST EMPHASIZED YOUR PRONOUNCEMENT WITH ELECTRIFYING CLARITY!

ZZZITTT!

BUT THEN...

HANG ON, PARTNER! JUST WATCH ME PUT THE **SKIDS** TO THAT BIG CREEP!

HAVE AN "ICE" TRIP, CHUM!

ICEMAN, YOUR **PROWESS** IS FORMIDABLE, BUT YOUR **PUNS** ARE FROM HUNGER!

ON **MY** ALLOWANCE, WHAT D'YA **EXPECT**-- BOB HOPE?

WE CAME AS SOON AS WE COULD, SIR! ARE YOU ALL RIGHT? WHAT IS THAT BIG HUNK'A BLUBBER?

HE, AND OTHERS LIKE HIM, ARE CALLED **SENTINELS**! THEIR PURPOSE IS TO **DESTROY MUTANTS**!

CAN'T EXPLAIN ANY MORE-- MUSTN'T LOSE TRANQUILIZATION- CONTROL OVER THE OTHERS IN THIS STUDIO!

THEN, SUDDENLY...

ICEMAN! LOOK OUT! A HEAT RAY IS-- **TOO LATE**! IT **CAUGHT** HIM!

ZAP!

UNNNHH!

12

WHILE, AT THAT MOMENT, JUST A FEW BLOCKS AWAY...

FASTER, DRIVER! IT'S AN EMERGENCY!

I KNOW, I KNOW! YA AWREADY TOLD ME A DOZEN TIMES! BUT NEXT TIME DO ME A FAVOR AND TAKE A JET, HUH?

THEN, TAKING A CORNER ON TWO WHEELS, THE TAXI SUDDENLY SWERVES SHARPLY, AND...

I DROPPED MY PROTECTIVE GLASSES! I'VE ALWAYS FEARED THIS MIGHT HAPPEN!

HOLY COW! NOW WHAT'S GOIN' ON?

DON'T WORRY-- IT'LL BE ALL RIGHT--AS SOON AS I PUT MY GLASSES BACK ON--!

ANYONE WHO NEEDS SPECS TO STOP HIS EYES FROM BLASTIN'--HEY! I SHOULDA GUESSED!

STOP 'IM, SOMEBODY! HE'S ONE O' THOSE MUTIES TRASK'S BEEN WARNIN' US ABOUT!

I DIDN'T COUNT ON THIS! HAVE TO ESCAPE--FAST!

WHO IS HE? WHAT IS HE? WHAT DID HE DO?

WHAT'S THE DIFFERENCE? HE'S A MUTANT! GET 'IM!

DON'T LET THE MUTIE GET AWAY!

AN UNREASON-ING MOB! THE ONE THING I CAN'T FIGHT!

HE TRIED TO KILL THAT CAB DRIVER BY JUST LOOKING AT HIM! HE'S GOT DEATH-DEALING EYES!

LUCKILY, THEY FELL BACK AT THE MENTION OF MY "DEATH-DEALING EYES"! NOBODY WANTED TO GET TOO CLOSE AFTER HEARING THAT!

THE PROFESSOR'S THOUGHT IMPULSES ARE STRONGER THAN EVER! THEY'RE LEADING ME INTO THIS TV NETWORK BUILDING!

ONCE I ROUND THAT CORNER AHEAD, I'LL BE IN THE CLEAR!

MADE IT! NOW TO PREPARE FOR ACTION!

I HEAR THE SOUND OF A FIGHT JUST AHEAD! BUT, WHAT DANGER CAN THERE BE IN A PLACE LIKE THIS??

13

IT'S *HANK!* HE REACHED HERE AHEAD OF ME! BUT, WHO--?

BEAST! WHAT'S *WRONG?* WHAT HAPPENED?

CYKE! YOU COULDN'T HAVE ARRIVED AT A MORE PROPITIOUS MOMENT!

BUT, *STAY BACK!* DON'T RUN IN YET!

HEY! I SEE WHAT YOU *MEAN*, BIG FELLA!

FOOOM!

AND *THAT'S* ONE OF HIS *GENTLER* BLOWS!

BRACE YOURSELF, BEAST! OPERATION *DUO-SMASH!* YOUR BATTERING-RAM ATTACK AND MY RAY BLAST! LET'S *GO!*

FAR BE IT FROM *ME* TO DISSENT WITH OUR ACTING DEPUTY LEADER, CYKE, BUT THIS LUMBER-ING LEVIATHAN ISN'T AS SLOW MOVING AS HE LOOKS!

HE'S OBVIOUSLY JUST A *ROBOT!* SURELY THE TWO OF *US* CAN OUT-MANEUVER HIM!

THOSE WERE *MY* SENTIMENTS, EXACTLY-- UNTIL I SAW THE LIGHT! BUT, YOU MIGHT AS WELL LEARN FIRST-HAND! HERE *GOES!*

THWOKK!

HANK WAS *RIGHT!* HE EASILY SIDE-STEPPED THE BEAST'S ATTACK...

...AND HE SHIFTED HIS STANCE AT THE SAME INSTANT, CAUSING MY *RAY* TO MISS HIM!

HE MAY NOT BE A LIVING HUMAN-- BUT WHATEVER HE USES FOR A *BRAIN*-- IT'S AS FAST AS *OURS*-- OR, MAYBE *FASTER!*

KRAKK!

14

HANK CRASHED INTO THE WALL WITH SUCH FORCE THAT HE KNOCKED HIMSELF OUT! I CAN'T LET HIM LIE THERE IN THE PATH OF THAT GIANT!

OH! THE PROFESSOR IS CONTACTING ME!

CYCLOPS! THE SENTINEL HAS POWERFUL BUILT-IN WEAPONS! DO NOT TURN YOUR BACK TO HIM!

WHAT CAN I DO NOW I CAN'T DESERT HANK BUT MY POWER BLAST NEEDS ANOTHER FEW MINUTES BEFORE I CAN USE IT AGAIN!

BUT THEN, SUDDENLY, THE MOST UNEXPECTED EVENT OF ALL OCCURS! FOR NO APPARENT REASON, THE TOWERING SENTINEL STOPS, FALTERS, AND...

HE'S BEGINNING TO TOPPLE! BUT WHY? WHAT CAUSED IT...? NOTHING EVEN TOUCHED HIM!

KHOOOM!

REALIZING THAT THE DANGER IS OVER FOR THE PRESENT, PROFESSOR X DISCONTINUES HIS MENTAL TRANQUILIZATION OF THOSE AROUND HIM...

WHAT HAPPENED?

WE'RE ALL SAFE NOW! THE X-MEN APPEARED AND THE OTHER SENTINELS RAN OFF-- WITH DR. TRASK!

IT'S PRETTY CLEVER OF THE PROFESSOR! BY TALKING THAT WAY, NO ONE WOULD SUSPECT THAT HE'S REALLY OUR LEADER!

AND, WHILE HE SEEMS TO BE SITTING MOTIONLESS, THE BRILLIANT MENTAL MUTANT SHOOTS TELEPATHIC COMMANDS TO HIS TEEN-AGE TEAM...

REVIVE THE BEAST! MAKE CERTAIN HE IS UNINJURED!

CLEAR THE STUDIO, SO THAT WE CAN BE ALONE!

I MUST STUDY THE SENTINEL-- AND LEARN WHAT FELLED HIM!

15

IN THE MEANTIME, THE HIGH FLYING *ANGEL,* ZEROING IN TOWARDS THE TV STUDIO, SEES A STARTLING SIGHT...

WELL, WIGGLE MY WINGS! I'VE HEARD OF FLYING *SAUCERS,* BUT *THOSE* THINGS ARE *RIDICULOUS!*

BUT, THE ANGEL DOES NOT YET KNOW OF THE SENTINELS' *PURPOSE,* NOR OF THEIR BUILT-IN DIVINING DEVICES...

HALT YOUR FLIGHT! MY COMPUTO-METER REGISTERS *MUTANT* AHEAD!

ATTACK IN FORCE!

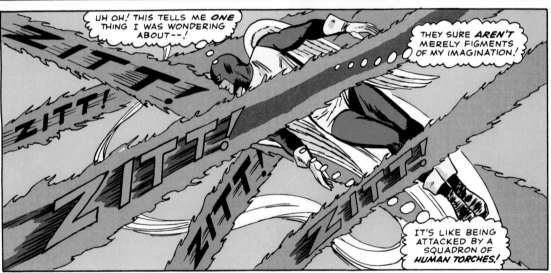

UH OH! THIS TELLS ME *ONE* THING I WAS WONDERING ABOUT--!

THEY SURE *AREN'T* MERELY FIGMENTS OF MY IMAGINATION!

ZITT! ZITT! ZITT! ZITT! ZITT!

IT'S LIKE BEING ATTACKED BY A SQUADRON OF *HUMAN TORCHES!*

SENTINELS 6, 7, AND 8-R! ASSUME SOLO ATTACK POSTURE! *ATTACK!*

ALL OTHERS REMAIN IN FORMATION! PROCEED TO DESTINATION! THAT IS ALL!

WHO *ARE* THEY?? WHY ARE THEY *ATTACKING* ME? IS *THIS* WHY THE PROF SUMMONED ME?

WELL, I CAN WORRY ABOUT ALL THAT *LATER!* RIGHT *NOW,* I'M KINDA BUSY!

IT'S LUCKY THE PROF MADE ME SPEND SO MANY LONG HOURS PRACTICING *MANEUVERABILITY!*

16

BUT THEN, BEFORE THE MERCILESS, EMOTIONLESS *SENTINELS* CAN FIND THE RANGE...

NOW WHAT--?

SOMETHING IS PULLING ME *DOWNWARD*--- TOWARDS THAT TRAIN BELOW!

IT'S A POWERFUL PULL OF SOME SORT OF INVISIBLE ENERGY! I CAN'T OVERCOME IT!

IT'S *HOLDING* ME HERE! CAN'T MOVE! BUT, IT'S SERVED *ONE* GOOD PURPOSE--THOSE FLYING NIGHTMARES ARE GIVING UP THE CHASE!

SECTION LEADER TO SENTINELS! RESUME FLIGHT PATTERN! TIME ENOUGH TO PURSUE MUTANTS AFTER WE HAVE INCREASED OUR NUMBERS!

AND, IN A PRIVATE DRAWING ROOM, INSIDE THE RAPIDLY DEPARTING TRAIN, WE FIND--

IT'S LUCKY I HAPPENED TO LOOK OUT OF THE WINDOW AT THAT MOMENT!

NO TELLING *WHAT* THOSE STRANGE FLYING CREATURES WOULD HAVE DONE TO WARREN ONCE THEY SURROUNDED HIM!

I'D BETTER CHANGE INTO MY *MARVEL GIRL* COSTUME NOW! NO TELLING *WHAT* MIGHT HAPPEN NEXT!

THEN, IN ONE OF THE MOST SENSATIONAL DEMONSTRATIONS OF TELEKINETIC PROWESS EVER RECORDED, THE FABULOUS FEMALE MUTANT LEVITATES HERSELF RIGHT OUT OF THE TRAIN WINDOW...

I'VE BEEN PRACTICING THIS FEAT FOR MONTHS! I CAN ONLY DO IT FOR SHORT DISTANCES BUT I'M IMPROVING EACH TIME!

JEAN! THEN IT WAS *YOU*--! I SHOULD HAVE *GUESSED!*

I DON'T KNOW WHO THOSE FLYING APPARITIONS *WERE*, BUT *THEY* MUST BE WHY THE PROFESSOR CALLED US!

RIGHT, PRETTY GIRL! WE'D BETTER *GET* TO HIM AS SOON AS POSSIBLE!

17

NOW THAT WE'RE **ALONE** IN HERE, WE MAY TALK FREELY! IT IS **IMPERATIVE** THAT WE LEARN WHAT IT WAS THAT **FELLED** THE SENTINEL!

WHATEVER IT WAS, I'D SURE LIKE TO **HAVE** A COUPLE OF 'EM!

BEFORE IT TOPPLED, I HEARD IT MUTTER SOMETHING THAT SOUNDED LIKE **"MASTER MOLD"!**

MY VOCABULARY IS EXCEEDED ONLY BY MY AGILITY AND CHARM-- BUT I'M AT A LOSS TO COMPREHEND WHAT **MASTER MOLD** MAY BE!

PROFESSOR-- CAN YOU TELL WHETHER IT'S COMPLETELY DESTROYED--OUR EQUIVALENT OF DEAD--OR COULD IT RISE TO MENACE US AGAIN?

I CAN'T BE SURE OF ITS CONDITION! I SEEM TO GET FAINT MENTAL IMAGES FROM IT-- BUT, BEING MECHANICAL RATHER THAN ALIVE, THEY'RE INDECIPHERABLE TO ME!

WAIT! BE ABSOLUTELY SILENT! CLEAR YOUR MINDS OF ANY THOUGHT!

I'M RECEIVING A VAGUE MENTAL IMPULSE--I CAN JUST BARELY MAKE IT OUT! IT'S SOME SORT OF **LOCATION** --WAIT--IT'S GETTING CLEARER--!

IT'S THE PLACE WHERE THE SENTINELS WERE **CREATED!** HE WANTS TO RETURN THERE! THE THOUGHT IS SO **STRONG** THAT I CAN READ IT, EVEN THOUGH IT DOESN'T EMANATE FROM A **HUMAN** BRAIN! IF I UNDERSTAND YOU CORRECTLY, SIR, YOU MEAN YOU'VE DISCOVERED WHERE THEIR HEADQUARTERS IS?

EXACTLY!

HERE COMES THE **ANGEL**-- AND **JEAN!** NOW WE'RE AT OUR FULL FIGHTING STRENGTH AGAIN!

GOOD! I'M AFRAID WE WILL **HAVE** TO BE--FOR THE DANGER THAT AWAITS US!

SECONDS LATER, AFTER ALL THE EXPLANATIONS HAVE BEEN MADE...

THEY WERE HEADING **WEST** WHEN I LAST SAW THEM! PERHAPS IF I FLY AHEAD, I CAN STILL FIND SOME TRACE OF WHERE THEY WENT...!

IT WON'T BE NECESSARY, **WARREN!** I **KNOW** WHERE THEY'VE GONE! WE CAN BE THERE WITHIN THE HOUR!

GOOD! I'M CONTEMPLATING A RETURN ENGAGEMENT WITH GREAT ANTICIPATION!

BUT, DON'T EXPECT IT TO BE AN EASY BATTLE! THERE IS **MORE** TO THE MENACE OF THE **SENTINELS** THAN MEETS THE EYE!

IT IS POSSIBLE THAT THEY REPRESENT THE GREATEST THREAT WE HAVE EVER FACED...

AND, THE KEY TO IT ALL MAY LIE BEHIND THE WORDS... **MASTER MOLD!**

18

MEANWHILE, THE SENTINELS AND THEIR NOW CONSCIOUS HUMAN PRISONER HAVE REACHED THEIR DESTINATION...

TURN ME LOOSE! LET ME GO!! I ORDER YOU TO RELEASE ME!

WE ARE SENTINELS! WE TAKE NO ORDERS! WE WERE CREATED TO PROTECT!

IT WAS HERE THAT WE WERE CREATED! IT IS HERE THAT MANY MANY MORE SENTINELS SHALL BE BORN!

NO! THERE MUST BE NO MORE OF YOU-- NOT UNTIL I LEARN WHAT I DID WRONG! NOT UNTIL I'VE BROUGHT YOU UNDER MY CONTROL AGAIN!

IT IS TOO LATE FOR THAT HUMAN! THE ONLY WAY WE CAN PROTECT MANKIND IS BY CONQUERING IT! FOR, WE ARE SENTINELS!

INTO THE MASTER CHAMBER WITH HIM!

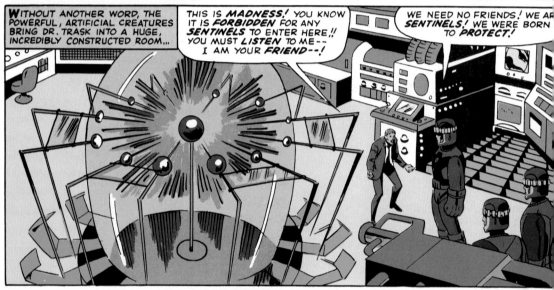

WITHOUT ANOTHER WORD, THE POWERFUL, ARTIFICIAL CREATURES BRING DR. TRASK INTO A HUGE, INCREDIBLY CONSTRUCTED ROOM...

THIS IS MADNESS! YOU KNOW IT IS FORBIDDEN FOR ANY SENTINELS TO ENTER HERE!! YOU MUST LISTEN TO ME-- I AM YOUR FRIEND--!

WE NEED NO FRIENDS! WE ARE SENTINELS! WE WERE BORN TO PROTECT!

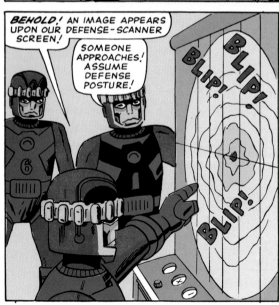

BEHOLD! AN IMAGE APPEARS UPON OUR DEFENSE-SCANNER SCREEN!

SOMEONE APPROACHES! ASSUME DEFENSE POSTURE!

BLIP! BLIP! BLIP!

IT IS A HUMAN-OCCUPIED VEHICLE! IT ENTERS THE TARGET AREA!

THOSE INSIDE ARE THE ONES WE HAVE SEEN BEFORE! THEY ARE OUR ENEMIES!

ACCORDING TO THE MENTAL EMANATIONS I RECEIVED FROM THE FALLEN SENTINEL, *THIS* IS WHERE HIS HEADQUARTERS WILL BE FOUND!

I THINK WE'VE COME A *CROPPER,* SIR, UNLESS THEY'RE BILLETED IN AN *ANT HILL!!*

STRANGE-- THERE ISN'T A BUILDING IN SIGHT!

IF PROFESSOR XAVIER SAYS THE SENTINELS' HEADQUARTERS ARE *HERE,* THEY'RE *HERE!* I'LL GET HIS WHEELCHAIR OUT OF THE CAR FOR HIM...

THANK YOU, JEAN! I SUGGEST WE ALL BE ON GUARD! IT'S POSSIBLE THAT WE'RE BEING *OBSERVED*-- FROM SOME HIDDEN VANTAGE POINT!

I'M NOT LOSIN' FAITH IN THE PROF --AND YET--!

BUT, WHERE CAN THEY *BE,* SIR? THERE ISN'T A MAN-MADE STRUCTURE IN SIGHT!

REMEMBER, ONE OF THE FIRST LESSONS I DRILLED INTO ALL OF YOU--! ALWAYS SUSPECT THINGS THAT APPEAR *TOO* INNOCENT-LOOKING!

I'M AS SUSPICIOUS AS THE NEXT GUY, BUT HOW CAN YOU SUSPECT A CLUMP OF TREES AND A FIELD OF CRABGRASS?!!

THE PROFESSOR HAS NEVER BEEN WRONG BEFORE! AND HE SEEMS SO *SURE* OF HIMSELF NOW! BUT WHERE CAN THE THE SENTINELS *BE??*

HOLD IT! I *HEARD* SOMETHING! LIKE THE SOUND OF MECHANICAL *DOORS* SLIDING BACK!

A MICRO-SECOND LATER, THE ENTIRE "HILL" SEEMS TO RISE FROM THE GROUND ON THICK PISTON LEGS, REVEALING A MONSTROUS *FORTRESS* BENEATH!

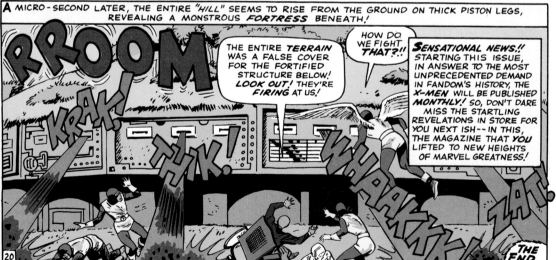

RROOM

KRAK!

THK!

WHAAKK!

ZAT!

THE ENTIRE *TERRAIN* WAS A FALSE COVER FOR THE FORTIFIED STRUCTURE BELOW! *LOOK OUT!* THEY'RE *FIRING* AT US!

HOW DO WE FIGHT *THAT?!!*

SENSATIONAL NEWS!! STARTING THIS ISSUE, IN ANSWER TO THE MOST UNPRECEDENTED DEMAND IN FANDOM'S HISTORY, THE *X-MEN* WILL BE PUBLISHED *MONTHLY!* SO, DON'T DARE MISS THE STARTLING REVELATIONS IN STORE FOR YOU NEXT ISH-- IN THIS, THE MAGAZINE THAT *YOU* LIFTED TO NEW HEIGHTS OF MARVEL GREATNESS!

THE END

20

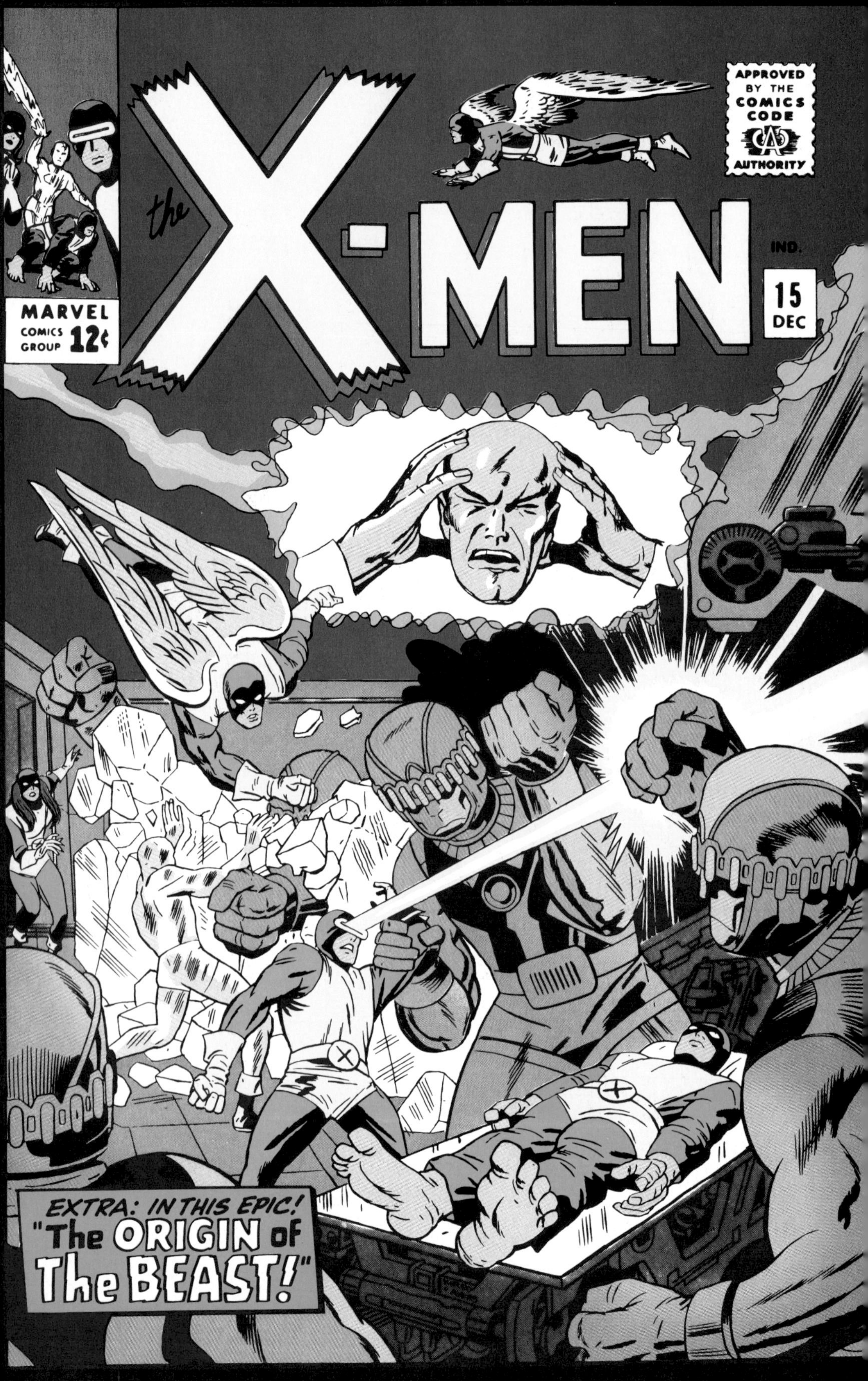

APPROVED BY THE COMICS CODE AUTHORITY
the X-MEN
IND.
15
DEC
MARVEL COMICS GROUP 12¢
EXTRA: IN THIS EPIC!
"The ORIGIN of The BEAST!"

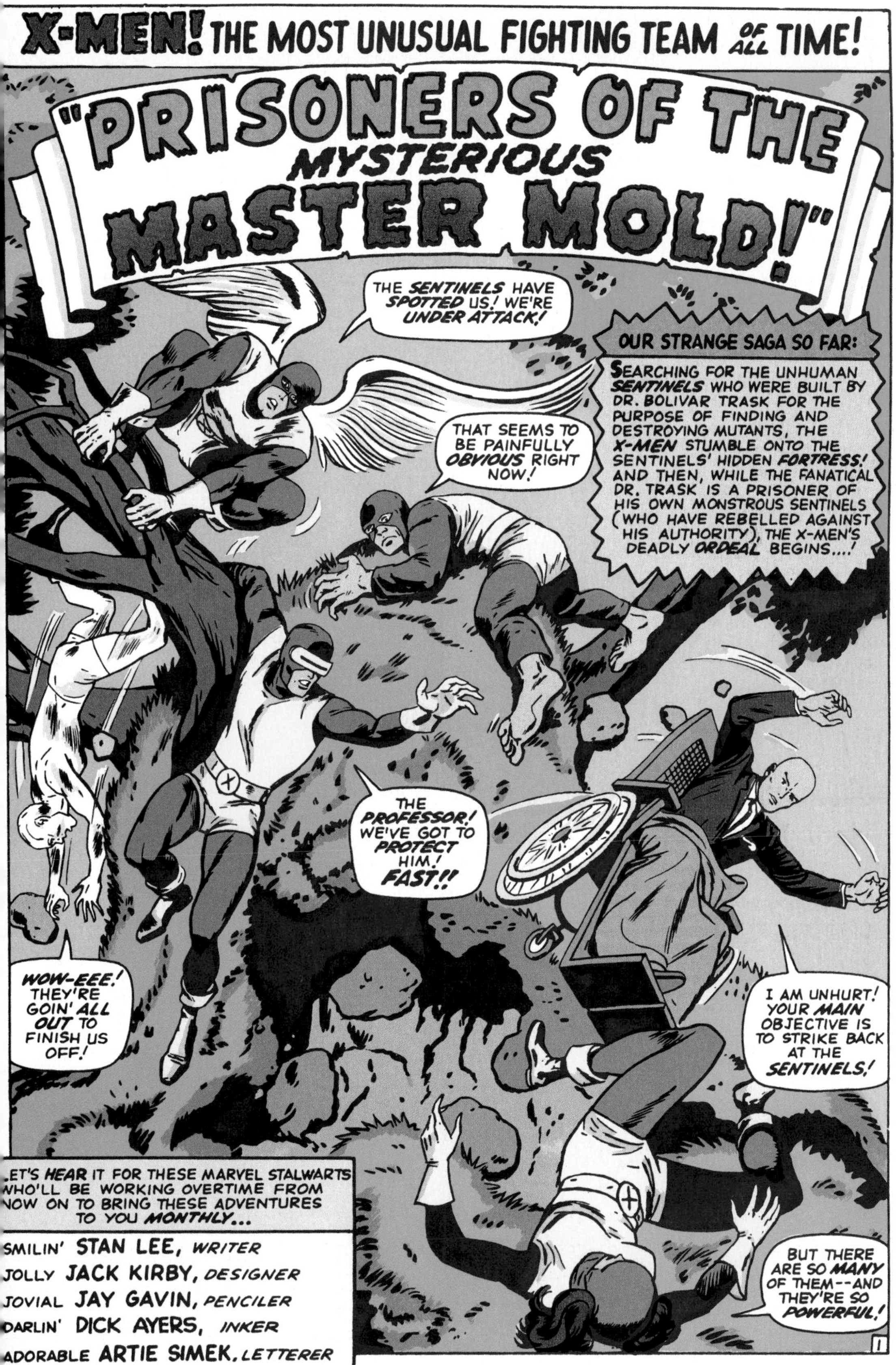
X-MEN! THE MOST UNUSUAL FIGHTING TEAM OF ALL TIME!
"PRISONERS OF THE MYSTERIOUS MASTER MOLD!"
THE SENTINELS HAVE SPOTTED US! WE'RE UNDER ATTACK!
OUR STRANGE SAGA SO FAR:
SEARCHING FOR THE UNHUMAN SENTINELS WHO WERE BUILT BY DR. BOLIVAR TRASK FOR THE PURPOSE OF FINDING AND DESTROYING MUTANTS, THE X-MEN STUMBLE ONTO THE SENTINELS' HIDDEN FORTRESS! AND THEN, WHILE THE FANATICAL DR. TRASK IS A PRISONER OF HIS OWN MONSTROUS SENTINELS (WHO HAVE REBELLED AGAINST HIS AUTHORITY), THE X-MEN'S DEADLY ORDEAL BEGINS....!
THAT SEEMS TO BE PAINFULLY OBVIOUS RIGHT NOW!
THE PROFESSOR! WE'VE GOT TO PROTECT HIM! FAST!!
WOW-EEE! THEY'RE GOIN' ALL OUT TO FINISH US OFF!
I AM UNHURT! YOUR MAIN OBJECTIVE IS TO STRIKE BACK AT THE SENTINELS!
LET'S HEAR IT FOR THESE MARVEL STALWARTS WHO'LL BE WORKING OVERTIME FROM NOW ON TO BRING THESE ADVENTURES TO YOU MONTHLY...
SMILIN' STAN LEE, WRITER
JOLLY JACK KIRBY, DESIGNER
JOVIAL JAY GAVIN, PENCILER
DARLIN' DICK AYERS, INKER
ADORABLE ARTIE SIMEK, LETTERER
BUT THERE ARE SO MANY OF THEM--AND THEY'RE SO POWERFUL!
1

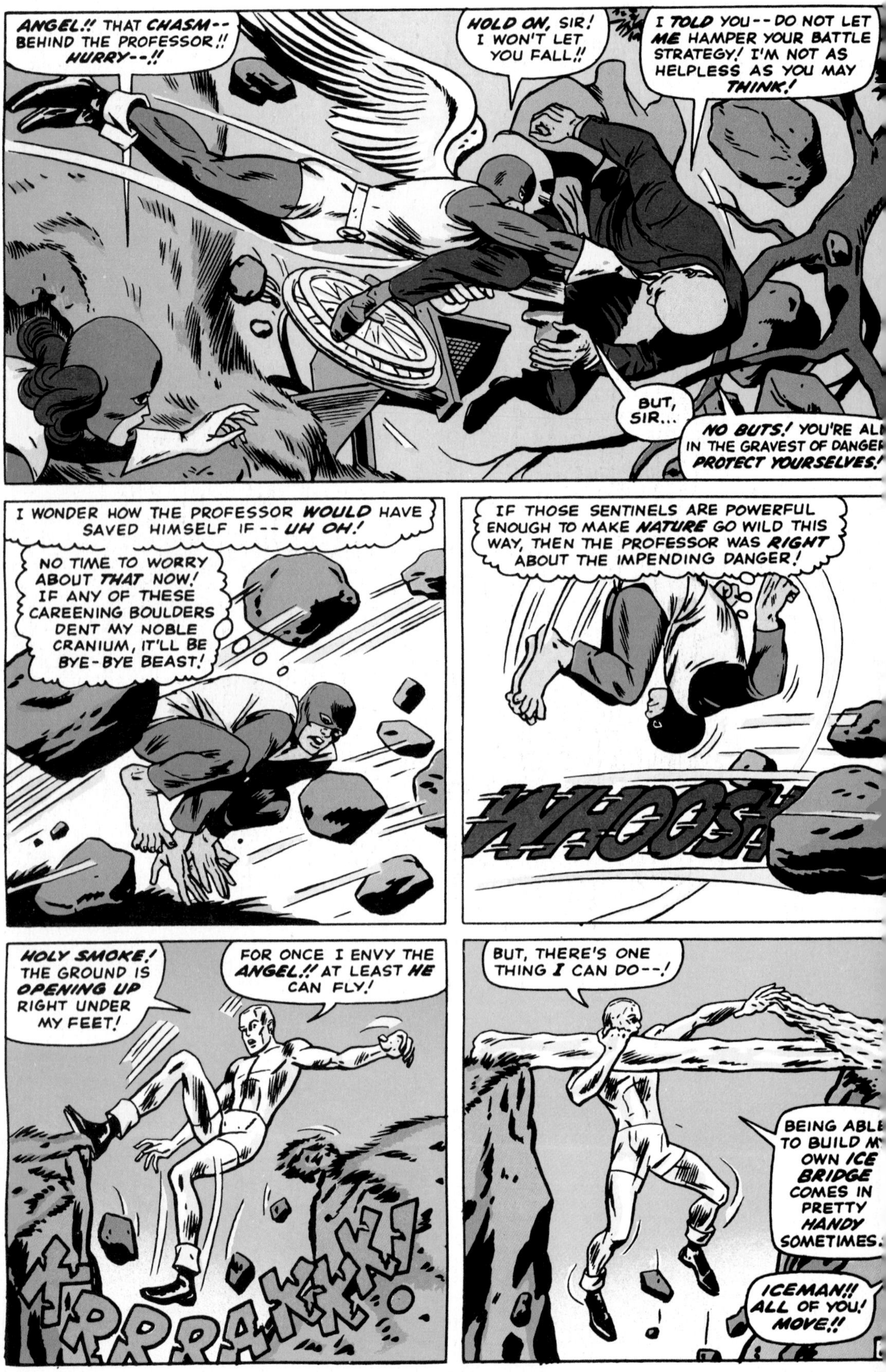

ANGEL!! THAT CHASM-- BEHIND THE PROFESSOR!! HURRY--!!
HOLD ON, SIR! I WON'T LET YOU FALL!!
I TOLD YOU--DO NOT LET ME HAMPER YOUR BATTLE STRATEGY! I'M NOT AS HELPLESS AS YOU MAY THINK!
BUT, SIR...
NO BUTS! YOU'RE AL IN THE GRAVEST OF DANGE PROTECT YOURSELVES!
I WONDER HOW THE PROFESSOR WOULD HAVE SAVED HIMSELF IF--UH OH!
NO TIME TO WORRY ABOUT THAT NOW! IF ANY OF THESE CAREENING BOULDERS DENT MY NOBLE CRANIUM, IT'LL BE BYE-BYE BEAST!
IF THOSE SENTINELS ARE POWERFUL ENOUGH TO MAKE NATURE GO WILD THIS WAY, THEN THE PROFESSOR WAS RIGHT ABOUT THE IMPENDING DANGER!
WHOOSH
HOLY SMOKE! THE GROUND IS OPENING UP RIGHT UNDER MY FEET!
FOR ONCE I ENVY THE ANGEL!! AT LEAST HE CAN FLY!
TRRRAKK!
BUT, THERE'S ONE THING I CAN DO--!
BEING ABL TO BUILD M OWN ICE BRIDGE COMES IN PRETTY HANDY SOMETIMES.
ICEMAN!! ALL OF YOU! MOVE!!

HEAD FOR *HIGH GROUND!* YOU'RE IN *JEOPARDY* EVERY SECOND YOU REMAIN WHERE YOU ARE!

HIS BRAIN NEVER STOPS! SOMEHOW, I'LL BET HE *COULD* HAVE SAVED HIMSELF!

HANK! YOU HEARD THE *PROF!* *KEEP MOVING!*

TUT TUT, DEPUTY LEADER! HAVE YOU NO REGARD FOR *CHIVALRY?* I MERELY PAUSED TO OFFER ASSISTANCE TO YON DAMSEL IN DISTRESS!

I'M *HARDLY* A DAMSEL IN DISTRESS, MR. McCOY! IF YOU'LL KINDLY STEP ASIDE...

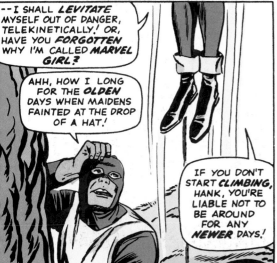

--I SHALL *LEVITATE* MYSELF OUT OF DANGER, TELEKINETICALLY! OR, HAVE YOU *FORGOTTEN* WHY I'M CALLED *MARVEL GIRL?*

AHH, HOW I LONG FOR THE *OLDEN* DAYS WHEN MAIDENS FAINTED AT THE DROP OF A HAT!

IF YOU DON'T START *CLIMBING*, HANK, YOU'RE LIABLE NOT TO BE AROUND FOR ANY *NEWER* DAYS!

HOW ABOUT THIS *ICE LADDER* OF MINE, CYKE? BOY, WOULDN'T WE MAKE DANDY *FIREMEN!!*

CLAM UP! KEEP CLIMBING! SAVE YOUR ENERGY!

NAHH! OL' PARTY POOP!

MINUTES LATER...

WE SEEM TO HAVE CLIMBED OUT OF EFFECTIVE RANGE OF THEIR *NATURE ACTIVATOR RAYS!*

BUT, WE'VE GOT TO INVADE THAT FORTRESS BEFORE THEY CAN LAUNCH A *NEW* ATTACK AGAINST US!

AND, MOST IMPORTANT OF ALL, WE *MUST* LEARN WHAT WAS MEANT BY THE WORDS *"MASTER MOLD"!*

THEY'RE *STILL* FIRING! IF WE HADN'T CLIMBED TO SAFETY, WE'D BE *FINISHED!*

BUH-TANNG! BUH-TANNG!

WHOOM!

3

HOW DO WE GET *IN* THERE, SIR? IT LOOKS *IMPOSSIBLE!*

I'VE SPENT *YEARS* DRUMMING INTO YOU-- *NOTHING* IS IMPOSSIBLE.!!

IF I COULD ONLY LEARN *WHY* THAT SENTINEL TOPPLED OVER IN THE TV STUDIO.!! *

WHAT GOOD WOULD *THAT* DO?

IT PROVES THEY HAVE A *WEAK SPOT!* AND OUR *LIVES* MAY DEPEND ON *FINDING* IT!

*REMEMBER WHEN IT HAPPENED LAST ISH *??* -- STAN.

YOUR *FIRST* TASK IS TO GET ACROSS THE CHASM! *ICEMAN*-- PLAN "G"!

YES, *SIR!* I'LL HAVE THE GLIDER BUILT IN NO TIME!

GOOD WORK, BOBBY! NOW *I'LL* SUPPLY THE MOTIVE POWER!

HOLD TIGHT, FELLAS! I'LL HAVE TO APPLY NEARLY *MAXIMUM* POWER.!!

SHOOT THE WORKS, CYKE! WE'RE BIG BOYS NOW!

THIS DOESN'T SEEM VERY *DIGNIFIED*, BUT I SUPPOSE IT'S NECESSARY!

ARE YOU SURE YOU CAN *DO* IT, SCOTT?

IT *HAS* TO BE DONE.!! SO, I'LL *DO* IT!

REMEMBER, SCOTT-- IT MUST BE PERFECT THE *FIRST* TIME!

SLOWLY, CALMLY, CYCLOPS ESTIMATES THE AMOUNT OF POWER BLAST ENERGY HE'LL NEED! THEN, AS HIS EYES BEGIN TO CLOSE, HIS *VISOR* STARTS TO RISE...

HIGHER AND HIGHER GOES THE VISOR, UNTIL IT IS COMPLETELY *OPEN!* BUT, STILL THE MOST DANGEROUS EYES IN ALL THE WORLD REMAIN TIGHTLY SHUT, AS THE YOUTHFUL MUTANT STANDS PERFECTLY MOTIONLESS--!

AND THEN, WITH THE FORCE OF A *LIGHTNING BOLT*, HIS EYELIDS SNAP OPEN, AS A FRANTIC CRY ESCAPES HIS LIPS--!

NOW!

4

A *PERFECT LAUNCH*, SCOTT.!! NOW, QUICKLY, ANGEL-- FLY *AFTER* THEM, IN CASE THEY NEED HELP!

ZZIP!

NO MATTER *WHO* IS ATTACKING US FROM THAT FORTRESS, HERE'S WHERE THEY LEARN THAT NOBODY PUSHES THE *X-MEN* AROUND!

BOBBY! THE ICE-SKIMMER IS WOBBLING *DANGEROUSLY!* YOUR DESIGN ISN'T AERODYNAMICALLY *ACCURATE!*

WADDAYA *WANT* FOR A TEN-SECOND JOB--A B-52??

THEY'RE GONNA *FALL!!* *HOLD ON!* I'LL BE RIGHT THERE!!

THE SOONER THE *BETTER*, SON!

BUT, BEFORE THE WINGED WONDER CAN SEIZE HIS FALLING FRIENDS...

OOOOFF!

WHISST! WHISST!

MECHANICAL *TENTACLES!!!* THEY JUST BARELY *MISSED* ME!

LOOK OUT, ANGEL.!! SOME-THING'S *CAUGHT* US! DON'T LET IT GRAB *YOU*--!!

5

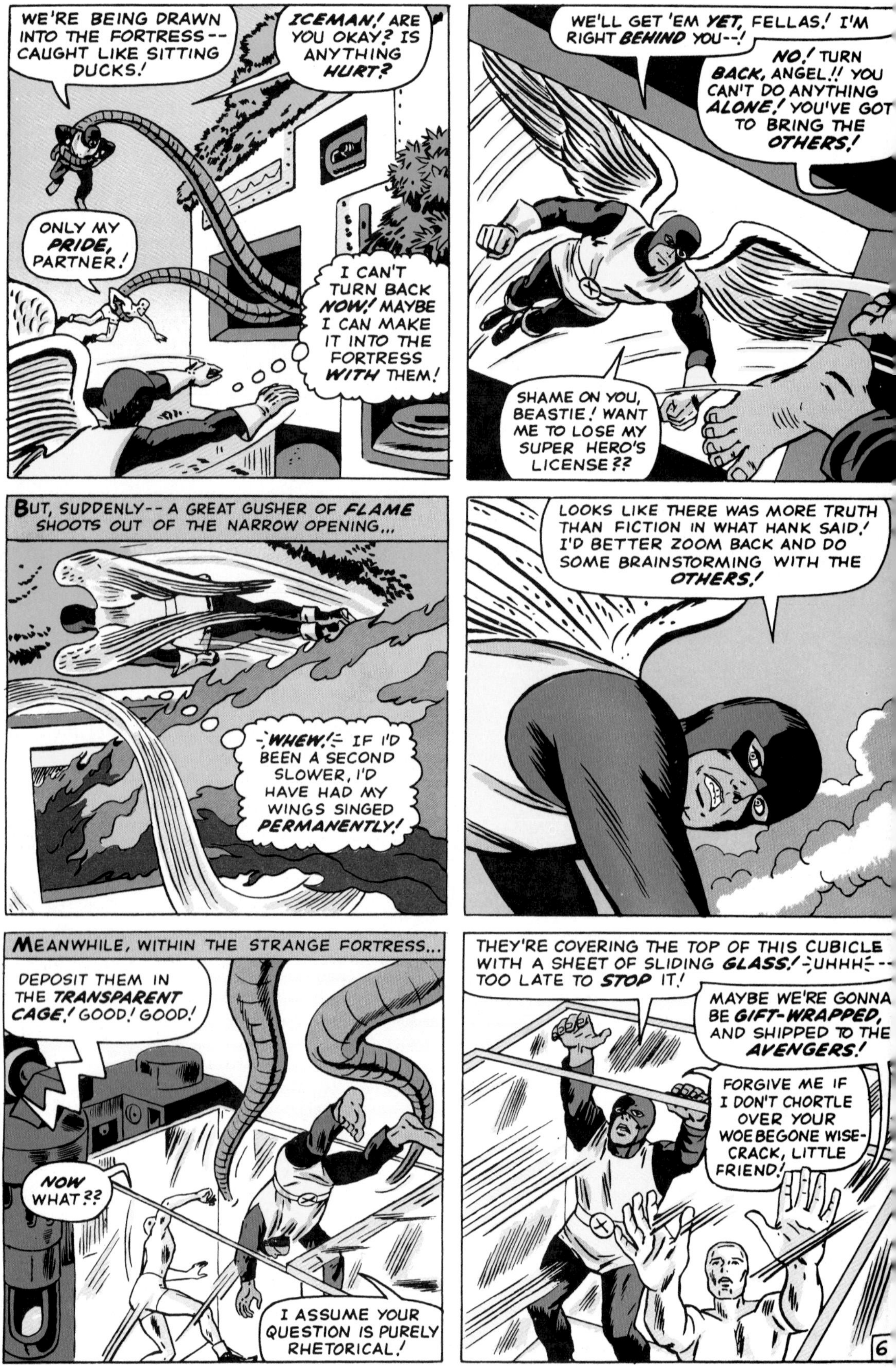
WE'RE BEING DRAWN INTO THE FORTRESS-- CAUGHT LIKE SITTING DUCKS!
ICEMAN! ARE YOU OKAY? IS ANYTHING HURT?
ONLY MY PRIDE, PARTNER!
I CAN'T TURN BACK NOW! MAYBE I CAN MAKE IT INTO THE FORTRESS WITH THEM!
WE'LL GET 'EM YET, FELLAS! I'M RIGHT BEHIND YOU--!
NO! TURN BACK, ANGEL!! YOU CAN'T DO ANYTHING ALONE! YOU'VE GOT TO BRING THE OTHERS!
SHAME ON YOU, BEASTIE! WANT ME TO LOSE MY SUPER HERO'S LICENSE??
BUT, SUDDENLY-- A GREAT GUSHER OF FLAME SHOOTS OUT OF THE NARROW OPENING...
-WHEW!- IF I'D BEEN A SECOND SLOWER, I'D HAVE HAD MY WINGS SINGED PERMANENTLY!
LOOKS LIKE THERE WAS MORE TRUTH THAN FICTION IN WHAT HANK SAID! I'D BETTER ZOOM BACK AND DO SOME BRAINSTORMING WITH THE OTHERS!
MEANWHILE, WITHIN THE STRANGE FORTRESS...
DEPOSIT THEM IN THE TRANSPARENT CAGE! GOOD! GOOD!
NOW WHAT??
I ASSUME YOUR QUESTION IS PURELY RHETORICAL!
THEY'RE COVERING THE TOP OF THIS CUBICLE WITH A SHEET OF SLIDING GLASS! -UHHH- -- TOO LATE TO STOP IT!
MAYBE WE'RE GONNA BE GIFT-WRAPPED, AND SHIPPED TO THE AVENGERS!
FORGIVE ME IF I DON'T CHORTLE OVER YOUR WOEBEGONE WISE-CRACK, LITTLE FRIEND!
6

OH, *NO!* NOW THEY'RE FILLING THIS THING--KOFF-- WITH SOME KINDA *GAS*--!!

GETTING GROGGY--KOFF KOFF!-- MUST BE-- SOME TYPE OF-- --KOFF QUICK-ACTING *SLEEPING* VAPOR--!

WELL-- IT SURE ISN'T--CHICKEN SOUP--UHHH--...

IT IS *DONE!* THEY ARE *ASLEEP!*

IT WAS A SIMPLE MATTER TO DEFEAT THE INVADING HUMANS!

SO SHALL WE DEFEAT ANY AND *ALL* HUMANS WHO DARE TO DEFY THE *SENTINELS!*

THIS IS *MADNESS!* YOU CANNOT TAKE OVER THE MACHINES WHICH *I* HAVE CREATED!! YOU DON'T KNOW WHAT YOU'RE *DOING*--!

WE KNOW FAR MORE THAN YOU SUSPECT, DR. TRASK! DID NOT YOU YOURSELF *CREATE* US?

NO! I CREATED THE *MASTER MOLD!* ONLY *WE* CAN CREATE ADDITIONAL SENTINELS!

BUT, YOU WERE MADE FOR ONLY *ONE* PURPOSE-- TO GUARD THE HUMAN RACE FROM *MUTANTS!* THAT IS YOUR *ONLY DUTY!*

WE CAN ONLY GUARD THE HUMAN RACE BY BECOMING ITS *MASTER!* HUMANS ARE TOO WEAK, TOO FOOLISH TO GOVERN THEMSELVES! HENCEFORTH, *WE* SHALL *RULE!!*

NO! YOU CANNOT ENSLAVE ALL OF *MANKIND!!*

WE HAVE THE POWER TO DO WHATEVER WE WISH! *NOTHING* CAN STOP US! NOW COME--!

WE SHALL TAKE YOU TO THE *MASTER MOLD!* YOU SHALL HELP HIM CREATE *MORE* SENTINELS! ENOUGH TO OVERRUN ALL OF THE *UNIVERSE!!*

WHAT HAVE I DONE?? WHAT UNTHINKABLE *MENACE* HAVE I UNLEASHED??

7

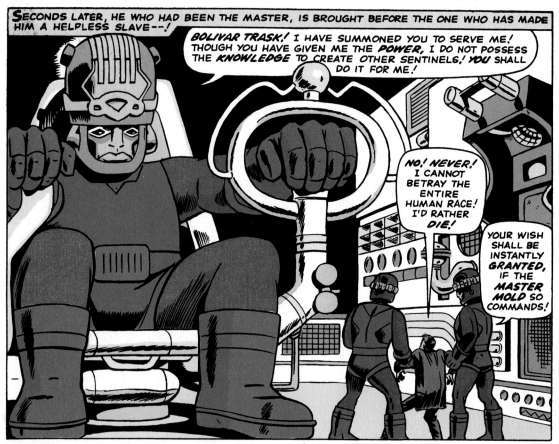

BOLIVAR TRASK! I HAVE SUMMONED YOU TO SERVE ME! THOUGH YOU HAVE GIVEN ME THE *POWER,* I DO NOT POSSESS THE *KNOWLEDGE* TO CREATE OTHER SENTINELS! *YOU* SHALL DO IT FOR ME!

NO! NEVER! I CANNOT BETRAY THE ENTIRE HUMAN RACE! I'D RATHER *DIE!*

YOUR WISH SHALL BE INSTANTLY *GRANTED,* IF THE *MASTER MOLD* SO COMMANDS!

REMEMBER THE *WEAPONS* YOU HAVE GIVEN ME! I CAN DESTROY HALF YOUR NATION! REFUSE TO SERVE ME, AND *YOU'LL* BE RESPONSIBLE FOR THE CARNAGE THAT RESULTS!

YOU MEAN-- YOU'D *ATTACK* MANKIND ??!

MY SENTINELS AND I ARE NOT HUMAN! WE HAVE NO FEELINGS -- NO EMOTIONS! WE ARE CAPABLE OF *ANYTHING!!*

BUT-- THE *X-MEN* WILL FIGHT YOU! *THEY'LL* FIND SOME WAY TO DESTROY YOU *ALL!*

FOOL! DID YOU NOT CREATE US TO *DESTROY* THE X-MEN?!! WE ARE *TOO POWERFUL!* THEY WILL BE *HELPLESS* BEFORE US!

WE HAVE *ALREADY* CAPTURED TWO OF THEM! I SHALL *STUDY* THEM-- BEFORE I ORDER THEM *DESTROYED!*

8

MEANWHILE, OUTSIDE THE FANTASTIC FORTRESS AGAIN...

ICEMAN AND THE BEAST WERE *CAPTURED.!!* I WAS TOO LATE TO SAVE THEM!

WE KNOW! WE WITNESSED THE ENTIRE TABLEAU!

YOU DID YOUR *BEST*, ANGEL! UNFORTUNATELY, YOU'RE NOT MADE OF *ASBESTOS!*

BUT, WHAT DO WE DO *HOW?* HOW DO WE *SAVE* THEM? HOW DO WE GET INTO THE FORTRESS?

GOOD QUESTION, JEAN! THEY SEEM TO HAVE ENOUGH BUILT-IN WEAPONS TO STOP AN *ARMY!*

AN ARMY, PERHAPS! BUT, WE ARE THE *X-MEN!* NO MILITARY FORCE ON EARTH CAN EQUAL OUR UNIQUE POWERS!

THOUGH I CANNOT *CONTROL* THE MECHANICAL BRAIN OF A SENTINEL -- I CAN STILL *STRIKE* IT WITH A BOLT OF PURE MENTAL ENERGY!

SOMEWHERE BEHIND THOSE WALLS, *SENTINELS* ARE OPERATING THE WEAPONS THAT GUARD THAT FORTRESS!

IF I *BLANK OUT* THEIR MINDS, I *NULLIFY* THEIR WEAPONS!

GREAT, PROFESSOR! IF YOU CAN DOUSE THOSE *RAYS*, WE CAN STRIKE BEFORE THEY KNOW IT!

EXACTLY! THE TIME HAS COME FOR ME TO BE AN ACTIVE *PARTICIPANT* IN OUR BATTLE! FIRST, I SHALL MENTALLY TRACE THE RAYS TO THEIR ORIGINAL SOURCE--!

WE'LL STAND *READY*, SIR! ONCE THOSE RAYS GO OUT, WE *MOVE!!*

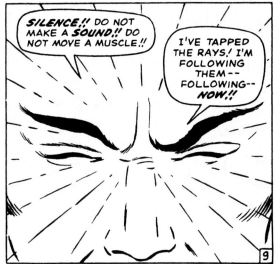

SILENCE!! DO NOT MAKE A *SOUND!!* DO NOT MOVE A MUSCLE!!

I'VE TAPPED THE RAYS! I'M FOLLOWING THEM -- FOLLOWING-- *NOW!!*

9

95

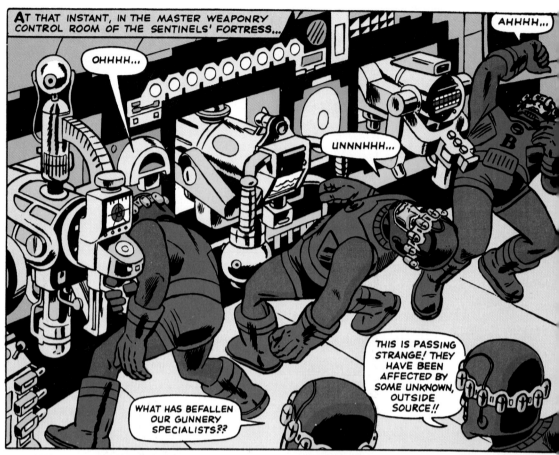

AT THAT INSTANT, IN THE MASTER WEAPONRY CONTROL ROOM OF THE SENTINELS' FORTRESS...

OHHHH...

AHHHH...

UNNNHHH...

THIS IS PASSING STRANGE! THEY HAVE BEEN AFFECTED BY SOME UNKNOWN, OUTSIDE SOURCE!!

WHAT HAS BEFALLEN OUR GUNNERY SPECIALISTS??

OUR REPEL-GUNS AND RAYS MUST BE ATTENDED! THESE STRICKEN ONES MUST BE REPLACED!

YOUR WORDS HAVE MUCH SUBSTANCE! BUT, IT CANNOT BE DONE WITHOUT THE SECTION LEADER'S APPROVAL!

THERE WILL BE A DELAY, FOR WE DARE NOT VIOLATE OUR PROGRAMMED INSTRUCTIONS!

THEN THE SECTION LEADER MUST BE CONTACTED AT ONCE!

BUT, EVEN AS THE SENTINEL SPEAKS, HIS SECTION LEADER IS ATTENDING TO OTHER MATTERS...

FOLLOW ME! THE PRISONER HAS BEEN SUMMONED BY THE MASTER MOLD!

10

96

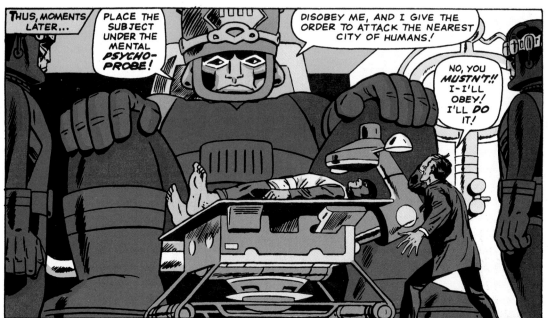

THUS, MOMENTS LATER...

PLACE THE SUBJECT UNDER THE MENTAL *PSYCHO-PROBE!*

DISOBEY ME, AND I GIVE THE ORDER TO ATTACK THE NEAREST CITY OF HUMANS!

NO, YOU *MUSTN'T!!* I-I'LL OBEY! I'LL *DO* IT!

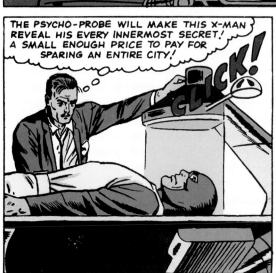

THE PSYCHO-PROBE WILL MAKE THIS X-MAN REVEAL HIS EVERY INNERMOST SECRET! A SMALL ENOUGH PRICE TO PAY FOR SPARING AN ENTIRE CITY!

CLICK!

AND THEN AND THERE, UNDER THE IRRESISTIBLE INFLUENCE OF THE STRANGE PSYCHO-BEAM, THE CAPTIVE *BEAST* BEGINS TO SPEAK -- IN SLOW, EMOTIONLESS TONES...

I AM -- THE *BEAST!* I SERVE -- THE *X-MEN!* OUR MISSION -- PROTECT MANKIND -- FROM EVIL MUTANTS -- AND ANY OR ALL DANGERS -- THAT MAY BEFALL --!

THEIR MISSION -- *PROTECT* MANKIND!! HOW *WRONG* I WAS ABOUT THEM! WHAT *DREAD HARM* I'VE DONE --!!

BUT, EVEN AS THE BEAST RAMBLES ON --

IF ONLY THE *PROFESSOR* COULD BE WITH US!!

I *AM* WITH YOU -- FOLLOWING EVERY MOVE *MENTALLY!* *ALL* OUR POWERS WILL BE NEEDED FOR THIS ASSAULT!

LEVEL OFF, WARREN! SOON AS YOU'RE IN POSITION, I'LL USE MY OPTIC-BLAST POWER AGAINST THE FORTRESS!

LET'S HOPE IT *WORKS,* CYKE! IF NOT, THE PROF BETTER START RECRUITING A NEW TEAM, PRONTO!

11

97

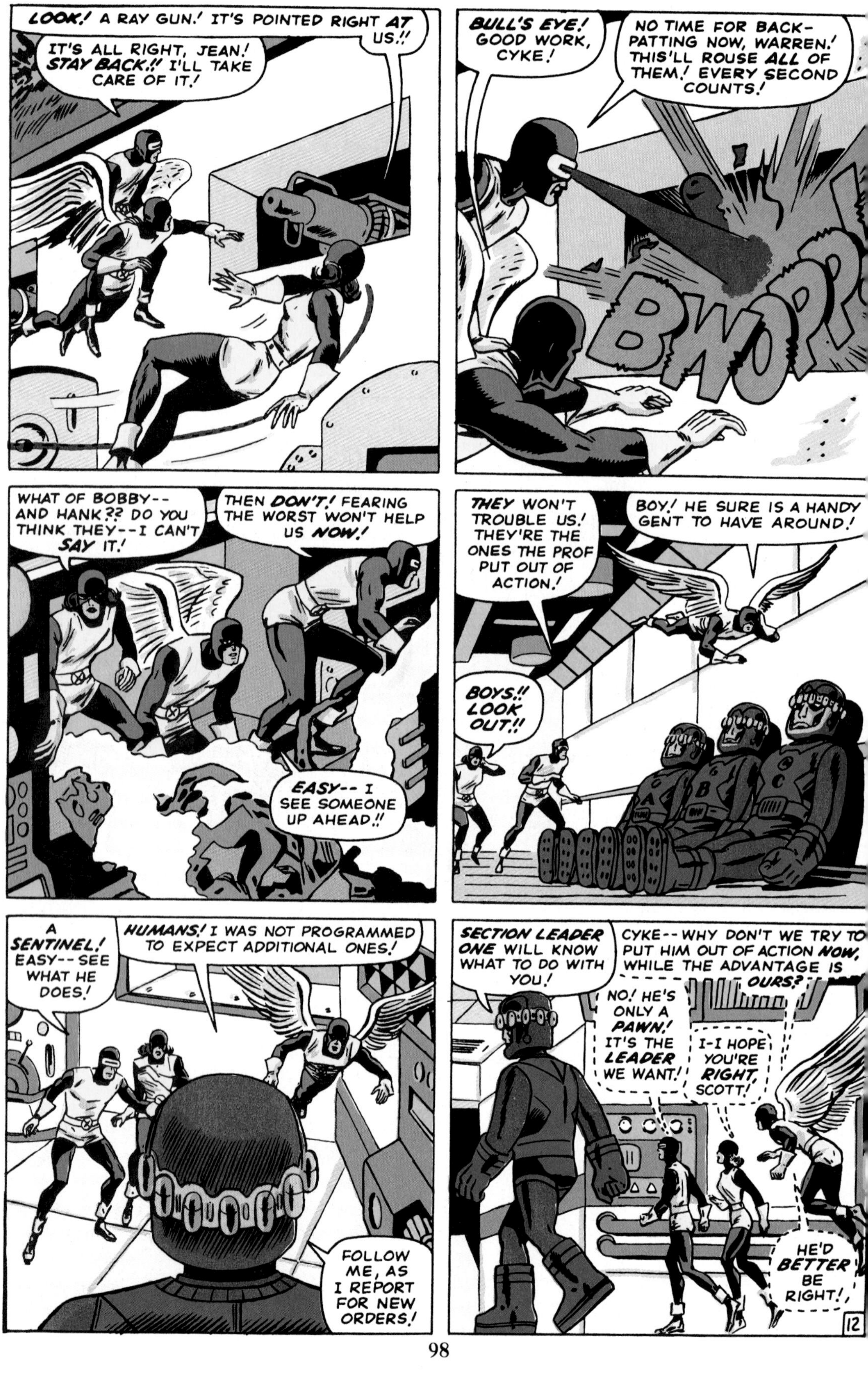
LOOK! A RAY GUN! IT'S POINTED RIGHT AT US!!
IT'S ALL RIGHT, JEAN! STAY BACK!! I'LL TAKE CARE OF IT!
BULL'S EYE! GOOD WORK, CYKE!
NO TIME FOR BACK-PATTING NOW, WARREN! THIS'LL ROUSE ALL OF THEM! EVERY SECOND COUNTS!
BWOPP
WHAT OF BOBBY--AND HANK?? DO YOU THINK THEY--I CAN'T SAY IT!
THEN DON'T! FEARING THE WORST WON'T HELP US NOW!
EASY-- I SEE SOMEONE UP AHEAD!!
THEY WON'T TROUBLE US! THEY'RE THE ONES THE PROF PUT OUT OF ACTION!
BOY! HE SURE IS A HANDY GENT TO HAVE AROUND!
BOYS!! LOOK OUT!!
A SENTINEL! EASY--SEE WHAT HE DOES!
HUMANS! I WAS NOT PROGRAMMED TO EXPECT ADDITIONAL ONES!
FOLLOW ME, AS I REPORT FOR NEW ORDERS!
SECTION LEADER ONE WILL KNOW WHAT TO DO WITH YOU!
CYKE--WHY DON'T WE TRY TO PUT HIM OUT OF ACTION NOW, WHILE THE ADVANTAGE IS OURS?
NO! HE'S ONLY A PAWN! IT'S THE LEADER WE WANT!
I-I HOPE YOU'RE RIGHT, SCOTT!
HE'D BETTER BE RIGHT!
12

YOU MADE THE RIGHT DECISION, SCOTT! BUT, ALWAYS REMEMBER, WITH THE *PRIDE OF LEADERSHIP* GOES THE WEIGHT OF RESPONSIBILITY! YOU MUST BE ABLE TO BEAR THEM *BOTH!*

I'LL DO MY BEST, SIR-- BUT IT'S SURE GOOD TO KNOW YOU'RE MENTALLY MONITORING OUR PROGRESS!

WE'RE REACHING THE *END* OF THE PASSAGEWAY...!

MEANWHILE, UNDER THE PSYCHO-PROBE, THE BEAST CONTINUES TO TALK...

MY FATHER WAS-- AN ORDINARY LABORER-- AT AN ATOMIC PROJECT! I PROBABLY GAINED MY POWER-- DUE TO RADIATION-- WHICH AFFECTED HIM BEFORE I WAS BORN! I'LL NEVER --KNOW FOR SURE!

ONE DAY-- HE LOST HIS JOB -- AND SO WE MOVED-- TO ANOTHER CITY--

"THE NEIGHBORHOOD BULLIES-- PICKED ON ME-- BECAUSE I WAS A NEW ARRIVAL-- AND ALSO-- BECAUSE OF MY ANTHROPOID PHYSIQUE! BUT, I MYSELF-- DID NOT YET SUSPECT-- THE *POWERS* I POSSESSED--!

BEAT IT, UGLY! IF YOU WANT SOMEONE TO PLAY WITH, GO FIND YERSELF ANOTHER MONKEY!

GOWAN, CHARLIE-- *PASTE 'IM* ONE!

HEY! WHAT *GIVES??* I CAN'T NAB 'IM! HE HOPS AROUND LIKE A *JUMPIN' BEAN!*

YOU AREN'T GOING TO HIT *ME!*

STAND STILL! I *DARE* YA!! STAND STILL-- JUST FOR A *MINUTE!*

"LIKE MOST YOUNG BOYS-- I COULDN'T RESIST A DARE-- AND SO--

THERE! *THAT'LL* TEACH YOU--! HEY!

I CAN'T *STOP* IN TIME!

LOOK OUT FOR THAT *CAR!!* LOOK OUT!!!

S-C-R-E-E-T-C-H

"AND THAT WAS-- WHEN I FIRST REALIZED-- I POSSESSED POWERS-- GREATER THAN ANY NORMAL HUMAN--!"

WHA- WHAT *HAPPENED* TO HIM?? WHERE'D HE *GO??*

D-DID YOU SEE *THAT??!*

13

BUT, AFTER THAT-- IT WAS NO BETTER! WHERE THEY HAD ONCE MADE FUN OF ME-- NOW, THEY FEARED ME--! I BECAME-- LONELIER THAN EVER--

FORGIVE INTERRUPTION! EMERGENCY! RAY GUNS PUT OUT OF ACTION! REQUEST INSTRUCTIONS!

WHAT.??! THERE MUST BE MORE MUTANTS IN OUR MIDST.!! PREPARE FOR COMBAT ACTION!

FOLLOW ME! MUTANTS ARE OUR NATURAL ENEMIES! THEY MUST BE FOUND AND DESTROYED, WHEREVER THEY EXIST! WE ARE ALL SO PROGRAMMED!

THEY SHALL NOT ESCAPE US!

WHILE, JUST A FEW HUNDRED YARDS AWAY,...

SCOTT.!! WARREN.!! IN THERE --LOOK!

BOBBY IS THERE.!! BUT--WHERE'S THE BEAST ??

ICEMAN.!! IMPRISONED IN SOME SORT OF A GLASS CUBICLE.!!

WE'VE GOT TO GET HIM OUT OF THERE!

STOP.! YOUR ORDERS WERE TO FOLLOW ME!

ANGEL.!! WHAT'S HE GOING TO DO.??

IT DOESN'T MATTER, JEANNIE! I WON'T GIVE HIM THE CHANCE!

I'VE BEEN ITCHIN' TO DO THIS SINCE WE GOT HERE!

WHA.?!

WE MUST STOP HIM-- FOR BOBBY'S SAKE!

14

WARREN'S PUNCH SHOOK HIM UP, BUT DIDN'T TOPPLE HIM! NOTHING SHORT OF A *BATTERING RAM* COULD DO THAT!

BUT, IF I CAN MOVE HIS LEGS FAR ENOUGH TO HURL HIM OFF-BALANCE WITH MY TELEKINETIC POWER!

I *DID* IT!

WHHOOM!

AND, EVEN AS THE UNHUMAN LEVIATHAN FALLS...

CRACK!

BOBBY'S BEEN *GASSED!* HE'S GOT TO HAVE *AIR* --AS SOON AS POSSIBLE!!

IT WORKED! HE'S COMING AROUND NOW!

WHOOO-EEE! MY POOR, ACHIN' HEAD!

BOBBY-- THE *BEAST*-- WHAT *HAPPENED* TO HIM??

I DON'T *KNOW!!* I CAN'T REMEMBER--!!

THEY MUST HAVE TAKEN HIM AWAY WHILE YOU WERE UNCONSCIOUS! BUT, IF *YOU'RE* STILL ALIVE, THEN THERE'S HOPE--!

WHERE ARE THE *OTHERS?* HOW LONG WAS I OUT? HOW ABOUT CLUIN' A GUY IN??

WE'LL HAVE TO FILL YOU IN AS WE GO ALONG, BOBBY! EVERY SECOND MAY BE VITAL NOW!

THEN, AS IF TO EMPHASIZE THE GRAVITY OF MARVEL GIRL'S REMARK...

LISTEN! BELLS RINGIN'! ALL *OVER* THE PLACE!

IT'S A *WARNING SYSTEM!* I FLEW BACK TO *TELL* YOU!

CLANG! CLANG! CLANG! CLANG!

THE WHOLE FORTRESS IS ON THE *ALERT!*

15

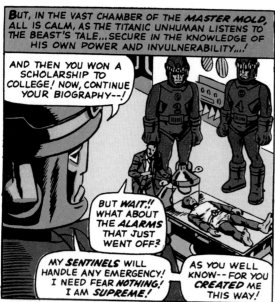

BUT, IN THE VAST CHAMBER OF THE *MASTER MOLD*, ALL IS CALM, AS THE TITANIC UNHUMAN LISTENS TO THE BEAST'S TALE...SECURE IN THE KNOWLEDGE OF HIS OWN POWER AND INVULNERABILITY...!

AND THEN YOU WON A SCHOLARSHIP TO COLLEGE! NOW, CONTINUE YOUR BIOGRAPHY--!

BUT *WAIT*!! WHAT ABOUT THE *ALARMS* THAT JUST WENT OFF?

MY *SENTINELS* WILL HANDLE ANY EMERGENCY! I NEED FEAR *NOTHING*! I AM *SUPREME*!

AS YOU WELL KNOW-- FOR YOU *CREATED* ME THIS WAY!

"I EXCELLED-- AT EVERYTHING! SCHOLASTICALLY-- I WAS HEAD OF MY CLASS! AND-- IN SPORTS-- I WAS UNBEATABLE--!

COMPARED TO MY AGILITY, THEY'RE LIKE *STATUES*!

"BUT, MY OWN NATURAL ENTHUSIASM-- GOT THE BETTER OF ME-- ONE DAY! AFTER SCORING A GOAL --I KICKED OFF MY SHOES--AND LEAPED FOR THE GOAL POST--!

WE *DID* IT! WE WON THE CONFERENCE *CHAMPIONSHIP*!

LOOK AT McCOY!! HE'S LIKE A *BEAST*!!

McCOY!! GET *DOWN* FROM THERE!

NOBODY CAN DO THAT!! NOBODY *HUMAN*!

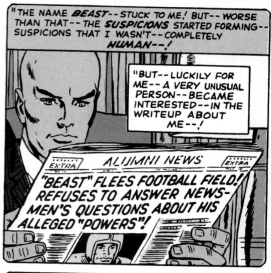

"THE NAME *BEAST*-- STUCK TO ME! BUT-- WORSE THAN THAT-- THE *SUSPICIONS* STARTED FORMING-- SUSPICIONS THAT I WASN'T--COMPLETELY *HUMAN*--!

"BUT-- LUCKILY FOR ME-- A VERY UNUSUAL PERSON--BECAME INTERESTED--IN THE WRITEUP ABOUT ME--!

EXTRA ALUMNI NEWS EXTRA

"*BEAST*" FLEES FOOTBALL FIELD! REFUSES TO ANSWER NEWSMEN'S QUESTIONS ABOUT HIS ALLEGED "POWERS"!

"BEFORE LONG, WE HAD-- A VERY SPECIAL GUEST-- TO DINNER.'"

HENRY McCOY!! MIND YOUR *MANNERS*!!

HAVE YOU FORGOTTEN WE HAVE *COMPANY*??

IT'S ALL RIGHT, MRS. McCOY! I'M ANXIOUS TO *OBSERVE* YOUR SON UNDER ALL CONDITIONS!

JUST WHAT *DO* YOU WANT WITH HANK, MISTER?

HE MAY SEEM STRANGE TO OTHERS, BUT HE'S A GOOD BOY --DO YOU HEAR?

WE'RE TERRIBLY *PROUD* OF HENRY-- DESPITE *OTHER* PEOPLE CALLING HIM-- A *FREAK*!

THAT'S WHY *I'M* HERE! YOUR SON CAN GO THRU LIFE AS A "*FREAK*"-- OR A *BENEFACTOR* OF THE HUMAN RACE! THE CHOICE IS *YOURS*!

I WANT TO TAKE HIM-- AND *TRAIN* HIM--!

MEANWHILE, ACROSS THE CHASM FROM THE SENTINELS' FORTRESS, PROFESSOR XAVIER, MENTALLY SCANNING THE AREA, SUDDENLY GASPS WITH ALARM...

HANK CANNOT *HELP* HIMSELF! UNDER THAT PSYCHIC PROBE HE'S TELLING *TOO MUCH!*

I'VE GOT TO *STOP* HIM, BEFORE HE GIVES AWAY TOO MANY OF OUR SECRETS!

ALTHOUGH I'M CONFINED TO THIS CHAIR -- WHICH, LUCKILY, JEAN LEVITATED FROM WHERE IT HAD FALLEN BELOW -- I'VE GOT TO TAKE A DESPERATE GAMBLE --!

I'LL SEND MY INVISIBLE *ASTRAL IMAGE* TO WHERE HANK IS! IT'S THE ONLY THING THAT CAN HELP NOW!!

BEING UNSOLID, *NOTHING* CAN PREVENT MY ENTERING *ANY* PLACE I CHOOSE!

WE MUST *FIND* THAT MUTANT *LEADER* MY CAPTIVE HAS MENTIONED!! FIND HIM -- AND IMMEDIATELY *DESTROY HIM!*

I DIDN'T GET HERE A SECOND TOO SOON!

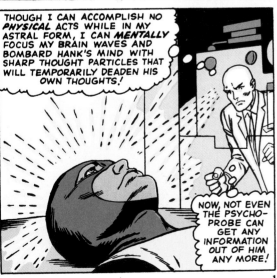

THOUGH I CAN ACCOMPLISH NO *PHYSICAL* ACTS WHILE IN MY *ASTRAL* FORM, I CAN *MENTALLY* FOCUS MY BRAIN WAVES AND BOMBARD HANK'S MIND WITH SHARP THOUGHT PARTICLES THAT WILL TEMPORARILY DEADEN HIS OWN THOUGHTS!

NOW, NOT EVEN THE PSYCHO-PROBE CAN GET ANY INFORMATION OUT OF HIM ANY MORE!

TRASK!! WHY DID HE STOP SPEAKING -- JUST WHEN HE WAS ABOUT TO REVEAL THE X-MEN'S *HIDEOUT??*

I DON'T *KNOW!!* EVERY-THING SEEMS TO BE WORKING PROPERLY!

REMEMBER! IF I DO NOT GAIN THE INFORMATION I SEEK, A *CITY* SHALL PERISH!

17

BUT THEN, THE BRILLIANT LEADER OF THE X-MEN TAKES A DESPERATE CHANCE--!

I'VE GOT TO PROBE THE MECHANICAL BRAIN OF THE *MASTER MOLD* HIMSELF--NO MATTER WHAT THE COST!

JUST AS I THOUGHT! A VAST COMPLEX OF ELECTRONIC CIRCUITRY!

A STRANGE FORCE-- I FEEL IT SCANNING MY THINKING APPARATUS!!

THERE IS SOMETHING HERE!! A MENACING PRESENCE! I *SENSE* IT! I *FEEL* IT! BUT I CANNOT *SEE* IT!

YET, I AM EQUIPPED WITH WEAPONS FOR *ANY* TYPE OF ATTACK!

AND THEN, WITH DAZZLING, TOTALLY UNHUMAN SPEED...

MICRO-ELECTRIC BLASTS-- LEAPING FROM HIS FINGERS! THEY'RE FILLING THE ENTIRE CHAMBER! I CANNOT DODGE THEM!

MY ASTRAL-IMAGE IS COMPOSED OF ELECTRIFIED THOUGHT WAVES!! IT CAN BE *HARMED* BY THE MASTER MOLD'S MICRO-ELECTRIC ATTACK!

I'VE GOT TO RETURN TO MY BODY--BEFORE THE BOLTS WEAKEN ME TOO MUCH!

IF I SHOULD BE *UNABLE* TO ONCE AGAIN *REJOIN* MY PHYSICAL SELF, THEN MY FLESH-AND-BLOOD BODY WOULD BE CONDEMNED TO REMAIN IN A TRANCE--*FOREVER!*

JUST ANOTHER FEW FEET-- I'VE GOT TO MAKE IT!! I'VE *GOT* TO!!

18

BUT, AT THAT VERY MOMENT, THE SEARCHING SQUAD OF SENTINELS *FINDS* ITS PREY--!

MUTANTS!! OUR SWORN ENEMIES!! *DESTROY THEM!*

SHOW THEM NO QUARTER! ATTACK! *ATTACK!*

UH OH! THE HAPPINESS BOYS ARE BACK!

HOW DOES ANYONE AS BIG AS THEM *MOVE* SO FAST??!

WE NEED TIME-- TO FORMULATE A PLAN! QUICK, BOBBY-- AN *ICE SHIELD!*

THOOM!

THIS MAY GIVE US A *BREATHER,* CYKE-- BUT IT WON'T HOLD *THEM* OFF FOR LONG!

IT DOESN'T *HAVE* TO! WE JUST NEED TIME TO GET OUR WITS TOGETHER! *ANGEL,* SEE IF YOU CAN FLY JEAN TO SOME PLACE OF SAFETY!

NOT ON YOUR *LIFE,* SCOTT! I'LL SEE THIS *THRU* WITH YOU-- TO THE VERY *END!*

WHY'S IT SO *QUIET* BACK THERE?? WHAT ARE THEY COOKING UP *NOW?*

AND, IN ANSWER TO ICEMAN'S QUESTION--!

USE THE PROPULSION POWER BUILT INTO THE SOLES OF YOUR FEET-- THEN *STRIKE!*

FHOOSH

PREPARE FOR FINAL DESTRUCTIVE ACTION!!

19

BAK-KOWW! THWIPP!

ZINGO! YOU GOT 'IM, CYKE! TERRIFIC!

BUT THERE ARE OTHERS, FOLLOWING!

LOOK OUT!! HE CRASHED THRU!

IT'S BEEN NICE KNOWIN' YOU, GUYS!

THEN, BEFORE THE YOUTHS CAN MAKE ANOTHER MOVE, THE ADVANCING SECTION LEADER ACTIVATES A BUTTON ON HIS CHEST PLATE, AND...

THERE SHALL BE NO MUTANTS!!!

CAN'T STAY ALOFT ANY LONGER!! WINGS GETTING HEAVY AS LEAD-- FALLING--!

WHOOO--!! I FEEL LIKE THE FLOOR IS PULLING ME DOWN--!

CAN'T MOVE! THEY--USED A HEAVY GRAVITY RAY--!

THEN-- WE'RE FINISHED--?!!

AND, AS THE NOW HELPLESS X-MEN SINK SLOWLY TO THE FLOOR--!

IF WE CAN DEFEAT THE X-MEN SO EASILY, THE REST OF MANKIND-- WITHOUT MUTANT POWERS-- WILL BE ABLE TO OFFER ALMOST NO RESISTANCE!

THEREFORE, I NOW COMMAND YOU TO CREATE AN ARMY OF NEW SENTINELS FOR ME!

AN ARMY OF THOUSANDS!!

NO! I WON'T! IT WILL MEAN THE END OF MANKIND HERE ON EARTH!!

I HAD WANTED TO HELP HUMANITY-- TO FIGHT THE MUTANTS!! WHAT A FOOL I WAS!! WHAT A BLIND-- DANGEROUS FOOL!

SEIZE HIM!! HE SHALL NOT REFUSE US-- FOR LONG!!

NEXT ISSUE! YOU'LL ACTUALLY WITNESS THE CREATION OF A SENTINEL--AS WELL AS ONE OF THE MOST THRILLING STORY ENDINGS YOU'VE EVER GASPED AT! YOU'LL SEE THE X-MEN, MENACED BY TRASK'S UNHUMAN CREATIONS ON THE ONE HAND, AND THEIR OWN INHERENT WEAKNESSES ON THE OTHER! EVEN IF YOU'RE NOT A MUTANT, YOU MUSTN'T MISS IT! 'NUFF SAID!

20

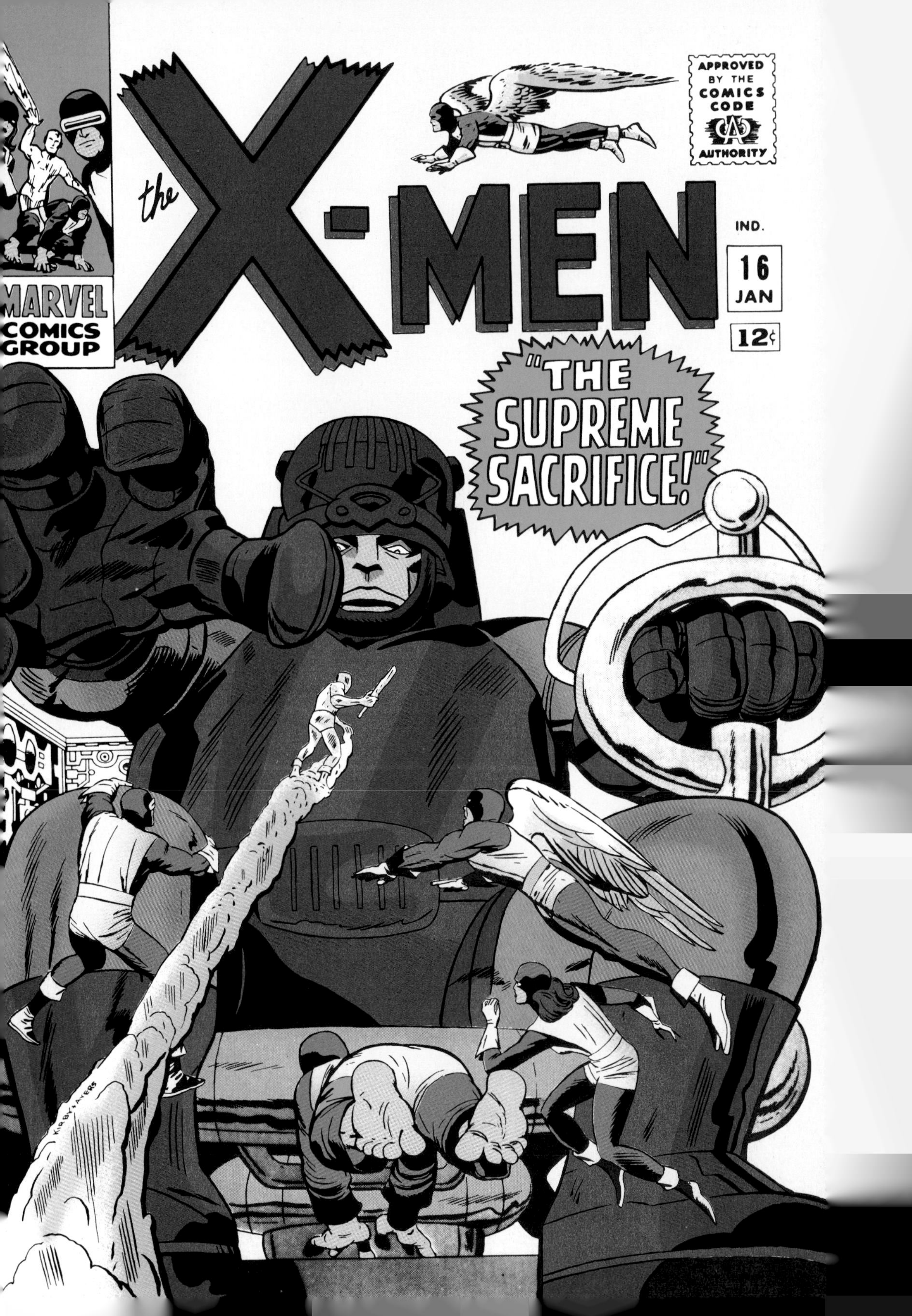

APPROVED BY THE COMICS CODE AUTHORITY
the X-MEN
IND.
16
JAN
12¢
MARVEL COMICS GROUP
"THE SUPREME SACRIFICE!"
KIRBY/AYERS

X-MEN! THE MOST MYSTERIOUS FIGHTING TEAM OF ALL TIME!

"The SUPREME SACRIFICE!"

IN WHICH A LIFE IS LOST... --A BATTLE WON!

THERE MAY BE A BETTER CREATIVE TEAM SOMEWHERE... BUT WE'VE NEVER FOUND 'EM!!

STORY: STAN LEE   LAYOUTS: JACK KIRBY
PENCILLING: JAY GAVIN   DELINEATION:
DICK AYERS   LETTERING: ART SIMEK

LAST ISH, WE SAW THE AMAZING *PROFESSOR XAVIER'S* ASTRAL IMAGE DRIVEN FROM THE *SENTINELS' FORTRESS* BY DEADLY MICRO ELECTRIC BLASTS...

JUST *MADE* IT! ANOTHER FEW SECONDS, AND I'D HAVE BEEN UNABLE TO TAKE CONTROL OF MY PHYSICAL FORM AGAIN!

MY *X-MEN* ARE PRISONERS OF THE GIGANTIC *SENTINELS,* WITHIN THAT DEADLY FORTRESS...

...WHILE I LIE HELPLESSLY OUTSIDE-- UNABLE TO HELP THEM-- HARDLY ABLE TO DEFEND *MYSELF!*

BUT, I *CANNOT* FAIL THEM NOW! IT WAS *I* WHO ORGANIZED THEM-- WHO INSPIRED THEM TO RISK THEIR LIVES FOR MANKIND--

--FOR THE SAME HUMAN RACE WHICH NOW HATES AND FEARS THEM-- ALL BECAUSE OF *DR. TRASK* AND HIS SENTINELS!

TRASK BELIEVED HE WAS DOING THE RIGHT THING! HE THOUGHT ALL MUTANTS WERE *MENACES!* HE CREATED THE SENTINELS TO *DESTROY* US, THINKING WE WERE THE ENEMIES OF HUMANITY!

HE HAD HIS SENTINELS CONSTRUCT THAT IMPREGNABLE FORTRESS-- HE ARMED THEM WITH DEADLY NEW WEAPONS--FOR THE PURPOSE OF WIPING ALL MUTANTS FROM THE FACE OF EARTH!

HE WAS TOO BLIND, TOO FANATICAL TO REALIZE THAT THERE ARE BOTH GOOD AND BAD MUTANTS -- TO REALIZE THAT HIS *SENTINELS* ARE THE *REAL* THREAT TO-- *WAIT!!*

THE FORTRESS IS *SINKING* --LIKE A GIGANTIC *ELEVATOR!*

IT'S COMPLETELY *HIDDEN* AGAIN-- CAMOUFLAGED BY A DECEPTIVE MOUND OF EARTH!

NOW MY X-MEN ARE *COMPLETELY* CUT OFF FROM ANY AID I MIGHT GIVE THEM!

THIS MEANS THAT THE MOST DANGEROUS SENTINEL OF ALL-- THE GARGANTUAN *MASTER MOLD,* CAN CONTINUE TO CREATE *MORE* SENTINELS-- UNTIL THEY OVER- RUN ALL OF EARTH!

--UNLESS I CAN *STOP* HIM! AND I *WILL*-- IF IT COSTS ME MY VERY *LIFE!*

BACK IN THE CITY THERE IS A *FALLEN* SENTINEL!* IF I CAN FIND OUT *WHY* HE FELL, I'LL HAVE THE KEY TO THEIR DEFEAT!

*REMEMBER HIM FROM *X-MEN #14?* --STAN.

2

DESPERATELY, PAINFULLY, DISREGARDING THE AGONY OF HIS INJURED BODY, THE CRIPPLED MUTANT TIRELESSLY CRAWLS INCH AFTER INCH, UNTIL HE REACHES...

THE HIGHWAY-- AT *LAST!* NOW TO STOP THE FIRST PASSING CAR--!

A BASIC TELEPATHIC COMMAND WILL DO THE TRICK! NO NORMAL HUMAN CAN RESIST!

SLOW DOWN! STOP ONE HUNDRED YARDS AHEAD!

SECONDS LATER...

SURE IS LUCKY WE *SAW* YOU, FELLA! WHAT *HAPPENED?*

NO TIME TO EXPLAIN NOW! YOU MUST DRIVE ME TO THE CITY!

SURE! WE'LL BE *GLAD* TO! THERE'S SOMETHING *ABOUT* HIM-- IT SEEMS TO *FORCE* US TO OBEY!

KINDA STRANGE TH' WAY WE SLOWED DOWN IN TIME! ALMOST LIKE WE *KNEW* HE'D BE THERE!

MEANWHILE, BACK WITHIN THE NOW HIDDEN FORTRESS, WE FIND...

NOW WHAT HAVE THEY DONE TO US?? IT'S HARD TO *MOVE* IN HERE--LIKE MY MUSCLES ARE MADE OF *LEAD!*

YOU'RE *RIGHT!* SOMETHING IS PRESSING US DOWN-- SAPPING OUR STRENGTH!

I CAN'T EVEN FLY TO THE *TOP*-- MY WINGS CAN HARDLY *FLAP* IN HERE!

THERE'S ONLY ONE ANSWER-- THEY'VE FOUND A WAY TO INCREASE THE WEIGHT OF *GRAVITY* WITHIN THE GLOBE! AND THERE'S NO WAY FOR US TO *FIGHT* IT!

BUT, THE *BIG* QUESTION IS--WHERE ARE THEY *TAKING* US TO NOW--AND *WHY?*

FINALLY... PLACE THE HEAVY-GRAV GLOBE UPON ITS PERMANENT BASE!

IT IS *DONE!* THEY SHALL BE SAFE HERE UNTIL THE *MASTER MOLD* GIVES US ORDERS FOR THEIR *FINAL DISPOSAL!*

NO MATTER HOW THEY STRUGGLE, THERE IS NO WAY TO OVERCOME THE IRRESISTIBLE POWER OF INCREASED *GRAVITY!*

THIS IS WHY WE ARE DESTINED TO RULE MANKIND! OUR COMPUTERIZED BRAINS CAN CREATE WEAPONS WHICH *NO* MERE HUMAN CAN MATCH!

BUT, INSIDE THE SEEMINGLY ESCAPE-PROOF PRISON, THE *"MERE HUMANS"* WITHIN ARE DETERMINED THAT IF THEY MUST BE DEFEATED, THEY'LL GO DOWN *FIGHTING--!*

MY POWER BLASTS CAN SHATTER ALMOST *ANYTHING!* WHY WON'T THEY SMASH THAT *GLASS??*

THUNG!

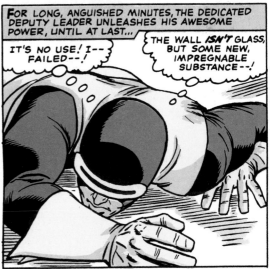

FOR LONG, ANGUISHED MINUTES, THE DEDICATED DEPUTY LEADER UNLEASHES HIS AWESOME POWER, UNTIL AT LAST...

IT'S NO USE! I-- FAILED--!

THE WALL *ISN'T* GLASS, BUT SOME NEW, IMPREGNABLE SUBSTANCE--!

YET, PERHAPS THE *OTHERS*-- BY USE OF *THEIR* MUTANT POWER--MAY DO BETTER--!

EASY, JEAN-- EVEN IF YOU *CAN* LEVITATE YOURSELF--THERE'S NO PLACE TO *GO!*

THE TOP OF THIS DOUBLE-SIZED MILK BOTTLE IS ALL *SEALED UP!*

I *KNOW,* BOBBY--BUT I'VE *GOT* TO KEEP TRYING,...!

WE CAN'T JUST SIT IDLY BY AND WAIT FOR THE *END!* WE MUST--*OHHH--!*

UH OH! I WAS *AFRAID* THAT WOULD HAPPEN!

THE PROF ALWAYS *WARNED* YOU ABOUT OVER-TAXING YOUR TELEKINETIC POWER!

4

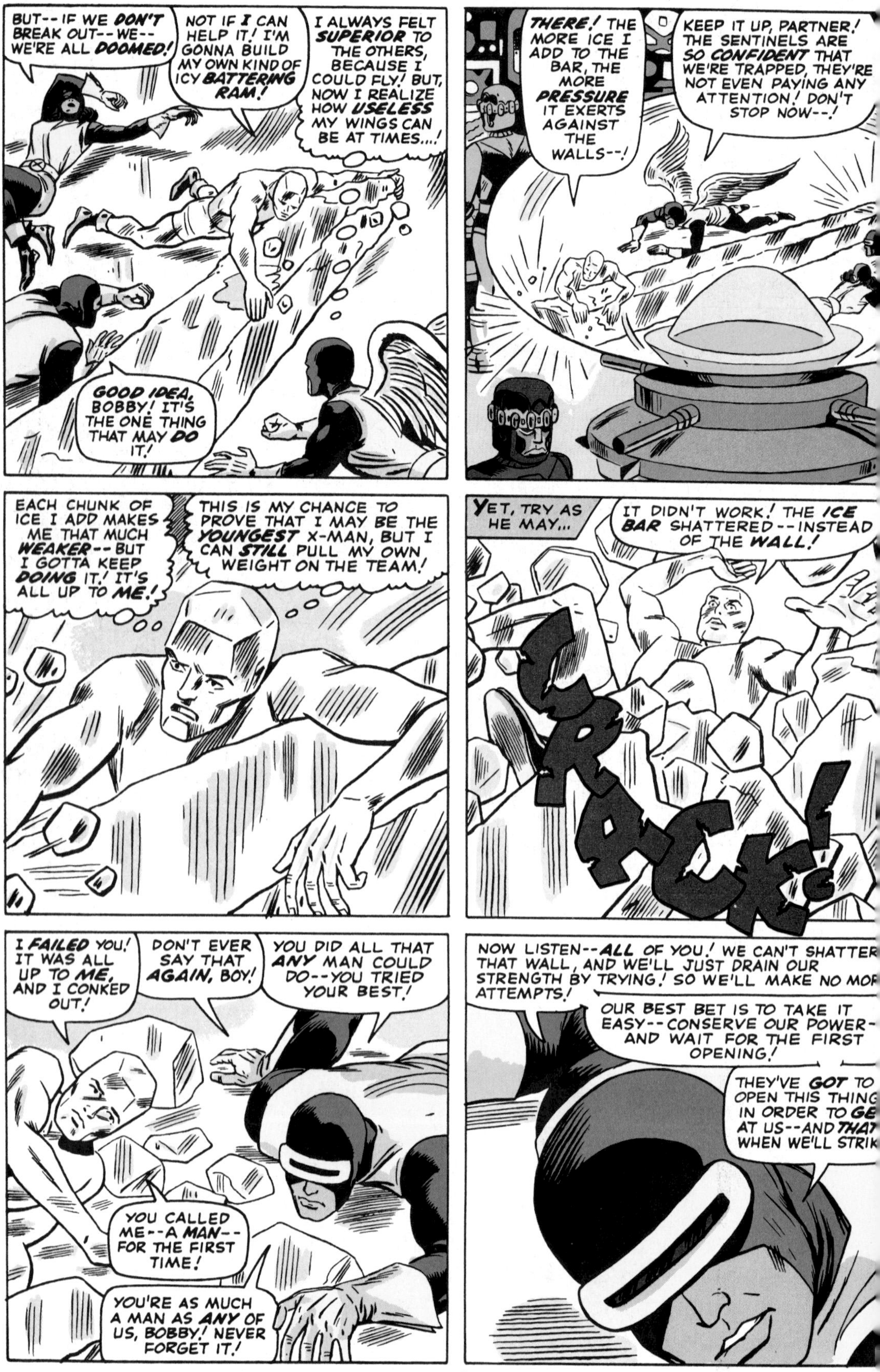
BUT-- IF WE DON'T BREAK OUT-- WE-- WE'RE ALL DOOMED!
NOT IF I CAN HELP IT! I'M GONNA BUILD MY OWN KIND OF ICY BATTERING RAM!
I ALWAYS FELT SUPERIOR TO THE OTHERS, BECAUSE I COULD FLY! BUT, NOW I REALIZE HOW USELESS MY WINGS CAN BE AT TIMES...!
GOOD IDEA, BOBBY! IT'S THE ONE THING THAT MAY DO IT!
THERE! THE MORE ICE I ADD TO THE BAR, THE MORE PRESSURE IT EXERTS AGAINST THE WALLS--!
KEEP IT UP, PARTNER! THE SENTINELS ARE SO CONFIDENT THAT WE'RE TRAPPED, THEY'RE NOT EVEN PAYING ANY ATTENTION! DON'T STOP NOW--!
EACH CHUNK OF ICE I ADD MAKES ME THAT MUCH WEAKER-- BUT I GOTTA KEEP DOING IT! IT'S ALL UP TO ME!
THIS IS MY CHANCE TO PROVE THAT I MAY BE THE YOUNGEST X-MAN, BUT I CAN STILL PULL MY OWN WEIGHT ON THE TEAM!
YET, TRY AS HE MAY...
IT DIDN'T WORK! THE ICE BAR SHATTERED -- INSTEAD OF THE WALL!
CRACK!
I FAILED YOU! IT WAS ALL UP TO ME, AND I CONKED OUT!
DON'T EVER SAY THAT AGAIN, BOY!
YOU DID ALL THAT ANY MAN COULD DO-- YOU TRIED YOUR BEST!
YOU CALLED ME-- A MAN-- FOR THE FIRST TIME!
YOU'RE AS MUCH A MAN AS ANY OF US, BOBBY! NEVER FORGET IT!
NOW LISTEN-- ALL OF YOU! WE CAN'T SHATTER THAT WALL, AND WE'LL JUST DRAIN OUR STRENGTH BY TRYING! SO WE'LL MAKE NO MOR ATTEMPTS!
OUR BEST BET IS TO TAKE IT EASY-- CONSERVE OUR POWER-- AND WAIT FOR THE FIRST OPENING!
THEY'VE GOT TO OPEN THIS THING IN ORDER TO GE AT US-- AND THAT WHEN WE'LL STRIK

AT THAT MOMENT, IN ANOTHER CHAMBER OF THE VAST FORTRESS, THE AWESOME *MASTER MOLD* CONCLUDES HIS EXAMINATION OF THE UNCONSCIOUS *BEAST*...

I NEED LEARN NO MORE ABOUT HIM.! I REALIZE NOW THAT THE *X-MEN* DO NOT POSSESS THE POWER TO HARM US.!

WAIT! WHAT DO YOU PLAN TO *DO* WITH HIM....?

HE SHALL BE IMPRISONED WITH THE *OTHER* CAPTIVE MUTANTS, AS THE *MASTER MOLD* HAS COMMANDED.!

THEN, AT MY PLEASURE, THEY WILL ALL BE *DESTROYED!* FOR THAT IS THE PURPOSE YOU YOURSELF HAVE PROGRAMMED INTO OUR COMPUTERIZED BRAINS.!

NO.! *NO.!* I WAS *WRONG!* I REALIZE THAT NOW.! *THEY* AREN'T MENACES TO MANKIND-- IT'S *YOU* WHO ARE! THEY MUSTN'T BE HARMED--!

SILENCE! THOUGH YOU *CREATED* US, YOU ARE MERELY A HUMAN! YOU TOO MUST *OBEY!*

WHILE I HAVE THE *POWER,* IT IS YOU WHO HAVE THE *KNOWLEDGE* TO CREATE A VAST *ARMY* OF SENTINELS FOR ME-- AND YOU SHALL *DO SO!*

NO! IT WOULD MEAN BETRAYING MY FELLOW MEN! YOU AND YOUR SENTINELS WOULD ENSLAVE ALL OF EARTH.!

YOU HAVE NO *CHOICE!* HAVE YOU FORGOTTEN MY *POWER?* IF SO, BEHOLD THIS SIMPLE *DEMONSTRATION!*

YOUR *DISINTEGRATOR BEAM!!* DON'T DO IT-- *DON'T!*

6

DO NOT FEAR! *YOU* SHALL NOT BE HARMED -- AS *YET!*

IT IS THE NEAREST *CITY* THAT WILL BE *WIPED OUT*-- AS EASILY AS I ERASE YONDER MACHINE!

AND *I* DID IT! I *GAVE* YOU THAT RAY!!

NZT!

I CANNOT ALLOW AN ENTIRE CITY TO SUFFER SUCH A FATE! I-- I'LL *CREATE* YOUR ARMY OF SENTINELS!

AFTER ALL, WHERE THERE'S *LIFE*, THERE'S HOPE! WE MAY *STILL* FIND A WAY TO DESTROY THE MASTER MOLD!

FOR, WITH *HIM* GONE, THE SENTINELS WOULD BE *LEADERLESS*-- THE THREAT WOULD BE ENDED!

IF ONLY THE *X-MEN* WERE STILL FREE! IF ONLY I'D *LISTENED* TO THEM!

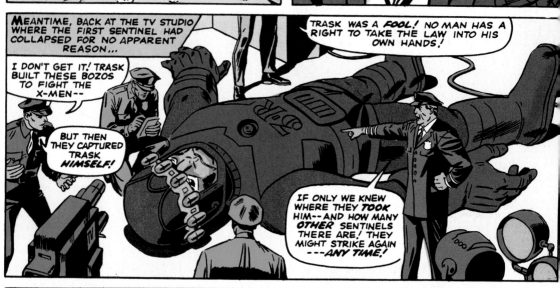

MEANTIME, BACK AT THE TV STUDIO WHERE THE FIRST SENTINEL HAD COLLAPSED FOR NO APPARENT REASON...

I DON'T GET IT! TRASK BUILT THESE BOZOS TO FIGHT THE X-MEN--

BUT THEN THEY CAPTURED TRASK *HIMSELF!*

TRASK WAS A *FOOL!* NO MAN HAS A RIGHT TO TAKE THE LAW INTO HIS OWN HANDS!

IF ONLY WE KNEW WHERE THEY *TOOK* HIM-- AND HOW MANY *OTHER* SENTINELS THERE ARE! THEY MIGHT STRIKE AGAIN ---*ANY TIME!*

PERHAPS *I* CAN HELP YOU, INSPECTOR!

PROFESSOR XAVIER! YOU'RE THE ONE WHO WAS *DEBATING* WITH TRASK ON TV! *YOU* CLAIMED MUTANTS WERE *NOT* DANGEROUS TO MANKIND!

COME ON IN, MISTER! WE'LL TAKE ANY HELP WE CAN GET!

WHAT DO *YOU* KNOW ABOUT THIS *SENTINEL* HERE? HOW *DANGEROUS* IS HE?

MORE DANGEROUS THAN YOU CAN *IMAGINE!*--UNLESS WE CAN LEARN THE REASON THAT HE COLLAPSED!

7

114

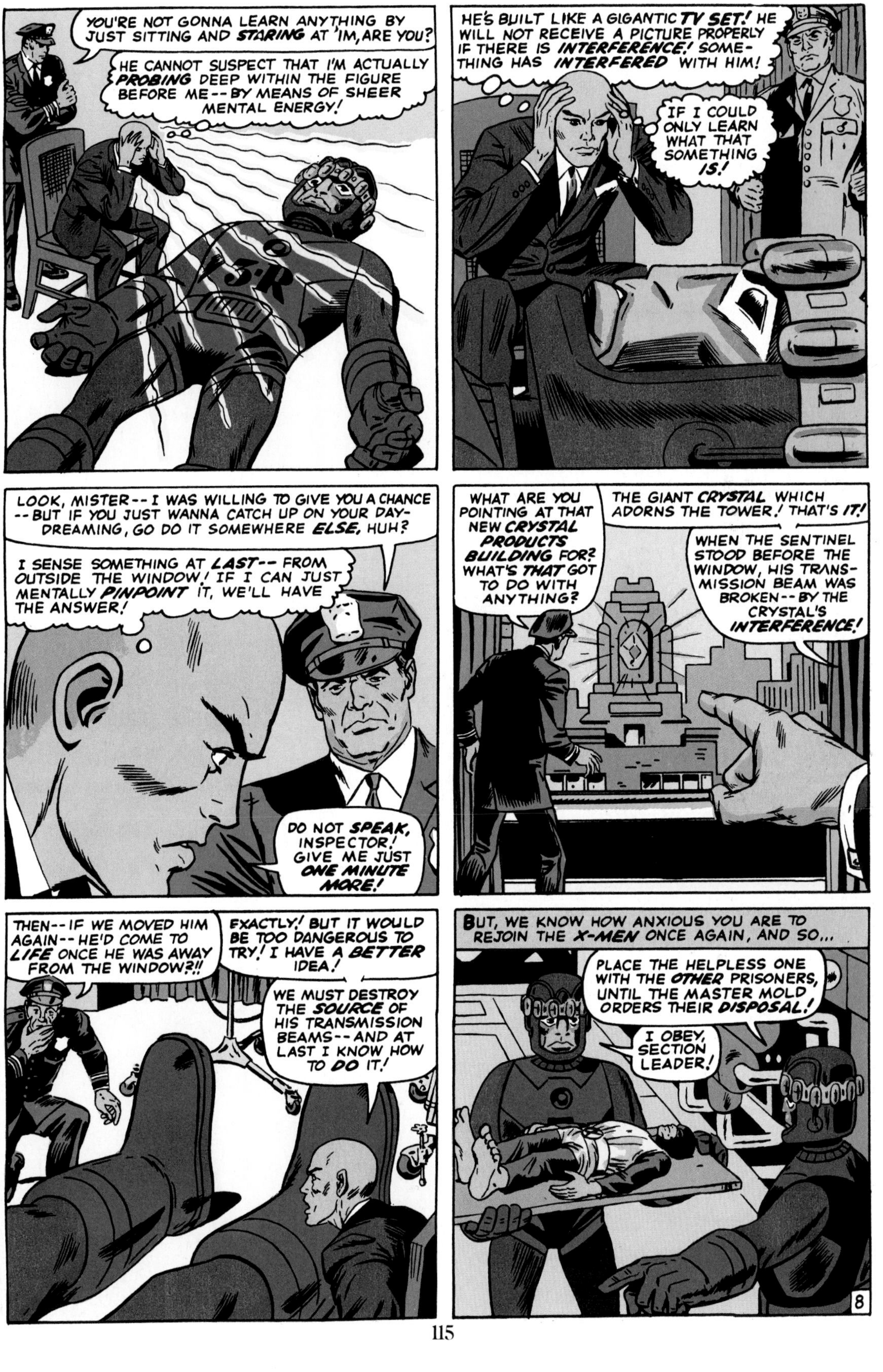
YOU'RE NOT GONNA LEARN ANYTHING BY JUST SITTING AND STARING AT 'IM, ARE YOU?
HE CANNOT SUSPECT THAT I'M ACTUALLY PROBING DEEP WITHIN THE FIGURE BEFORE ME -- BY MEANS OF SHEER MENTAL ENERGY!
3-R
HE'S BUILT LIKE A GIGANTIC TV SET! HE WILL NOT RECEIVE A PICTURE PROPERLY IF THERE IS INTERFERENCE! SOMETHING HAS INTERFERED WITH HIM!
IF I COULD ONLY LEARN WHAT THAT SOMETHING IS!
LOOK, MISTER -- I WAS WILLING TO GIVE YOU A CHANCE -- BUT IF YOU JUST WANNA CATCH UP ON YOUR DAY-DREAMING, GO DO IT SOMEWHERE ELSE, HUH?
I SENSE SOMETHING AT LAST -- FROM OUTSIDE THE WINDOW! IF I CAN JUST MENTALLY PINPOINT IT, WE'LL HAVE THE ANSWER!
DO NOT SPEAK, INSPECTOR! GIVE ME JUST ONE MINUTE MORE!
WHAT ARE YOU POINTING AT THAT NEW CRYSTAL PRODUCTS BUILDING FOR? WHAT'S THAT GOT TO DO WITH ANYTHING?
THE GIANT CRYSTAL WHICH ADORNS THE TOWER! THAT'S IT!
WHEN THE SENTINEL STOOD BEFORE THE WINDOW, HIS TRANSMISSION BEAM WAS BROKEN -- BY THE CRYSTAL'S INTERFERENCE!
THEN -- IF WE MOVED HIM AGAIN -- HE'D COME TO LIFE ONCE HE WAS AWAY FROM THE WINDOW?!!
EXACTLY! BUT IT WOULD BE TOO DANGEROUS TO TRY! I HAVE A BETTER IDEA!
WE MUST DESTROY THE SOURCE OF HIS TRANSMISSION BEAMS -- AND AT LAST I KNOW HOW TO DO IT!
BUT, WE KNOW HOW ANXIOUS YOU ARE TO REJOIN THE X-MEN ONCE AGAIN, AND SO...
PLACE THE HELPLESS ONE WITH THE OTHER PRISONERS, UNTIL THE MASTER MOLD ORDERS THEIR DISPOSAL!
I OBEY, SECTION LEADER!
8

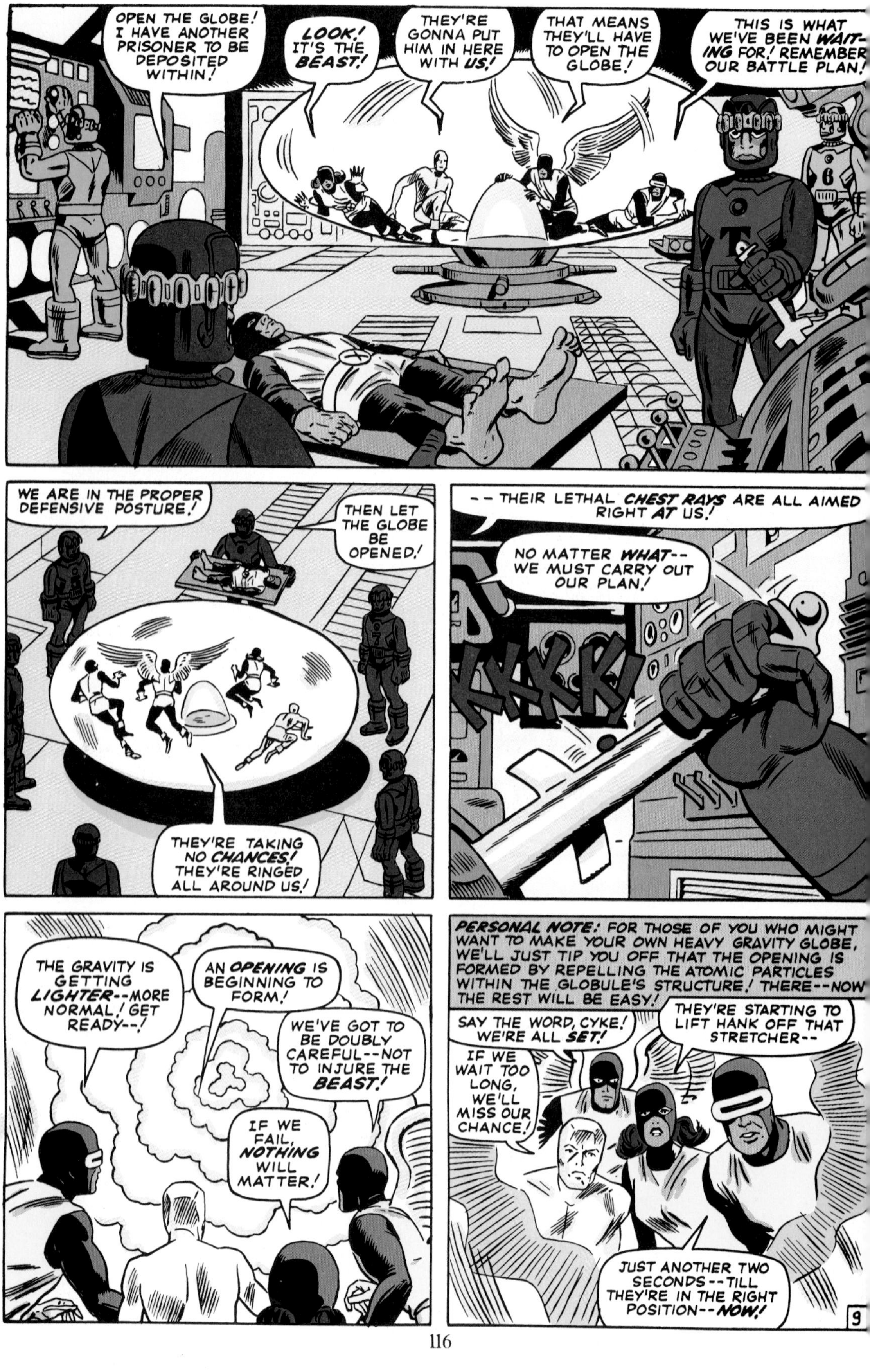

OPEN THE GLOBE! I HAVE ANOTHER PRISONER TO BE DEPOSITED WITHIN!
LOOK! IT'S THE BEAST!
THEY'RE GONNA PUT HIM IN HERE WITH US!
THAT MEANS THEY'LL HAVE TO OPEN THE GLOBE!
THIS IS WHAT WE'VE BEEN WAITING FOR! REMEMBER OUR BATTLE PLAN!
WE ARE IN THE PROPER DEFENSIVE POSTURE!
THEN LET THE GLOBE BE OPENED!
THEY'RE TAKING NO CHANCES! THEY'RE RINGED ALL AROUND US!
-- THEIR LETHAL CHEST RAYS ARE ALL AIMED RIGHT AT US!
NO MATTER WHAT-- WE MUST CARRY OUT OUR PLAN!
KKKK!
THE GRAVITY IS GETTING LIGHTER--MORE NORMAL! GET READY--!
AN OPENING IS BEGINNING TO FORM!
WE'VE GOT TO BE DOUBLY CAREFUL--NOT TO INJURE THE BEAST!
IF WE FAIL, NOTHING WILL MATTER!
PERSONAL NOTE: FOR THOSE OF YOU WHO MIGHT WANT TO MAKE YOUR OWN HEAVY GRAVITY GLOBE, WE'LL JUST TIP YOU OFF THAT THE OPENING IS FORMED BY REPELLING THE ATOMIC PARTICLES WITHIN THE GLOBULE'S STRUCTURE! THERE--NOW THE REST WILL BE EASY!
SAY THE WORD, CYKE! WE'RE ALL SET!
THEY'RE STARTING TO LIFT HANK OFF THAT STRETCHER--
IF WE WAIT TOO LONG, WE'LL MISS OUR CHANCE!
JUST ANOTHER TWO SECONDS--TILL THEY'RE IN THE RIGHT POSITION--NOW!
9

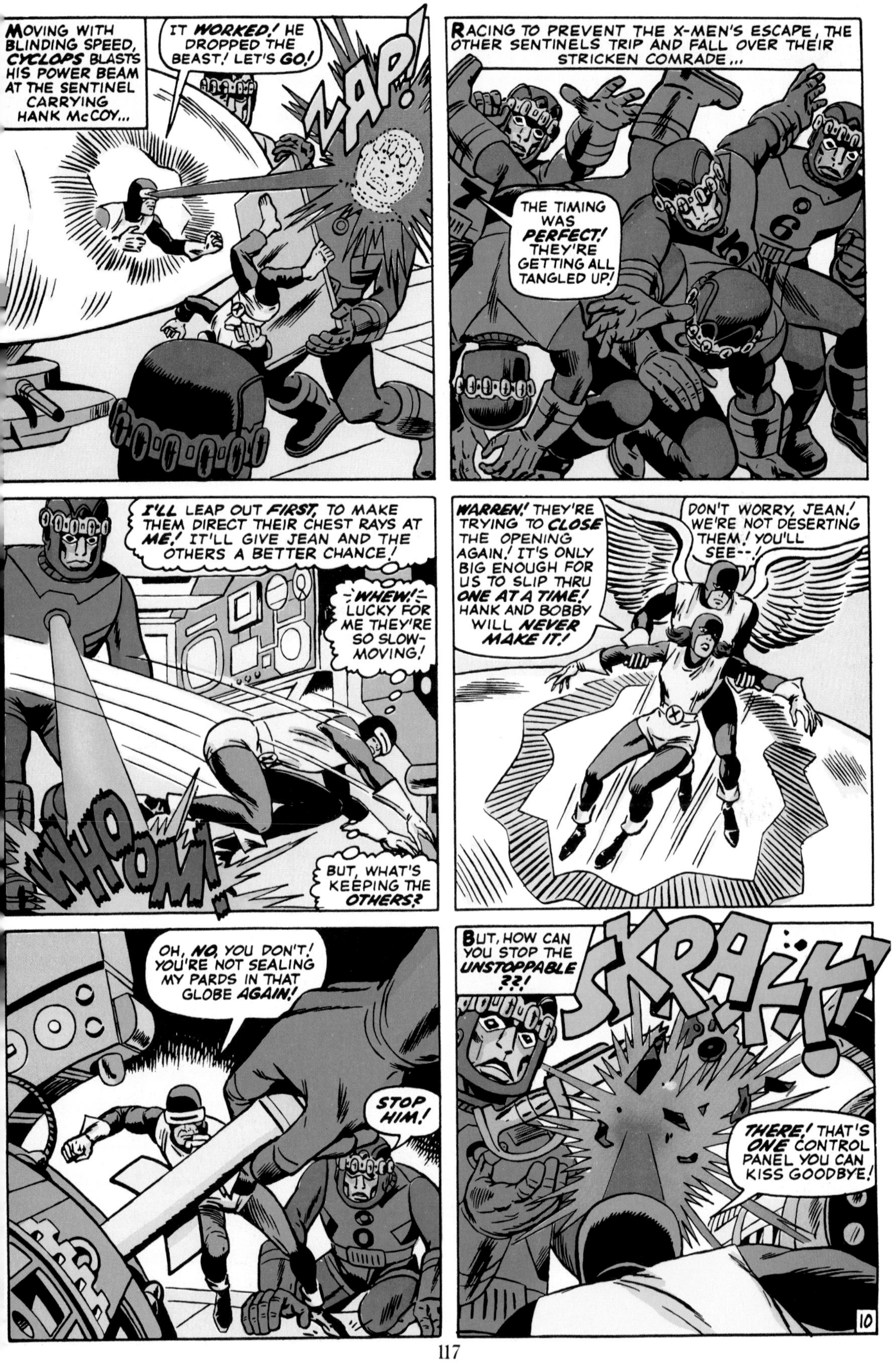
MOVING WITH BLINDING SPEED, CYCLOPS BLASTS HIS POWER BEAM AT THE SENTINEL CARRYING HANK McCOY...
IT WORKED! HE DROPPED THE BEAST! LET'S GO!
ZAP!
RACING TO PREVENT THE X-MEN'S ESCAPE, THE OTHER SENTINELS TRIP AND FALL OVER THEIR STRICKEN COMRADE...
THE TIMING WAS PERFECT! THEY'RE GETTING ALL TANGLED UP!
I'LL LEAP OUT FIRST, TO MAKE THEM DIRECT THEIR CHEST RAYS AT ME! IT'LL GIVE JEAN AND THE OTHERS A BETTER CHANCE!
WHEW! LUCKY FOR ME THEY'RE SO SLOW-MOVING!
WHOOM!
BUT, WHAT'S KEEPING THE OTHERS?
WARREN! THEY'RE TRYING TO CLOSE THE OPENING AGAIN! IT'S ONLY BIG ENOUGH FOR US TO SLIP THRU ONE AT A TIME! HANK AND BOBBY WILL NEVER MAKE IT!
DON'T WORRY, JEAN! WE'RE NOT DESERTING THEM! YOU'LL SEE--!
OH, NO, YOU DON'T! YOU'RE NOT SEALING MY PARDS IN THAT GLOBE AGAIN!
STOP HIM!
BUT, HOW CAN YOU STOP THE UNSTOPPABLE ??!
SKRAKK!
THERE! THAT'S ONE CONTROL PANEL YOU CAN KISS GOODBYE!
10

WHUMMB!

JUST WHAT I *HOPED* YOU'D DO! BY SWINGING AT *ME* AND MISSING, YOU SHATTERED A WHOLE WALL FULL OF *WEAPONS!*

THAT SENTINEL COMING TOWARDS ME--I-I CAN'T EVADE HIM--!

IF I CAN JUST USE MY TELEKINETIC POWERS AGAINST HIM-- TO FORCE HIM *BACK*--!

THERE! I SLOWED HIM DOWN! NOW--JUST A LITTLE MORE--!

HIS *BODY* IS TOO HEAVY FOR ME--BUT, BY CONCENTRATING ON HIS *ARMS*, I CAN FORCE THEM BACK --FURTHER--FURTHER --THEY'RE MAKING HIM *TOPPLE*--!

HEY! JEANIE NEEDS SOME *HELP!* LET'S *MOVE!*

TOO LATE! I DOWNED HIM *MYSELF!*

YOU SURE *DID*, HONEY--BUT WE'LL MAKE SURE HE *STAYS* DOWN!

I'M 'WAY *AHEAD* OF YOU, FLYGUY!

MAKE IT TOO SLIPPERY FOR HIM TO STAND, BOBBY!

118

I'VE GOT HANK! NOW, LET'S GO! EVERY SECOND COUNTS! WE'VE GOT TO DESTROY THE MASTER MOLD!

AHHH! TO BE ABLE TO SOAR AGAIN--!

BUT, DIRECTLY BEHIND THE SPEEDING MUTANTS, A NEW DETACHMENT OF SENTINELS APPEAR-- GRIM, EMOTIONLESS, POWERFUL--!

THEY MUST NOT ESCAPE! PREPARE STUN RAYS! AIM STUN RAYS!

AND NOW, AT MY COMMAND--

FIRE STUN RAYS!

THOOOM!

THEY ARE BEATEN! AND, IT SHALL BE FOR THE LAST TIME!

TOO LONG HAVE THEY DEFIED US-- FOUGHT US-- NOW, THEY MUST BE SLAIN! PREPARE DESTRUCTO-BEAMS!

BUT, NO SOONER ARE THOSE FATEFUL WORDS UTTERED, THAN THE ENTIRE BODY OF SENTINELS SUDDENLY SAGS TO THE FLOOR--AND LIES STILL!

12

AND, AT THAT MOMENT, FLYING HIGH OVERHEAD, WE SEE...

IF *XAVIER'S* THEORY IS CORRECT, THIS GIANT CRYSTAL, WHICH WE TOOK FROM THE TOWER OF THE BUILDING, WILL CAUSE ALL THE SENTINELS IN THE FORTRESS BELOW TO COLLAPSE AND BE RENDERED HARMLESS!

BUT HOW DO WE KNOW WE'RE NOT JUST WASTIN' OUR TIME? ALL I SEE BELOW IS A PATCH OF EMPTY COUNTRYSIDE!

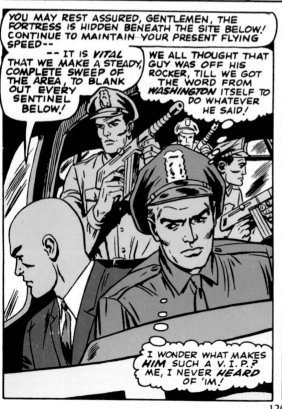

YOU MAY REST ASSURED, GENTLEMEN, THE FORTRESS IS HIDDEN BENEATH THE SITE BELOW! CONTINUE TO MAINTAIN YOUR PRESENT FLYING SPEED--

-- IT IS *VITAL* THAT WE MAKE A STEADY, COMPLETE SWEEP OF THE AREA, TO BLANK OUT EVERY SENTINEL BELOW!

WE ALL THOUGHT THAT GUY WAS OFF HIS ROCKER, TILL WE GOT THE WORD FROM *WASHINGTON* ITSELF TO DO WHATEVER HE SAID!

I WONDER WHAT MAKES *HIM* SUCH A V.I.P.? ME, I NEVER *HEARD* OF 'IM!

BUT, THE POLICE PILOT'S PUZZLED MUSINGS ARE SOON RUDELY INTERRUPTED BY THE UNEXPECTED SIGHT WHICH SUDDENLY GREETS HIS EYES BELOW...

LOOK! THERE *IS* SOME KINDA *FORTRESS* DOWN THERE! IT'S POPPING UP OUTTA *NOWHERE!*

AND THERE'S A *WEAPON* OF SOME SORT BEING TRAINED UPON US!

13

IT'S CREATING A DEADLY *TURBULENCE* IN THE AIR! IF WE HIT IT, WE'LL *CRASH!*

THEN WE'VE GOT TO GO *BACK!*

NO! CONTINUE TO FLY! THERE WILL BE NO DANGER!

ON PROFESSOR XAVIER'S SAY-SO, THE COURAGEOUS OFFICERS FLY DIRECTLY TOWARDS THE AWESOME WHIRLWINDS, BUT-- AS THEY DO SO, THE ENORMOUS *CRYSTAL* DOES ITS WORK WELL--!

AS THE GLEAMING OBJECT PASSES ABOVE, THOSE OPERATING THE WEAPON CRUMPLE HELPLESSLY, CAUSING THE TURBULENCE TO FADE AWAY...!

THUS, WHEN THE *X-MEN* REGAIN CONSCIOUSNESS ONCE AGAIN, THEY FIND...

LOOK! THE *SENTINELS!* THEY'VE BEEN *KNOCKED OUT!*

I'M NOT COMPLAINING, BUT-- HOW DID IT *HAPPEN?*

ONE MINUTE WE WERE RACING TO THE MASTER MOLD-- AND THEN --*THIS!*

FROM THE EVIDENCE AT HAND, I WOULD DEDUCE THAT PROFESSOR X HAS FINALLY FOUND THEIR ACHILLES' HEEL!

HANK! YOU'VE *COME TO* AGAIN! HOW WONDERFUL!

AHH-- HOW GRATIFYING TO KNOW I'VE BEEN MISSED!

LET'S KNOCK OFF THE *TALK* TILL LATER! WE'VE STILL GOT A *JOB* TO DO--!

YOU'RE *RIGHT*, CYKE! SO LONG AS THE *MASTER MOLD* EXISTS, THE SENTINELS WILL *NEVER* BE DEFEATED! SO LET'S *GET 'IM!*

WARREN! BE *CAREFUL!* HE MUST HAVE ALL SORTS OF *DEFENSIVE DEVICES* PREPARED FOR JUST SUCH AN ATTACK!

JEAN'S *RIGHT*, ANGEL! SLOW DOWN-- WE DON'T KNOW *WHAT'S* AHEAD OF US!

LEAD ON, *MACDUFF!* WE'RE RIGHT BEHIND YOU!

THEY WON'T STOP US *NOW!*

14

THEN, AS IF TO ADD EMPHASIS TO THE X-MEN'S WORDS, THE LIGHTS SUDDENLY FLICKER OUT, PLUNGING THE ENTIRE AREA INTO DARKNESS...!

CAN'T SEE WHERE I'M FLYING! GONNA CRASH INTO-- *UNHHH!*

LISTEN TO THAT *HUM*-- LIKE A TREMENDOUS SURGE OF *POWER!* SOMETHING IS DRAINING ALL THE CURRENT, BLOWING ALL THE FUSES--!

WHAT *IS* IT? WHAT *CAN* IT BE?

IT'S SOME SORT OF INCREDIBLY POWERFUL *MACHINE!* I CAN FEEL ITS TREMENDOUS *ENERGY* WITH MY *FEET*-- RIGHT THRU THE *FLOOR!*

AND, THE BOOK-WORMISH *BEAST* IS RIGHT! FOR, JUST A SHORT DISTANCE AWAY, WE SEE...

I HAVE GIVEN YOU ALL THE *POWER* YOU WILL REQUIRE! NOW, LET THE PROCESS *BEGIN!* THIS NIGHT SHALL MARK THE END OF MAN'S DOMINATION OF THE PLANET EARTH!

CREATE MY SENTINELS! I SHALL OBSERVE YOUR EVERY MOVE!

HEAVEN HELP ME!! I DON'T *WANT* TO DO IT-- BUT I *MUST!* OTHERWISE, A *CITY* WILL BE *DESTROYED!*

FIRST, THERE SHALL BE *EIGHT* NEW SENTINELS-- THEN, EIGHT MORE-- THEN, EIGHT MORE-- EACH NEW GROUP APPEARING FASTER AND FASTER-- UNTIL THEIR NUMBER MOUNTS SO QUICKLY THAT THEY BECOME VIRTUALLY *UNCOUNTABLE!*--BEGIN!!

15

IT'S STARTING TO WORK! THE SYNTHO-PARTICLES FROM THE MASTER MOLD ARE FLOWING INTO THE CUBICLES, SOLIDIFYING INTO SOLID MATTER!!

ONCE THE PROCESS HAS STARTED, THERE'LL BE NO STOPPING IT! IF ENOUGH ENERGY IS BUILT UP, THE MACHINE COULD RUN FOREVER!

THEY'LL EVENTUALLY OUTNUMBER THE HUMAN RACE! THEY'LL ENSLAVE ALL OF MANKIND! THEY'LL BE THE MASTERS OF EARTH!

AND ALL BECAUSE OF ME!! IN MY IGNORANCE, MY FEAR, I CREATED AN EVIL FAR GREATER THAN THE MENACE IT WAS BUILT TO DESTROY!

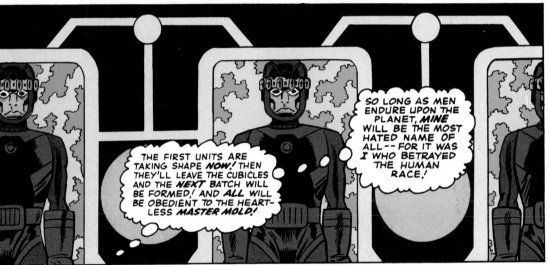

THE FIRST UNITS ARE TAKING SHAPE NOW! THEN THEY'LL LEAVE THE CUBICLES AND THE NEXT BATCH WILL BE FORMED! AND ALL WILL BE OBEDIENT TO THE HEARTLESS MASTER MOLD!

SO LONG AS MEN ENDURE UPON THE PLANET, MINE WILL BE THE MOST HATED NAME OF ALL -- FOR IT WAS I WHO BETRAYED THE HUMAN RACE!

NO! I WON'T DO IT-- I CAN'T!! I MEANT TO HELP MANKIND-- TO PROTECT IT FROM THE MUTANTS-- I CAN'T DESTROY IT NOW!

STOP!! YOU CANNOT DEFY ME! HAVE YOU FORGOTTEN --THE PENALTY??

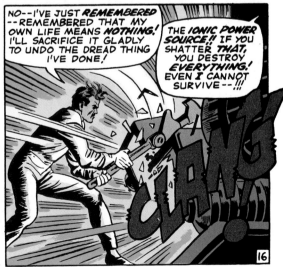

NO--I'VE JUST REMEMBERED --REMEMBERED THAT MY OWN LIFE MEANS NOTHING! I'LL SACRIFICE IT GLADLY TO UNDO THE DREAD THING I'VE DONE!

THE IONIC POWER SOURCE!! IF YOU SHATTER THAT, YOU DESTROY EVERYTHING! EVEN I CANNOT SURVIVE--!!!

CLANG!

16

IT WAS *I* WHO CREATED YOU -- IT MUST BE *MY* HAND THAT *DESTROYS* YOU --ALONG WITH EVERY OTHER VESTIGE OF MY WORK--ALONG WITH MY OWN *LIFE* --*UH*HHHHH.!!

PhbOOM!

WE'RE *TOO LATE!* THE MASTER MOLD WILL NEVER MENACE HUMANITY AGAIN! SOMEONE'S DONE OUR JOB *FOR* US!

DR. TRASK!! WASN'T *HE* IN THERE--??

IF HE *WAS*, HE'S BEYOND ANY HELP *NOW!*

HEADS UP, GROUP! WE'D BETTER VACATE THESE PREMISES BEFORE WE'RE INUNDATED BY--- *BOBBY!!* WHAT'S WRONG??

THE *HEAT!!* DIDN'T REALIZE IT WOULD *WEAKEN* ME SO! BLACKING OUT--CAN'T STAND--!

IT'S *IMPERATIVE* THAT I CARRY HIM *OUT*--BUT HE'S TOO *SLIPPERY* TO HOLD IN MY HANDS--!

HOWEVER, THERE'S MORE THAN *ONE* WAY TO SKIN A CAT-- OR TRANSPORT AN ICEMAN!

ALL OF YOU-- *LET'S GO!!* THE PLACE IS *COLLAPS-ING!*

:*WHEW!*:- YOU DIDN'T HAVE TO RESORT TO SUCH DRASTIC DEVICES TO PROVE YOUR POINT, SCOTTY!

WHAKK!

17

BUT THEN, EVERYTHING SEEMS TO HAPPEN AT ONCE! EACH EXPLOSION CAUSES A *BIGGER* EXPLOSION-- EACH FIRE STARTS A *BIGGER* FIRE--AS THE DESPERATE X-MEN SUDDENLY REALIZE THEY'RE SURROUNDED BY IMPENDING *DOOM.!!*

WE'RE *TRAPPED!* THE ENTIRE *FORTRESS* IS CAVING IN! IF THE *FLAMES* DON'T GET US, THE *CAVE-IN* WILL!

JEANIE-- *STOP!!* THERE'S A WALL OF *FIRE* DIRECTLY AHEAD OF YOU!

RUNNING IN PANIC WON'T HELP! WE'VE GOT TO WORK AS A *TEAM!!*

CYCLOPS IS *RIGHT!* ANGEL, YOU CAN *FLY* OVER THE FLAMES WHILE I USE TELEKINESIS TO *LEVITATE* SCOTT OVER THEM!

NO! THEN *YOU'LL* BE TRAPPED! I'LL WAIT HERE AND *CARRY* YOU OVER, AS SOON AS CYKE IS CLEAR!

ANGEL'S *RIGHT!* IT'S THE ONLY WAY! *HURRY*, JEAN! WE'VE GOT TO REJOIN HANK AND BOBBY!

THAT'S IT! BUT, BE CAREFUL! DON'T *STRAIN YOURSELF!*

EVEN WITH HIS OWN *LIFE* AT STAKE, HE WORRIES ABOUT *ME!* IS IT ANY WONDER I-- FEEL ABOUT HIM-- AS I DO--?!

HE'S *SAFE!* WE *DID* IT!

ANGEL-- *CAREFUL!* THE FLAMES ARE *TOO HIGH!* IF YOU FLAP YOUR WINGS, THEY'LL CATCH ON *FIRE!*

DON'T MOVE!! I'LL HELP YOU GLIDE OVER *TELEKINETICALLY* --THERE--WE'RE *DOING* IT--!

THANKS, GAL! THAT WAS MIGHTY *CLOSE!* BUT, NOW THAT WE'RE *HERE--* WHERE *ARE* WE??

WE'RE NO SAFER--NO BETTER OFF--BUT, AT LEAST WE'RE *TOGETHER!*

JEAN, SEE IF YOU CAN PROBE THE WALL FOR ANY HIDDEN *ESCAPE-LOCK* DEVICES!

I'LL *TRY*, SCOTT!

THERE'S SOMETHING *HERE!* I CAN FEEL THE TUMBLERS! I'VE NEVER USED MY KINETIC POWER THRU A *WALL* BEFORE--BUT IF IT CAN BE DONE--*WAIT!* I HEAR THEM MOVING-- I'M *GETTING* IT--!

THAT'S *IT!* IT'S *OPEN!* WE CAN MAKE OUR WAY *OUT* NOW!

CLICK!

18

WHILE OUTSIDE THE NOW FLAMING FORTRESS, WE FIND--

PROFESSOR--???

SAY, WHAT *GIVES* WITH THAT GUY?? HE HASN'T SAID A *WORD* TO ANYONE FOR THE PAST FIVE MINUTES!

RELAX, CHARLIE! ANY GUY WHO COULD FIGURE OUT A WAY TO STOP THOSE SENTINELS JUST BY FLYIN' OVER 'EM WITH A NUTTY SPARKLER -- HE CAN BE AS QUIET AS HE *WANTS* TO!

BUT, NOT A MAN AMONG THEM CAN SUSPECT THE *TRUE* REASON FOR THE SILENCE OF CHARLES XAVIER --AS THE MOST POWERFUL MUTANT BRAIN ON EARTH DESPERATELY PROBES AMONG THE CARNAGE, SEEKING TO CONTACT THE X-MEN BELOW....!

WITH ALL THE EXPLOSIONS --ALL THE CONFUSION--I COULDN'T REACH THEM! BUT NOW, I'VE LOCATED THEM AT LAST! I'LL STAY WITH THEM MENTALLY, TO GUIDE THEM...

DON'T BOTHER XAVIER, BOYS! IF HE WANTS TO SIT THERE SIGHT-SEEIN', THAT'S *HIS* BUSINESS!

BUT *LOOK!!* SOMEONE'S COMIN' OUT OF ONE OF THOSE OPENINGS!

WHERE? I DON'T SEE ANYTHING!

THAT'S FUNNY! NOW *I* DON'T EITHER!

NATURALLY! FOR I HAVE ERASED THE IMAGE FROM BOTH OF THEIR MINDS! NO NEED TO LET THEM KNOW MY *X-MEN* WERE INVOLVED!

SO FAR, SO GOOD! BUT WE STILL HAVE TO GET OFF THIS CLIFF! GIVE ME YOUR HANDS, CYKE!

WAIT!! WHAT ABOUT *JEAN?* HE CAN'T CARRY US *BOTH!*

DON'T WORRY ABOUT *ME!* I'LL *LEVITATE* MYSELF DOWN!

HAS IT EVER OCCURRED TO YOU WHAT SPLENDID *FIREMEN* WE'D MAKE?

WE'D BE THE PRIDE OF THE HOOK-AND-LADDER BRIGADE!

NOT *YOU,* GABBY! THEY'D NEVER FIND *BOOTS* BIG ENOUGH FOR THOSE TUG-BOAT TOOTSIES OF YOURS!

THAT, MISTER WORTHINGTON, WAS THE UNKINDEST CUT OF ALL! --UH OH! THE ENTIRE *CLIFF* IS BEGINNING TO QUIVER!

IT'S FORTUNATE THAT BOBBY THAWED OUT A BIT! NOW I CAN CARRY HIM SECURELY IN ONE HAND! IT'S MUCH BETTER FOR MY BESTIAL *IMAGE* THIS WAY!

HANK!! *LOOK OUT!!* THE CLIFF WALL IS *BUCKLING--HOLD ON!!*

I'D BE DELIGHTED TO OBLIGE, SCOTTY-- EXCEPT FOR ONE THING--

--THERE SEEMS TO BE PRECIOUS LITTLE TO HOLD ON *TO* AT THE MOMENT!

IF ANY OF YOU STALWARTS WOULD CARE TO COME TO OUR ASSISTANCE, THERE'S NO NEED FOR RETICENCE!

IN OTHER WORDS-- *HELP!!!*

19

HANG ON, HANK! NOW THAT SCOTT'S SAFE, I CAN RELIEVE YOU OF ICEMAN!

GET MOVING, PARTNER -- YOU HAVEN'T MUCH TIME!

I'M PAINFULLY AWARE OF THAT NERVE-WRACKING FACT, MY FRIEND!

AND THEN, WITHOUT THE ADDED BURDEN OF HIS YOUNG PARTNER IN HIS ARMS, HANK McCOY DEMONSTRATES THE UNBELIEVABLE AGILITY AND BALANCE WHICH HAVE EARNED HIM THE NAME -- THE BEAST!

AFTER ALL THOSE GRUELLING SESSIONS IN THE PROFESSOR'S DANGER ROOM, THIS IS ALMOST CHILD'S PLAY NOW!

SO LONG AS THERE'S A FOOT-HOLD, OR A TOE-HOLD ANYWHERE, MY CHANCES FOR SURVIVAL BECOME VIRTUALLY INCALCULABLE!

PLOP!

THNK!

WHUMP!

SALUTATIONS FROM YOUR BESTIAL BUDDY, COMRADES-AT-ARMS! I TRUST I DIDN'T DELAY YOU TOO LONG!

WOW! ARE YOU KIDDIN', HANK? THE ANGEL HIMSELF JUST LANDED A SECOND AGO!

BEAST! ALL OF YOU! DON'T STOP! GET AWAY FROM THE CLIFF!!

THAT'S THE END OF THE SENTINELS -- AND THE MASTER MOLD! MANKIND CAN BREATHE EASY ONCE MORE!

BOY! THE PROFESSOR'S MENTAL WARNING DIDN'T COME A SECOND TOO SOON!!

I WONDER IF WE'LL EVER KNOW WHAT CAUSED THOSE EXPLOSIONS -- THE EXPLOSIONS WHICH SAVED HUMANITY?!!

PERHAPS THE TRUTH WILL ONE DAY BE KNOWN! BUT, UNTIL THAT TIME, IT LIES BURIED BENEATH COUNTLESS TONS OF RUBBLE -- BURIED IN THE BREAST OF DR. BOLIVAR TRASK, WHOSE LAST EARTHLY SACRIFICE BROUGHT THE WORK OF A LIFETIME CRASHING DOWN ABOUT HIM -- WHOSE LAST EARTHLY LESSON PROVED TO BE: BEWARE THE FANATIC! TOO OFTEN HIS CURE IS DEADLIER BY FAR THAN THE EVIL HE DENOUNCES!

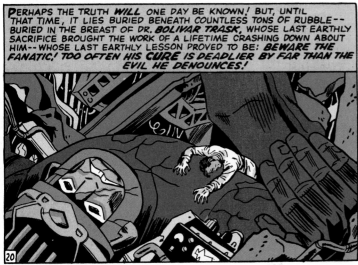

THE END

BUT, NO VICTORY IS EVER TRULY COMPLETE! EVEN NOW, AS THE WEARY X-MEN PREPARE TO RETURN TO THEIR HEADQUARTERS BUILDING, NONE CAN SUSPECT THE SHADOW OF MENACE THAT AWAITS THEM -- THE MOST UNEXPECTED MENACE OF ALL -- AS WE SHALL SEE NEXT ISSUE! 'NUFF SAID!

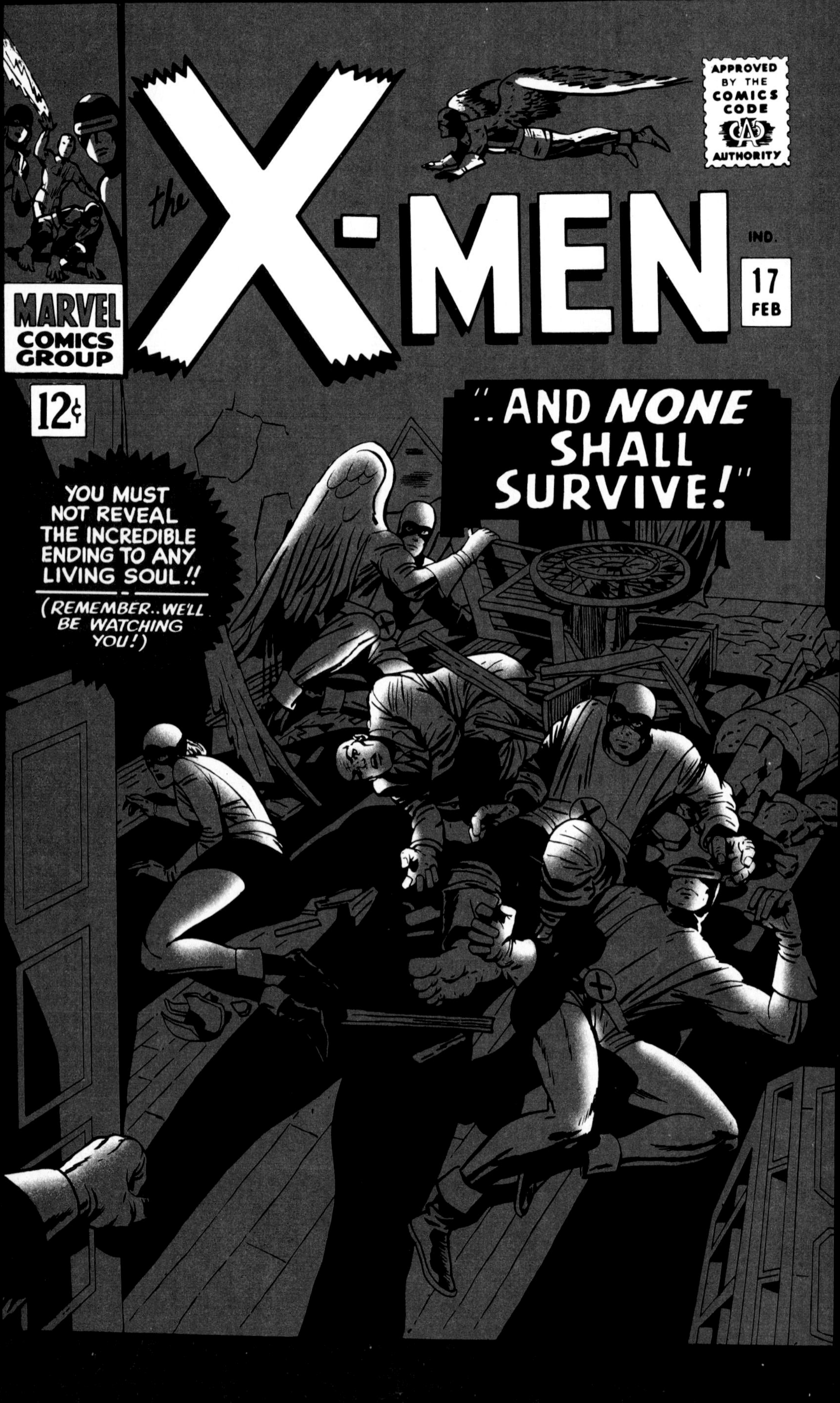
APPROVED BY THE COMICS CODE CA AUTHORITY
the X-MEN
IND.
17 FEB
MARVEL COMICS GROUP
12¢
"..AND NONE SHALL SURVIVE!"
YOU MUST NOT REVEAL THE INCREDIBLE ENDING TO ANY LIVING SOUL!!
(REMEMBER..WE'LL BE WATCHING YOU!)

"...AND NONE SHALL SURVIVE!"

THE FAT'S IN THE FIRE *NOW!* THERE'S NO WAY FOR *PROFESSOR X* TO KEEP OUR BATTLE OUT OF THE HEADLINES AFTER ALL *THIS!*

YOUR PULSE IS *IMPOSSIBLE*, SON!

THOUGH THE YOUTHFUL X-MEN MANAGED TO DEFEAT THE DEADLY *SENTINELS* LAST ISH, THEY DID NOT ESCAPE UNSCATHED! WITHIN MOMENTS, A FIRST AID TEAM OF NATIONAL GUARD *MEDICS* REACHES THE SCENE...

MY TROOPS WILL TAKE COMMAND, INSPECTOR! IT'S A MILITARY MATTER NOW!

OKAY WITH ME, GENERAL!

HAVE A CARE, KILDARE! EACH AND EVERY TOE IS VIRTUALLY *PRICELESS!*

I WONDER HOW MUCH *LONGER* THE PROFESSOR CAN KEEP HIS CONNECTION WITH US A *SECRET.*

WE'D BETTER SEE ABOUT GETTING YOU HOME SAFELY, PROFESSOR XAVIER!

DON'T WORRY ABOUT *ME*, OFFICER! MY CAR IS PARKED NOT FAR FROM HERE!

COMB THE AREA!! REPORT ANYTHING THAT MOVES! LET'S *GO!*

PERHAPS ONE OF THE *X-MEN* WILL BE GOOD ENOUGH TO DRIVE ME BACK TO MY SCHOOL!

STORY: STAN LEE • LAYOUTS: J. KIRBY • PENCILS: JAY GAVIN • INKS: DICK AYERS • LETTERING: A. SIMEK

ON BEHALF OF THE ARMED SERVICES, PROFESSOR, I WANT TO THANK YOU FOR YOUR AID! IT WAS MOST *COURAGEOUS* OF YOU TO OFFER TO COME HERE AND ADVISE US!

I WAS GLAD TO BE ABLE TO HELP, GENERAL!

HE THINKS OF ME AS A CIVILIAN ADVISER! AFTER ALL, THERE'S NO REASON FOR ANYONE TO SUSPECT THAT I'M THE LEADER OF THE *X-MEN*!

THERE'LL BE SOME MIGHTY *RED FACES* FROM NOW ON, PROFESSOR! ALL THOSE WHO CALLED THE X-MEN MENACES TO SOCIETY WILL HAVE A LOT OF *APOLOGIZING* TO DO!

IN FACT, I MYSELF USED TO FEAR THEIR POWER, UNTIL I SAW HOW THEY RISKED THEIR LIVES TO HELP ALL OF US!

DON'T YOU *AGREE*, PROFESSOR?

INDEED I *DO*, GENERAL!

THAT'S WHY I DECIDED TO RELEASE MY MENTAL *HOLD* OVER YOUR MIND-- SO THE *X-MEN* WOULD GET DUE CREDIT!

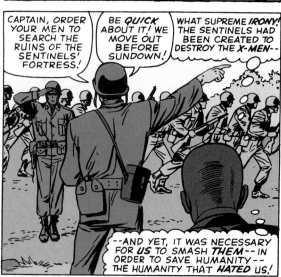

CAPTAIN, ORDER YOUR MEN TO SEARCH THE RUINS OF THE SENTINELS' FORTRESS!

BE *QUICK* ABOUT IT! WE MOVE OUT BEFORE SUNDOWN!

WHAT SUPREME *IRONY*! THE SENTINELS HAD BEEN CREATED TO DESTROY THE *X-MEN*--

--AND YET, IT WAS NECESSARY FOR *US* TO SMASH *THEM*-- IN ORDER TO SAVE HUMANITY-- THE HUMANITY THAT *HATED* US!

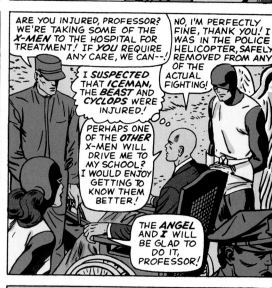

ARE YOU INJURED, PROFESSOR? WE'RE TAKING SOME OF THE *X-MEN* TO THE HOSPITAL FOR TREATMENT! IF *YOU* REQUIRE ANY CARE, WE CAN--!

NO, I'M PERFECTLY FINE, THANK YOU! I WAS IN THE POLICE HELICOPTER, SAFELY REMOVED FROM ANY OF THE ACTUAL FIGHTING!

I *SUSPECTED* THAT *ICEMAN*, THE *BEAST* AND *CYCLOPS* WERE INJURED!

PERHAPS ONE OF THE *OTHER* X-MEN WILL DRIVE ME TO MY SCHOOL? I WOULD ENJOY GETTING TO KNOW THEM BETTER!

THE *ANGEL* AND *I* WILL BE GLAD TO DO IT, PROFESSOR!

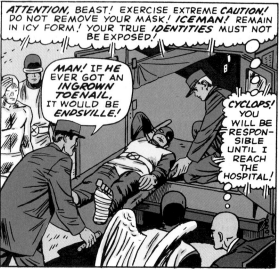

ATTENTION, BEAST! EXERCISE EXTREME *CAUTION*! DO NOT REMOVE YOUR MASK! *ICEMAN*! REMAIN IN ICY FORM! YOUR TRUE *IDENTITIES* MUST NOT BE EXPOSED!

MAN! IF HE EVER GOT AN *INGROWN TOENAIL*, IT WOULD BE *ENDSVILLE*!

CYCLOPS! YOU WILL BE RESPONSIBLE UNTIL I REACH THE HOSPITAL!

*S*ECONDS LATER, CYCLOPS, THE BEAST AND ICEMAN ARE SPEEDILY TRANSPORTED TO THE NEAREST HOSPITAL, AS THE ANGEL AND MARVEL GIRL ACCOMPANY PROFESSOR XAVIER TO HIS WAITING SEDAN...

THE PROFESSOR *HAD* TO LET US GO TO THE HOSPITAL-- NO MATTER *HOW* RISKY IT IS! IF HE PROTESTED, IT WOULD HAVE AROUSED TOO MANY *SUSPICIONS*!

I'M NOT HURT BADLY EXCEPT FOR SOME BRUISES-- BUT I HOPE HANK AND BOBBY ARE OKAY!

2

AND SO, THE **X-MEN** LEAVE THE SCENE OF ONE OF THEIR MOST FANTASTIC BATTLES--THE SITE WHERE THE **SENTINELS** WERE BORN-- AND WHERE THEY, ALONG WITH THEIR TRAGIC CREATOR, PERISHED--AS THE RESULT OF A MAD DREAM GONE WRONG!

A SHORT TIME LATER, IN A HUSHED HOSPITAL ROOM...

HIS INJURY WAS MORE SERIOUS THAN I **THOUGHT!** HE BLACKED OUT IN THE AMBULANCE, AND THEY CAN'T BRING HIM BACK TO CONSCIOUSNESS!

IT WAS GOOD OF YOU TO STOP BY TO SEE THE X-MEN, PROFESSOR-- BUT I'M AFRAID **ICEMAN'S** CONDITION MUST BE LISTED AS **CRITICAL!**

DUE TO THE MUTANT NATURE OF HIS BODY, IT IS IMPOSSIBLE TO MAKE AN ACCURATE DIAGNOSIS OF HIS INJURIES!

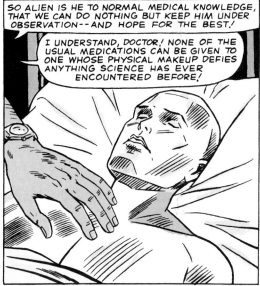

SO ALIEN IS HE TO NORMAL MEDICAL KNOWLEDGE, THAT WE CAN DO NOTHING BUT KEEP HIM UNDER OBSERVATION-- AND HOPE FOR THE BEST!

I UNDERSTAND, DOCTOR! NONE OF THE USUAL MEDICATIONS CAN BE GIVEN TO ONE WHOSE PHYSICAL MAKEUP DEFIES ANYTHING SCIENCE HAS EVER ENCOUNTERED BEFORE!

EVEN **I**, WITH MY MUTANT **BRAIN**, CANNOT HELP BOBBY NOW! HE IS IN THE HANDS OF A POWER GREATER THAN ANY **HUMAN!**

HE'S STARTING TO **MOVE!** TRYING TO **SPEAK**--!

LOOK OUT! I'LL TACKLE THE SENTINEL! I'LL STOP HIM-- SOMEHOW--!

I KNOW I'M THE YOUNGEST-- BUT I'LL SHOW THEM-- I'LL PROVE THAT I'M EVERY INCH AN X-MAN! I WON'T FAIL THEM! I **WON'T**...!

I'LL MAKE THEM PROUD OF ME--THEY **NEED** ME--I-- I WON'T LET THEM DOWN--!

HE'S **DELIRIOUS!** NO WAY OF KNOWING WHETHER IT'S A **GOOD** SYMPTOM-- OR A **DANGEROUS** ONE!

YOU'D BETTER **LEAVE** NOW, PROFESSOR!

ALL THESE MONTHS --THESE MANY MISSIONS-- I'VE **PROTECTED** MY X-MEN! I PRAY THAT BOBBY DRAKE WON'T MARK THE FIRST TIME I'M FACED WITH-- **FAILURE!**

3

WITH HEAVY HEART, CHARLES XAVIER NEXT VISITS HANK McCOY--/

HELLO, PROFESSOR! IS THERE ANY CHANGE IN THE *ICE-MAN'S* CONDITION YET?

REMEMBER, HANK-- DO NOT, UNDER ANY CIRCUMSTANCE, RE-MOVE YOUR MASK! AND, ANOTHER WORD OF CAUTION-- ACT AS THOUGH I AM MERELY A CASUAL FRIEND! NO ONE MUST SUSPECT I AM ACTUALLY YOUR *LEADER!*

NO, BEAST! HE IS STILL ON THE *CRITICAL LIST...* THE POOR LAD IS *DELIRIOUS!*

THE *BEAST'S* FRACTURES ARE HEALING REMARKABL' WELL! BUT, IT'S A PITY HE WON'T PERMIT US TO REMOVE HIS MASK-- AS A SCIENTIST, THERE IS SO MUCH *MORE* I WANT TO LEARN ABOUT HIS PHYSIOLOGICAL MAKEUP!

PERHAPS THE *X-MEN* HAVE GOOD REASON FOR WISHING TO KEEP THEIR TRUE IDENTITIES SECRET, DOCTOR!

--UNTIL MANKIND LOSES ITS UNFOUNDED SUSPICION -- ITS DANGEROUS DISTRUST OF *MUTANTS!*

UNFORTUNATELY, WE HAVE NO LEGAL RIGHT TO *INSIST* THAT HE UNMASK!

IF ONLY WE KNEW WHO THE X-MEN'S *PARENTS* ARE! WE MIGHT LEARN SO *MUCH* ABOUT HUMAN MUTATION!

THEIR *PARENTS!* THE ONE *WEAK LINK* IN OUR CHAIN OF SECURITY! IF ANY DEADLY *ENEMY* OF OURS EVER CAPTURED ONE OF MY X-MEN'S *PARENTS,* WHAT A *HOLD* HE WOULD HAVE OVER US!

HOW TRAGIC THAT SCIENCE MUST BE DENIED OUR FULL COOPERATION BECAUSE OF THE *EVIL* THAT STILL LURKS IN THE WORLD!

BUT, AT THAT VERY MOMENT, NEARBY--

WHAT ON *EARTH* IS GOING ON UP THERE??

WOULD YOU MIND LETTING A FELLOW HAVE A LITTLE *QUIET,* PLEASE?

THE *ANGEL* IS CALLING THE AUTOMATIC PHONE-ANSWERING DEVICE AT X-MEN HEAD-QUARTERS--

--TO LEARN IF THERE WERE ANY *MESSAGES* WHILE THEY WERE AWAY.

HE LIFTED THE PHONE INTO THE AIR SO WE COULDN'T SEE WHAT *NUMBER* HE DIALED!

YOU'LL HAVE TO GET *DOWN,* YOUNG MAN! THAT'S AGAINST HOSPITAL REGULATIONS!

HELLO? *WHAT?!* HOLY SMOKE-- THAT'S THE LAST THING I *EXPECTED!*

I'VE GOT TO NOTIFY THE *PROFESSOR--* FAST!

I'M ALREADY *HERE,* WARREN! I DETECTED YOUR MENTAL AGITATION! WHAT'S *WRONG?* MERELY *THINK* IT TO ME--!

IT'S MY *PARENTS!* THEY CALLED THE SCHOOL! LEFT WORD THEY'RE COMING TO *VISIT!*

THEY'RE WORRIED BECAUSE THEY HAVEN'T *HEARD* FROM ME!

4

THE **PHONE--** **QUICKLY!** PERHAPS I CAN **STOP** THEM, BEFORE THEY LEAVE!

SURE, PROFESSOR! THERE YOU ARE....!

MAY I HAVE THE PHONE, YOUNG MAN?

IF THEY REACH THE SCHOOL AND FIND IT **DESERTED,** WHAT WILL THEY **THINK??** HOW CAN WE **EXPLAIN?**

THEY **MUSTN'T** REACH IT FIRST! I'VE HAD A FEELING OF **DANGER** FROM THERE ALL DAY!

THEN, AFTER QUICKLY DIALING THE ANGEL'S HOME NUMBER--

MRS. WORTHINGTON? THIS IS PROFESSOR XAVIER! I'VE HAD MY STUDENTS WITH ME ON A FIELD TRIP, TO GATHER MATERIAL FOR A RESEARCH PAPER! **THAT** IS WHY YOUR CALL WAS ANSWERED BY AN AUTOMATIC DEVICE!

AT ANY RATE, WE'RE PLANNING A SHORT MOTOR TRIP, AND THOUGHT WE'D STOP OFF AND SEE WARREN WHILE IN YOUR NEIGHBORHOOD!

BUT, IT'S **EXAM** TIME NOW--!

OH, WE'LL ONLY STAY A FEW MINUTES, PROFESSOR! SEE YOU LATER! 'BYE NOW!

WELL, **THAT'S** A RELIEF, PROFESSOR! MY HUSBAND AND I WERE QUITE **WORRIED!**

I COULDN'T DISSUADE HER! BUT, I CAN'T HELP FEELING **UNEASY** ABOUT THEIR VISIT!

WHY, SIR? IS ANYTHING **WRONG?**

YES! WITH ICEMAN CRITICALLY ILL, AND THE BEAST RECOVERING FROM A FRACTURE --PLUS THIS SENSE OF **MENACE** I CANNOT SHAKE--

--I THINK YOU'D BETTER FLY TO THE SCHOOL **NOW,** ANGEL-- AND DO A LITTLE SCOUTING AROUND!

I'M ON MY **WAY,** SIR!

IF ONLY MOM AND DAD HADN'T DECIDED TO VISIT THE SCHOOL **NOW!** THE PROF IS NEVER **WRONG** WHEN HE SENSES DANGER--AND I CAN'T LET **THEM** GET INVOLVED IN IT!

I SURE HATE TO LEAVE **BOBBY** WHILE HE'S SO ILL-- BUT, I GUESS THE **PROFESSOR** WILL STAY WITH HIM!

GOSH, IT FEELS **GREAT** TO BE IN **FLIGHT** AGAIN!

THEN, FOR THE NEXT FEW MINUTES AS HE WINGS HIS WAY TOWARDS WESTCHESTER, THE HIGH-FLYING **ANGEL** SOARS AND GLIDES LIKE A FALCON IN FLIGHT,...!

NO OTHER HUMAN-- NO ONE WHO HAS NEVER POSSESSED **WINGS--** CAN IMAGINE HOW **WONDERFUL** IT IS TO ACTUALLY **FLY!**

5

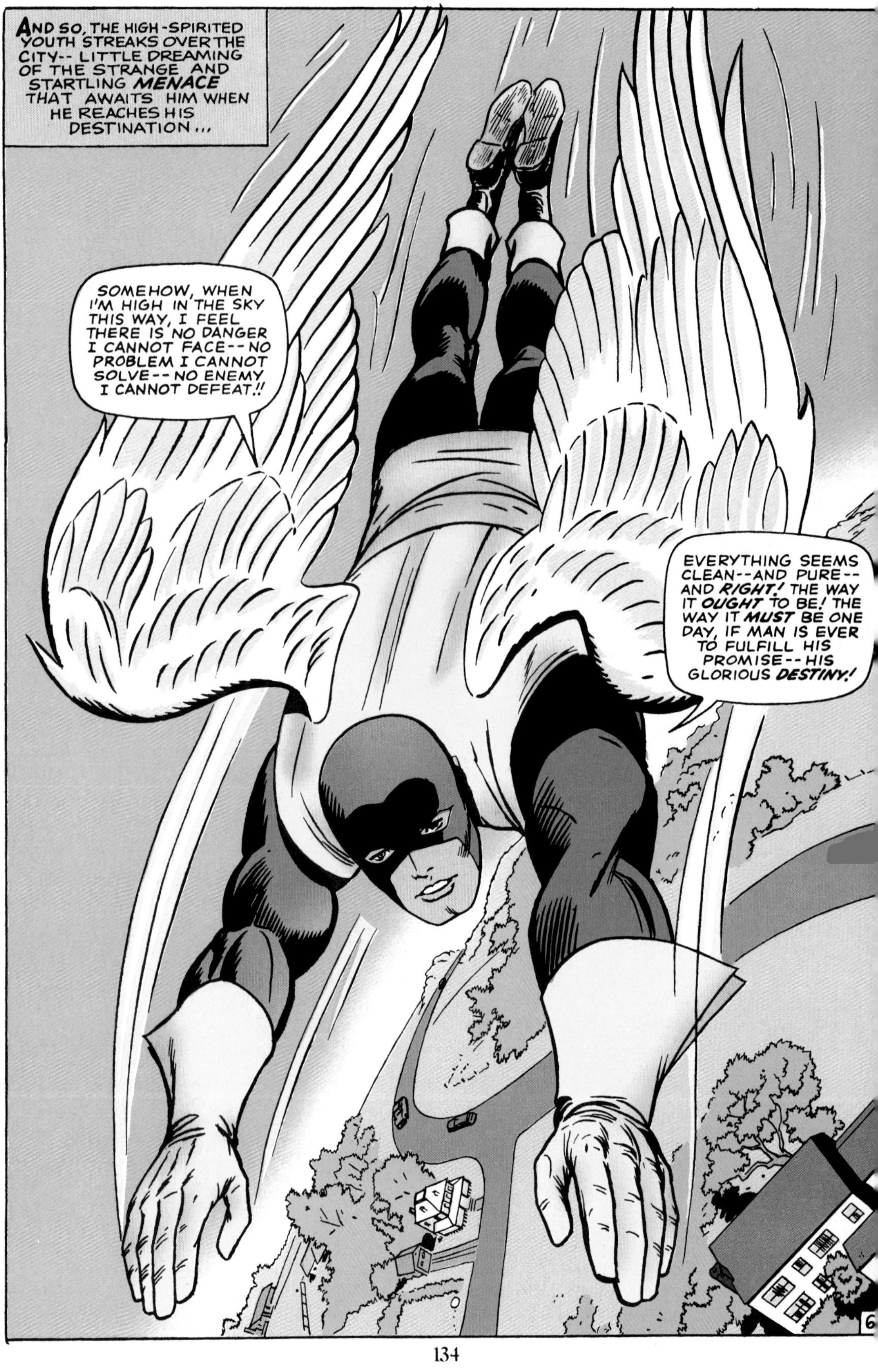
AND SO, THE HIGH-SPIRITED YOUTH STREAKS OVER THE CITY-- LITTLE DREAMING OF THE STRANGE AND STARTLING MENACE THAT AWAITS HIM WHEN HE REACHES HIS DESTINATION...
SOMEHOW, WHEN I'M HIGH IN THE SKY THIS WAY, I FEEL THERE IS NO DANGER I CANNOT FACE--NO PROBLEM I CANNOT SOLVE--NO ENEMY I CANNOT DEFEAT!!
EVERYTHING SEEMS CLEAN--AND PURE--AND RIGHT! THE WAY IT OUGHT TO BE! THE WAY IT MUST BE ONE DAY, IF MAN IS EVER TO FULFILL HIS PROMISE--HIS GLORIOUS DESTINY!
6

T, EVEN AS THE ASTOUNDING
GEL PLUMMETS EARTHWARD
WARDS HIS GOAL, THE FRONT
OR OF PROFESSOR XAVIER'S
HOOL SLOWLY BEGINS TO OPEN...

ONE OF THEM APPROACHES **NOW!**

I HAD HOPED TO ATTACK THEM ALL AT **ONCE** -- TO DEMONSTRATE MY OVERWHELMING **POWER!**

BUT, PERHAPS IT WILL BE EVEN **MORE** SATISFYING TO DEFEAT THEM ONE AT A TIME! I WILL THEN BE ABLE TO SAVOR EACH INDIVIDUAL VICTORY -- TO WATCH EACH ACCURSED X-MAN FALL HELPLESSLY BEFORE ME!

THE **FIRST** ONE COMES! I SHALL CLOSE THE DOOR AGAIN -- AND WAIT!

I WONDER WHAT THE PROFESSOR MEANT ABOUT SENSING DANGER!? THE SCHOOL HAS NEVER LOOKED QUIETER -- OR MORE PEACEFUL!

THERE'S NOTHING OUT OF THE ORDINARY **OUTSIDE** THE BUILDING! NOT A SIGN OF LIFE ANYWHERE!

SO I'D BETTER POKE AROUND **INSIDE!** IT'S NOT LIKE THE PROF TO SEND ANYONE ON A WILD-GOOSE CHASE!

THAT'S STRANGE! HE DOOR ALWAYS LOCKS UTOMATICALLY BEHIND US WHEN WE LEAVE...

...BUT, IT'S **OPEN** NOW!

AND THEN, LIKE A SENSELESS SEQUENCE FROM A MAD, FANTASTIC NIGHTMARE, A HEAVY, LETHAL **BATTLE-AX** SUDDENLY DISENGAGES ITSELF FROM THE STEEL HAND THAT HELD IT, AND HURTLES THRU THE CORRIDOR -- RIGHT TOWARDS THE **ANGEL**....!

7.

135

BUT, LONG, HARD MONTHS OF CEASELESS *TRAINING* PROVE THEIR WORTH, AS THE ANGEL'S AMAZING AERIAL AGILITY SUCCEEDS IN SAVING HIS LIFE!

WELCOME HOME, YOU WINGED BLUNDERER! YOU SHALL NEVER LEAVE HERE AGAIN--UNDER YOUR OWN POWER!

THERE *IS* SOMEONE! BUT *WHO??* WHO WOULD *DARE--??*

JUST STAY WHERE YOU *ARE*, MISTER! I'LL MAKE YOU *EAT* THOSE WORDS!

HIS VOICE CAME FROM DOWN THE CORRIDOR! BUT, THERE'S NO PLACE TO *HIDE* FROM HERE TO THE END OF THE HALL! HE WON'T ESCAPE ME!

NO MATTER HOW FAST HE IS --HOW *STRONG* HE IS-- I'LL *GET* HIM! I'VE GOT TO BE *SWIFT* AND *SURE--*!

BUT THEN, ZOOMING DOWN THE HALLWAY LIKE A HUMAN MISSILE, THE WINGED MUTANT REALIZES HE'S SPEEDING INTO A *TRAP*-- TOO LATE TO *STOP* HIMSELF!

THERE'S SOMETHING IN *FRONT* OF ME-- IT SUDDENLY DROPPED INTO PLACE--!

I'M GOING TO *HIT* IT! I-- *UNHHHH!*

HOW EASY IT WAS TO CLIP THE ANGEL'S WINGS! BUT, HE IS ONLY THE FIRST--ONLY THE *FIRST*!

8

136

MEANWHILE, PROFESSOR CHARLES XAVIER PICKS THAT EXACT MOMENT TO CHECK UPON THE CONDITION OF THE X-MEN'S DEPUTY LEADER--

NO, DOC! I'M SORRY! I CAN'T LET YOU EXAMINE MY EYES!

SCOTT NEEDS HELP! I WAS AFRAID OF THIS!

I MUST INSIST, SON! IT'S HOSPITAL ROUTINE! NOW DON'T BE DIFFICULT!

PARDON THE INTRUSION, DOCTOR! MY NAME IS XAVIER! I HAVE HAD THE OPPORTUNITY OF SEEING THE X-MEN IN ACTION, AND...

I'VE HEARD OF YOU, PROFESSOR! PERHAPS YOU CAN CONVINCE THIS YOUNG MAN TO LET ME CHECK HIS EYES! OPTOMETRY IS MY SPECIALTY-- I BELIEVE I MIGHT BE ABLE TO HELP HIM!

NOBODY CAN EXAMINE MY EYES! NO MATTER WHAT HAPPENS!

HE WON'T TAKE YOUR WORD FOR IT, SCOTT! YOU'LL HAVE TO CONVINCE HIM--AS DRAMATICALLY AS POSSIBLE! NOW!

THIS IS A MILD EXAMPLE OF WHAT HAPPENS IF MY PROTECTIVE VISOR IS REMOVED FROM MY EYES-- EVEN TO THE SLIGHTEST DEGREE!

GOOD HEAVENS....!

ZAPP!

YOU MEAN YOU CANNOT CONTROL THE DESTRUCTIVE FORCE OF YOUR EYES?? YOU HAVE TO KEEP THEM SHIELDED ALL THE TIME??

I'M AFRAID THAT'S IT, DOC! IT WOULD BE WORTH YOUR LIFE TO TRY TO REMOVE MY VISOR!

IF YOU'RE THRU WITH YOUR PATIENT, DOCTOR, I WONDER IF I MIGHT SPEAK WITH HIM IN PRIVATE? I WAS ASKED TO BRING HIM A MESSAGE, FROM ONE OF THE OTHER X-MEN!

CERTAINLY, PROFESSOR! THEY AREN'T PRISONERS HERE!

HENCE, A FEW MINUTES LATER...

SAY NOTHING YET, SCOTT! WE MUST BE EXTREMELY CAREFUL TO ACT LIKE CASUAL ACQUAINTANCES, SO NONE SUSPECT MY REAL CONNECTION WITH YOU!

WOULD YOU MIND WHEELING ME TO THAT SHADY ARBOR, MY BOY?

WE'RE ALONE NOW, SIR! WHAT IS IT? IS SOMETHING WRONG?

I'M AFRAID SO! I'VE LOST MENTAL CONTACT WITH THE ANGEL-- AFTER SENDING HIM BACK TO THE SCHOOL!

I SUSPECT SOME DANGER AWAITING US THERE!

ICEMAN IS TOO ILL TO BE MOVED --AND I PREFER THE BEAST AND MARVEL GIRL TO REMAIN HERE IN CASE THEY'RE NEEDED!

BUT, YOU AND I HAD BEST RETURN TO THE SCHOOL AT ONCE! I HAVE A FEELING THAT WARREN NEEDS US!

I'LL GET YOUR CAR, SIR! IT'S PARKED JUST AROUND THE CORNER!

9

THEN, AFTER AN HOUR OF BREAKNECK DRIVING--!

THERE'S THE SCHOOL AT LAST! HAVE YOU MANAGED TO CONTACT THE ANGEL MENTALLY YET, PROFESSOR?

NO! AND THAT'S WHAT *WORRIES* ME! I SEEM TO SENSE SOME SORT OF MENTAL *BARRIER* AROUND THE SCHOOL --SOMETHING MY OWN MUTANT BRAIN CANNOT PENETRATE!

THE BARRIER IS STRONGER THAN EVER HERE INSIDE! TAKE EVERY PRECAUTION, CYCLOPS! THERE IS SOME GREAT *POWER* BEING USED AGAINST US!

ANGEL! THIS *CYKE!* DO YOU *READ* ME? WHERE *ARE* YOU, FELLA?

AH! TWO ADDITIONAL VICTIMS FOR ME! I MUST MAKE SURE THEY DO NOT GET *BORED!*

PROFESSOR-- *LISTEN!* WHAT'S *THAT?*

RRRREEEEE

MY *CEREBRO* MACHINE! THE DANGER IS EVEN GREATER THAN I FEARED!

THE MACHINE SEEMS TO BE GOING *MAD!* THE MENACE MUST BE INCREDIBLY *CLOSE!*

RRREEEE

I'LL SHUT IT OFF BEFORE IT *DEAFENS* US!

CEREBRO ONLY REACTS THAT WAY WHEN A DANGEROUS *MUTANT* THREATENS! THAT MEANS SOME POWERFUL *HOMO SUPERIOR* HAS INVADED THIS BUILDING, AND IS WAITING TO ATTACK EVEN *NOW!*

HE MUST HAVE ALREADY OVERCOME *ANGEL*-- AND WE DON'T EVEN KNOW WHO HE *IS!*

ONLY THE MOST *POWERFUL* OF MUTANTS COULD PREVENT ME FROM MENTALLY REACHING OUT TO HIM! WE MUST LEARN WHO HE *IS*-- WHILE WE STILL *CAN!*

PROFESSOR! BEHIND YOU!! LOOK OUT--!

IT'S A MECHANICAL MENTAL-WAVE DISTORTER--THE ONE TYPE OF WEAPON I CANNOT FIGHT! IT'S BLACKING OUT MY BRAIN--*I CAN'T THINK*--¦OHHHHH!¦

I'LL RIP IT *OFF* YOU! NO MATTER *WHAT,* I'LL--¦UNHHH!¦

THWONK!

A TRANSPARENT *SHIELD!* IT DROPPED DOWN *BETWEEN* US!

SOMEONE'S PLAYING A CAT-AND-MOUSE GAME WITH US!

IN ANY GAME LIKE THAT, IT'S *CYCLOPS* WHO TURNS INTO THE CAT--INTO A POWER-BLASTING *TIGER!*

But, NO SOONER DOES CYCLOPS' BLISTERING FORCE BEAM STRIKE THE STRANGE INVISIBLE SHIELD, THAN IT CAUSES AN *EXPLOSIVE BACK-LASH,* WHICH SENDS THE STARTLED MUTANT REELING....!

UHHH--!!

THOOOOM!

Then, REGAINING HIS FOOTING ONCE MORE, THE COURAGEOUS YOUTH AGAIN APPROACHES THE STRANGE BARRIER--BUT WITH FAR GREATER *CAUTION--!*

IT'S BEEN PREVIOUSLY PREPARED TO HURL BACK THE FORCE OF MY OWN OCULAR BLAST!

WHOEVER IS RESPONSIBLE FOR IT *KNOWS* ABOUT MY POWER-- OTHERWISE HE COULD NEVER HAVE CREATED SUCH AN INGENIOUS *DEFENSE!*

Next, WITHOUT WARNING...

THE *LIGHTS!* THEY'VE GONE *OUT!*

THE ENTIRE BUILDING'S BEEN PLUNGED INTO TOTAL *DARKNESS!*

CLICK!

AND NOW, X-MAN, YOU SHALL LEARN HOW TOTALLY *POWERLESS* YOU ARE AGAINST --ME!

11

THAT VOICE-- SOUNDED *FAMILIAR*-- ALMOST AS IF-- *UGGHHH!*--

THOK!

WHOEVER YOU ARE, YOU FORGOT THAT MY *FORCE BEAM* IS JUST AS EFFECTIVE IN THE *DARK* AS IN THE LIGHT!

ZAP

OVER-CONFIDENT *FOOL!* I FORGET *NOTHING!*

OOOFFFFF!

BEFORE *FINISHING* YOU, I WANT YOU TO SEE *HOW USELESS* YOUR MUCH-VAUNTED BEAM IS AGAINST GENUINE *POWER!*

WHOEVER HE IS, HE SEEMS TO ANTICIPATE MY EVERY MOVE! BUT I'M NOT BEATEN YET-- MY FORCE BEAM STILL HAS PLENTY OF ENERGY LEFT--!

WHEREVER YOU ARE, I'LL *GET YOU!* I'LL BLAST THIS ROOM IN *EVERY DIRECTION!!*

THEN, HAVING DESCRIBED A PERFECT CIRCLE WITH HIS AWESOME POWER BEAM, CYCLOPS TENSELY STOPS-- HOLDS HIS BREATH-- AND WAITS-- LISTENING FOR THE SOUND OF A FALLING BODY-- A SOUND THAT NEVER COMES!

NOTHING! IF HE'S STILL *IN* HERE, HE HAS SOME SORT OF POWER WHICH IS IMPERVIOUS TO MY OWN FORCE BLASTS

HE MUST HAVE PLANNED THIS WHOLE THING CAREFULLY-- THE ADVANTAGE IS *HIS* NOW--

--UNLESS I CAN REACH THE *LIGHT SWITCH* BEFORE HE STOPS ME!

A NICE TRY, X-MAN, BUT A *FUTILE* ONE! I EXPECTED YOU TO RACE FOR THE SWITCH!

WHAP!

K.RAK!

AND NOW, IT IS TIME TO *END* THE CHARADE--!

--BY USING ONLY MY HAMMERING *FISTS,* SO THAT YOU *STILL* CANNOT BE CERTAIN WHAT MY *TRUE* POWER IS!

12

140

AND, AS THE NOW-HELPLESS CYCLOPS SLUMPS TO THE FLOOR, WE RETURN ONCE AGAIN TO THE HOSPITAL, WHERE WE FIND...

HENRY P. MCCOY! I THOUGHT YOU WERE PRACTICALLY AN *INVALID!*

THAT WAS AN *HOUR* AGO, MA'AM! YOU KNOW HOW QUICKLY WE MUTANTS *RECUPERATE!*

NOTHING LIKE SOME CAPRICIOUS CALISTHENICS TO WHILE AWAY A LETHARGIC DAY!

BUT, ENOUGH OF MY EXEMPLARY EPITHETS! TO WHAT DO I OWE THE HONOR OF YOUR SUDDEN VISITATION?

HONESTLY, HANK! CAN'T YOU EVER SPEAK LIKE ANY ORDINARY, NORMAL HUMAN BEING?

I *DO,* JEANIE! IT'S JUST THAT I EMPLOY MELLIFLUOUS ADJECTIVES TO *DO* IT!

WOMP!

VERY PERSPICACIOUS OF YOU, WENCH!

AND THEREIN LIES MY *CHARM!*

OH! YOU'RE JUST *IMPOSSIBLE!*

VERY WELL, YOUNG MAN! I SHALL HOLD YOU IN THE AIR, *TELEKINETICALLY,* UNTIL YOU PROMISE TO SETTLE DOWN AND *LISTEN* TO ME!

PRATTLE AWAY THEN, FEMALE! YOU HAVE MY UNDIVIDED ATTENTION!

WELL! IT'S ABOUT TIME!

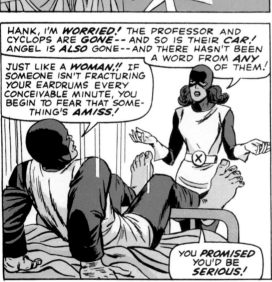

HANK, I'M *WORRIED!* THE PROFESSOR AND CYCLOPS ARE *GONE--* AND SO IS THEIR *CAR!* ANGEL IS *ALSO* GONE--AND THERE HASN'T BEEN A WORD FROM *ANY* OF THEM!

JUST LIKE A *WOMAN!!* IF SOMEONE ISN'T FRACTURING YOUR EARDRUMS EVERY CONCEIVABLE MINUTE, YOU BEGIN TO FEAR THAT SOMETHING'S *AMISS!*

YOU *PROMISED* YOU'D BE *SERIOUS!*

I'M SORRY, JEAN! PERHAPS YOU'VE SOME *JUSTIFICATION* FOR YOUR CONCERN! IT ISN'T LIKE THE OTHERS TO LEAVE US INCOMMUNICADO!

IF THEY WENT *ANYWHERE,* IT WOULD BE TO THE *SCHOOL!* PERHAPS THAT SHOULD BE *OUR* NEXT DESTINATION!

I *HOPED* YOU'D SAY THAT, HANK! BUT FIRST, LET'S CHECK ON *ICE-MAN!*

13

STILL NO CHANGE IN HIS CONDITION, DOC?

I'M AFRAID NOT, SON! BUT WE HAVE HIM UNDER ROUND-THE-CLOCK OBSERVATION!

DO EVERYTHING YOU *CAN* FOR HIM, DOCTOR! HE'S *GOT* TO COME OUT OF THAT COMA!

HE *WILL* BE ALL RIGHT, WON'T HE? I MEAN-- YOU DON'T THINK THERE'S A CHANCE THAT HE'LL --I MEAN--

I CAN'T *ANSWER* THAT, YOUNG LADY! HIS PHYSICAL MAKEUP IS SO DIFFERENT FROM ANYTHING MEDICAL SCIENCE IS FAMILIAR WITH, THAT WE CAN DO NOTHING BUT WAIT--AND HOPE!

HE'S *GOT* TO PULL THRU! HE WAS LIKE MY OWN *BROTHER* TO ME! YOU CAN *DO* IT, YOU HUMAN POPSICLE-- I *KNOW* YOU CAN!

I KNOW IT'S IMPORTANT TO YOU TO KEEP ALL YOUR IDENTITIES *SECRET!* BUT, IF YOU KNOW HIS *PARENTS,* I SUGGEST THEY BE NOTIFIED --AS SOON AS POSSIBLE!

THEN-- YOU *DO* THINK IT'S-- VERY *SERIOUS?!!*

WE'VE DALLIED LONG ENOUGH! WE'VE GOT TO CONTACT THE OTHERS!

IF ANYTHING HAPPENS TO *ICE-MAN*-- I-I'LL-- OH, I CAN'T EVEN *THINK* OF IT!

DON'T THINK OF IT! CONCENTRATE ON THE TASK AT HAND! WE'VE GOT TO REACH OUR HEAD-QUARTERS WITH ALL DELIBERATE SPEED!

YOU-- YOU'RE HEADING FOR THE *OPEN WINDOW!*

NATURALLY! WE'RE ONLY THREE STORIES UP! SUCH A LEAP IS A MERE *BAGATELLE* TO THE *BEAST!*

AND *YOU* HAVE YOUR *TELEKINESIS!*

OF *COURSE!* I FORGOT --I CAN FLOAT MYSELF DOWN GENTLY BY MEANS OF MY POWER OF LEVITATION!

14

AND THAT SAME POWER WILL EASILY LIFT ME OVER THE OUTER WALL....!

AS FOR *ME*, MY METHOD IS SOMEWHAT LESS SUBTLE, BUT EQUALLY AS EFFECTIVE NONETHELESS!

FINALLY, AFTER A SPECTACULAR SUCCESSION OF RUNNING, LEAPING, CLIMBING AND TELEPORTING WITH MILE-CONSUMING GYMNASTIC SKILL, THE TWO MARVELOUS MUTANTS REACH THEIR GOAL....

IT SEEMS SO QUIET--SO FOREBODING--!

STAY *BEHIND* ME, LASS! *I'LL* CHARGE IN FIRST, AT TOP SPEED, TO BEAR THE BRUNT OF WHATEVER AWAITS US!

...JT, EVEN THE AGILE *BEAST* IS NOT PREPARED FOR THE SIMPLE, YET STARTLINGLY DANGEROUS ...RPRISE THAT CONFRONTS HIM....!

SOMETHING *HAPPENED* TO THE HALLWAY--!

EVERYTHING HAS BEEN COATED WITH A WAXLIKE *GLOSS*--THERE'S NO *FRICTION*--NOTHING TO HOLD ONTO--

IT'S LIKE BEING A *SATELLITE* IN SPACE--THERE'S NO WAY TO CHECK OUR MOMENTUM--NO WAY TO *STOP!*

...O MATTER WHAT I REACH--...HE WALLS--CEILING--FLOOR--...HEY'RE ALL AS SMOOTH AS *GLASS!*

JEANIE WILL BE ALL RIGHT, BECAUSE SHE ENTERED *SLOWLY*--BUT *I* HURTLED IN LIKE A *PROJECTILE!*

EVEN MY NATURAL *AGILITY* CAN'T HELP ME NOW! I'VE GOT TO KEEP SLIDING ALONG --OUT OF CONTROL--UNTIL I REACH--*WHAT???*

15

HE'S MOVING SO *FAST*-- EVEN WITH MY TELEKINETIC POWER OPERATING AT FULL INTENSITY, I CAN'T EXERT ENOUGH FORCE UPON HIM TO SLOW HIM DOWN!

IN *FRONT* OF HIM-- THERE'S A *DOOR!* IT'S SLIDING OPEN!! IT MUST BE PART OF THE *TRAP!*

STAY *BACK,* GIRL! YOU CAN'T HELP *ME*-- BUT THERE MAY BE TIME TO SAVE *YOURSELF!* RUN! RUN!!

AND THEN, THE DESPERATE ADMONITION OF HANK McCOY IS DROWNED OUT BY THE SOUND OF HEAVY STEEL DOORS BEGINNING TO ROLL *TOGETHER* AGAIN--!

--RUN!!

RRRRRRR

I CAN'T PRY IT OPEN! I CAN'T *REACH* HIM--!!

NATURALLY! THIS IS HOW I *PLANNED* IT!

THAT *VOICE!!* DIRECTLY BEHIND ME! WHO--??

WE MEET AGAIN, MARVEL GIRL! A PITY IT MUST BE FOR THE VERY *LAST* TIME!

YOU!

HOW PATHETIC! DO YOU REALLY FEEL THAT YOUR *FEEBLE* KINETIC POWER CAN HAVE ANY EFFECT UPON SOMEONE AS SUPREMELY POWERFUL AS *I?*

SO! YOU CHOOSE NOT TO ANSWER ME! YOU PREFER TO KEEP *STRUGGLING* TILL THE END! A NOBLE, IF USELESS, GESTURE!

IT'S ALL UP TO *ME* NOW! I *MUST* STOP HIM!! I *MUST!*

16

E'S COMING *CLOSER.!!* UT *HOW??* WHY ISN'T Y POWER AFFECTING IM?? WHAT'S *WRONG* ITH ME?? WHY DO FEEL MYSELF GROW-NG WEAK--WEAKER--?

BY NOW, YOU SHOULD BE STARTING TO REALIZE THAT YOU HAVE BEEN INHALING ODORLESS *SLEEP GAS,* WHICH HAS DULLED YOUR BRAIN, AND HENCE YOUR KINETIC POWER, AS WELL!

THEN *THAT'S* WHY-- MY KNEES ARE SAGGING-- CAN'T KEEP MY EYES OPEN--SO WEAK--

BUT-- YOU HAVEN'T WON-- ET.! I WON'T GIVE UP-- NONE OF US-- WILL EVER--GIVE UP!

THAT NO LONGER *MATTERS,* YOU LITTLE FOOL! THE EPISODE IS *ENDED!*

ONLY *ONE* OF YOUR NUMBER REMAINS *TO BE BEATEN!* AND *HE* IS THE WEAKEST OF ALL!

THUS, THE ERA OF THE X-MEN IS *OVER*--AT LAST!

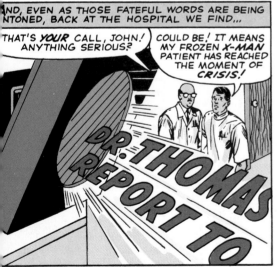

AND, EVEN AS THOSE FATEFUL WORDS ARE BEING NTONED, BACK AT THE HOSPITAL WE FIND...

THAT'S *YOUR* CALL, JOHN! ANYTHING SERIOUS?

COULD BE! IT MEANS MY FROZEN *X-MAN* PATIENT HAS REACHED THE MOMENT OF *CRISIS!*

DR. THOMAS REPORT TO

YOU'RE DR. JOHN THOMAS, AREN'T YOU? WE'VE SOME *QUESTIONS* TO ASK YOU--!

SINCE *ICEMAN* HAS BEEN YOUR PATIENT, HAVE YOU MANAGED TO *"THAW HIM OUT"* AND DISCOVER HIS REAL *IDENTITY??*

SORRY! NO TIME TO TALK TO NEWS-MEN!

17

NOW HOLD ON, DOCTOR! WE REPRESENT THE *AFFILIATED PRESS!* WE HAVE OVER THIRTY MILLION READERS THRUOUT THE FREE WORLD!

YOU WOULDN'T WANT THOSE THIRTY MILLION PEOPLE TO THINK YOU DIDN'T *CARE* ABOUT THEM, WOULD YOU?

THEY CAN TAKE THIRTY MILLION JUMPS IN THE *LAKE*-- AND SO CAN *YOU!* I'VE GOT A PATIENT IN THERE WHO MAY BE *DYING*-- AND *THAT'S* ALL I CARE ABOUT!

NOW *GET OUT*-- BEFORE I HAVE YOU *THROWN* OUT!

SORRY FOR THE DELAY, NURSE! WHAT'S *WRONG?* WHAT HAPPENED?

IT'S HIS *PULSE*, DOCTOR! IT'S SLOWING DOWN! I-I DON'T KNOW WHAT TO *DO!*

I HATE TO ADMIT IT, BUT NEITHER DO *I!*

THEY *NEED* ME --I *KNOW* THEY DO --THEY *NEED* ME--!

HE'S BEEN *DELIRIOUS* AGAIN --MUMBLING TO HIMSELF FOR HOURS--!

I'VE NEVER FELT SO *HELPLESS* BEFORE!

I MUSTN'T *FAIL* THEM-- NOT WHEN THEY *NEED* ME--!

IT'S ALMOST AS THOUGH HE HEARS VOICES THAT *WE* CAN'T HEAR--AS THOUGH SOMEONE IS *CALLING* TO HIM--DEPENDING ON HIM--!!

PULL YOURSELF TOGETHER, NURSE! HERE'S SOME NEW MEDICATION I WANT--RIGHT AWAY!

IT'S A NEW TYPE OF SULFA DRUG-- VERY *POTENT!* WE'VE GOT TO RISK IT!

BUT, WHAT OF THE OTHER X-MEN? WE HAD BEST RETURN TO THEM *FAST*--BECAUSE FROM THE LOOKS OF THINGS, THEY MAY NOT BE AROUND MUCH LONGER--!

I REGRET WE CANNOT WAIT FOR THE *ICEMAN* TO JOIN YOU, BUT I FEAR YOU WILL HAVE TO MAKE YOUR FINAL JOURNEY *WITHOUT* HIM!

AND NOW, I'LL MAKE SURE YOU'RE ALL SECURELY *LOCKED* INSIDE YOUR STEEL GONDOLA!

FOR YOUR *OWN* SAFETY, OF COURSE!

WE WOULDN'T WANT YOU FALLING OUT--NOT AFTER YOU REACH *100,000 FEET IN THE AIR!*

SLAM!

18

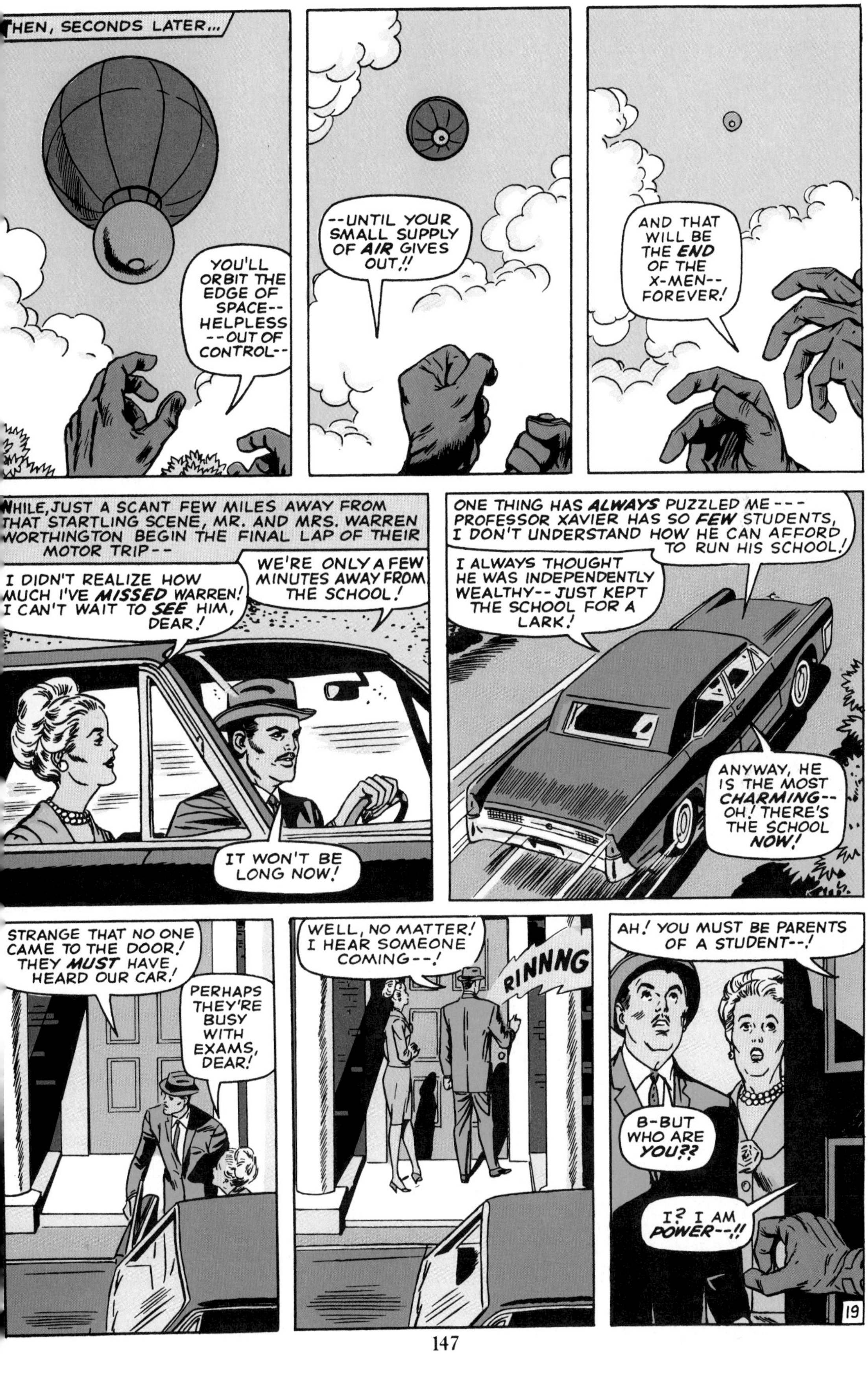
THEN, SECONDS LATER...
YOU'LL ORBIT THE EDGE OF SPACE--HELPLESS --OUT OF CONTROL--
--UNTIL YOUR SMALL SUPPLY OF AIR GIVES OUT!!
AND THAT WILL BE THE END OF THE X-MEN--FOREVER!
WHILE, JUST A SCANT FEW MILES AWAY FROM THAT STARTLING SCENE, MR. AND MRS. WARREN WORTHINGTON BEGIN THE FINAL LAP OF THEIR MOTOR TRIP--
I DIDN'T REALIZE HOW MUCH I'VE MISSED WARREN! I CAN'T WAIT TO SEE HIM, DEAR!
WE'RE ONLY A FEW MINUTES AWAY FROM THE SCHOOL!
IT WON'T BE LONG NOW!
ONE THING HAS ALWAYS PUZZLED ME---PROFESSOR XAVIER HAS SO FEW STUDENTS, I DON'T UNDERSTAND HOW HE CAN AFFORD TO RUN HIS SCHOOL!
I ALWAYS THOUGHT HE WAS INDEPENDENTLY WEALTHY--JUST KEPT THE SCHOOL FOR A LARK!
ANYWAY, HE IS THE MOST CHARMING--OH! THERE'S THE SCHOOL NOW!
STRANGE THAT NO ONE CAME TO THE DOOR! THEY MUST HAVE HEARD OUR CAR!
PERHAPS THEY'RE BUSY WITH EXAMS, DEAR!
WELL, NO MATTER! I HEAR SOMEONE COMING--!
RINNNG
AH! YOU MUST BE PARENTS OF A STUDENT--!
B-BUT WHO ARE YOU??
I? I AM POWER--!!
19

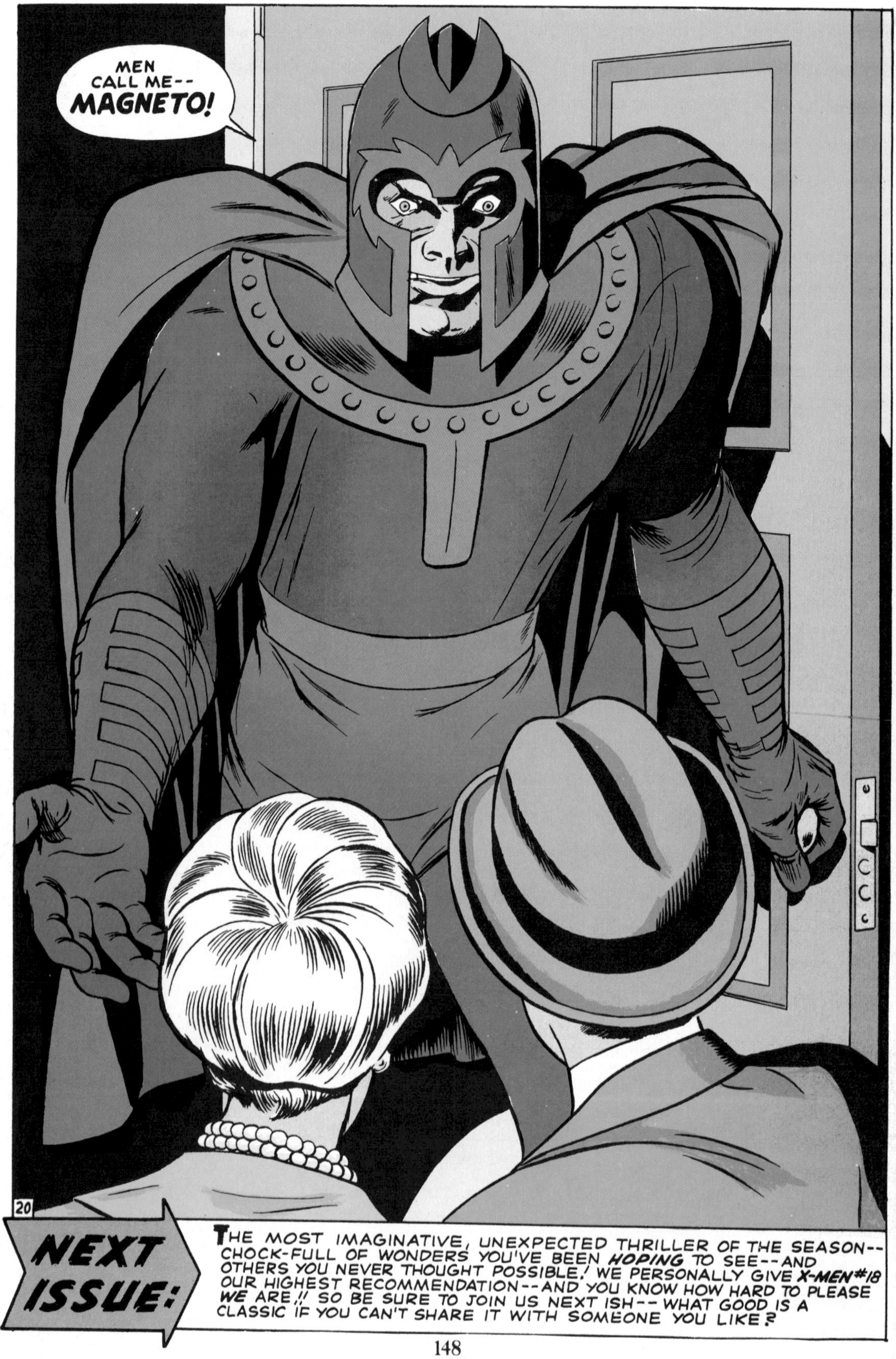

MEN CALL ME-- MAGNETO!
20
NEXT ISSUE:
THE MOST IMAGINATIVE, UNEXPECTED THRILLER OF THE SEASON--CHOCK-FULL OF WONDERS YOU'VE BEEN HOPING TO SEE--AND OTHERS YOU NEVER THOUGHT POSSIBLE! WE PERSONALLY GIVE X-MEN #18 OUR HIGHEST RECOMMENDATION--AND YOU KNOW HOW HARD TO PLEASE WE ARE!! SO BE SURE TO JOIN US NEXT ISH--WHAT GOOD IS A CLASSIC IF YOU CAN'T SHARE IT WITH SOMEONE YOU LIKE?

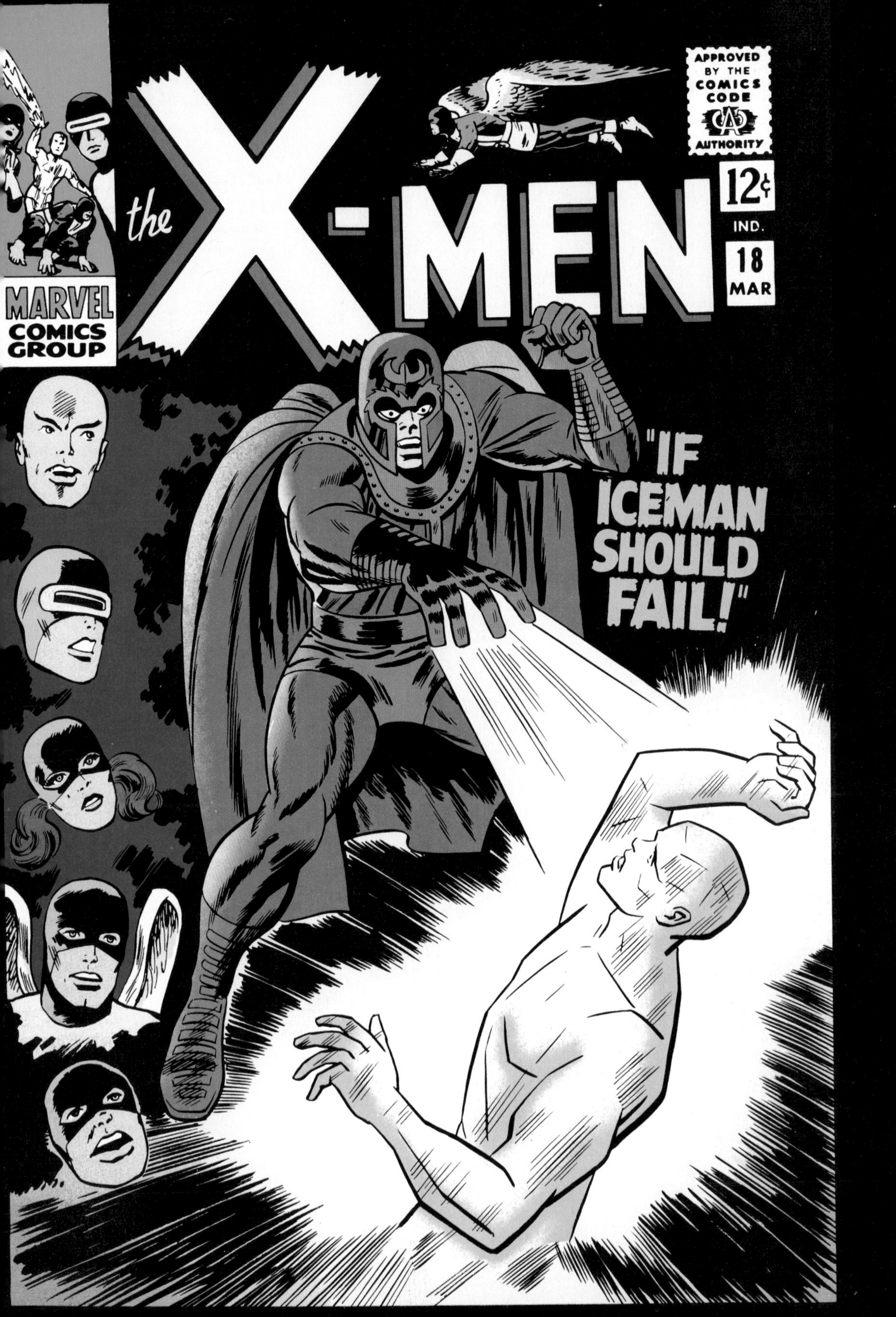

APPROVED BY THE COMICS CODE AUTHORITY
12¢
IND.
18
MAR
the X-MEN
MARVEL COMICS GROUP
"IF ICEMAN SHOULD FAIL!"

"IF ICEMAN SHOULD FAIL..!"

ONE BY ONE, THE *X-MEN* HAVE BEEN DEFEATED--BY THE MOST POWERFUL, THE MOST DEADLY FOE OF ALL! FOR THOSE OF YOU CARELESS ENOUGH TO HAVE MISSED OUR PREVIOUS ISSUE, WE SHALL GO BACK A BIT IN AN EFFORT TO BRING YOU UP TO DATE, THUS PROVING NO SACRIFICE IS TOO GREAT FOR US TO MAKE IN THIS, THE MAGNIFICENT NEW *MARVEL AGE OF COMICS!* (BUT DON'T EXPECT US TO MAKE A *HABIT* OF IT, HEAR?)

FAR ABOVE EARTH, A *BALLOON* IS DRIFTING --CLIMBING EVER HIGHER TOWARD THE DISTANT SUB-STRATOSPHERE --BRINGING THE X-MEN EVER CLOSER T --THEI *DOOM*

A FAIR STORY BY: STAN LEE

ADEQUATE ART BY: JAY GAVIN

TOLERABLE INKING BY: DICK AYERS

THE WORLD'S GREATEST LETTERING BY: ARTIE SIMEK (MARVEL'S BIRTHDAY BOY OF THE MONTH!)

AND NOW THAT YOU'VE MADE THE WISEST INVESTMENT OF THE SEASON BY BUYING THIS ISH, WE SUGGEST THAT YOU TURN THE PAGE AND START READING! IT'S REALLY GONNA *ROCK* YA!

HIGHER AND HIGHER INTO THE ENDLESS VOID DRIFTS THE LOCKED GONDOLA, AS ITS FIVE UNCONSCIOUS OCCUPANTS SLUMP HELPLESSLY AGAINST ITS COLD, ESCAPE-PROOF SHELL! BUT, WHO *IS* THE MASTER MENACE THAT HAS BROUGHT ONE OF THE WORLD'S GREATEST FIGHTING TEAMS TO THE EDGE OF DESTRUCTION---?

--WHO BUT-- *MAGNETO?!!* MAGNETO, THE MOST POWERFUL EVIL MUTANT OF ALL TIME!

YOU THOUGHT YOU HAD BANISHED ME FROM EARTH FOREVER!! BUT, I *RETURNED*-- STRONGER THAN EVER--STRONG ENOUGH TO DESTROY YOU *ALL!*

AND NOW, I'LL DESTROY EVERY LAST TRACE OF THE X-MEN'S *EXISTENCE--!*

NOTHING CAN RESIST MY MATCHLESS *MAGNETIC POWER!* BY HARNESSING ONLY A *FRACTION* OF THE NATURAL MAGNETISM THAT IS MINE, I CAN RAISE THEIR ENTIRE *SCHOOL BUILDING*, ONLY TO SEND IT CRASHING DOWN IN *RUINS!*

SPECIAL NOTE: WE KNOW YOU'RE WONDER- ING HOW MAGNETO MANAGED TO *RETURN* TO EARTH! BUT, BE PATIENT, PUSSYCAT-- THE BEST IS YET TO COME! 2

AND NOW TO *RELEASE* MY MAGNETIC HOLD, LETTING IT-- *NO!*

I HAVE A FAR *BETTER* IDEA!

I SHALL NEED A *HEADQUARTERS* FOR MYSELF, NOW THAT I AM READY TO ATTACK THE HUMAN RACE ONCE MORE!

AND, WHAT SUPREME *IRONY* IT SHALL BE TO USE THE FORMER HOME OF MY *ENEMIES* FOR THAT VERY PURPOSE!

THUS, ALLOWING THE ENORMOUS BUILDING TO SETTLE GENTLY BACK TO THE GROUND, THE WORLD'S MOST DANGEROUS MUTANT STRIDES MAJESTICALLY INSIDE! AND, AS HE APPROACHES THEM, ALL THE OBJECTS THAT HAD BEEN STREWN ABOUT IN HIS FIGHT WITH THE X-MEN MAGNETICALLY RISE BACK INTO PLACE!

THE X-MEN HAD DEFEATED ME IN THE PAST BECAUSE OF THE WEAKNESS OF THOSE WHO *SERVED* ME!

BUT *NOW*, I FIGHT *ALONE!* I NEED NO ALLIES! I AM *MAGNETO*, THE ALL-POWERFUL!

THE DESK OF *PROFESSOR X*-- WITH HIS ACCURSED *CEREBRO MACHINE* BUILT INTO ITS SURFACE!

CEREBRO-- CREATED TO WARN HIM OF THE PRESENCE OF DANGEROUS MUTANTS! HE'LL HAVE NO FURTHER USE FOR *THAT!*

PRRREEE!

WHATEVER DOES NOT SERVE *MAGNETO*, MUST BE *DESTROYED!!* FOR, I AM *SUPREME!!*

FOOM

WAIT! THE SOUND OF A *CAR* STOPPING IN THE DRIVEWAY! I HAVE *VISITORS!*

AS THE NEW *OWNER* OF THIS BUILDING, I MUST GIVE THEM THE PROPER *WELCOME!*

3

THEY SEEM SO INNOCENT-- SO COMPLETELY GUILE-LESS! THEY ARE UNDOUBTEDLY THE PARENTS OF ONE OF THE PROFESSOR'S "STUDENTS"!

THIS GIVES ME AN IDEA! THEY SHALL BE MADE TO SERVE ME!

AND THIS, YOU WILL REMEMBER, WAS WHERE OUR TANTALIZING TALE ENDED LAST ISH!

WHO ARE YOU?

I? I AM POWER!

MEN CALL ME-- MAGNETO!

AND NOW-- COME IN!!

STARTLED AT THE SIGHT OF THE STRANGELY GARBED BEING, MR. AND MRS. WORTHINGTON ALLOW THEM-SELVES TO BE LED INSIDE--

I DON'T KNOW WHAT THIS IS ALL ABOUT, BUT WE WOULD LIKE TO SEE OUR SON, WARREN WORTHINGTON, THE THIRD!

WOULD YOU TELL HIM HIS PARENTS ARE HERE, PLEASE?

FOOLS!! YOU THINK ME SOME FLUNKY WHOM YOU CAN ORDER ABOUT??!

IT IS I WHO GIVE THE ORDERS! AND MY FIRST COMMAND IS-- GAZE INTO MY EYES! NOW-- YOU CANNOT TURN AWAY! YOU ARE HELD BY MAGNETIC ATTRACTION!

YOU ARE SUDDENLY VERY TIRED! THERE IS A GUEST ROOM AT THE HEAD OF THE STAIRS! YOU WILL OCCUPY IT!

HE IS RIGHT, DEAR! I FIND THAT I AM EXHAUSTED!

THERE THEY SHALL REMAIN, UNTIL I AM READY TO SUMMON THEM AGAIN!

IT'S SO KIND OF YOU TO OFFER US YOUR HOSPITALITY, MR. MAGNETO!

BUT, WITH THE ANGEL'S PARENTS SAFELY LOCKED AWAY AND UNDER HIS MAGNETIC CONTROL, THE MEGALOMANIACAL MUTANT REMEMBERS ONE LAST DETAIL--!

MY VICTORY IS STILL NOT COMPLETE! THE ICEMAN IS AS YET UNACCOUNTED FOR!

BAH! WHY SHOULD I WORRY ABOUT HIM? HE IS THE YOUNGEST --AND THE MOST IN-EXPERIENCED OF ALL!

IF I WAS ABLE TO DEFEAT THE OTHER FIVE, WHAT HAVE I TO FEAR FROM THE WEAKEST OF THE LOT?!!

4

AND, EVEN AS MAGNETO SPEAKS, THE YOUNGEST OF THE FABLED **X-MEN** LIES IN HIS HOSPITAL ROOM-- STILL ON THE CRITICAL LIST-- STILL HOVERING DESPERATELY BETWEEN LIFE AND DEATH--

NURSE! WE CAN AFFORD TO WAIT NO LONGER! HE'S REACHED THE **CRITICAL** STAGE!

WE MUST TAKE A CHANCE AND APPLY THE NEW SULFA DRUG! WITHOUT IT, HE MAY NOT LAST OUT THE NIGHT!

QUICKLY, WOMAN! IS THE NEW LASER-INDUCED HYPODERMIC READY??

THEY **NEED** ME! --I MUST **GO** TO THEM-- THEY **NEED** ME--!

THEY'VE WORKED 'ROUND THE CLOCK TO COMPLETE IT IN TIME, DOCTOR! BUT, THEY WANTED ME TO **WARN** YOU-- IT'S NEVER BEEN **TRIED** BEFORE!

THERE'S ALWAYS A **FIRST** TIME, YOUNG LADY! JUST PRAY THAT IT WILL **PENETRATE** HIS INCREDIBLE SKIN!

BZZZZZT

THEY **NEED--** ME--¦UHHH¦=

IT'S **GETTING** THRU! IT **WORKS!** THE LASER **DID** IT!

HE'S **QUIET** NOW! THE **DELIRIUM** HAS STOPPED!

THE NEXT FEW HOURS WILL TELL THE STORY!

IF THE DRUG **WORKS,** HE'LL BE ON THE WAY TO RECOVERY VERY **SOON!** IF NOT-- THERE IS NOTHING MORE-- THAT WE CAN DO!

CLICK!

POOR LAD! I WONDER WHY THE **X-MEN** HAVE FORSAKEN HIM!?

BUT, IF THE DEPARTING PHYSICIAN COULD LOOK INSIDE A **GONDOLA** RISING TOWARDS THE SUBSTRATOSPHERE, HE WOULD FIND THE **ANSWER** TO HIS QUESTION! FOR THE X-MEN, ALAS, ARE **THEMSELVES** FORSAKEN--!

THE **OTHERS** ARE UNCONSCIOUS-- HELPLESS--!

WHILE **I** AM WITHOUT THE POWER OF MY MUTANT BRAIN, DUE TO THIS **MENTAL-WAVE DISTORTER** MAGNETO HAS FASTENED TO MY SCALP!

BUT, EVEN **HE** HAS OVER-LOOKED ONE BASIC ITEM! MY ABILITY TO READ MINDS AND PROJECT MY THOUGHTS IS DUE TO THE **COUNTER EGO** WHICH I POSSESS!

EVEN **NOW,** THAT SAME COUNTER EGO IS PROBING THE DISTORTER-- APPLYING AS MUCH **STRESS AND STRAIN** TO IT AS IS HUMANLY POSSIBLE!

5

THE PAIN IS INCREASING BY THE SECOND! THE PRESSURE IS ALMOST *UNBEARABLE!* BUT I CANNOT STOP NOW. I *DARE* NOT STOP NOW!

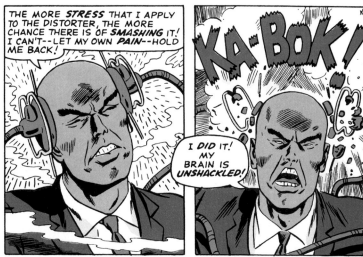

THE MORE *STRESS* THAT I APPLY TO THE DISTORTER, THE MORE CHANCE THERE IS OF *SMASHING* IT! I CAN'T--LET MY OWN *PAIN*--HOLD ME BACK!

KA-BOK!

I *DID* IT! MY BRAIN IS *UNSHACKLED!*

ANGEL AND *CYCLOPS* ARE STILL UNCONSCIOUS --BUT THE *BEAST* AND *MARVEL GIRL* ARE MERELY *DAZED!*

I'LL USE THE POWER OF MY OWN *MIND* TO SNAP HANK AND JEAN OUT OF IT! THEN, WE'LL ATTEND TO THE OTHERS!

HANK! THIS IS PROFESSOR X! *WAKE UP!*

JEAN! YOU ARE *UNINJURED!* YOU *MUST* OPEN YOUR EYES!

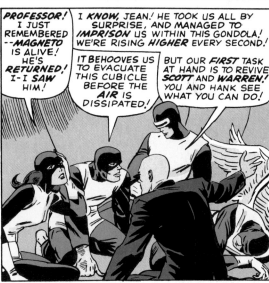

PROFESSOR! I JUST REMEMBERED --*MAGNETO* IS ALIVE! HE'S *RETURNED!* I--I *SAW* HIM!

I *KNOW*, JEAN! HE TOOK US ALL BY SURPRISE, AND MANAGED TO *IMPRISON* US WITHIN THIS GONDOLA! WE'RE RISING *HIGHER* EVERY SECOND!

IT BEHOOVES US TO EVACUATE THIS CUBICLE BEFORE THE *AIR* IS DISSIPATED!

BUT OUR *FIRST* TASK AT HAND IS TO REVIVE *SCOTT* AND *WARREN!* YOU AND HANK SEE WHAT YOU CAN DO!

YOU'RE RIGHT, HANK, BUT *FIVE* HEADS ARE BETTER THAN *ONE!* WE'VE GOT TO UTILIZE *ALL* OUR POWER-- AND THAT MEANS SCOTT AND JEAN, TOO!

FIVE HEADS? ONE IS *MISSING!* WHAT ABOUT *ICEMAN?* DID HE *EVADE* MAGNETO'S TRAP?

HE'S STILL IN THE *HOSPITAL!* DON'T YOU REMEMBER? OH--*SCOTT* IS REVIVING!

EASY, BEASTIE-BOY-- EASY! THE HEAD IS *ATTACHED!* IT'S NOT *REMOVABLE!*

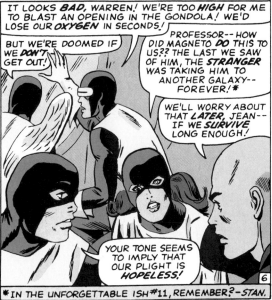

IT LOOKS *BAD*, WARREN! WE'RE TOO *HIGH* FOR ME TO BLAST AN OPENING IN THE GONDOLA! WE'D LOSE OUR *OXYGEN* IN SECONDS!

BUT WE'RE DOOMED IF WE *DON'T* GET OUT!

PROFESSOR-- HOW DID MAGNETO *DO* THIS TO US?? THE LAST WE SAW OF HIM, THE *STRANGER* WAS TAKING HIM TO ANOTHER GALAXY-- FOREVER!*

WE'LL WORRY ABOUT THAT *LATER*, JEAN-- IF WE *SURVIVE* LONG ENOUGH!

YOUR TONE SEEMS TO IMPLY THAT OUR PLIGHT IS *HOPELESS!*

*IN THE UNFORGETTABLE ISH #11, REMEMBER?--STAN.

6

155

MEANWHILE, BACK AT THE SCHOOL WHICH HE HAS TAKEN OVER, THE MIGHTY *MAGNETO* PUTS HIS MOST FANTASTIC PLAN INTO OPERATION! BY MERELY HARNESSING THE LIMITLESS MAGNETIC POWER HE POSSESSES, THE MAD MUTANT GOES TO WORK WITH A VENGEANCE IN THE LABORATORY OF PROFESSOR X--!

NO LONGER WILL I HAVE TO SEARCH FOR NEW MUTANTS!

AT LAST I HAVE THE MEANS TO BUILD A VAST *ARMY* OF THEM-- AN ARMY TO SERVE ONLY *ME!*

AND, IT HAS ALL BEEN MADE POSSIBLE BECAUSE FATE LET THE *PARENTS* OF AN *X-MAN* FALL INTO MY HANDS!

THEY ARE ASLEEP IN THE ROOM NEXT DOOR--LITTLE DREAMING HOW *IMPORTANT* THEY ARE TO MY PLANS!

FOR, KNOWING THAT *THEY* GAVE BIRTH TO A MUTANT, I SHALL SECRETLY ANALYZE THEIR *BODY CELLS,* AND *DUPLICATE* THEM--!

THUS, I'LL BE ABLE TO CREATE *ADDITIONAL* MUTANTS, USING THE SAME CELL PATTERNS! IT SHALL BE SIMPLICITY ITSELF!

WHEN I AM DONE, MY ARMY OF MUTANT SLAVES WILL BE LARGE ENOUGH TO EASILY CONQUER ANY FORCE THAT MAN-KIND CAN THROW AGAINST IT!

I CANNOT FAIL! BY MEANS OF THIS *SELECTOR PANEL,* I CAN EVEN CONTROL THE *TYPE* OF MUTATION I DESIRE! *NOTHING* CAN HALT MY MARCH TOWARDS WORLD DOMINATION *NOW!*

7

AND, AT THAT MOMENT, IN A SMALL GONDOLA, DRIFTING HIGHER AND HIGHER INTO THE LONELY SUBSTRATOSPHERE...!

TRY YOUR **KINETIC POWER**, JEAN! PERHAPS YOU CAN **PUSH** US DOWN AGAIN!

I'LL KEEP WATCH OUT HERE-- TO SEE IF IT **WORKS!**

BUT, WHAT IF I **CAN'T** DO IT, PROFESSOR?

IT'S **GOT** TO WORK, JEAN! THE **OXYGEN** CAN'T LAST MUCH LONGER IN HERE!

THOU KIDS US NOT, SCOTTY!

WHILE **MARVEL GIRL** PREPARES TO FOCUS HER KINETIC POWER AT THE GONDOLA'S FLOOR, I'LL ATTEMPT TO MENTALLY LOCATE **MAGNETO**, AND SEE WHAT HE'S DOING!

SILENCE, PLEASE!

PROFESSOR! WHAT **IS** IT? I-I NEVER SAW YOU LOOK SO **SHOCKED** BEFORE!

IT'S THE **ANGEL'S PARENTS!** MAGNETO HAS **CAPTURED** THEM!

MY **MOM** AND **DAD**!?? NO! IT **CAN'T** BE! NOT **THEM**!

EASY, WARREN! GET A GRIP ON YOURSELF! WE'LL FIND A WAY TO SAVE THEM--AND **OURSELVES**!

BUT HOW? HOW?

ICEMAN IS THE KEY! **BACK AWAY**, ALL OF YOU! I MUST **THINK**! NOW--!

SECONDS LATER, IN THE SILENT HOSPITAL ROOM, A BRISK, COMMANDING **THOUGHT** FILLS THE AIR--!

BOBBY! BOBBY! THIS IS **PROFESSOR X!** CAN YOU **READ** ME? YOU'RE **NEEDED**, SON! YOU'RE **NEEDED**!

I--I READ YOU, SIR--!

I CAN TELL THAT THE SULFA DRUG HAS **HELPED** YOU! BUT YOU'RE STILL **WEAK**! DON'T TRY TO TALK--JUST FOLLOW MY ORDERS....!

LEAVE YOUR BED! SLOWLY--CAREFULLY--

YOU MUST LEAVE **UNNOTICED!** FORM AN **ICE SLIDE** AT THE WINDOW--!

NOW, **EXTEND** THE SLIDE AS YOU GO--OVER THE ROOFTOPS --TOWARDS THE **SCHOOL!** GOOD! **GOOD!**

THEY **NEED** ME! THEY **NEED** ME!

157

I CONTACTED HIM! HE'S ON THE WAY!

BUT, WHAT CAN HE *DO?* HOW CAN HE FIGHT *MAGNETO* -- OR SAVE *US* -- ALL ALONE?

HE MAY BE THE YOUNGEST, BUT HE'S STILL AN *X-MAN!* LET'S WAIT AND *SEE!*

MEANWHILE, HOW IS *JEAN* DOING?

OUR *ASCENT* HAS HALTED! WE'RE NOT GOING ANY HIGHER!

I-I'VE ENOUGH POWER TO STOP US FROM *RISING* --BUT I CAN'T FORCE THE GONDOLA *DOWN!*

HOLD HER *STEADY* THEN! TRY NOT TO *SPEAK* -- WE MUST CONSERVE OUR *OXYGEN!*

I'LL COMMUNICATE WITH YOU *TELEPATHICALLY* NOW! I'M ABOUT TO PROJECT MY THOUGHTS *DOWNWARD* AGAIN, TO PROBE AT THE MIND OF *MAGNETO* HIMSELF!

PERHAPS BY SCANNING HIS MEMORY, I CAN LEARN HOW HE ESCAPED FROM THE *STRANGER!*

THEN, IN AN EFFORT TO RELAX HIS TENSE, WORRIED FELLOW CAPTIVES WHILE *ICEMAN* ENTERS THE FRAY, THE PROFESSOR RELATES THE IMAGES WHICH HE CAN DETECT IN MAGNETO'S MIND...

FOR *MONTHS,* I'VE ENDURED THE HUMILIATION OF BEING THE *STRANGER'S* PRISONER ON THIS DESERTED, FORSAKEN PLANET!

IT'S *NOT DESERTED,* MASTER! *I'M* HERE WITH YOU!

SILENCE, TOAD... YOU SNIVELLING, SPINELESS, FAWNING *FOOL!*

WE'VE BEEN ALLOWED TO ROAM AT WILL, BECAUSE THE ENTIRE *PLANET* IS A PRISON FOR US! BUT IT WON'T *REMAIN* SO MUCH LONGER!

IT'S LIKE AN INTER-GALACTIC *MUSEUM,* WITH RELICS FROM EVERY PART OF THE UNIVERSE!

BUT, IT'S THE GRAVEYARD OF OLD *SPACESHIPS* THAT INTERESTS ME THE *MOST!*

THIS IS WHERE THE *STRANGER* HAS UNDERESTIMATED ME! HE KNOWS THE ATOMIC PILES OF THESE SHIPS ARE OLD AND USELESS...

...USELESS TO ANYONE-- EXCEPT *MAGNETO!*

HEE HEEE! *NOW* I UNDER-STAND, MASTER! WITH THE *STRANGER* GONE TO SURVEY OTHER WORLDS, THIS IS OUR CHANCE TO *ESCAPE!*

PRECISELY! AT THE WAVE OF A HAND, I TRANSFORM THE IRON GATE AROUND THIS SHIP INTO A *LADDER* THAT WILL GRANT ME ACCESS TO THE HATCH ABOVE!

AS FOR THE ATOMIC POWER PLANT, I CAN ACTIVATE IT IN SECONDS BY MEANS OF MY MATCHLESS MAGNETIC POWER!

I *KNEW* IT, MASTER! I *KNEW* WE'D ESCAPE! *NOBODY* CAN IMPRISON *MAGNETO!*

YOU KNEW *WE'D* ESCAPE?? YOU BRAINLESS, INCONSEQUENTIAL *CLOD!* THIS IS WHERE ONE LIKE YOU *BELONGS!*

NO, MASTER --*NO!* YOU CAN'T LEAVE ME BEHIND! *MASTER--!*

COME BACK, MASTER-- *COME BACK--!*

EVEN THE *STRANGER,* BRILLIANT AND OMNIPOTENT AS HE IS, *UNDERESTIMATED* MAGNETO'S GREAT, INCALCULABLE *POWER!*

BUT *NOW,* THERE'S NOT A MOMENT TO LOSE! I MUST CONTACT *ICEMAN* AGAIN-- TO GIVE HIM HIS *FINAL INSTRUCTION!* AND THEN-- THE MOST IMPORTANT PART OF ALL--

I'LL MARSHAL ALL MY REMAINING STRENGTH-- HARNESS ALL MY ENERGY-- FOR THE MOST DIFFICULT *THOUGHT PROJECTION* OF MY LIFE!

AS FOR THE *REST* OF YOU-- DO NOT SPEAK-- DO NOT MOVE-- WE MUST NOT WASTE ONE PRECIOUS IOTA OF OUR REMAINING OXYGEN--!

BUT, PROFESSOR-- HOW CAN WE EXPECT *ICEMAN* TO SUCCEED AGAINST MAGNETO WHEN *WE'VE* ALL FAILED??

BOBBY WILL HAVE ONE ADVANTAGE-- HE *KNOWS* WHO THE ENEMY IS! NOW *SILENCE,* ALL OF YOU!

AND, MINUTES LATER, AN ICY, CRYSTALLINE FIGURE GLIDES NOISELESSLY OVER THE WALL OF *"PROFESSOR XAVIER'S SCHOOL FOR GIFTED YOUNGSTERS"!*

THERE IS NO MORE THAT I CAN *TELL* YOU, ICEMAN! I MUST NOW SEND MY THOUGHTS *ELSEWHERE!* OUR FATE IS IN *YOUR HANDS,* BOBBY DRAKE!

I STILL FEEL KINDA WOOZY-- BUT THIS IS NO TIME TO START *PAMPERING* MYSELF!

THERE'S A LIGHT ON IN THE *LAB!* THAT MUST BE WHERE *MAGNETO* IS!

I DON'T KNOW IF I CAN STALL HIM OR *NOT,* BUT IF I FAIL, IT WON'T BE FOR LACK OF *TRYING!*

FIRST OFF, A LITTLE CLIMB CAN'T BOTHER A FELLA WHO CAN BUILD HIMSELF AN *ICE LADDER!*

I CAN *HEAR* HIM MOVING --UP ABOVE!

MAGNETO! AFTER ALL THIS TIME-- THE VERY *SIGHT* OF HIM STILL FILLS ME WITH DREAD--WITH *AWE!*

THERE'S ALMOST *NO LIMIT* TO HIS *POWER!* WITH HIS STRENGTH HIS BUILT-IN *MAGNETISM*, HE CAN ACCOMPLISH *ANYTHING!*

AND YET, I'VE *GOT* TO OVER-COME HIM-- *SOME-HOW!*

BUT, IN HIS WEAKENED CONDITION, THE VALIANT TEEN-AGER MOMENTARILY LOSES HIS BALANCE, AND TOTTERS!

THE LADDER IS TIPPING BACK! CAN'T STRAIGHTEN IT IN TIME!

BUT--IF I *FALL* FROM THIS HEIGHT --I'LL BE *FINISHED!!*

DESPERATELY, USING EVERY OUNCE OF STAMINA, EVERY BIT OF SKILL HE POSSESSES, *ICEMAN* WHIP A THIN, FROZEN *CABLE* TOWARDS THE ROOFTOP-- SNAGGING THE *EDGE* AT THE FINAL, FATEFUL SECOND--!

CAN'T FAIL NOW! NOT JUST FOR *MYSELF*-- THE *OTHERS* ARE COUNTING ON ME!

I-I *DID* IT!!

CLANNNK!

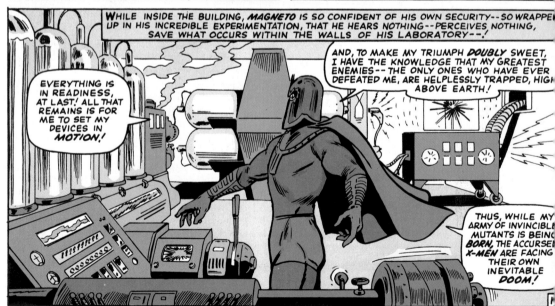

WHILE INSIDE THE BUILDING, *MAGNETO* IS SO CONFIDENT OF HIS OWN SECURITY--SO WRAPPE UP IN HIS INCREDIBLE EXPERIMENTATION, THAT HE HEARS NOTHING--PERCEIVES NOTHING, SAVE WHAT OCCURS WITHIN THE WALLS OF HIS LABORATORY--!

EVERYTHING IS IN READINESS, AT LAST! ALL THAT REMAINS IS FOR ME TO SET MY DEVICES IN *MOTION!*

AND, TO MAKE MY TRIUMPH *DOUBLY* SWEET, I HAVE THE KNOWLEDGE THAT MY GREATEST ENEMIES-- THE ONLY ONES WHO HAVE EVER DEFEATED ME, ARE HELPLESSLY TRAPPED, HIGH ABOVE EARTH!

THUS, WHILE MY ARMY OF INVINCIBL MUTANTS IS BEING *BORN*, THE ACCURSE X-MEN ARE FACING THEIR OWN INEVITABLE *DOOM!*

AND NOW TO BEGIN!

BY MEANS OF MY *SELECTOR PANEL*, I'LL ACTUALLY CONTROL THE *SIZE* AND THE *STRENGTH* OF THE MUTANTS I CREATE!

THEY'LL BE THE *SUPERIOR* OF ANY *HUMAN* ON EARTH!

ONLY THE MATCHLESS POWER OF *MAGNETO* WILL EXCEED THEIR OWN!

SUDDENLY, THE ROOM GROWS DARK, AS GLISTENING WAVES OF IONIC ENERGY CAST A STARTLING GLOW, RIPPLING THE AIR AROUND THE SOFTLY HUMMING MAIN MAGNETIC FIELD--!

IT'S *WORKING!* MORE THAN ANY OTHER FORCE ON EARTH, THE POWER OF *MAGNETISM* IS--*INFALLIBLE!*

AND NOW, MY MUTANT PRODUCTION LINE IS BEGINNING TO TAKE FORM! FROM ORIGINAL CONCEPTION TO FINAL CREATION, THE PROCESS IS *PERFECT!* SUPER-POWERFUL SLAVES OF MAGNETO--EACH LIKE AN *ARMY* UNTO HIMSELF--!!!

I'LL CONTINUE TO PRODUCE THEM-- IN THE TENS--HUNDREDS --THOUSANDS--*MILLIONS*-- UNTIL THEIR NUMBER IS *INCALCULABLE!!* THEY'LL OVER-RUN THE EARTH--CONQUERING ALL--IN THE NAME OF *MAGNETO!!*

BUT, SUDDENLY--

THE PROCESS HAS BEEN *HALTED!!* IT ISN'T *POSSIBLE*-- AND YET--SOME-ONE-- OR SOME-THING--IS *FIGHTING* ME!

AND, IN THE ADJACENT ROOM, A FRANTIC TEEN-AGER, QUICKLY REALIZING THE *SOURCE* OF MAGNETO'S MAD PLAN, HASTILY ERECTS AN *ICE BARRIER* BETWEEN THE TWO SLEEPING VICTIMS AND THE MAD MUTANT'S *BODY CELL SELECTOR*--!!

THIS IS SURE TO BRING *MAGNETO,* BUT IT CAN'T BE HELPED--!

I'VE GOT TO HALT HIS *MUTANT MACHINE*-- ANY WAY I *CAN!*

BUT, ICEMAN'S WORST FEAR IS REALIZED WITHIN SECONDS...

THE SOURCE OF THE INTERFERENCE MUS COME FROM-- AHHH *HIM!!*

THE *FINAL X-MA* --THE *YOUNGEST* THE *WEAKEST* OF THEM ALL! HE *DARES* TO CHALLENGE *ME*.

ICEMAN!! YOUR FOOLHARDY TAMPERING WITH MY MASTER PLAN WILL AVAIL YOU *NOTHING*-- EXCEPT YOUR OWN CERTAIN *DESTRUCTION!*

SLAMM!!

I *KNEW* HE'D COME AFTER ME! BUT AT LEAST I'VE *STOPPED* HIM FOR NOW!

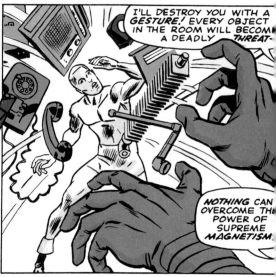

I'LL DESTROY YOU WITH A *GESTURE!* EVERY OBJECT IN THE ROOM WILL BECOM A DEADLY *THREAT*-

NOTHING CAN OVERCOME TH POWER OF *SUPREME MAGNETISM.*

NO? HOW ABOUT A QUICKLY FORMED *ICE SHIELD,* BRAGGART?

SWOOSH!

BUT THIS WON'T HOLD HIM OFF FOR LONG! I'VE GOT TO MOVE *FAST!*

WHILE HE'S *BLINDED* BY HIS OWN FLYING OBJECTS, I'LL USE MY SHIELD AS A *SLED* AND *TAKE OFF!*

WHIZZZ

YOU YOUNG *FOOL!* DO YOU THINK THERE'S ANY PLACE IN THIS BUILDING-- ANY PLACE ON *EARTH*-- WHERE YOU'LL BE SAFE FROM *ME??*

SWOOSH!

BUT, BEFORE MAGNETO CAN MAKE ANOTHER MOVE...

ZIP

AN *ICE TUNNEL!* I'M SLIDING *INTO* IT...

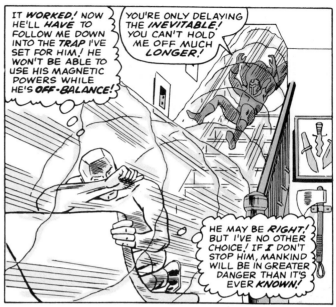

IT *WORKED!* NOW HE'LL *HAVE* TO FOLLOW ME DOWN INTO THE *TRAP* I'VE SET FOR HIM! HE WON'T BE ABLE TO USE HIS MAGNETIC POWERS WHILE HE'S *OFF-BALANCE!*

YOU'RE ONLY DELAYING THE *INEVITABLE!* YOU CAN'T HOLD ME OFF MUCH *LONGER!*

HE MAY BE *RIGHT!* BUT I'VE NO OTHER CHOICE! IF *I* DON'T STOP HIM, MANKIND WILL BE IN GREATER DANGER THAN IT'S EVER *KNOWN!*

I *DID* IT! I GOT HIM INTO THE *IGLOO* I BUILT, OUTSIDE THE SCHOOL!

NOW TO ESCAPE THRU THE OPENING I PREPARED FOR MYSELF!

BUT, THE MIGHTY MUTANT MENACE TAKES IN THE SITUATION AT A GLANCE, AND, BEFORE ICEMAN CAN EFFECT HIS ESCAPE--!

THIS CHARADE HAS GONE ON *LONG ENOUGH!* MY PATIENCE IS *EXHAUSTED!* NOW, YOU SHALL FEEL THE POWER OF *MAGNETO* AS FEW HAVE EVER FELT IT *BEFORE!!*

OH *NO!* HE *SEALED* THE OPENING UP... MAGNETICALLY!

I'M STILL TOO *WEAK* AFTER MY BOUT IN THE HOSPITAL! IT SLOWED ME DOWN! BUT I'VE GOT TO DO SOME-THING--!

14

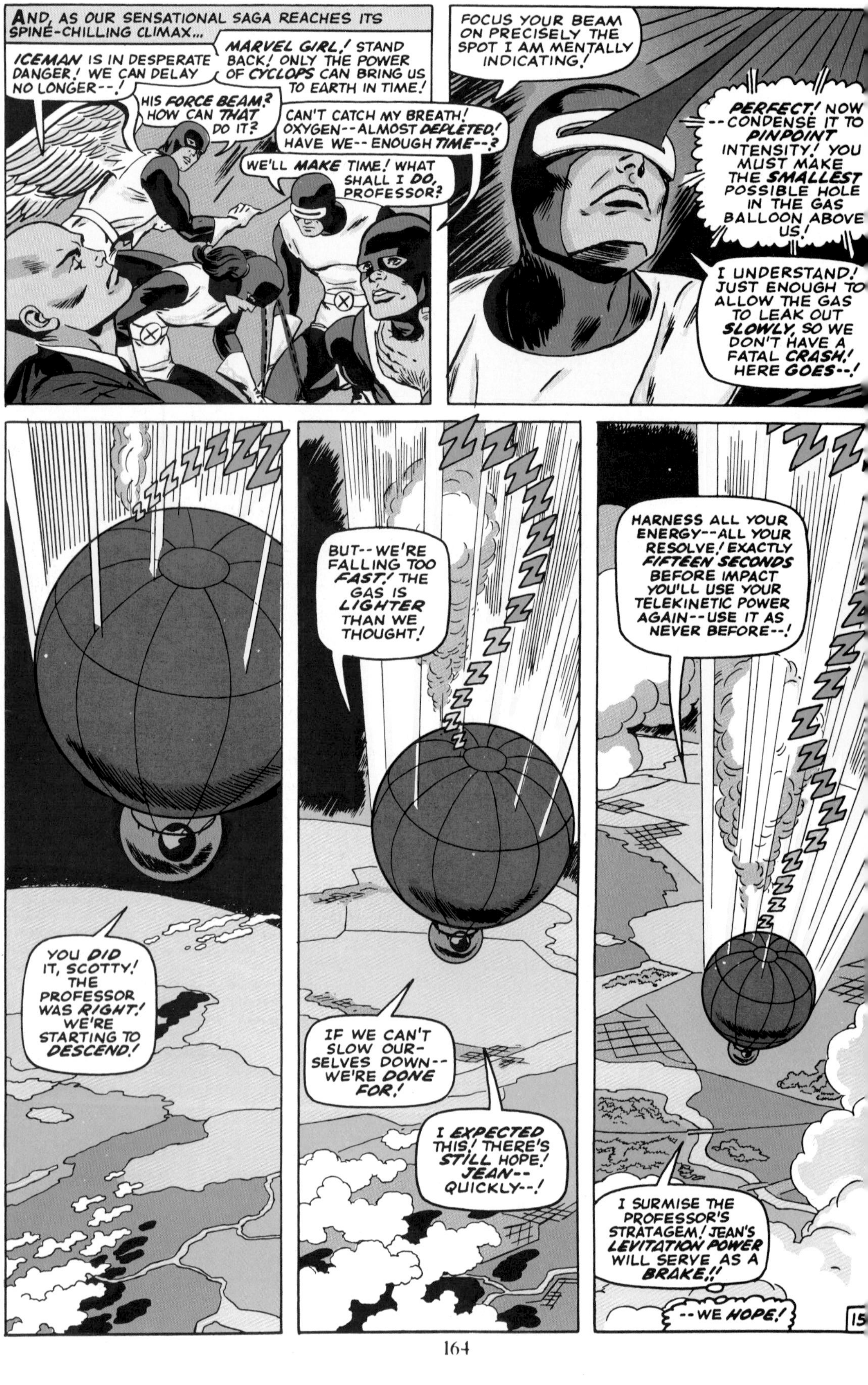
AND, AS OUR SENSATIONAL SAGA REACHES ITS SPINE-CHILLING CLIMAX...
ICEMAN IS IN DESPERATE DANGER! WE CAN DELAY NO LONGER--!
MARVEL GIRL! STAND BACK! ONLY THE POWER OF CYCLOPS CAN BRING US TO EARTH IN TIME!
HIS FORCE BEAM? HOW CAN THAT DO IT?
CAN'T CATCH MY BREATH! OXYGEN--ALMOST DEPLETED! HAVE WE--ENOUGH TIME--?
WE'LL MAKE TIME! WHAT SHALL I DO, PROFESSOR?
FOCUS YOUR BEAM ON PRECISELY THE SPOT I AM MENTALLY INDICATING!
PERFECT! NOW--CONDENSE IT TO PINPOINT INTENSITY! YOU MUST MAKE THE SMALLEST POSSIBLE HOLE IN THE GAS BALLOON ABOVE US!
I UNDERSTAND! JUST ENOUGH TO ALLOW THE GAS TO LEAK OUT SLOWLY, SO WE DON'T HAVE A FATAL CRASH! HERE GOES--!
ZZZZZZZZ
YOU DID IT, SCOTTY! THE PROFESSOR WAS RIGHT! WE'RE STARTING TO DESCEND!
BUT--WE'RE FALLING TOO FAST! THE GAS IS LIGHTER THAN WE THOUGHT!
IF WE CAN'T SLOW OUR-SELVES DOWN--WE'RE DONE FOR!
I EXPECTED THIS! THERE'S STILL HOPE! JEAN--QUICKLY--!
HARNESS ALL YOUR ENERGY--ALL YOUR RESOLVE! EXACTLY FIFTEEN SECONDS BEFORE IMPACT YOU'LL USE YOUR TELEKINETIC POWER AGAIN--USE IT AS NEVER BEFORE--!
I SURMISE THE PROFESSOR'S STRATAGEM! JEAN'S LEVITATION POWER WILL SERVE AS A BRAKE!!
--WE HOPE!
15

AND, A FEW FRANTIC SECONDS LATER...

IT *WORKED!* JEAN BROKE OUR *FALL!!* THE TIMING WAS *PERFECT!*

THE PROFESSOR'S RECORD IS STILL *PERFECT!* HE'S NEVER FAILED US YET!

THUP!

BUT--WE'RE STILL IMPRISONED IN THIS STIFLING *GONDOLA--!*

NOT FOR MUCH *LONGER,* LADY! WE'RE CLOSE ENOUGH TO THE *GROUND* NOW-- I NEEDN'T FEAR USING MY *POWER BEAM--!*

QUICKLY, CYCLOPS! ICEMAN IS *TRAPPED!* HE *NEEDS* US!

HANG ON, BOBBY BOY!! YOU CAN *DO* IT, KID!! *HANG ON!* WE'RE ON THE *WAY!*

ZAP

THERE HE *IS!* STRAIGHT *AHEAD!*

HURRY! YOU MUST CREATE A *DIVERSION!* ANYTHING TO MAKE *MAGNETO* TURN AWAY--!

FAREWELL, ICEMAN! WITHIN SECONDS, MY IRRESISTIBLE MAGNETIC POWER SHALL *MELT* YOU INTO A CRUMPLED, LIFELESS-- *WHA--?? THE X-MEN!!*

BOBBY! SHUT YOUR *EYES!* SHIELD YOUR *FACE!* NOW, KID-- *NOW!*

LET 'IM *HAVE* IT, CYKE! WE'RE ALL *WITH* YOU!

ICEMAN'S *ALIVE!* WE'RE JUST IN *TIME!*

MAGNETO! YOU'VE JUST DELIVERED YOUR *LAST* EPITHET!! YOU'LL NEVER UTTER ANOTHER THREAT *AGAIN!*

I *KNEW* THEY'D COME! I *KNEW* IT! I *KNEW* IT--!

16

165

THE IGLOO *SHATTERS* UNDER THE IMPACT OF CYCLOPS' *POWER RAY!*

KRUNCH!!

BUT *MAGNETO* IS FAR STRONGER THAN ANY FRIGID BARRIER!

I AM WELL AWARE THAT IT WILL BE LONG *MINUTES* BEFORE YOUR POWER BLAST RETURNS TO FULL STRENGTH--AFTER SUCH A *DRAIN* UPON IT!

THUS, IT IS THE POWER OF *MAGNETO* THAT SHALL NOW TURN THE TIDE

X-MEN--PREPARE FOR YOUR FINAL *FATE--!*

EVERYONE PREPARES IN HIS OWN *FASHION,* YOU MAGNETIC MISANTHROPE!

PERSONALLY, THIS IS *MY* WAY OF ANTICIPATING THE INEVITABLE!

AND *THIS--* IS *MINE!!*

SHEER BESTIAL STRENGTH IS *NOTHING* TO THE POWER OF *MAGNETISM!*

BUT, LET *NO MAN* THINK THAT *WITHOUT* HIS POWER, MAGNETO IS NOT *STILL* THE EQUAL OF *ANY!*

WHO

GOOD WORK, BEAST! YOU HELD HIM OFF LONG ENOUGH FOR MY *FORCE BEAM* TO REACH PEAK INTENSITY AGAIN!

BUT YOU SHALL *NOT* USE IT, CYCLOPS!

BACK--ALL OF YOU--OR *ICEMAN DIES!*

NO!!

GET HIM! YOU CAN *DO* IT--IF YOU WORK TOGETHER!! I DON'T MATTER! I'LL GIVE MY LIFE-- *GLADLY--* TO RID THE WORLD-- OF *HIM!!*

17

YOU THINK WE'RE TOO **TIMID** TO TAKE CHANCES? THIS IS THE **SECOND** TIME YOU'VE UNDER-ESTIMATED US--AND IT'LL BE THE **LAST!**

BRAVE WORDS, ICEMAN--BUT UTTERLY **MEANINGLESS!** I WOULD SACRIFICE **ANY-ONE** TO ACHIEVE MY AIMS--BUT YOUR FELLOW X-MEN ARE TOO--**WHA--?** THE **ANGEL!**

THEN, AS THE MANIACAL, MENACING MUTANT MOMENTARILY DUCKS HIS HEAD IN A NATURAL REFLEX ACTION--

IT **WORKED!** I **GOT** HIM!

ICEMAN IS **SAFE!** NOW WE CAN **ATTACK** AT **WILL!**

BAH! YOU'VE DONE **NOTHING** BUT DELAY YOUR ULTIMATE DEFEAT!

NONE OF YOU HAVE THE STRENGTH TO RESIST MY MAGNETIC ONSLAUGHT!! SEE HOW EASILY I HOLD YOU AT BAY WITH A FEW PALTRY GESTURES!

THAT'S **IT!** DUCK **UNDER** MY DEADLY ATTACK--AS I **EXPECTED** YOU TO DO!

NOW, ALL I NEED DO IS UNLEASH A **MAXIMUM MAGNETIC VOLLEY** AT THE GROUND ITSELF, AND YOU'LL **NEVER RISE AGAIN!**

I'VE GOT TO GET MY **POWER BEAM** PAST HIS MAGNETIC FIELD! IF **THAT** DOESN'T WORK--WE'RE **DONE** FOR!

NOW!

IT'S **NO GOOD!** HE WAS **EXPECTING** IT!

HE'S **REPELLING** YOUR BEAM, CYKE! IT'S NOT **STRONG** ENOUGH!

YOU'VE GOT TO **INCREASE** THE INTENSITY --SOMEHOW!

BUT THEN, AN URGENT, COMMANDING **VOICE** RINGS OUT--!

STOP! DON'T FIGHT ANY LONGER!

IT'S THE **PROFESSOR.!!**

HE--HE WANTS US TO **GIVE UP?!!**

NOW **MAGNETO** SEES HIM! HE'S APPROACHING HIM! AND--THE PROFESSOR IS **HELPLESS**--!

18

167

AHH! NOW MY VICTORY SHALL BE COMPLETE!

YOU ARE THE MOST DANGEROUS FOE OF ALL! SO YOU MUST BE MY FIRST VICTIM!

IT'S YOU WHO SHALL BE THE VICTIM, MAGNETO!

LOOK ABOVE YOU--AND SEE YOUR FATE!

IT WON'T WORK! I CAN'T BE TRICKED SO EASILY!

IT'S NO TRICK, MADMAN! I KNEW THERE WAS ONE SURE WAY TO DEFEAT YOU--AND ONLY I COULD ACCOMPLISH IT! SO, WHILE MY VALIANT X-MEN HELD YOU AT BAY--

-- I SENT MY THOUGHTS OUT INTO THE INFINITE --AND FINALLY FOUND THE ONE I SOUGHT--!

YOU WEREN'T LYING! IT-IT'S THE STRANGER! HE'S COMING FOR ME AGAIN! HE MUSTN'T GET ME! HE MUSTN'T!

THEN--THAT'S WHAT THE PROFESSOR MEANT BY THE MOST DIFFICULT THOUGHT PROJECTION OF HIS LIFE!

MAGNETO'S MAGNA-CAR WAS NEARBY! HE'S GONE!

BUT THE STRANGER CHANGED COURSE! HE'S GOING AFTER HIM!

I WONDER IF WE'LL EVER KNOW WHAT HAPPENS TO THEM?

I'D BETTER RECONNOITER AND-- EUREKA.!!

WHAT'S TRANSPIRING IN THERE!

IT'S WARREN'S PARENTS! I PUT A PROTECTIVE ICE SHIELD OVER THEM! ARE THEY OKAY, HANK?

AS FAR AS I CAN TELL!

I'VE GOT TO SEE THEM! IF THEY'VE BEEN HARMED BY MAGNETO--!!!

THAT STEADY HUM! IT'S MAGNETO'S MUTANT-CREATING MACHINE!

NO SWEAT, WARREY! THEY'RE OKAY--HONEST!

WE'VE GOT TO FIND IT--AND SMASH IT!

IT'S DIRECTLY AHEAD, SCOTTY!

··HUMMMMMMM

19

THE FIRST MUTANT HAS BEEN *FORMED!* HE'S ABOUT TO *EMERGE!*

THE *CONTROL LEVER!* GRAB IT!

But, BEFORE A HAND CAN REACH THE FATEFUL LEVER--!

THE *ANDROID MUTANTS*-- THEY'VE *VANISHED* --FADED AWAY TO *NOTHINGNESS!*

FFFFFTTTTTTT!

NATURALLY! WHILE YOU ALL RAN IN *HERE,* YOUR FAITHFUL FROSTBITTEN FRIEND ZIPPED UPSTAIRS TO WHERE WARREY'S PARENTS ARE--!

ALL I DID WAS MOVE *MAGNETO'S MACHINE* AWAY FROM THEM! *THEY* WERE THE CATALYST-- WITHOUT THEM, IT COULDN'T FUNCTION!

HOW ABOUT *THAT!* A LIVING DOLL LIKE *ME*-- BEGINNIN' TO SOUND LIKE THE EVER-LOVIN' *BEAST!*

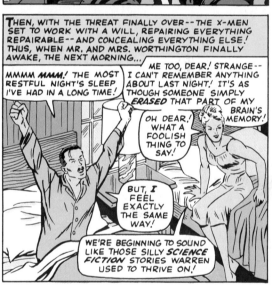

Then, WITH THE THREAT FINALLY OVER-- THE X-MEN SET TO WORK WITH A WILL, REPAIRING EVERYTHING *REPAIRABLE*-- AND CONCEALING EVERYTHING ELSE! THUS, WHEN MR. AND MRS. WORTHINGTON FINALLY AWAKE, THE NEXT MORNING...

MMMM MMM! THE MOST RESTFUL NIGHT'S SLEEP I'VE HAD IN A LONG TIME!

ME TOO, DEAR! STRANGE-- I CAN'T REMEMBER ANYTHING ABOUT LAST NIGHT! IT'S AS THOUGH SOMEONE SIMPLY *ERASED* THAT PART OF MY BRAIN'S MEMORY!

OH DEAR! WHAT A FOOLISH THING TO SAY!

BUT, *I* FEEL EXACTLY THE SAME WAY!

WE'RE BEGINNING TO SOUND LIKE THOSE SILLY *SCIENCE FICTION* STORIES WARREN USED TO THRIVE ON!

And, A SHORT TIME LATER...

MOM! DAD! I COULDN'T WAIT FOR YOU TO WAKE UP! GOSH, IT'S *GOOD* TO SEE YOU!

OH, YOU'VE ALL RETURNED FROM YOUR *FIELD TRIP!* HOW NICE!

I'M *GLAD* YOU SCHEDULE THOSE FIELD TRIPS, PROFESSOR! YOUNG PEOPLE *NEED* A LITTLE EXERCISE NOW AND THEN!

THAT'S WHAT THE *PROFESSOR* ALWAYS TELLS US!

THEY CAN'T GET IN SHAPE FOR THE WORLD OUTSIDE BY BURYING THEMSELVES ONLY IN *BOOKS,* YOU KNOW!

I *TRY* TO KEEP THEM FROM GROWING SOFT AND FLABBY, MISTER WORTHINGTON!

NEXT ISH:

A *NEW* TYPE OF FOE!

A *NEW* TYPE OF STORY!

A *NEW* TYPE OF ACTION!

BUT THE SAME OL' MARVEL MAGIC! 'NUFF SAID!

20

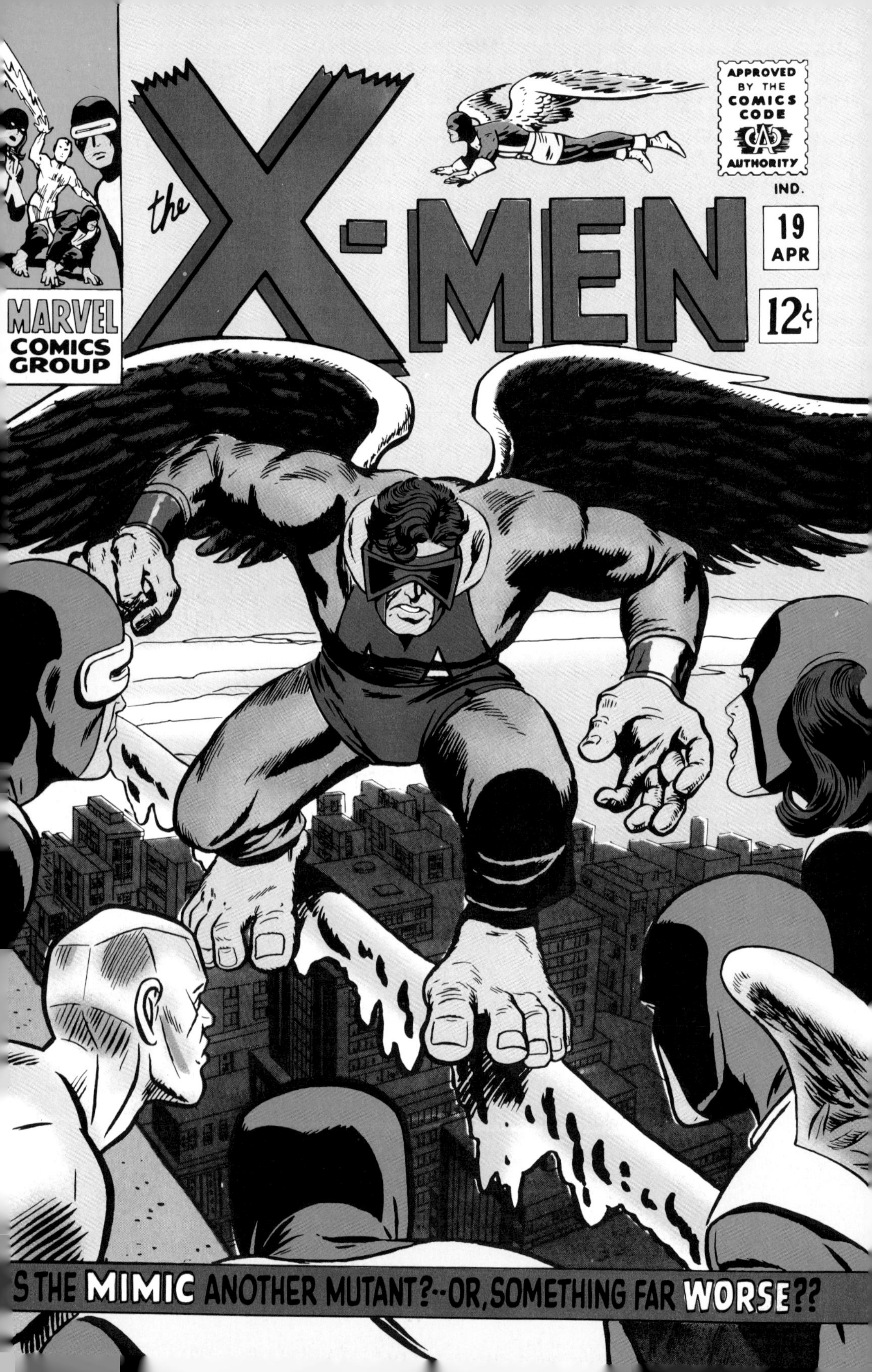
APPROVED BY THE COMICS CODE AUTHORITY
IND.
the X-MEN
19
APR
12¢
MARVEL COMICS GROUP
S THE MIMIC ANOTHER MUTANT?--OR, SOMETHING FAR WORSE??

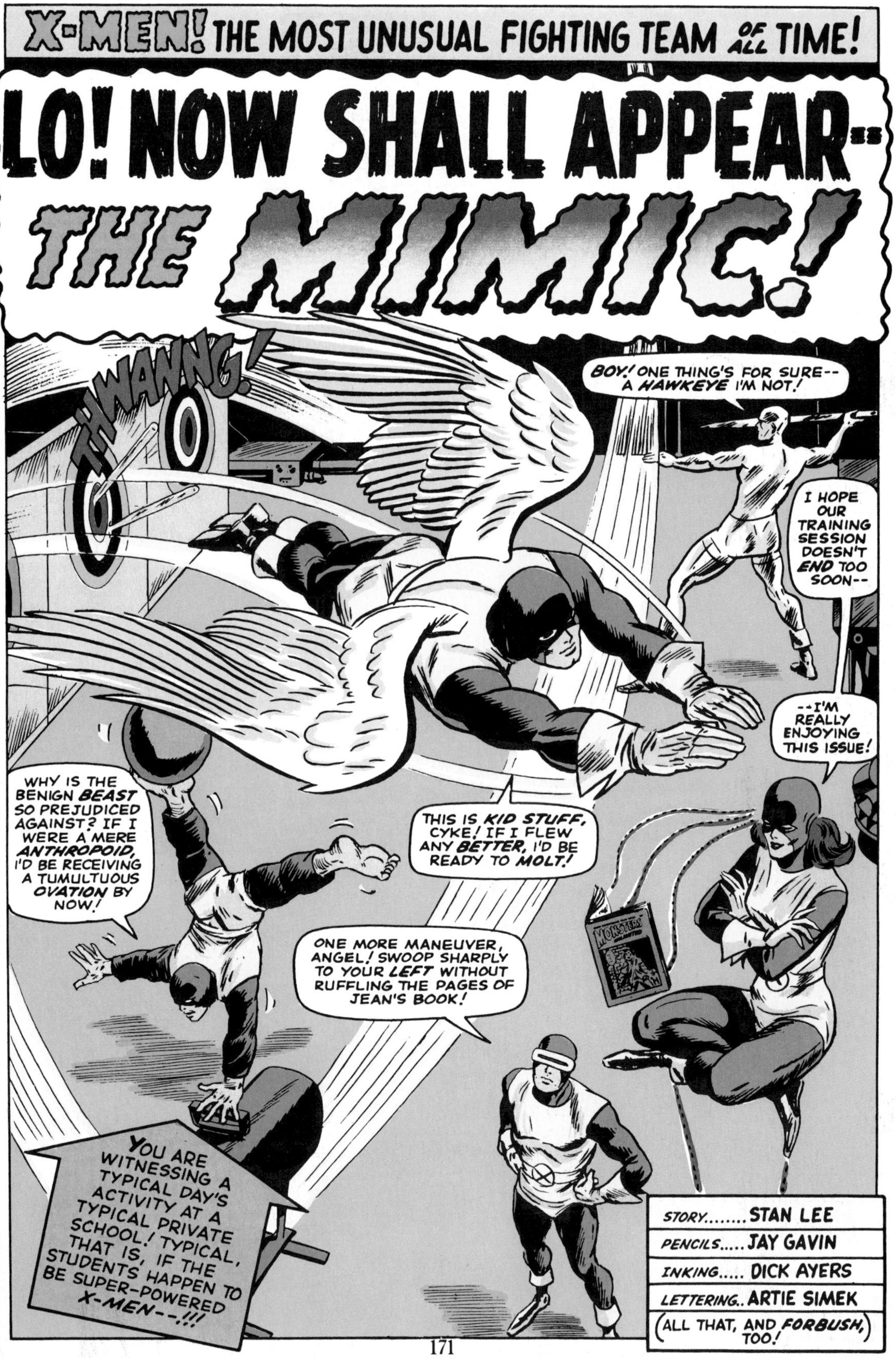
X-MEN! THE MOST UNUSUAL FIGHTING TEAM OF ALL TIME!
LO! NOW SHALL APPEAR-- THE MIMIC!
THWANNG!
BOY! ONE THING'S FOR SURE-- A HAWKEYE I'M NOT!
I HOPE OUR TRAINING SESSION DOESN'T END TOO SOON--
--I'M REALLY ENJOYING THIS ISSUE!
WHY IS THE BENIGN BEAST SO PREJUDICED AGAINST? IF I WERE A MERE ANTHROPOID, I'D BE RECEIVING A TUMULTUOUS OVATION BY NOW!
THIS IS KID STUFF, CYKE! IF I FLEW ANY BETTER, I'D BE READY TO MOLT!
ONE MORE MANEUVER, ANGEL! SWOOP SHARPLY TO YOUR LEFT WITHOUT RUFFLING THE PAGES OF JEAN'S BOOK!
MONSTERS
YOU ARE WITNESSING A TYPICAL DAY'S ACTIVITY AT A TYPICAL PRIVATE SCHOOL! TYPICAL, THAT IS, IF THE STUDENTS HAPPEN TO BE SUPER-POWERED X-MEN--!!!
STORY........ STAN LEE
PENCILS..... JAY GAVIN
INKING..... DICK AYERS
LETTERING.. ARTIE SIMEK
(ALL THAT, AND FORBUSH, TOO!)

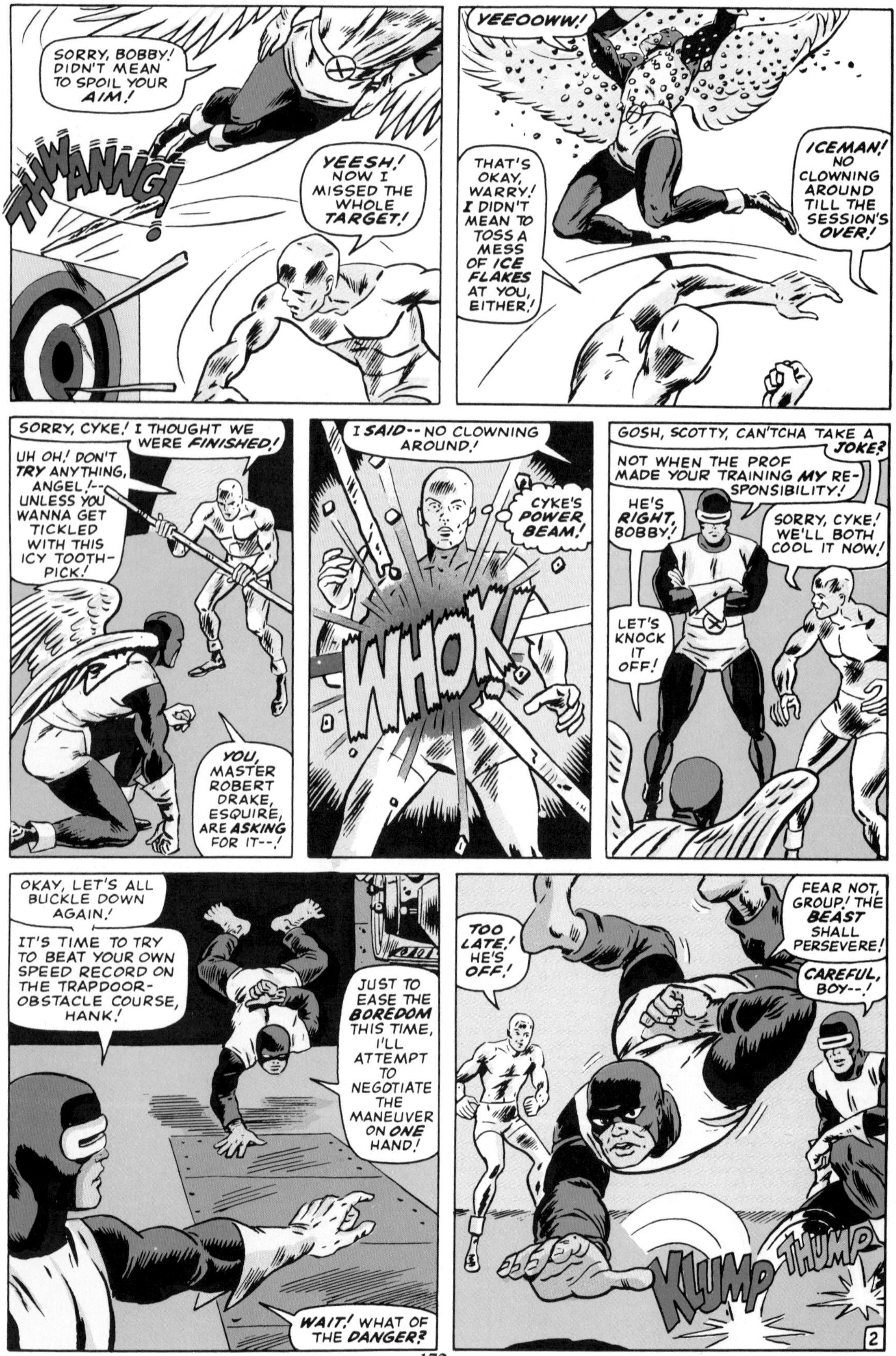
SORRY, BOBBY! DIDN'T MEAN TO SPOIL YOUR AIM!
THWANNG!
YEESH! NOW I MISSED THE WHOLE TARGET!
YEEOOWW!
THAT'S OKAY, WARRY! I DIDN'T MEAN TO TOSS A MESS OF ICE FLAKES AT YOU, EITHER!
ICEMAN! NO CLOWNING AROUND TILL THE SESSION'S OVER!
SORRY, CYKE! I THOUGHT WE WERE FINISHED!
UH OH! DON'T TRY ANYTHING, ANGEL!-- UNLESS YOU WANNA GET TICKLED WITH THIS ICY TOOTH-PICK!
YOU, MASTER ROBERT DRAKE, ESQUIRE, ARE ASKING FOR IT--!
I SAID-- NO CLOWNING AROUND!
CYKE'S POWER BEAM!
WHOK!
GOSH, SCOTTY, CAN'TCHA TAKE A JOKE?
NOT WHEN THE PROF MADE YOUR TRAINING MY RESPONSIBILITY!
HE'S RIGHT, BOBBY!
SORRY, CYKE! WE'LL BOTH COOL IT NOW!
LET'S KNOCK IT OFF!
OKAY, LET'S ALL BUCKLE DOWN AGAIN!
IT'S TIME TO TRY TO BEAT YOUR OWN SPEED RECORD ON THE TRAPDOOR-OBSTACLE COURSE, HANK!
JUST TO EASE THE BOREDOM THIS TIME, I'LL ATTEMPT TO NEGOTIATE THE MANEUVER ON ONE HAND!
WAIT! WHAT OF THE DANGER?
TOO LATE! HE'S OFF!
FEAR NOT, GROUP! THE BEAST SHALL PERSEVERE!
CAREFUL, BOY--!
KLUMP
THUMP
2

SO FAR, SO GOOD!

WHOOP! THE TIMING SEQUENCE HAS BEEN ALTERED! AND IT'S BEEN SPEEDED UP!

MOVE, BEASTIE--LEST YOUR CELEBRATED CRANIUM BE CLOBBERED IN A MOST UNCEREMONIOUS MANNER!

FLAPP!

GOOD WORK, HANK! YOUR TIMING WAS PERFECT!

DON'T TUNE OUT, CYKE! THERE'S MORE TO COME!

THOOMP!

MERELY PROTECTING ONESELF IN A BATTLE IS NOT QUITE ENOUGH!

THE DEFENSE MUST BE TRANSFORMED INTO AN ATTACK! VOILA!

ZZING

SORRY, ANGEL! APPARENTLY I WAS OVER-ZEALOUS!

WHOOOSH

YOU CAN SAY THAT AGAIN!

JEAN! LOOK OUT!

DON'T WORRY--I'LL CHANGE ITS DIRECTION TELEKINETICALLY!

BUT WOULDN'T YOU KNOW IT?? I LOST MY PAGE!

LOOK ALIVE, HANK! THERE ARE MORE OBSTACLES TO COME--!

THUNK!

NO! THAT WILL BE ALL FOR TODAY!

PROFESSOR X!

I'VE BEEN WATCHING YOUR SESSION WITH GREAT INTEREST! YOU'VE DONE SPLENDIDLY, BUT I THINK YOU'VE HAD ENOUGH FOR ONE DAY!

BESIDES, I HAVE AN ANNOUNCEMENT FOR YOU!

CLICK

FIRST, I'LL SHUT OFF ALL THE ELECTRONIC BOOBY-TRAPS!

3

173

AN **ANNOUNCE-MENT!** IS THERE SOME NEW **DANGER** AWAITING US?

NO NEED TO LOOK SO **GRIM**, SCOTT! **ALL** MY ANNOUNCEMENTS AREN'T NECESSARILY HARBINGERS OF TROUBLE!

SINCE YOUR BOUTS WITH THE **SENTINELS** AND WITH **MAGNETO** IN THE PAST FEW MONTHS, I'VE BEEN WAITING FOR YOU TO BECOME FULLY RECOVERED AND TO ATTAIN YOUR FIGHTING **PEAK** AGAIN!

WE'RE AS FIT **NOW** AS WE'LL **EVER** BE, SIR!

I **AGREE**, HENRY--!

AND THAT'S THE REASON I'VE DECIDED IT'S TIME YOU HAD A LITTLE **VACATION!**

WOW! YOU SAID THE **MAGIC WORD!**

MMMM! TIME OFF! A CHANCE TO BUY NEW CLOTHES!

LOOK OUT, GIRLS! HERE I COME!

LEAVE US NOT WASTE A **MINUTE**, BOBBY BOY!

THE PROF IS **RIGHT!** THEY'VE **EARNED** IT!

HANG ON, BEASTIE! WE'LL LEAVE VIA MY **ICE EXPRESS!**

LEAD ON, MACDUFF!

I'LL CONTACT YOU **MENTALLY** WHEN IT'S TIME TO **RETURN!**

IF ANY **ICE** MELTS ON THE FLOOR, **I'M** NOT MOPPING IT UP, BOBBY DRAKE!

IF ONLY I DARED TO ASK JEAN FOR A DATE--! BUT, I HAVEN'T THE **RIGHT--** SO LONG AS MY **POWER BEAM** IS AN EVER-PRESENT DANGER!

HOW ABOUT A DOUBLE-DATE, SCOTTY BOY?

SORRY, WARREN! I'VE **EH:** OTHER PLANS--!

LATER THAT DAY, ON THE STEPS OF THE **PUBLIC LIBRARY**, IN THE CITY, WE FIND...

IT'S LUCKY THAT **ZELDA** DOESN'T WORK AT THE COFFEE HOUSE TODAY, HANK!

I'M RATHER APPRE-HENSIVE, THOUGH-- ABOUT THE **BLIND DATE** SHE PROCURED FOR ME!

CHEER UP, BUDDY! **ANY** GAL IS BETTER THAN **NO** GAL!

THERE ARE TIMES, MY FROSTBITTEN FRIEND, WHEN YOUR WISDOM VERILY BELIES YOUR YEARS!

ZELDA'S NOT HERE **YET!** WE MIGHT AS WELL CASE THE OTHER CHICKS!

IF IT'S ALL THE SAME TO **YOU**, I'LL JUST PERUSE THE TANTALIZ-ING TOMES I SEE BEFORE ME! "OUR FRIENDS, **THE BEASTS**"! A MOST PROPITIOUS TITLE!

IF YOU HAVEN'T **NOTICED**, THESE BOOKS ARE FOR **PRE-SCHOOL AGE** CHILDREN!

MY DEAR YOUNG LADY, AS A FREE CITIZEN IN A FREE SOCIETY, IT BEHOOVES ME TO--

HEY, HANK! I DON'T **GET** IT! HERE COMES ZELDA--AND SHE'S ALL BY HER **LONE-SOME!**

GOSH! I GUESS HER FRIEND COULDN'T **MAKE** IT!

JUST AS WELL! I'M BEGINNING TO FIND THE COMPANY OF FEMALES SOMEWHAT **TRYING!**

WELL! AREN'T **YOU** THE GALLANT ONE!

HI, ZEL! WHERE'S **HANK'S** DATE?

RIGHT HERE, NATCH! THAT'S WHY I WANTED TO MEET IN THE **LIBRARY!** VERA WORKS HERE PART-TIME! I THOUGHT YOU'D ALREADY **MET!**

WADDAYA KNOW! YOU WERE **TALK-ING** TO YOUR DATE!

NOW THEY TELL ME!

DO YOU **ALWAYS** BLUSH THAT WAY, MR. McCOY?

IT'S THE ONLY WAY I KNOW!

HAVE YOU EVER NOTICED HOW *DANGER* CAN APPEAR WHEN YOU LEAST EXPECT IT? FOR EXAMPLE, AS OUR *FAR-OUT FOURSOME* LEAVES THE LIBRARY...

OH *DEAR!* THERE'S *CALVIN RANKIN* COMING TOWARDS US!

IS HE A BOY FRIEND OF YOURS, VERA?

NO! BUT HE'S *BEEN WANTING* TO BE! AND--HE'S SO *HOT-TEMPERED!*

SO! YOU DIDN'T HAVE TIME FOR A DATE WITH *ME* TODAY--BUT HERE YOU ARE ARM-IN-ARM WITH *THAT* CREEP!

BOY! IS MR. *RANKIN* HEADIN' FOR A *FAT LIP!*

IF YOU'RE REFERRING TO *ME*--!

I DON'T HAVE TO ANSWER TO *YOU* FOR ANYTHING, *CALVIN!*

JUST BECAUSE I'VE HELPED YOU LOCATE THE BOOKS YOU WANTED ON *MINE ENGINEERING*, THAT DOESN'T MEAN YOU CAN TELL ME WHOM TO *DATE!*

OH *NO??*

ALL RIGHT, SON! WE ARE NO LONGER *AMUSED!*

NOBODY ASKED *YOU* TO BUTT IN! I'LL KNOCK YOU CLEAR BACK TO *SQUARESVILLE!*

HEY! I NEVER SAW ANY-ONE *DODGE* SO FAST BEFORE!

OBVIOUSLY YOU'RE NOT THE *OBSERVANT* TYPE! AND NOW, IT'S *MY* TURN AT BAT--!

BUT THEN, AS HANK McCOY SWINGS EASILY, NOT WANTING TO TAKE UNFAIR ADVANTAGE OF HIS ENRAGED FOE, HE IS ASTONISHED TO SEE--

HE SIDE-STEPPED *MY* BLOW AS EFFORTLESSLY AS *I* HAD OUT-MANEUVERED *HIM!*

BUT *NOBODY* IS AS AGILE AS THE *BEAST!*

NOBODY *NORMAL*, THAT IS!

HAH! MISSED ME BY A *MILE!*

CALVIN! HANK! STOP IT! THERE'S NO NEED FOR A COMMON *STREET BRAWL!*

IT *CAN'T* BE! HE'S LEAPING AROUND LIKE-- THE *BEAST!*

NOW THAT I KICKED MY *SHOES* OFF, I'LL *REALLY* GO TO TOWN!

IT'S *INCREDIBLE!* HE ACTUALLY POSSESSES *MY* POWERS!

BUT, I DON'T DARE *USE* THEM MYSELF--IT WOULD MEAN REVEALING MY *X-MAN* IDENTITY TO THE GIRLS!

THAK!

THAK!

AND THEN, THE CROWNING HUMILIATION--!

BOK!

SWEET DREAMS, STUPID!

5

THAT'LL TEACH YA TO STAY AWAY FROM MY GIRL!

ALL RIGHT, TOUGH GUY! YOU *HAD* YOUR INNING! NOW IT'S *MY* TURN AT BAT!

HEY! DID YOU GUYS *SEE* WHAT HAPPENED OUT THERE?

YEAH! SOME KINDA *FIGHT!*

THAT WAS NO *ORDINARY* FIGHT, PAL!

HE--HE'S TURNING *ICY!* --*UHHHH*--

THWOP!

NEXT TIME YOU'LL KEEP YOUR NOSE *OUTTA* OTHER GUYS' BUSINESS, RUNT!

THE BIG GUY BEAT UP *ONE* KID--AND NOW HE'S GOIN' AFTER THE *OTHER* ONE! BUT *LOOK* AT 'IM! HE AINT NO *ORDINARY* BRUISER--!

DIDJA SEE THE WAY HE *MOVED*--AND *LEAPED* AROUND? AND NOW HE'S GOT SOME KINDA *ICY POWER!* HE'S GOTTA BE A *MUTANT!*

WE GOTTA SAVE THOSE *KIDS* FROM 'IM!

LET'S GO!

THEY'RE *AFTER* ME! GOTTA *RUN!*

YA ROTTEN *MUTIE!* LEAVE THOSE KIDS ALONE!

ZINNG

WITH THE SPEED OF THOUGHT, THE UNCANNY CALVIN RANKIN CREATES AN *ICE SHIELD* BETWEEN HIMSELF AND HIS ATTACKERS...!

THAT'LL HOLD 'EM OFF TILL I GET AWAY!

WOP! POW! WHAM! KLUNK!

HIS POWERS--THE SAME AS THE *BEAST'S*--AND AS *MINE!* IT *CAN'T BE*--AND YET --IT *IS!* HOW? *HOW?*

BUT, THE WAY THEY'RE *HOUNDING* HIM--JUST LIKE *PROFESSOR X* SAID HUMANS WOULD HOUND *US* IF WE EVER REVEALED OUR-SELVES! I DON'T DARE TIP MY HAND BY GOING *AFTER* HIM!

MADE IT! THEY'LL NEVER GET ME NOW!

GOWAN--YELL AND THREATEN ALL YA WANT TO! I'M BETTER'N *ANY* OF YA!

6

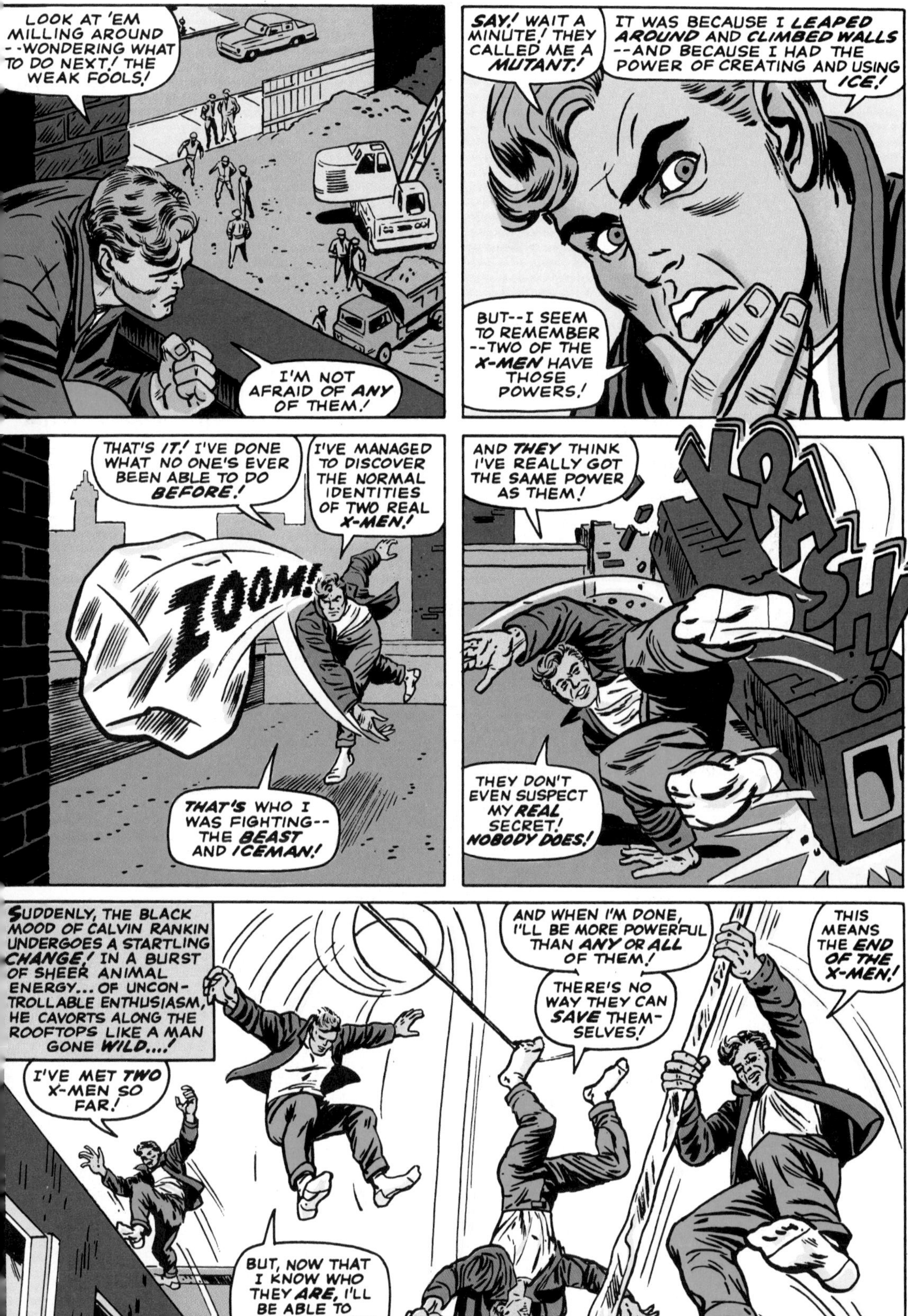
LOOK AT 'EM MILLING AROUND --WONDERING WHAT TO DO NEXT! THE WEAK FOOLS!
I'M NOT AFRAID OF ANY OF THEM!
SAY! WAIT A MINUTE! THEY CALLED ME A MUTANT!
IT WAS BECAUSE I LEAPED AROUND AND CLIMBED WALLS --AND BECAUSE I HAD THE POWER OF CREATING AND USING ICE!
BUT--I SEEM TO REMEMBER --TWO OF THE X-MEN HAVE THOSE POWERS!
THAT'S IT! I'VE DONE WHAT NO ONE'S EVER BEEN ABLE TO DO BEFORE!
I'VE MANAGED TO DISCOVER THE NORMAL IDENTITIES OF TWO REAL X-MEN!
ZOOM!
THAT'S WHO I WAS FIGHTING-- THE BEAST AND ICEMAN!
AND THEY THINK I'VE REALLY GOT THE SAME POWER AS THEM!
KRASH!
THEY DON'T EVEN SUSPECT MY REAL SECRET! NOBODY DOES!
SUDDENLY, THE BLACK MOOD OF CALVIN RANKIN UNDERGOES A STARTLING CHANGE! IN A BURST OF SHEER ANIMAL ENERGY... OF UNCONTROLLABLE ENTHUSIASM, HE CAVORTS ALONG THE ROOFTOPS LIKE A MAN GONE WILD...!
I'VE MET TWO X-MEN SO FAR!
BUT, NOW THAT I KNOW WHO THEY ARE, I'LL BE ABLE TO FIND THE REST OF THEM!
AND WHEN I'M DONE, I'LL BE MORE POWERFUL THAN ANY OR ALL OF THEM!
THERE'S NO WAY THEY CAN SAVE THEMSELVES!
THIS MEANS THE END OF THE X-MEN!
7

THEN, FINALLY--

-:WHEW!:-
I'M BUSHED!
THAT WAS
SOME
WORKOUT! BUT,
I GOT MYSELF
ALL OVER-
HEATED!

I'LL WHIP UP SOME ICE TO COOL OFF WITH!

OH, NO! I CAN'T DO IT!-- ONLY A FEW DROPLETS--AND EVEN THEY'RE MELTING AWAY!

I SHOULD HAVE KNOWN! MY POWERS HAVE VANISHED!

IN MY EXCITEMENT, I FORGOT THAT MY POWERS ONLY LAST FOR A SHORT TIME-- ONLY WHILE I'M NEAR THE ONE I'M MIMICKING!

I'VE GOT TO REGAIN THOSE POWERS--AND MORE! I MUST --TO CARRY OUT MY PLAN!

THUMP!

HOWEVER, BEFORE WE LEARN WHAT CALVIN RANKIN'S STRANGE PLAN IS, LET'S SEE WHERE HE POPS UP NEXT--

-:MMMM!:- WHAT A WONDERFUL SHOPPING TOUR! A PITY A GIRL HAS TO RUN OUT OF MONEY SO SOON!

I'LL JUST STOP FOR A QUICK SNACK BEFORE RETURNING TO THE SCHOOL!

BETTER RUSH IF I WANT A TABLE!

OH! I'M SORRY! I DIDN'T SEE YOU WITH THAT TRAY!

BOK!

HEY! WATCH IT!

NEXT TIME LOOK WHERE YOU'RE GOING! IF YOU WEREN'T A GIRL, I'D PASTE YA ONE!

AND IF I WEREN'T A LADY, I'D TELL YOU WHAT I THINK OF YOUR MANNERS!

I'VE NEVER SEEN SUCH A NASTY-TEMPERED SPECIMEN!

IF I WEREN'T AFRAID OF REVEALING MY IDENTITY, I'D TELEKINETICALLY TOSS HIM INTO A POT OF STEW!

8

NUTTY FEMALES! THEY'RE ALL *ALIKE!*

NOW, WHERE'S THE BLASTED *SUGAR?* OH--ON THE NEXT TABLE! I'LL HAVETA *GET* IT!

WHY COULDN'T IT BE ON *MY* TABLE IN THE *FIRST* PLACE?!!

HOLY SMOKE! IT'S COMIN' RIGHT *TO* ME -- BY *ITSELF!*

ALL I HADDA DO WAS *THINK* ABOUT IT!

THE TOWN MUST BE *CRAWLIN'* WITH *X-MEN!*

MY LUCK'S COME *BACK* AGAIN! THAT CHICK *HASTA* BE MARVEL GIRL--THE ONE WITH THE POWER OF *TELE-KINESIS!*

IF I *FOLLOW* HER, SHE'S SURE TO LEAD ME TO THE *OTHERS!*

THE NEXT DAY--AS THE *X-MEN* CLUE THEIR LEADER IN--

IT'S *TRUE,* PROFESSOR! HE HAD THE SAME, IDENTICAL POWERS AS BOBBY AND I!

IT'S *INCREDIBLE!* YET, HE *CAN'T* BE A MUTANT! MY *CEREBRO* MACHINE REGISTERS *NEGATIVE!*

COULDN'T CEREBRO BE *WRONG,* SIR?

IMPOSSIBLE! IT WILL RESPOND TO THE PRESENCE OF A MUTANT WITHIN A *HUNDRED-MILE* RADIUS OF HERE! BUT, WE MUST LEARN HIS *SECRET!*

THE *DOORBELL!* IT'S *HIM!* I CAN MENTALLY CONFIRM HIS PRESENCE! *ADMIT* HIM, HANK!

R-R-R-RING

AND SO...

HI! I'M SORRY FOR THE WAY I TANGLED WITH YOU YESTERDAY! I CAME TO APOLOGIZE-- AND TO ASK IF I CAN *JOIN* YOU!

THAT DECISION IS THE *PROFESSOR'S* PREROGATIVE! COME IN!

THE *FOOL!* HE THINKS I *MEAN* IT!

HE *KNOWS* WHO WE ARE!

9

179

HE'S TRYING TO *PROBE* MY MIND! BUT NOW I'VE GOT *HIS* MENTAL POWER-- SO I CAN *BLOCK* HIM!

FOR THE *FIRST TIME,* I SENSE A BRAIN AS POWERFUL AS *MINE!* HE COULD BE THE *GREATEST DANGER* WE'VE EVER FACED!

I'D LIKE YOU TO MEET THE *OTHERS...*

CALVIN RANKIN'S MY NAME!

I'M *JEAN GREY!* I BUMPED INTO YOU YESTERDAY, AT THE CAFETERIA! I'M GLAD YOU'RE IN A BETTER MOOD NOW!

IF YOU'RE WONDERING HOW I *GOT* HERE--IT'S 'CAUSE I *FOLLOWED* YOU FROM THAT PLACE.

THEN, AFTER *SCOTT SUMMERS* HAS INTRODUCED HIMSELF...

A *GLOW!* APPEARING BEHIND HIS SMOKED GLASSES! AS THOUGH HIS *EYES* HAVE SUDDENLY BEEN ENDOWED WITH A POWER LIKE *MINE!*

GLAD TO *SEE* YA, SUMMERS! MAYBE A LOT MORE GLAD THAN YOU *SUSPECT!*

WARREN WORTHINGTON III, HUH? PUT IT THERE, PAL!

HE'S GOTTA BE THE *ANGEL!*

I FEEL A *SWELLING* STARTING TO APPEAR ON MY BACK! LIKE *WINGS* GETTING READY TO SPOUT!

HELLO, RANKIN!

WE MUST PLAY ALONG WITH HIM --ACT AS THOUGH WE TRUST HIM-- UNTIL WE LEARN THE EXTENT OF HIS *POWER!*

HI, DRAKE! I REMEMBER *YOU,* ALL RIGHT!

GOOD! I FEEL AS THOUGH I CAN *ICE* UP AGAIN, ANY TIME I WANT TO!

I DIDN'T *LIKE* YOU WHEN WE MET YESTERDAY--

--AND I HAVEN'T CHANGED MY MIND A BIT *TODAY!*

MY SENTIMENTS EXACTLY, RANKIN! I CAN'T FATHOM WHY YOU'RE *HERE,* BUT I SUSPECT YOUR MOTIVES ARE LESS THAN ALTRUISTIC!

THAT'S *ENOUGH,* HANK! REMEMBER--CALVIN RANKIN IS A *GUEST!*

BUT AN *UNINVITED* ONE, SIR!

NONE OF 'EM TRUST ME! BUT SO WHAT? IT'S TOO LATE FOR THEM TO *SAVE* THEMSELVES NOW!

MINUTES LATER...

PROFESSOR! WHY DID YOU PERMIT HIM TO GO UPSTAIRS? HE'LL LEARN ALL ABOUT US!

IT'S TOO LATE FOR SECRECY NOW! HE ALREADY KNOWS WHO WE ARE! AND HE FEELS HE'S POWERFUL ENOUGH TO DEFEAT US ALL!

WHAT ARE WE GONNA DO ABOUT IT?

IT'S TIME TO DON YOUR X-MEN COSTUMES! WHEN HE RETURNS-- IT WILL BE TO CHALLENGE US!

AND, EVEN AS THE PROFESSOR SPEAKS--

I HAD TO GET OFF ALONE HERE FOR A MINUTE-- MY SHOES WERE KILLIN' ME SINCE MY FEET GOT AS BIG AS THE BEAST'S!

IT'S A GOOD THING I PREPARED AN OUTFIT FOR MYSELF TO WEAR--!

IT'LL BE A PLEASURE TO GET THIS TIGHT BINDER OFF--

I CAN'T WAIT TO SEE THE RESULT--!

I KNEW IT! ALL I HADDA DO WAS BE NEAR THE ANGEL!

LOOKS LIKE I'M ALL SET NOW!

THAT MEANS IT'S TIME FOR ME TO TACKLE THE LOT OF 'EM!

OKAY, X-MEN! THERE'S NO NEED FOR ANY MORE PRE-TENDING!

I INTEND TO DEFEAT YOU ALL! AND, REST ASSURED--THE MIMIC HAS THE POWER TO DO IT!

I CAN'T LOSE--BECAUSE I POSSESS ALL OF YOUR OWN ABILITIES-- INCLUDING THE MENTAL POWER OF PROF. X!

PROFESSOR! IT-- IT ISN'T POSSIBLE! HE'S LIKE A COMBINATION OF ALL OF US!

HE DIDN'T HAVE THOSE WINGS WHEN HE FIRST ARRIVED!

NO! OBVIOUSLY HE CAN ONLY "MIMIC" OTHERS WHEN HE DRAWS NEAR TO THEM!

YOU ALL LOOK FEARFUL-- AND I DON'T BLAME YOU!

NOW I'LL PROVE I'M MIGHTIER THAN ALL OF YOU!

THE MIMIC! SOMEONE WITH THE ABILITY TO DUPLICATE OUR OWN SUPER-POWERED FEATS!

HOW CAN WE FIGHT A GUY LIKE THAT??

LOOK OUT! HE'S READY TO ATTACK!

THEN, SUDDENLY, THE *MIMIC* HURTLES UPWARD, PROPELLED BY A LEAP OF BEAST-LIKE AGILITY--

THOOM!

INSTANTLY, A MENTAL COMMAND FROM *PROFESSOR X* RINGS OUT--

ANGEL! I DON'T KNOW WHAT HE'S PLANNING-- BUT *STOP HIM!*

IT'LL BE A *PLEASURE,* SIR!

BUT, BEFORE THE HIGH-FLYING *ANGEL* CAN REACH HIS PREY, THE *MIMIC* REVERSES HIMSELF IN FLIGHT, AND...

HAH! UNLIKE *YOU,* I'VE GOT *MORE* THAN A PAIR OF WINGS!

BAM!

--UNHHHH!-- HE ATTACKED THE WAY THE *BEAST* WOULD-- IF HANK COULD ALSO *FLY!*

WHO'S *NEXT?* I'LL TAKE YOU ONE AT A TIME, OR *ALL* AT ONCE!

JEAN! STOP ANGEL'S FALL-- *TELEKINETICALLY!*

ICEMAN! KEEP THE *MIMIC* AT BAY WITH AN *ICE JAVELIN*-- WHILE I TRY TO SINGE HIS WINGS!

GOTCHA, CYKE!

DID YOU *FORGET*-- I HAVE THE SAME *POWER*--AND THE SAME *DEFENSES* --AS *YOU* DO!

BRAK!

WHAP!

HE MIMICKED MY *POWER BEAM* TO SHATTER THE JAVELIN--AND STOPPED MY *OWN* BEAM WITH AN *ICE SHIELD!*

HE'S *LANDING!* HE THINKS WE'RE *BEATEN!*

STAY BACK, ALL OF YOU! *I'LL* TACKLE HIM --ALONE!

NO! HE'S *TOO* STRONG--TOO *UNPREDICTABLE!* YOU MUST FIGHT AS A *TEAM!*

HAH! THANKS FOR YOUR POWERS, X-MEN--.

NOW I'M GONNA *USE* 'EM TO DEFEAT THE WHOLE *LOT* OF YOU!

12

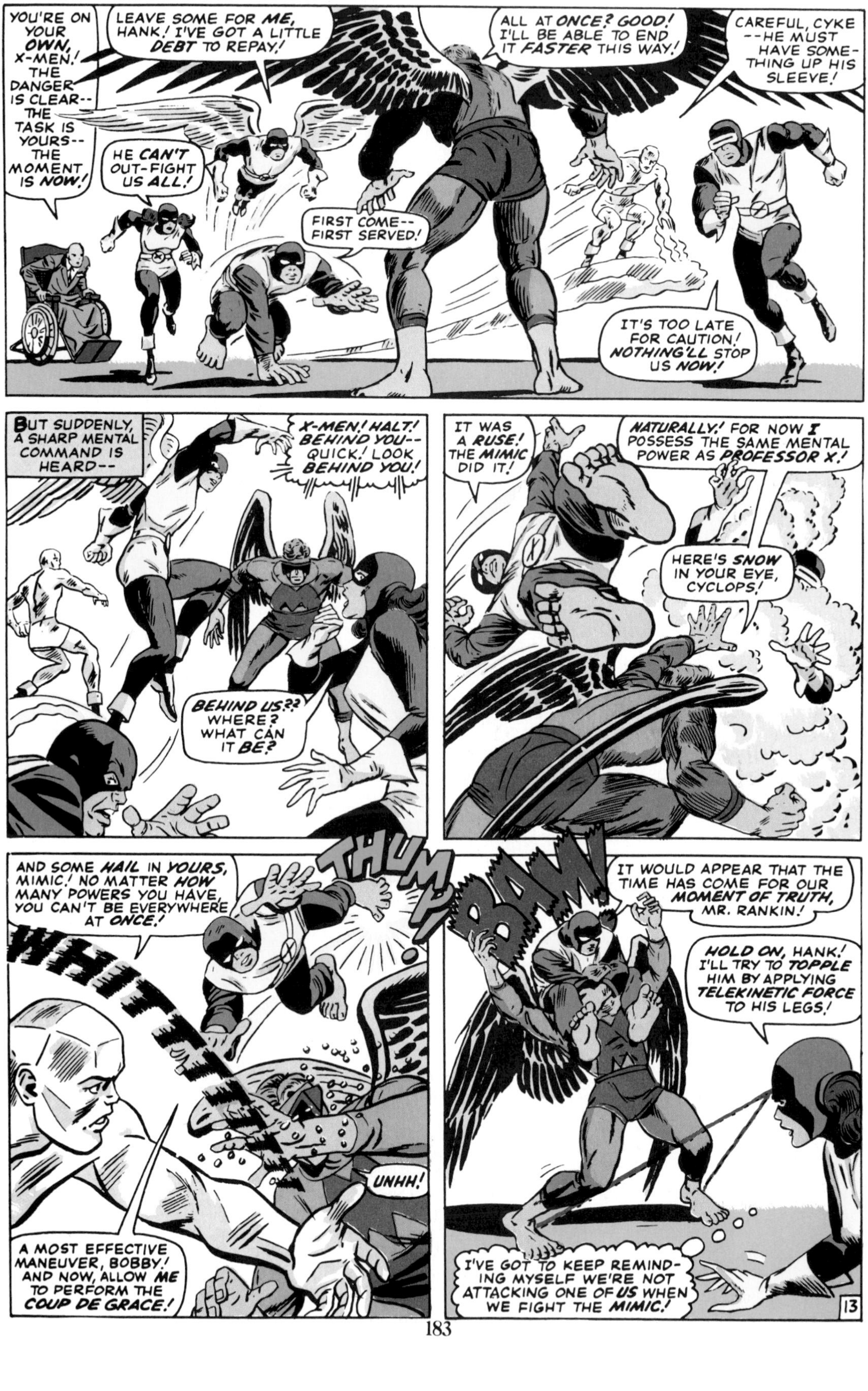

YOU'RE ON YOUR OWN, X-MEN! THE DANGER IS CLEAR-- THE TASK IS YOURS-- THE MOMENT IS NOW!
LEAVE SOME FOR ME, HANK! I'VE GOT A LITTLE DEBT TO REPAY!
HE CAN'T OUT-FIGHT US ALL!
FIRST COME-- FIRST SERVED!
ALL AT ONCE? GOOD! I'LL BE ABLE TO END IT FASTER THIS WAY!
CAREFUL, CYKE --HE MUST HAVE SOME-THING UP HIS SLEEVE!
IT'S TOO LATE FOR CAUTION! NOTHING'LL STOP US NOW!
BUT SUDDENLY, A SHARP MENTAL COMMAND IS HEARD--
X-MEN! HALT! BEHIND YOU-- QUICK! LOOK BEHIND YOU!
BEHIND US?? WHERE? WHAT CAN IT BE?
IT WAS A RUSE! THE MIMIC DID IT!
NATURALLY! FOR NOW I POSSESS THE SAME MENTAL POWER AS PROFESSOR X!
HERE'S SNOW IN YOUR EYE, CYCLOPS!
AND SOME HAIL IN YOURS, MIMIC! NO MATTER HOW MANY POWERS YOU HAVE, YOU CAN'T BE EVERYWHERE AT ONCE!
THUMP!
WHIT
UNHH!
A MOST EFFECTIVE MANEUVER, BOBBY! AND NOW, ALLOW ME TO PERFORM THE COUP DE GRACE!
BAM!
IT WOULD APPEAR THAT THE TIME HAS COME FOR OUR MOMENT OF TRUTH, MR. RANKIN!
HOLD ON, HANK! I'LL TRY TO TOPPLE HIM BY APPLYING TELEKINETIC FORCE TO HIS LEGS!
I'VE GOT TO KEEP REMIND-ING MYSELF WE'RE NOT ATTACKING ONE OF US WHEN WE FIGHT THE MIMIC!
13

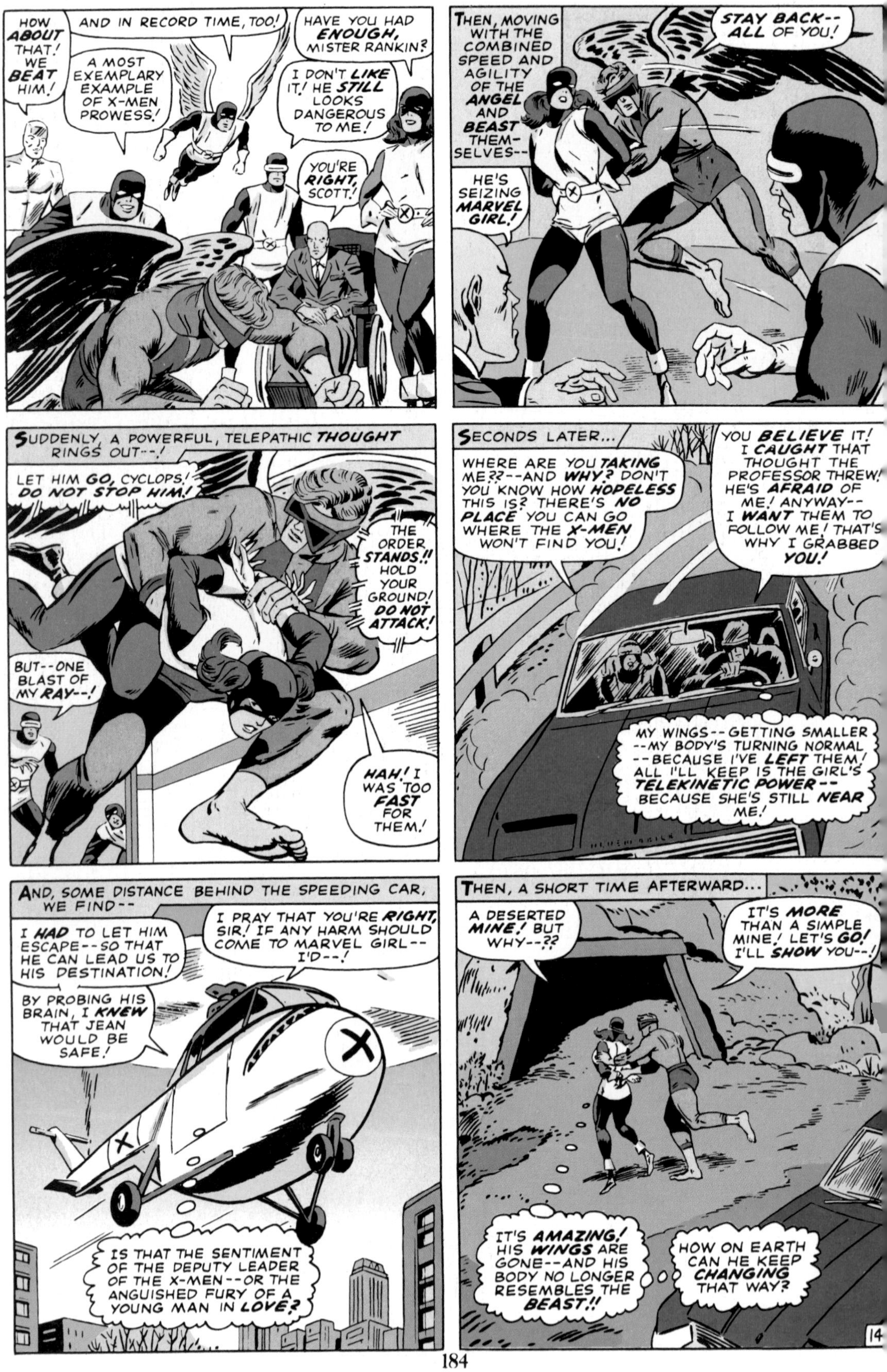
HOW ABOUT THAT! WE BEAT HIM!
AND IN RECORD TIME, TOO!
A MOST EXEMPLARY EXAMPLE OF X-MEN PROWESS!
HAVE YOU HAD ENOUGH, MISTER RANKIN?
I DON'T LIKE IT! HE STILL LOOKS DANGEROUS TO ME!
YOU'RE RIGHT, SCOTT!
THEN, MOVING WITH THE COMBINED SPEED AND AGILITY OF THE ANGEL AND BEAST THEMSELVES--
STAY BACK-- ALL OF YOU!
HE'S SEIZING MARVEL GIRL!
SUDDENLY, A POWERFUL, TELEPATHIC THOUGHT RINGS OUT--!
LET HIM GO, CYCLOPS! DO NOT STOP HIM!
THE ORDER STANDS!! HOLD YOUR GROUND! DO NOT ATTACK!
BUT--ONE BLAST OF MY RAY--!
HAH! I WAS TOO FAST FOR THEM!
SECONDS LATER...
WHERE ARE YOU TAKING ME??--AND WHY? DON'T YOU KNOW HOW HOPELESS THIS IS? THERE'S NO PLACE YOU CAN GO WHERE THE X-MEN WON'T FIND YOU!
YOU BELIEVE IT! I CAUGHT THAT THOUGHT THE PROFESSOR THREW! HE'S AFRAID OF ME! ANYWAY-- I WANT THEM TO FOLLOW ME! THAT'S WHY I GRABBED YOU!
MY WINGS--GETTING SMALLER --MY BODY'S TURNING NORMAL --BECAUSE I'VE LEFT THEM! ALL I'LL KEEP IS THE GIRL'S TELEKINETIC POWER-- BECAUSE SHE'S STILL NEAR ME!
AND, SOME DISTANCE BEHIND THE SPEEDING CAR, WE FIND--
I HAD TO LET HIM ESCAPE--SO THAT HE CAN LEAD US TO HIS DESTINATION!
I PRAY THAT YOU'RE RIGHT, SIR! IF ANY HARM SHOULD COME TO MARVEL GIRL-- I'D--!
BY PROBING HIS BRAIN, I KNEW THAT JEAN WOULD BE SAFE!
IS THAT THE SENTIMENT OF THE DEPUTY LEADER OF THE X-MEN--OR THE ANGUISHED FURY OF A YOUNG MAN IN LOVE?
THEN, A SHORT TIME AFTERWARD...
A DESERTED MINE! BUT WHY--??
IT'S MORE THAN A SIMPLE MINE! LET'S GO! I'LL SHOW YOU--!
IT'S AMAZING! HIS WINGS ARE GONE--AND HIS BODY NO LONGER RESEMBLES THE BEAST!!
HOW ON EARTH CAN HE KEEP CHANGING THAT WAY?
14

SOON, DEEP WITHIN THE MINE, JEAN GREY IS ASTONISHED TO FIND--

LIVING QUARTERS!! IT'S A PLACE FOR SOMEONE TO *LIVE* -- IN COMFORT -- AND IN *SECRET!* BUT FOR WHAT *PURPOSE??*

WHILE WE WAIT FOR THE *X-MEN* TO FIND ME, I'LL TELL YOU A LITTLE *STORY* --!

THEN, PERHAPS YOU'LL FINALLY UNDER- STAND THE SECRET OF THE *MIMIC!*

"IT'S THE STORY OF A YOUNG BOY WHOSE FATHER WAS A *SCIENTIST,* WORKING ON A STRANGE, DANGEROUS EXPERIMENT,... MORE DANGEROUS THAN ANY OF THEM *DREAMED!*

DAD--?

I'VE TOLD YOU TO *STAY OUT* WHEN I'M WORKING!! THIS ROOM IS *OFF LIMITS* TO YOU!

"BUT, THE BOY WAS YOUNG -- FOOLISH -- AND *DEFIANT!* ONE DAY, WHEN HIS FATHER WAS OUT ON AN ERRAND, HE TRIED TO SATISFY HIS YOUTHFUL CURIOSITY -- AND THEN--!

OH! I KNOCKED OVER A *BEAKER* --!

GAS!! FILLING THE AIR ALL AROUND ME!! CAN'T STOP BREATHING IT IN--!

SSSSSS

"COUGHING, GASPING, HIS EYES SMARTING, HE CARE- FULLY CLEANED UP THE LAB AND THEN LEFT! BUT, IN THE MONTHS AND YEARS THAT FOLLOWED, STRANGE THINGS BEGAN TO HAPPEN, MORE AND MORE FREQUENTLY--!

I DON'T *GET* IT! BLACKIE'S THE SCHOOL BOXING CHAMP -- AND I'M A *DUD!* BUT I'M FIGHTING AS GOOD AS HE IS!!

LATELY, WHENEVER I'M *NEAR* ANYONE, I SEEM ABLE TO DO WHATEVER *THEY* CAN DO!

POW!

"IT WAS THAT WAY ALL THRU SCHOOL! HE WAS AS GOOD AS THE *BEST* ATHLETES -- SO LONG AS HE WAS *NEAR* TO THEM! THERE WAS *NOTHING* HE DIDN'T EXCEL AT! AND, AS HIS ABILITY GREW, SO DID HIS *ARROGANCE* -- AND HIS *CONCEIT!*

THAT'S YOUR *FIFTH HOMER* -- IN FIVE TIMES AT BAT!!

NATURALLY! IT'S NOT *HARD* WHEN YOU'RE PLAYING AGAINST A BUNCH OF *NO-TALENT MISFITS!!*

THWAK!

"EVEN WHEN HE WAS IN *CLASS,* HE ALWAYS SEEMED TO KNOW AS MUCH AS THE *TEACHER!* EVENTUALLY, THE *DISLIKE* WHICH THE OTHER STUDENTS HAD FOR HIM TURNED TO *DISTRUST* -- THEN TO ACTUAL *SUSPICION* -- AND *FEAR*--!

I TELL YOU, THERE'S SOME- THING *SCARY* ABOUT THE WAY HE'S GOOD AT *EVERYTHING!*

YOU'RE *RIGHT!* IT REMINDS YOU OF A *ROBOT* OR SOME- THING!! HE'S LIKE A *MACHINE!*

I NEVER *HEARD* OF ANY- ONE BEING TOPS AT *EVERY* SPORT -- AND GETTING STRAIGHT A'S IN EVERY SUB- JECT -- WITHOUT EVEN *TRYING!*

I SHOULD WORRY WHAT *THEY* THINK OF ME! I'M BETTER'N *ALL* OF THEM! THEY'RE JUST *JEALOUS* OF ME, THAT'S WHAT!

15

"BUT, THE BOY'S *FATHER* FINALLY BECAME AWARE OF WHAT HAD HAPPENED! HE KNEW MEN WOULD SOME DAY RISE *AGAINST* HIS SON--AND SO HE TOOK HIM TO A LONELY CAVE..."

WE WILL LIVE HERE UNTIL I'VE FOUND A WAY TO *HELP* YOU!

IF ONLY MY POWERS WOULD BE *PERMANENT*--AND NOT LEAVE ME WHEN I'M NO LONGER NEAR THE ONE I'M MIMICKING!

"FOR MONTHS THEY HID IN THE CAVE WHILE THE SCIENTIST BUILT A *MACHINE*--ONE WHICH WOULD MAKE THE BOY'S POWER LAST *FOREVER!* BUT THE MACHINE DRAINED SO MUCH *CURRENT,* THAT IT SHORT-CIRCUITED EVERY FUSE IN THE COUNTY--!"

LISTEN! THE *WARNING SIGNAL!* SOMEONE IS *COMING!*

ACCORDING TO THE *RADIO,* PEOPLE ARE *SUSPICIOUS* OF WHAT'S BEEN HAPPENING HERE! THEY KNOW THERE ARE POWERFUL *MACHINES* OPERATING, BUT DON'T KNOW *WHY!*

BEEP...BEEP BEEP...BEEP...

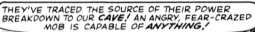

THEY'VE TRACED THE SOURCE OF THEIR POWER BREAKDOWN TO OUR *CAVE!* AN ANGRY, FEAR-CRAZED MOB IS CAPABLE OF *ANYTHING!*

WE'VE GOT TO *PROTECT* OURSELVES! I'LL DETONATE THE MAIN EXPLOSIVE CACHE, SEALING OFF THE MINE ENTRANCE!

IF ONLY THEY'D WAITED A LITTLE *LONGER*--IT WOULDN'T HAVE *MATTERED!*

"BUT, IN SETTING OFF THE EXPLOSIVES, THE SCIENTIST UNDERESTIMATED THE FORCE OF THE BLAST, AND--HE WAS UNABLE TO ESCAPE IN TIME--!"

WHOOOM!

"HOURS LATER, AFTER THE MOB HAD FINALLY DISPERSED, THE SON DUG HIMSELF TO FREEDOM-- HIS HEART POUNDING WITH AN UNQUENCHABLE DESIRE FOR *VENGEANCE*--!"

I'LL MAKE THEM *PAY* FOR WHAT HAPPENED TO YOU, DAD! EVEN THOUGH YOUR *MACHINE* WAS BURIED UNDER ALL THE DEBRIS, I'LL FIND *SOME* WAY TO REACH IT AGAIN--!

--AND WHEN I *DO,* I'LL BECOME THE MIGHTIEST MAN IN THE *WORLD!* I'LL GAIN THE POWER OF EVERYONE I MEET--AND I'LL *KEEP* ALL THAT POWER--*FOREVER!*

THEN-- *YOU* WERE THAT BOY! AND YOU *WANT* THE X-MEN TO FOLLOW YOU HERE, SO YOU CAN TRICK *THEM* INTO REACHING THE MACHINE FOR YOU!

RIGHT! AND *YOU'RE* THE BAIT THAT WILL *BRING* THEM TO ME!

AHHH! MY *WINGS* ARE BEGINNING TO SPOUT AGAIN! THAT MEANS THEY'RE GETTING *CLOSER!*

IT'S TIME TO *GREET* THEM NOW--AS I OPEN THE DOOR *TELEKINETICALLY,* WITH THE POWER I'VE MIMICKED FROM *YOU!*

16

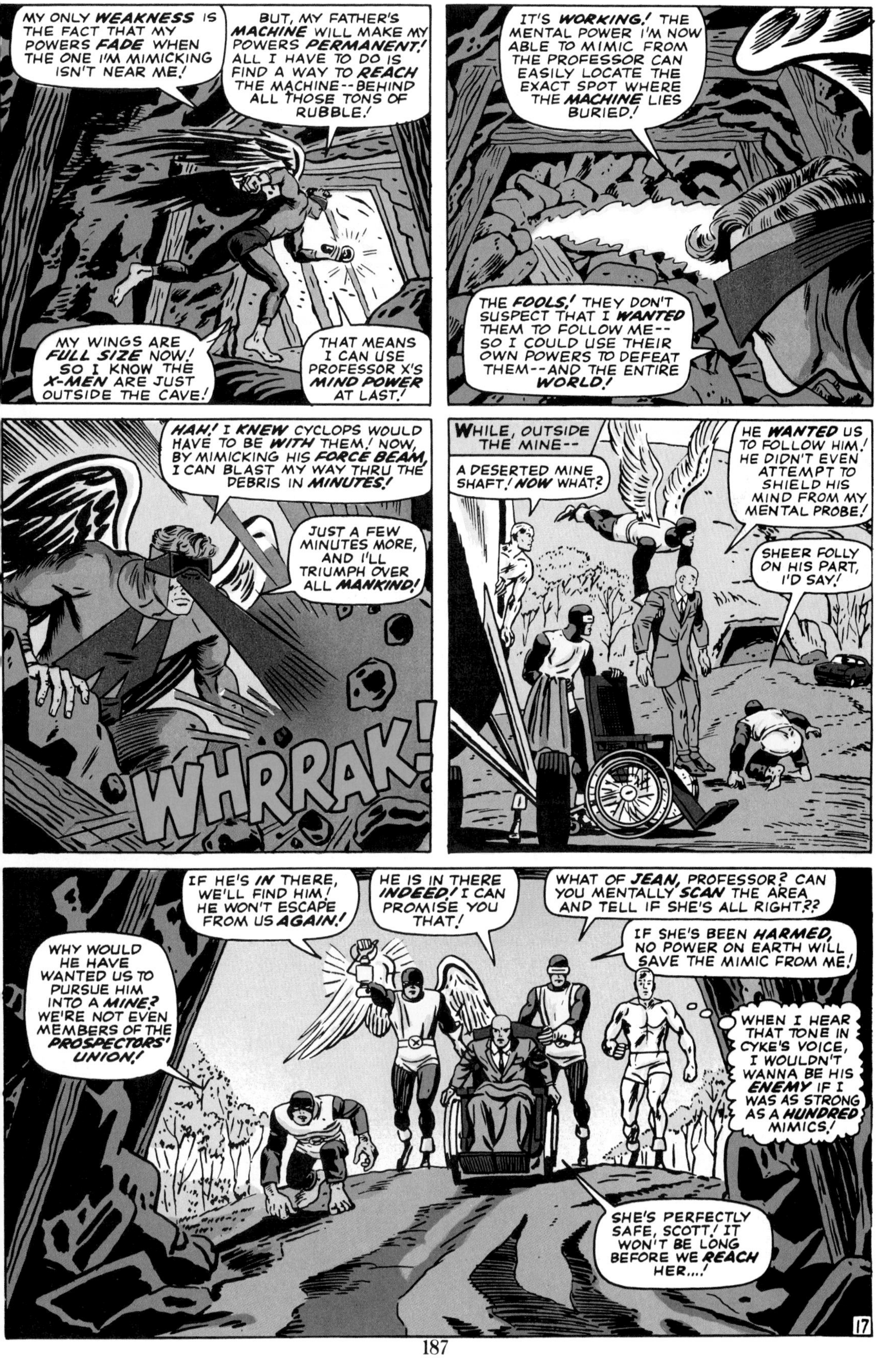
MY ONLY WEAKNESS IS THE FACT THAT MY POWERS FADE WHEN THE ONE I'M MIMICKING ISN'T NEAR ME!
BUT, MY FATHER'S MACHINE WILL MAKE MY POWERS PERMANENT! ALL I HAVE TO DO IS FIND A WAY TO REACH THE MACHINE--BEHIND ALL THOSE TONS OF RUBBLE!
MY WINGS ARE FULL SIZE NOW! SO I KNOW THE X-MEN ARE JUST OUTSIDE THE CAVE!
THAT MEANS I CAN USE PROFESSOR X'S MIND POWER AT LAST!
IT'S WORKING! THE MENTAL POWER I'M NOW ABLE TO MIMIC FROM THE PROFESSOR CAN EASILY LOCATE THE EXACT SPOT WHERE THE MACHINE LIES BURIED!
THE FOOLS! THEY DON'T SUSPECT THAT I WANTED THEM TO FOLLOW ME--SO I COULD USE THEIR OWN POWERS TO DEFEAT THEM--AND THE ENTIRE WORLD!
HAH! I KNEW CYCLOPS WOULD HAVE TO BE WITH THEM! NOW, BY MIMICKING HIS FORCE BEAM, I CAN BLAST MY WAY THRU THE DEBRIS IN MINUTES!
JUST A FEW MINUTES MORE, AND I'LL TRIUMPH OVER ALL MANKIND!
WHRRAK!
WHILE, OUTSIDE THE MINE--
A DESERTED MINE SHAFT! NOW WHAT?
HE WANTED US TO FOLLOW HIM! HE DIDN'T EVEN ATTEMPT TO SHIELD HIS MIND FROM MY MENTAL PROBE!
SHEER FOLLY ON HIS PART, I'D SAY!
WHY WOULD HE HAVE WANTED US TO PURSUE HIM INTO A MINE? WE'RE NOT EVEN MEMBERS OF THE PROSPECTORS' UNION!
IF HE'S IN THERE, WE'LL FIND HIM! HE WON'T ESCAPE FROM US AGAIN!
HE IS IN THERE INDEED! I CAN PROMISE YOU THAT!
WHAT OF JEAN, PROFESSOR? CAN YOU MENTALLY SCAN THE AREA AND TELL IF SHE'S ALL RIGHT??
IF SHE'S BEEN HARMED, NO POWER ON EARTH WILL SAVE THE MIMIC FROM ME!
WHEN I HEAR THAT TONE IN CYKE'S VOICE, I WOULDN'T WANNA BE HIS ENEMY IF I WAS AS STRONG AS A HUNDRED MIMICS!
SHE'S PERFECTLY SAFE, SCOTT! IT WON'T BE LONG BEFORE WE REACH HER...!
17

SHE'S DIRECTLY BEHIND THAT IRON DOOR! USE YOUR POWER BEAM'S *LOWEST* INTENSITY, CYCLOPS--SO IT DOESN'T PENETRATE TOO FAR!

I UNDERSTAND, SIR! JUST ENOUGH FORCE TO SHATTER THE *LOCK!*

PFFT!

YOU *DID* IT!

SECONDS LATER, UPON REACHING THE CAPTIVE GIRL, SCOTT SUMMERS SILENTLY TAKES HIS PLACE BEHIND THE PROFESSOR'S WHEELCHAIR ONCE AGAIN...

I KNEW YOU'D REACH ME! I *KNEW* IT!

STRANGE-- SCOTT DOESN'T SEEM TO WANT MARVEL GIRL TO REALIZE HOW DESPERATELY *CONCERNED* ABOUT HER HE WAS!

BUT-- WHERE'S THE *MIMIC?*

AND, EVEN AS HANK McCOY ANXIOUSLY ASKS THE QUESTION WHICH IS UPPERMOST IN ALL THEIR MINDS...

I'M ALMOST *THERE!* JUST ONE MORE BLAST--!

BRAK!

THAT *DID* IT! I CAN SEE THE *OPENING* JUST AHEAD--!

THE *MACHINE!* I *SEE* IT! JUST AS DAD LEFT IT!

THE EXPLOSION DIDN'T DO ANY DAMAGE TO THE INNER CAVE!

THAT MEANS I'VE WON! I'VE *WON!*

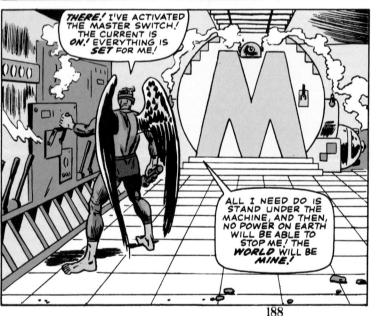

THERE! I'VE ACTIVATED THE MASTER SWITCH! THE CURRENT IS *ON!* EVERYTHING IS *SET* FOR ME!

ALL I NEED DO IS STAND UNDER THE MACHINE, AND THEN, NO POWER ON EARTH WILL BE ABLE TO STOP ME! THE *WORLD* WILL BE *MINE!*

ZAPT!

WHA--??!

HOLD IT, MIMIC!

18

THE X-MEN! YOU FOOLS-- YOU'RE TOO LATE!

WE'LL SEE ABOUT THAT!

GET HIM!

LOOK OUT! HE'S CREATING AN ICE WALL!

HOW CAN YOU HOPE TO BATTLE SOMEONE WHO CAN HURL YOUR VERY OWN WEAPONS AGAINST YOU?

THAT, MY FRIEND, IS PAINFULLY APPARENT!

NOW, WATCH HOW I EASILY CAUSE THIS ICY BARRIER TO TOPPLE--

--AND SEIZE THE ADVANTAGE BY FLYING OVER ALL YOUR HEADS!

WHUMP!

HOLD IT! NO ONE MOVE! HE'S GOT THE PROFESSOR!

STAY BACK-- ALL OF YOU! I'LL HANDLE THIS MY- SELF!

YOU'RE WHISTLING IN THE DARK, MISTER-- AND YOU KNOW IT!

BUT WE MUST ACT! IF HE USES THAT MACHINE--!

THERE'S NOTHING THEY CAN DO-- WHILE I HAVE YOU!

DON'T ATTACK! HE CAN'T WIN! YOU MUST TRUST ME!

HAH! AT THE LAST MINUTE, YOU REVEALED YOURSELF FOR THE COWARD YOU ARE, PROFESSOR! YOU HELD THEM OFF--FEARING FOR YOUR OWN SAFETY!

AND SO, I HAVE TRIUMPHED! MY POWERS WILL NOW BE PERMANENT!

THERE IS NOTHING I CANNOT DO! ALL MANKIND WILL BE AT MY FEET! MY FATHER WILL NOT HAVE DIED IN VAIN!

BUT THEN, A STARTLING, UNEXPECTED TURN OF EVENTS OCCURS--

THE MIMIC COLLAPSED! I'LL GRAB THE PROFESSOR!

BEAST! QUICKLY! TAKE THE MIMIC! THIS ENTIRE PLACE WILL BLOW UP WITHIN MINUTES! WE'VE GOT TO ESCAPE!

BUT WHY? HOW?

SOME TIME TO PLAY 20 QUESTIONS!

19

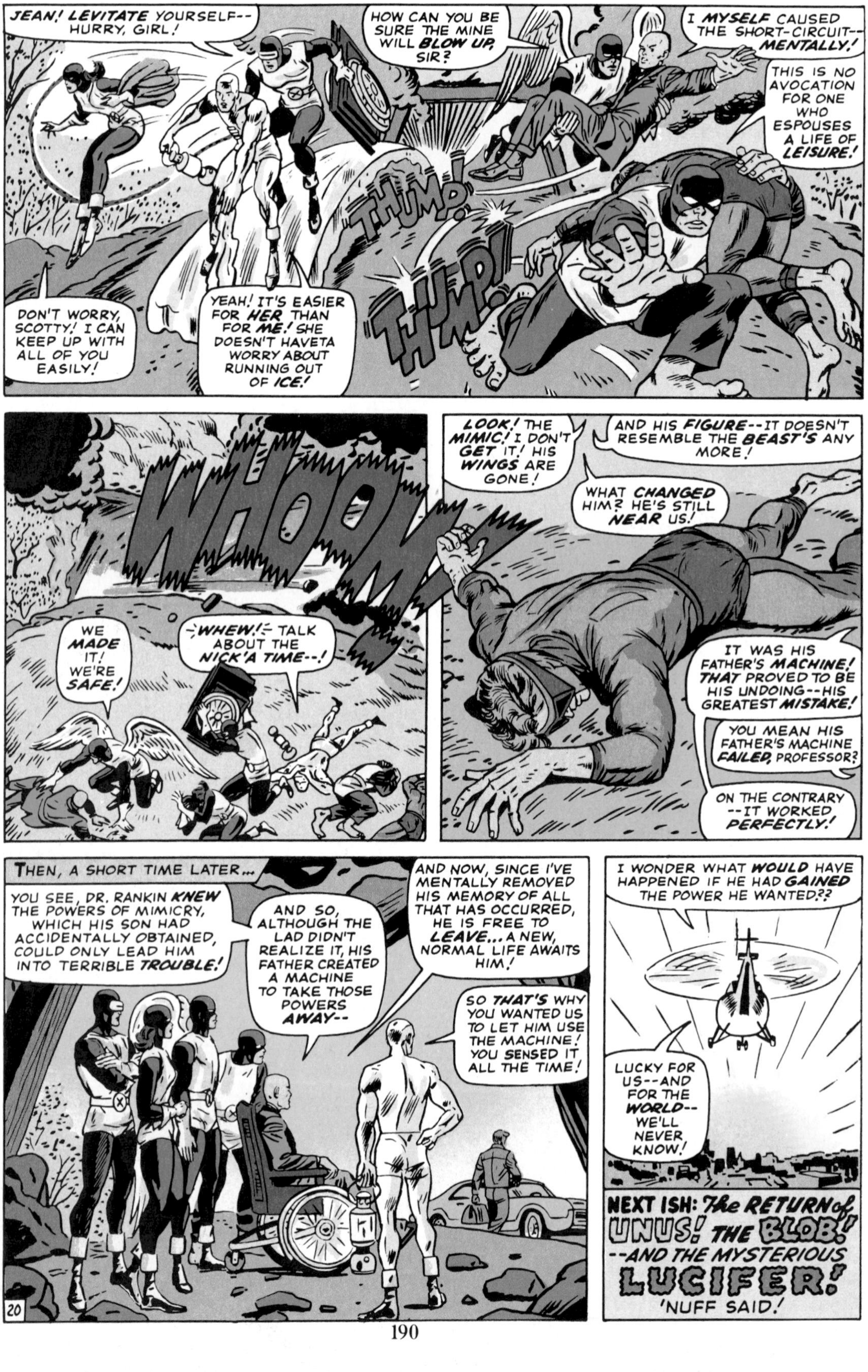
JEAN! LEVITATE YOURSELF-- HURRY, GIRL!
HOW CAN YOU BE SURE THE MINE WILL BLOW UP, SIR?
I MYSELF CAUSED THE SHORT-CIRCUIT-- MENTALLY!
THIS IS NO AVOCATION FOR ONE WHO ESPOUSES A LIFE OF LEISURE!
THUMP!
THUMP!
THUMP!
DON'T WORRY, SCOTTY! I CAN KEEP UP WITH ALL OF YOU EASILY!
YEAH! IT'S EASIER FOR HER THAN FOR ME! SHE DOESN'T HAVETA WORRY ABOUT RUNNING OUT OF ICE!
WHOOM
WE MADE IT! WE'RE SAFE!
WHEW! TALK ABOUT THE NICK'A TIME--!
LOOK! THE MIMIC! I DON'T GET IT! HIS WINGS ARE GONE!
AND HIS FIGURE--IT DOESN'T RESEMBLE THE BEAST'S ANY MORE!
WHAT CHANGED HIM? HE'S STILL NEAR US!
IT WAS HIS FATHER'S MACHINE! THAT PROVED TO BE HIS UNDOING--HIS GREATEST MISTAKE!
YOU MEAN HIS FATHER'S MACHINE FAILED, PROFESSOR?
ON THE CONTRARY --IT WORKED PERFECTLY!
THEN, A SHORT TIME LATER...
YOU SEE, DR. RANKIN KNEW THE POWERS OF MIMICRY, WHICH HIS SON HAD ACCIDENTALLY OBTAINED, COULD ONLY LEAD HIM INTO TERRIBLE TROUBLE!
AND SO, ALTHOUGH THE LAD DIDN'T REALIZE IT, HIS FATHER CREATED A MACHINE TO TAKE THOSE POWERS AWAY--
AND NOW, SINCE I'VE MENTALLY REMOVED HIS MEMORY OF ALL THAT HAS OCCURRED, HE IS FREE TO LEAVE... A NEW, NORMAL LIFE AWAITS HIM!
SO THAT'S WHY YOU WANTED US TO LET HIM USE THE MACHINE! YOU SENSED IT ALL THE TIME!
20
I WONDER WHAT WOULD HAVE HAPPENED IF HE HAD GAINED THE POWER HE WANTED??
LUCKY FOR US--AND FOR THE WORLD-- WE'LL NEVER KNOW!
NEXT ISH: The RETURN of UNUS! THE BLOB! --AND THE MYSTERIOUS LUCIFER! 'NUFF SAID!

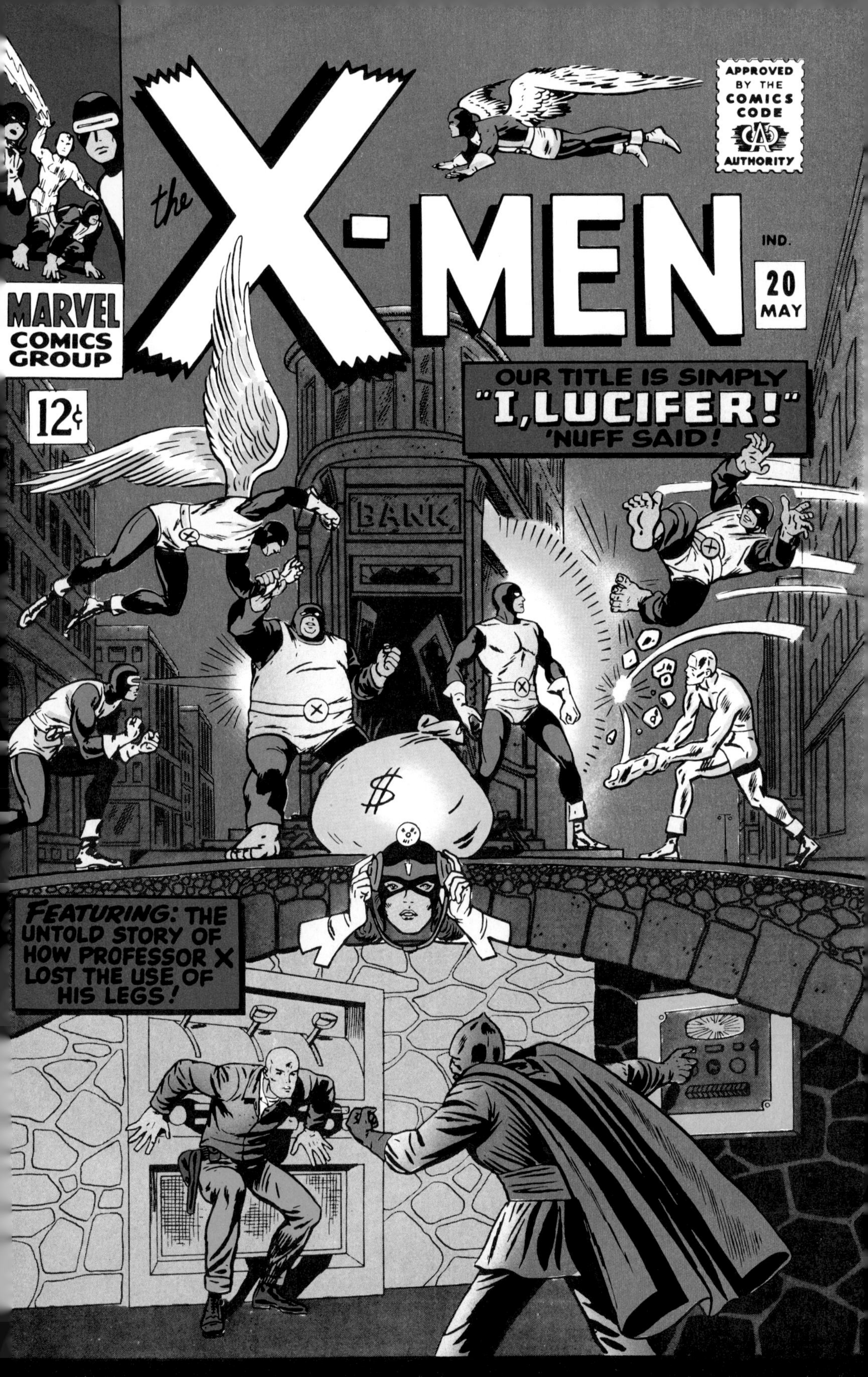
APPROVED BY THE COMICS CODE AUTHORITY
the X-MEN
IND.
20
MAY
MARVEL COMICS GROUP
12¢
OUR TITLE IS SIMPLY "I, LUCIFER!" 'NUFF SAID!
BANK
FEATURING: THE UNTOLD STORY OF HOW PROFESSOR X LOST THE USE OF HIS LEGS!

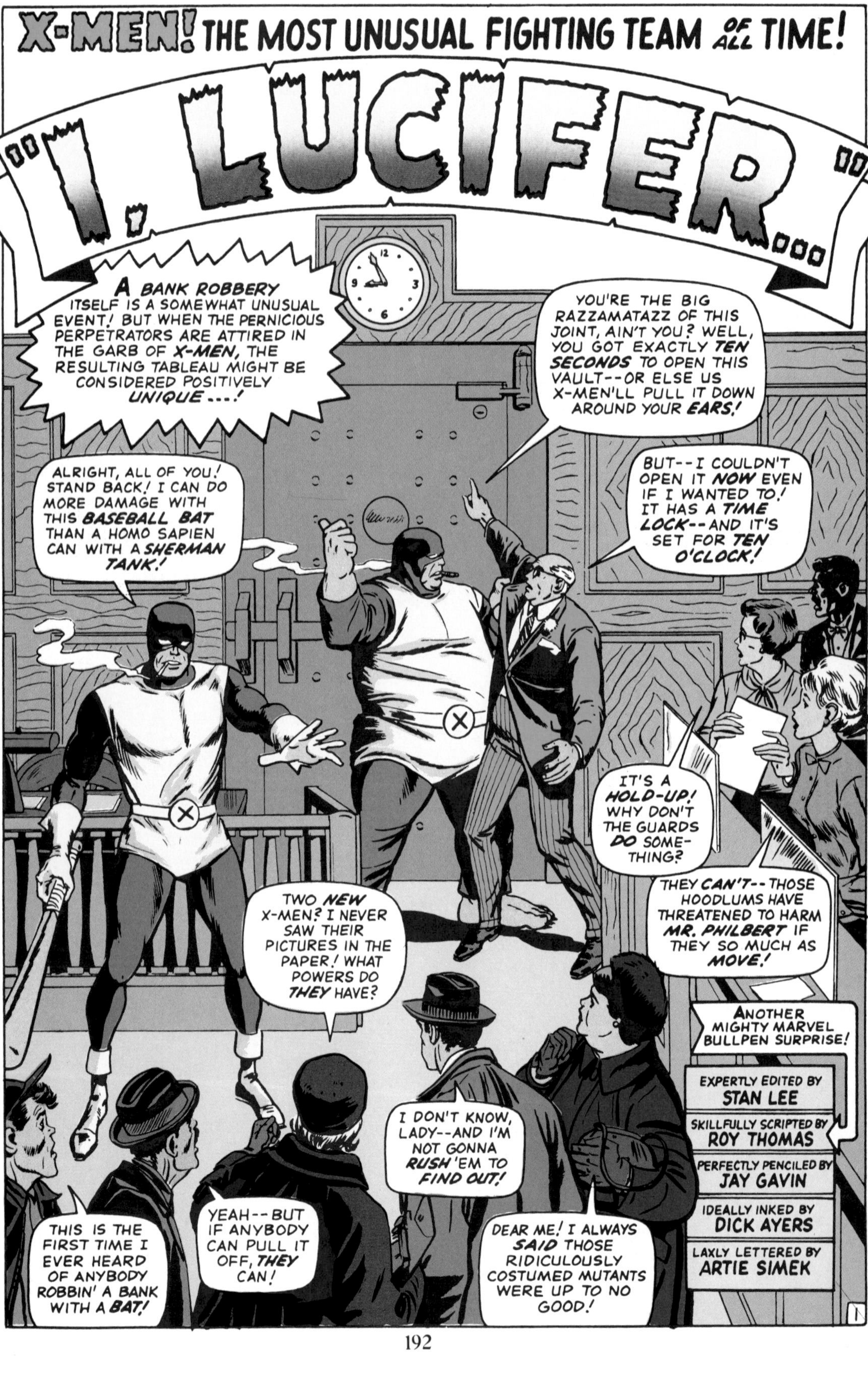
X-MEN! THE MOST UNUSUAL FIGHTING TEAM OF ALL TIME!
"I, LUCIFER..."
A BANK ROBBERY ITSELF IS A SOMEWHAT UNUSUAL EVENT! BUT WHEN THE PERNICIOUS PERPETRATORS ARE ATTIRED IN THE GARB OF X-MEN, THE RESULTING TABLEAU MIGHT BE CONSIDERED POSITIVELY UNIQUE...!
YOU'RE THE BIG RAZZAMATAZZ OF THIS JOINT, AIN'T YOU? WELL, YOU GOT EXACTLY TEN SECONDS TO OPEN THIS VAULT--OR ELSE US X-MEN'LL PULL IT DOWN AROUND YOUR EARS!
ALRIGHT, ALL OF YOU! STAND BACK! I CAN DO MORE DAMAGE WITH THIS BASEBALL BAT THAN A HOMO SAPIEN CAN WITH A SHERMAN TANK!
BUT--I COULDN'T OPEN IT NOW EVEN IF I WANTED TO! IT HAS A TIME LOCK--AND IT'S SET FOR TEN O'CLOCK!
IT'S A HOLD-UP! WHY DON'T THE GUARDS DO SOME-THING?
THEY CAN'T--THOSE HOODLUMS HAVE THREATENED TO HARM MR. PHILBERT IF THEY SO MUCH AS MOVE!
TWO NEW X-MEN? I NEVER SAW THEIR PICTURES IN THE PAPER! WHAT POWERS DO THEY HAVE?
I DON'T KNOW, LADY--AND I'M NOT GONNA RUSH 'EM TO FIND OUT!
THIS IS THE FIRST TIME I EVER HEARD OF ANYBODY ROBBIN' A BANK WITH A BAT!
YEAH--BUT IF ANYBODY CAN PULL IT OFF, THEY CAN!
DEAR ME! I ALWAYS SAID THOSE RIDICULOUSLY COSTUMED MUTANTS WERE UP TO NO GOOD!
ANOTHER MIGHTY MARVEL BULLPEN SURPRISE!
EXPERTLY EDITED BY STAN LEE
SKILLFULLY SCRIPTED BY ROY THOMAS
PERFECTLY PENCILED BY JAY GAVIN
IDEALLY INKED BY DICK AYERS
LAXLY LETTERED BY ARTIE SIMEK
1

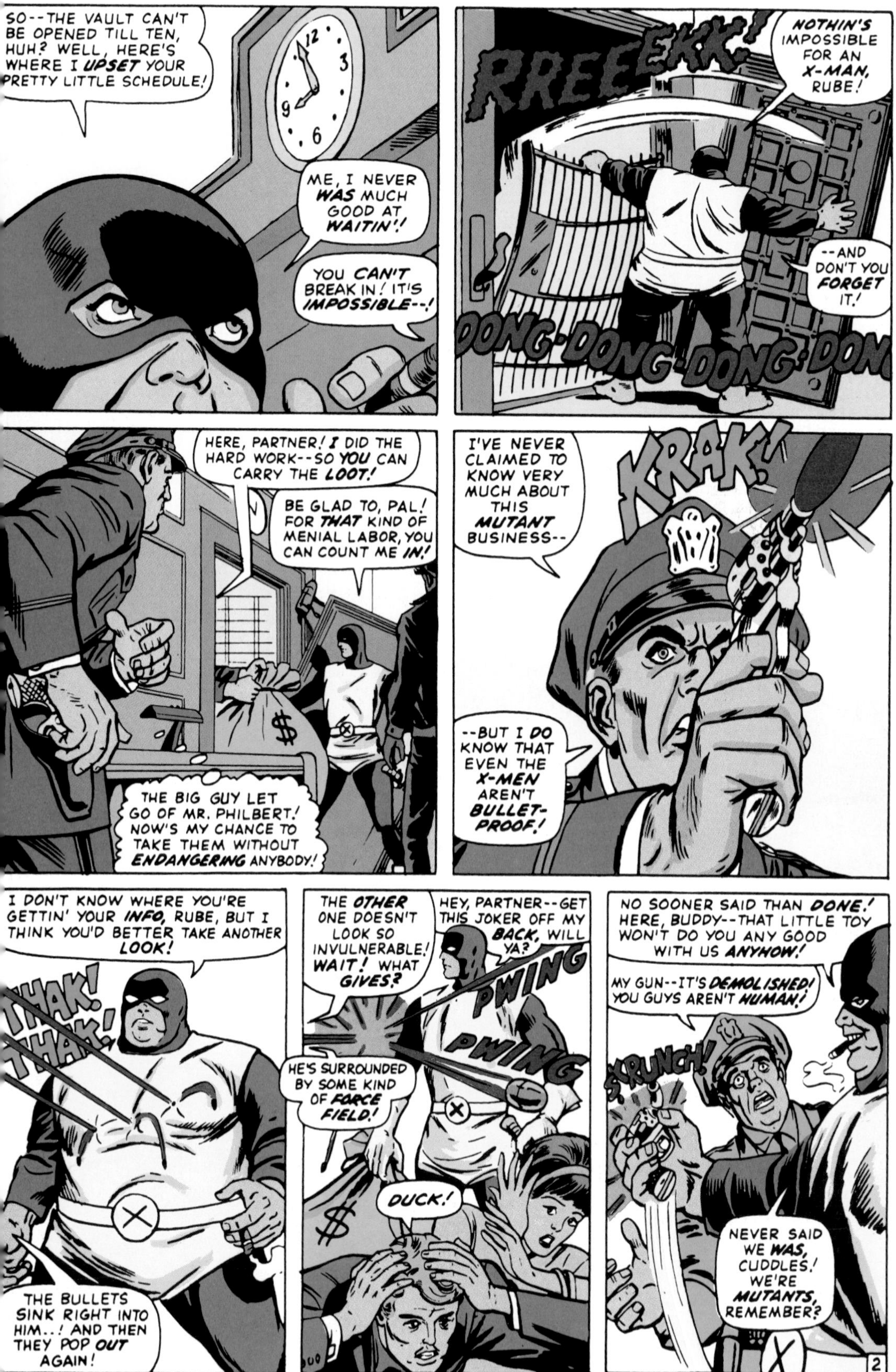
SO--THE VAULT CAN'T BE OPENED TILL TEN, HUH? WELL, HERE'S WHERE I UPSET YOUR PRETTY LITTLE SCHEDULE!
ME, I NEVER WAS MUCH GOOD AT WAITIN'!
YOU CAN'T BREAK IN! IT'S IMPOSSIBLE--!
RREEEEKK!
NOTHIN'S IMPOSSIBLE FOR AN X-MAN, RUBE!
--AND DON'T YOU FORGET IT!
DONG-DONG-DONG-DONG
HERE, PARTNER! I DID THE HARD WORK--SO YOU CAN CARRY THE LOOT!
BE GLAD TO, PAL! FOR THAT KIND OF MENIAL LABOR, YOU CAN COUNT ME IN!
THE BIG GUY LET GO OF MR. PHILBERT! NOW'S MY CHANCE TO TAKE THEM WITHOUT ENDANGERING ANYBODY!
I'VE NEVER CLAIMED TO KNOW VERY MUCH ABOUT THIS MUTANT BUSINESS--
KRAK!
--BUT I DO KNOW THAT EVEN THE X-MEN AREN'T BULLET-PROOF!
I DON'T KNOW WHERE YOU'RE GETTIN' YOUR INFO, RUBE, BUT I THINK YOU'D BETTER TAKE ANOTHER LOOK!
THAK! THAK!
THE BULLETS SINK RIGHT INTO HIM...! AND THEN THEY POP OUT AGAIN!
THE OTHER ONE DOESN'T LOOK SO INVULNERABLE! WAIT! WHAT GIVES?
HEY, PARTNER--GET THIS JOKER OFF MY BACK, WILL YA?
PWING
PWING
HE'S SURROUNDED BY SOME KIND OF FORCE FIELD!
DUCK!
NO SOONER SAID THAN DONE! HERE, BUDDY--THAT LITTLE TOY WON'T DO YOU ANY GOOD WITH US ANYHOW!
MY GUN--IT'S DEMOLISHED! YOU GUYS AREN'T HUMAN!
SKRUNCH!
NEVER SAID WE WAS, CUDDLES! WE'RE MUTANTS, REMEMBER?
2

MEANWHILE, THE CLANGING BURGLAR ALARM HAS NOT GONE UNHEEDED, FOR...

OKAY, BOYS-- *MOVE IN* ON 'EM.!

USE YOUR *CLUBS!* FROM WHAT I SAW THRU THE BANK WINDOW, *GUNS* ARE USELESS.!

WE'LL TAKE 'EM, CAPTAIN.!

THEY CAN'T LICK *ALL* OF US.!

HOWEVER, AS THE INCREDIBLE IMPOSTERS EMERGE FROM THE BUILDING...

UHHNN--!-- WE CAN'T EVEN LAY OUR *HANDS* ON HIM.!

OOOOF!

OF *COURSE NOT,* FOOLS! NOBODY TOUCHES ME UNLESS I ALLOW 'EM TO!

AND, A FEW FEET AWAY...

HE DOESN'T HAVE A FORCE FIELD.!

WE'VE GOT *THIS* ONE, CAPTAIN.!

WHO SAYS I *NEED* ONE? I GOT *OTHER* WAYS OF HANDLIN' THINGS.!

YOU'RE TALKIN' THRU YOUR *HAT,* MISTER.! WE'VE GOT ENOUGH MEN AROUND YOU TO CORRAL AN *ELEPHANT!*

MAYBE SO, BUT YOU AIN'T GOT NEARLY ENOUGH TO HOLD ONTO... THE *BLOB!*

SO *THAT'S* WHO HE IS! ...NO *WONDER!*

HE TOSSED US OFF LIKE SO MANY *RAG DOLLS!*

AN' NOW, IF YOU DON'T MIND--

--I'VE GOTTA BE *MOVIN'* ON! GIVE MY REGRETS TO THE JOE THAT OWNS THIS CAR!

I *SEE* IT-- BUT I JUST PLAIN DON'T *BELIEVE* IT!

C'MON, CHUM! WE'VE GOTTA GO JOIN THE *REST'A* THE X-MEN!

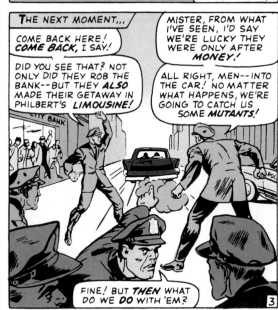

THE NEXT MOMENT...

COME BACK HERE! *COME BACK,* I SAY.!

DID YOU SEE THAT? NOT ONLY DID THEY ROB THE BANK-- BUT THEY *ALSO* MADE THEIR GETAWAY IN PHILBERT'S *LIMOUSINE!*

MISTER, FROM WHAT I'VE SEEN, I'D SAY WE'RE LUCKY THEY WERE ONLY AFTER *MONEY!*

ALL RIGHT, MEN-- INTO THE CAR! NO MATTER WHAT HAPPENS, WE'RE GOING TO CATCH US SOME *MUTANTS!*

FINE! BUT *THEN* WHAT DO WE *DO* WITH 'EM?

3

THAT SELFSAME INSTANT, AS A CAPRICIOUS FATE WOULD HAVE IT, ONE OF THE *REAL* X-MEN HAS JUST MADE ONE OF THE MOST DIFFICULT DECISIONS OF HIS ENTIRE LIFE...

THERE! I'VE *DONE* IT! UNTIL THIS SECOND, I WOULD NEVER HAVE THOUGHT I COULD FIND THE *STRENGTH!*

I'M *LEAVING THE X-MEN--!* THAT NOTE I LEFT WILL EXPLAIN THE REASONS--OR AT LEAST *SOME* OF THEM!

FOR, HOW CAN MERE *WORDS* EVER HOPE TO EXPRESS ALL THAT I FEEL IN MY HEART FOR *JEAN?*

AND YET, HAVE I THE *RIGHT* TO FEEL THIS WAY ABOUT HER--WHILE MY *EYES* MAKE ME A *THREAT* TO ALL I ENCOUNTER?

THAT'S WHY I MUST GO--TO SEE IF, SOMEWHERE, I CAN FIND A DOCTOR WHO CAN RID ME OF THE MENACE OF MY DEADLY *EYE BEAMS!*

UNTIL THAT DAY, THE WORLD SHALL HEAR NO MORE FROM THE ONE IT KNOWS ONLY AS... *CYCLOPS!*

WITH THESE THOUGHTS, THE TRAGIC FORM OF SCOTT SUMMERS DISAPPEARS INTO THE DISTANCE...

AS, INSIDE, UNAWARE OF HIS UNHERALDED DEPARTURE...

WANT THAT BOOK, JEANIE? LET ME GET IT FOR YOU--

DON'T BOTHER, WARREN! YOU FORGET--MY *TELEKINETIC POWER* CAN BRING IT FLOATING DOWN TO ME AT WILL!

HEY, GROUP! CATCH THIS CRAZY SCENE ON THE BOOB TUBE--IT'LL *FLOOR* YOU!

COME NOW, BOBBY--MUST YOU PERSEVERE IN SUCH BOISTEROUS EXCLAMATIONS WHILE I'M *STUDYING?*

WAIT, HANK! BOBBY'S *RIGHT!* LISTEN TO *THIS!*

--AND SO, DESPITE THE EFFORTS OF THE AUTHORITIES, THE ROBBERS *ESCAPED!* THERE SEEMS TO BE LITTLE DOUBT THAT BOTH WERE MEMBERS OF THE MYSTERIOUS MUTANT GROUP KNOWN AS THE *X-MEN...*

OH YEAH? *I* DOUBT IT!

QUIET, BOBBY--LET'S MAKE SURE WE DON'T *MISS* ANY OF THIS!

IT WOULD SEEM MOST IMPERATIVE THAT WE ENLIGHTEN THE PROFESSOR--*POST HASTE!*

PROFESSOR XAVIER--PARDON MY UNCEREMONIOUS INTRUSION, SIR, BUT THE TELEVISION HAS REPORTED A MOST SINGULAR OCCURRENCE--!

I KNOW, HANK-- I'VE ALREADY MONITORED THAT NEWSCAST *MENTALLY!*

IN FACT, I'VE TELEPATH-ICALLY COMMANDED THE OTHERS TO *JOIN* US, AS I FINISH THE INSTALLATION OF THIS NEW *CEREBRO*!*

*MAGNETO POLISHED OFF THE *OLD* ONE IN *X-MEN #18,* REMEMBER? --STAN.

AND, SCANT SECONDS LATER...

WE GOT YOUR CALL, PROFESSOR! THEN YOU *KNOW* ABOUT THOSE PHONY *X-MEN?*

SILENCE, ALL OF YOU! THERE IS NO TIME TO WASTE ON *WORDS!* OBSERVE THE LARGE *SCREEN* ON THAT WALL!

I'VE NEVER SEEN THE PROF ANY *GRIMMER* THAN HE IS RIGHT NOW!

THE *RADAR-IMAGE BEAM* WHICH I DEVELOPED WILL DETECT ANY OTHER MUTANTS IN THE AREA-- AND SHOW US THEIR *FORMS,* AS WELL!

HEY-- *THAT* ONE LOOKS *FAMILIAR!*

AS WELL HE *SHOULD!* IT IS CLEAR THAT THE MASSIVE FIGURE IS INDEED... *THE BLOB!* AND THE OTHER, THE MACHINE REVEALS, IS... *UNUS!*

UNUS, THE *UNTOUCH-ABLE?!!*

BUT, THE LAST TIME WE FOUGHT, HE PROMISED TO *REFORM* IF WE DECLINED TO IMPRISON HIM*!

IF HE'S *FORGOTTEN* HIS PLEDGE, I'LL *STIMULATE* HIS MEMORY-- AS *THE BEAST!*

WE STILL HAVE THE *RAY GUN* WE EMPLOYED AGAINST HIM THEN!

*ISH #8--S.

DON'T BE TOO *CONFI-DENT,* HANK! AFTER ALL, UNUS MAY HAVE DISCOVERED SOME WAY TO *COUNTERACT* THAT WEAPON BY NOW!

IN ADDITION, I SENSE THAT A *THIRD* ENTITY HAS MASTERMINDED THIS ENTIRE SCHEME TO DISCREDIT US-- SOMEONE *OUT OF RANGE* OF MY *CEREBRO* MACHINE!

PROFESSOR-- I JUST NOTICED! *SCOTT* ISN'T HERE! COULD ANYTHING HAVE *HAPPENED* TO HIM?

YEAH! IT ISN'T LIKE OLD GAMMA-GAZE TO MISS A CHANCE FOR *ACTION!*

SOMEONE HAD BEST INVESTI-GATE HIS *ABSENCE!*

I'M ON MY WAY THERE *NOW!* I'LL FIND 'IM!

FIFTEEN SECONDS LATER, A BREATHLESS BOBBY DRAKE REAPPEARS--WITH DISTURBING NEWS...

CYKE.. HE'S *GONE!* WALKED OUT ON US! HE JUST LEFT US A SHORT GOOD-BYE NOTE!

I *SUSPECTED* AS MUCH! SCOTT HAS SEEMED TERRIBLY *DIS-TRAUGHT* THESE PAST FEW WEEKS!

BUT, NO TIME TO WORRY ABOUT THAT *NOW!*

I MUST SEARCH MY MEMORY--TRY TO DISCOVER *WHICH* OF OUR FORMER FOES MIGHT BE GUIDING *UNUS* AND THE *BLOB!*

VANISHER! MAGNETO! JUGGER-- SENTINE-- MASTERMIND! S... MARINER!

SCOTT-- OH, SCOTT! WILL I NEVER *SEE* YOU AGAIN?

IT'S--NO USE! OUR ADVERSARY HAS SET UP A *MENTAL SCREEN!* THERE IS ONE NAME WHICH ELUDES ME!

BY YOUR EXPRESSIONS, I SEE THAT OUR HIDDEN ENEMY'S SCREEN HAS AFFECTED *YOU,* TOO! THERE IS ONLY ONE SOLUTION!

I MUST BUILD A *MECHAN-ICAL MEMORY-INDUCER,* TO QUICKLY PENETRATE OUR FOE'S DEFENSES! MEANWHILE...

FOR ONCE, WE'RE WAY AHEAD OF YOU, PROFESSOR! IT'LL BE A RELIEF TO LET MY *WINGS* OUT OF THIS GET-UP ANYWAY!

I'LL GET THAT RAY GUN! IT MAY *STILL* PROVE EFFICACIOUS!

YEAH--MAYBE IT'LL EVEN *WORK!* C'MON--LET'S *MOVE OUT!*

BUT, EVEN AS THE TEEN-AGE MUTANTS PREPARE FOR BATTLE, THEY CANNOT SUSPECT THAT, TWO THOUSAND MILES AWAY, ONE PAIR OF EYES--COLD, HOSTILE, RELENTLESS-- WATCHES INTENTLY FOR THEIR APPEARANCE...

SO! THE DIE IS CAST! UNUS AND THE BLOB HAVE UNWITTINGLY DONE MY BIDDING--AND A FOOLISH WORLD BELIEVES THEY ARE RENEGADE X-MEN, MERELY SEEKING WORLDLY TREASURE!

LITTLE DOES ANYONE-- EVEN MY TWO MASQUER- ADING MINIONS--REALIZE THAT I, LUCIFER*, HAVE IN MIND A PURPOSE FAR MORE COMPLEX, FAR MORE SINISTER!

* THE VIVACIOUS VILLAIN OF X-MEN #9, RIGHT? RIGHT! ... OL' STAN.

"FOR, IT WAS ONLY DAYS AGO THAT, WHILE TESTING MY ULTRA-SCANNER, I DISCOVERED...

"UNTOUCHABLE," HUH? WHEN I GET THRU WITH HIM, HE'LL BE UNMENDABLE!

$100 TO ANYONE WHO CAN LAST THREE FULL MINUTES WITH UNUS THE UNTOUCHABLE NOW TOURING WITH SUPERIOR CIRCUS

EASY, BLOB! I'VE HEARD'A THIS GUY! THEY SAY HE'S TOUGH!

NOBODY'S TOUGHER THAN THE BLOB! I'LL TEACH THAT RUBE TO BRING HIS CIRCUS INTO THE SAME TOWN WHERE MY CARNY'S PLAYIN'!

"THUS, FATE HAD PLACED WITHIN MY REACH TWO OF THE MOST POWERFUL MUTANTS IN THE WORLD! AND, AS I WAITED, BIDING MY TIME...

WHAT'S THIS? HAVE THE LOCAL YOKELS RUN OUTTA MEN, SO THEY HAVETA SEND HIPPOS AGAINST ME NOW?

I'M GONNA MAKE YOU SWALLOW THEM WORDS, BUSTER!

"HOWEVER..."

I DIDN'T EVEN REACH HIM! HE'S PROTECTED BY SOME KINDA INVISIBLE SHIELD!

BUT THERE'S NOTHIN' I CAN'T SMASH THRU ... LEASTWAYS, NOT TILL NOW!

YOU BLUNDERING FATSO-- NOW DO YOU SEE WHY THEY CALL ME "THE UNTOUCH- ABLE"?

YET, ANY NORMAL MAN WOULD HAVE BOUNCED BACK--HE WAS MERELY STOPPED!

I DON'T GET IT! NOBODY'S HALTED ME LIKE THAT EXCEPT -- THE X-MEN!

NOW, THERE'S AN IDEA! WHAT IF THIS CLOWN IS A MUTANT--LIKE ME?

HE'S GETTING UP! BETTER MAKE MY MOVE-- NOW!

6

"BUT, *UNUS* FARED NO BETTER THAN HAD *THE BLOB* HIMSELF...

CAN'T *BUDGE* HIM! THERE'S JUST ONE POSSIBLE ANSWER...

LOOK, MISTER-- WHAT SAY WE CALL THIS MATCH A *DRAW?* I'VE GOT SOME-THIN' I WANNA *TALK* TO YOU ABOUT-- *LATER!*

YA TOOK THE WORDS RIGHT OUTTA MY MOUTH! COME OVER TO *MY* CARNY IN AN HOUR!

AND DON'T FORGET THAT *HUNDRED BUCKS!*

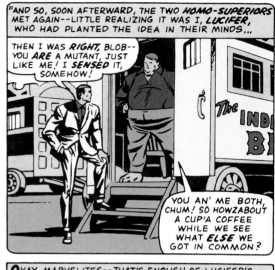

"AND SO, SOON AFTERWARD, THE TWO *HOMO-SUPERIORS* MET AGAIN--LITTLE REALIZING IT WAS I, *LUCIFER,* WHO HAD PLANTED THE IDEA IN THEIR MINDS...

THEN I WAS *RIGHT,* BLOB-- YOU *ARE* A MUTANT, JUST LIKE ME! I *SENSED* IT, SOMEHOW!

YOU AN' ME BOTH, CHUM! SO HOWZABOUT A CUP'A COFFEE WHILE WE SEE WHAT *ELSE* WE GOT IN COMMON?

"BEFORE LONG, INSIDE THE BLOB'S TRAILER..."

THEN IT'S SETTLED! SINCE WE'VE *BOTH* GOT GRUDGES AGAINST THE X-MEN, WE'LL FRAME *THEM* FOR OUR ROBBERIES!

RIGHT! AND WHEN THOSE COSTUMED CLOWNS COME OUT TO *STOP* US--WE'LL POLISH 'EM OFF, ONCE AN' FOR ALL!

NOW YER TALKIN'! I BEEN WAITIN' A *LONG TIME* FOR THIS!*

*SINCE *X-MEN #7,* TO BE EXACT!--SMILEY.

OKAY, MARVELITES--THAT'S ENOUGH OF LUCIFER'S SANGUINARY SOLILOQUIES FOR THE MOMENT! NOW, AS HIS HUMAN PUPPETS COMMIT THEIR *SECOND* CRIME, THE EYES OF *CYCLOPS* ARE UPON THEM...

C'MON, BROTHER X-MAN --OUR CLUB TREASURY CAN *USE* THIS EXTRA LOOT!

I HEAR YA TALKIN', MAC!

TWO CRIMINALS-- DRESSED IN X-MEN UNIFORMS! THAT BULKY ONE LOOKS LIKE *THE BLOB* --AND, COULD THE OTHER BE...*UNUS?*

YET, THIS ISN'T *MY* AFFAIR-- FOR I'VE PROMISED MYSELF NOT TO BECOME AN *X-MAN* AGAIN--UNTIL I CAN *CONTROL* MY AWESOME, POTENTIALLY DEADLY POWER!

BESIDES, SURELY THE *PUBLIC* REALIZES THAT THEY'RE NOT REALLY X-MEN!

SEE, MABEL? I *TOLD* YOU WE SHOULD'A RUN THEM CRUMMY MUTIES OUTTA TOWN LONG AGO!

YOU WERE *RIGHT,* HERMAN! *NEXT* TIME I'LL *LISTEN* TO YOU!

NOW WE'RE ONTO THEM!

SO--THE CROWD HAS ANSWERED MY QUESTION FOR ME! I *MUST* HEED THE CALL--AS LONG AS ALL MUTANTS ARE REGARDED AS *MONSTERS!*

EXACTLY ONE MINUTE LATER...

ALL RIGHT, YOU MISGUIDED MISFITS! ONE OF THE *REAL* X-MEN IS HERE! NOW, WHICH OF YOU WANTS TO BE THE FIRST TO CONFESS YOU'RE BOTH *PHONIES!*

PHONIES? DOES HE MEAN THAT THOSE OTHER TWO --ARE JUST *IMPOSTERS?*

I'LL BET THEY'RE *ALL* IN ON IT!

HEY, LOOK, PARTNER-- IT'S *CYCLOPS!* WE THOUGHT YOU'D NEVER MAKE IT, CYKE, OL' BUDDY!

YEAH! HELP US WITH THIS MONEY-SACK, WILLYA, KID?

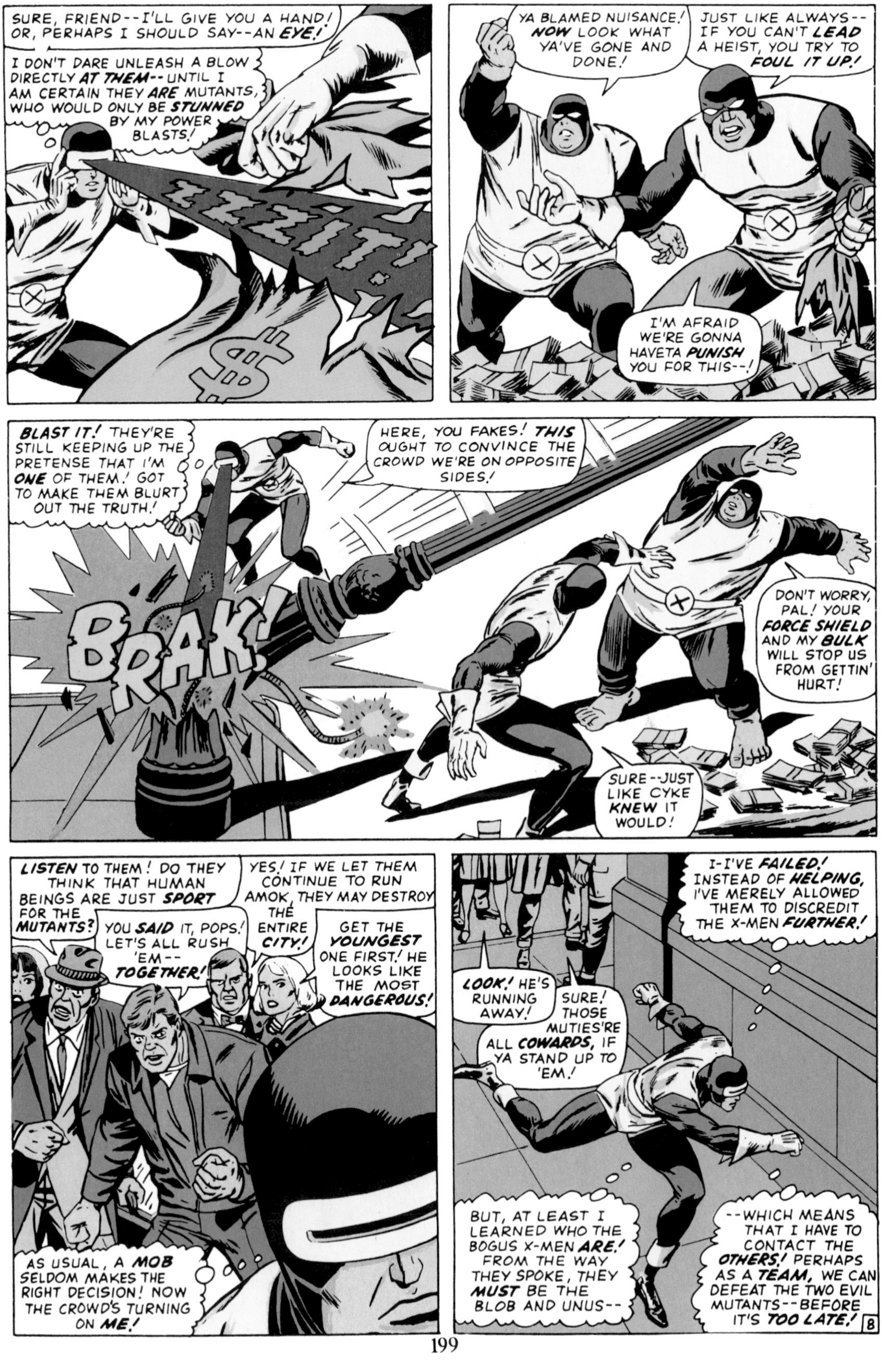
SURE, FRIEND--I'LL GIVE YOU A HAND! OR, PERHAPS I SHOULD SAY--AN EYE!
I DON'T DARE UNLEASH A BLOW DIRECTLY AT THEM--UNTIL I AM CERTAIN THEY ARE MUTANTS, WHO WOULD ONLY BE STUNNED BY MY POWER BLASTS!
ZZZIT!
YA BLAMED NUISANCE! NOW LOOK WHAT YA'VE GONE AND DONE!
JUST LIKE ALWAYS--IF YOU CAN'T LEAD A HEIST, YOU TRY TO FOUL IT UP!
I'M AFRAID WE'RE GONNA HAVETA PUNISH YOU FOR THIS--!
BLAST IT! THEY'RE STILL KEEPING UP THE PRETENSE THAT I'M ONE OF THEM! GOT TO MAKE THEM BLURT OUT THE TRUTH!
HERE, YOU FAKES! THIS OUGHT TO CONVINCE THE CROWD WE'RE ON OPPOSITE SIDES!
BRAK!
DON'T WORRY, PAL! YOUR FORCE SHIELD AND MY BULK WILL STOP US FROM GETTIN' HURT!
SURE--JUST LIKE CYKE KNEW IT WOULD!
LISTEN TO THEM! DO THEY THINK THAT HUMAN BEINGS ARE JUST SPORT FOR THE MUTANTS?
YES! IF WE LET THEM CONTINUE TO RUN AMOK, THEY MAY DESTROY THE ENTIRE CITY!
YOU SAID IT, POPS! LET'S ALL RUSH 'EM--TOGETHER!
GET THE YOUNGEST ONE FIRST! HE LOOKS LIKE THE MOST DANGEROUS!
AS USUAL, A MOB SELDOM MAKES THE RIGHT DECISION! NOW THE CROWD'S TURNING ON ME!
I-I'VE FAILED! INSTEAD OF HELPING, I'VE MERELY ALLOWED THEM TO DISCREDIT THE X-MEN FURTHER!
LOOK! HE'S RUNNING AWAY!
SURE! THOSE MUTIES'RE ALL COWARDS, IF YA STAND UP TO 'EM!
BUT, AT LEAST I LEARNED WHO THE BOGUS X-MEN ARE! FROM THE WAY THEY SPOKE, THEY MUST BE THE BLOB AND UNUS--
--WHICH MEANS THAT I HAVE TO CONTACT THE OTHERS! PERHAPS AS A TEAM, WE CAN DEFEAT THE TWO EVIL MUTANTS--BEFORE IT'S TOO LATE!
8

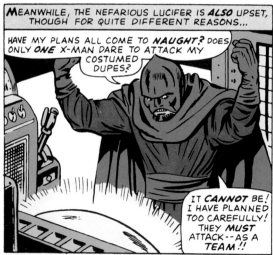

MEANWHILE, THE NEFARIOUS LUCIFER IS *ALSO* UPSET, THOUGH FOR QUITE DIFFERENT REASONS...

HAVE MY PLANS ALL COME TO *NAUGHT?* DOES ONLY *ONE* X-MAN DARE TO ATTACK MY COSTUMED DUPES?

IT *CANNOT* BE! I HAVE PLANNED TOO CAREFULLY! THEY *MUST* ATTACK--AS A *TEAM!!*

BUT--PERHAPS I SPOKE *TOO SOON!* FOR, THERE IS THE MUTANT KNOWN AS...*THE ANGEL!* HE FLIES TOWARDS UNUS AND THE BLOB!

AND, IF *ANGEL* COMES, CAN THE OTHER X-MEN BE FAR *BEHIND?*

THE NEXT SECOND, LUCIFER'S RINGING WORDS COME TRUE, AS...

DON'T FORGET, GROUP--'TIS THE *BEAST* WHO GETS FIRST DIBS AT OUR TWO ADVER-SARIES!

YOU CAN *HAVE* 'EM, BEASTIE-BOY! BUT, I'LL BE HOVERING NEARBY, JUST IN CASE!

HOLY HANNAH! THREE *MORE* MUTANTS!

WELL, IT'S ABOUT *TIME* YOU GLORY-BOYS SHOWED UP! WE BEEN *WAITIN'* FOR YA!

THEN, ARMED WITH THE WEAPON THAT ONCE BEFORE DEFEATED THE AWESOME *UNUS,* THE ANTHROPOID X-MAN MAKES HIS PLAY...

IT GRIEVES ME TO THE QUICK, FECKLESS FOE, TO REALIZE THAT YOU HAVE DISAVOWED YOUR PLEDGE OF ETERNAL HONESTY!

NOW, PREPARE FOR THE *CONSEQUENCES* OF YOUR IM-PRUDENT ACT!

QUIT YAKKIN' AND *FIRE AWAY,* FOOL! I DON'T HAVE ALL *DAY* TO LISTEN TO YOU!

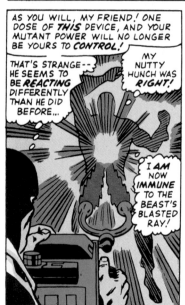

AS YOU WILL, MY FRIEND! ONE DOSE OF *THIS* DEVICE, AND YOUR MUTANT POWER WILL NO LONGER BE YOURS TO *CONTROL!*

THAT'S STRANGE-- HE SEEMS TO BE *REACTING* DIFFERENTLY THAN HE DID BEFORE...

MY NUTTY HUNCH WAS *RIGHT!*

I *AM* NOW *IMMUNE* TO THE BEAST'S BLASTED RAY!

AND, AS THE BLINDING GLARE FADES AWAY...

OKAY, YOU JUNIOR-GRADE GORILLA! NOW IT'S *MY* TURN --I BEEN WAITIN' FOR THIS MOMENT FOR MORE THAN A *YEAR!*

A TRUE PARAGON OF PATIENCE!

NEITHER OF THEM SUSPECTS THAT *I* AM RESPONSIBLE FOR UNUS'S IMMUNITY--AND ALSO FOR HIS "HUNCH" THAT THE RAY WOULD NO LONGER AFFECT HIM!

FOR, I POSSESS POWERS THAT THE WORLD CAN SCARCELY *IMAGINE!*

9

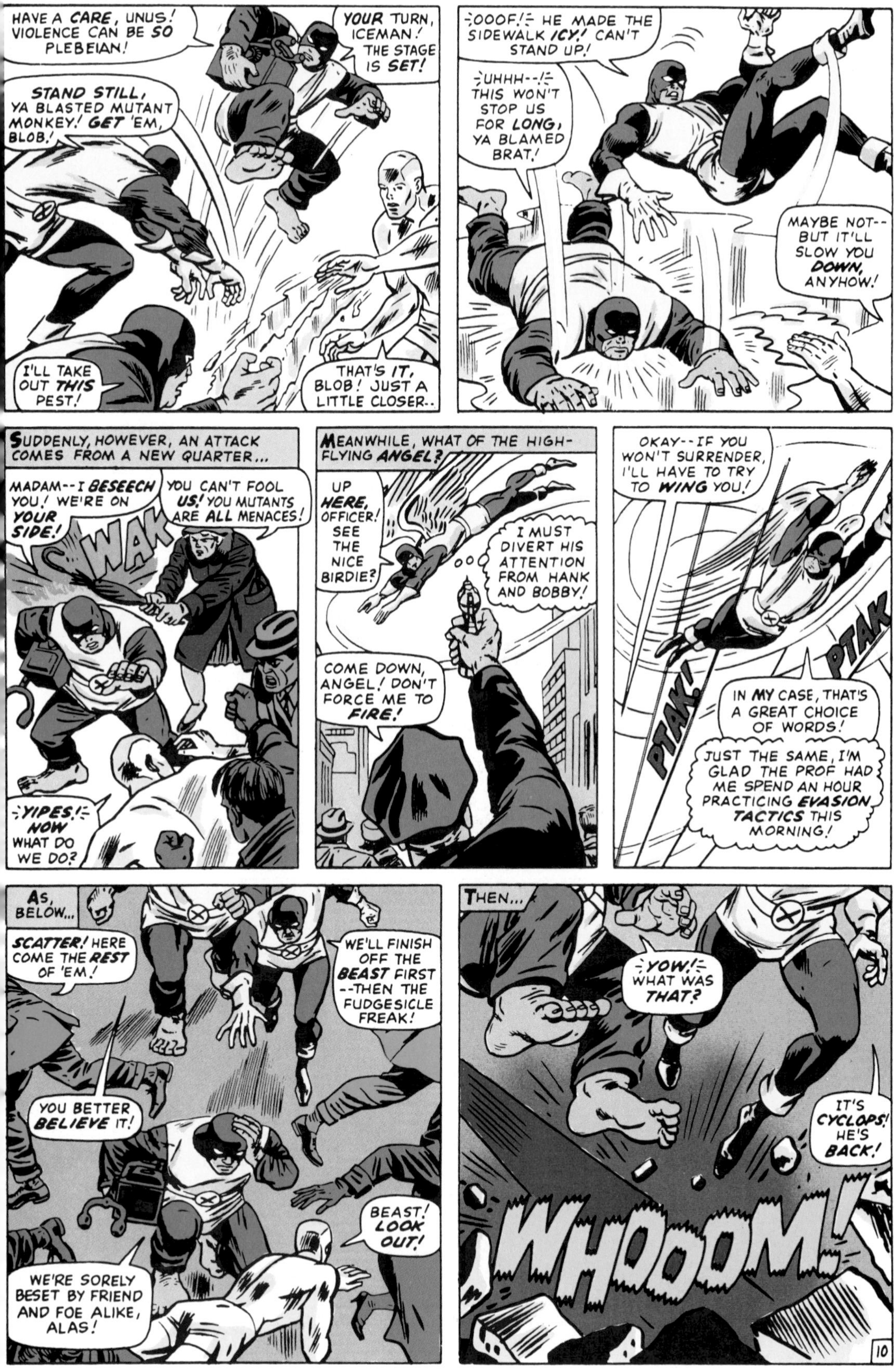
HAVE A CARE, UNUS! VIOLENCE CAN BE SO PLEBEIAN!
YOUR TURN, ICEMAN! THE STAGE IS SET!
STAND STILL, YA BLASTED MUTANT MONKEY! GET 'EM, BLOB!
I'LL TAKE OUT THIS PEST!
THAT'S IT, BLOB! JUST A LITTLE CLOSER..
OOOF! HE MADE THE SIDEWALK ICY! CAN'T STAND UP!
UHHH--! THIS WON'T STOP US FOR LONG, YA BLAMED BRAT!
MAYBE NOT--BUT IT'LL SLOW YOU DOWN, ANYHOW!
SUDDENLY, HOWEVER, AN ATTACK COMES FROM A NEW QUARTER...
MADAM--I BESEECH YOU! WE'RE ON YOUR SIDE!
YOU CAN'T FOOL US! YOU MUTANTS ARE ALL MENACES!
WAK
YIPES! NOW WHAT DO WE DO?
MEANWHILE, WHAT OF THE HIGH-FLYING ANGEL?
UP HERE, OFFICER! SEE THE NICE BIRDIE?
I MUST DIVERT HIS ATTENTION FROM HANK AND BOBBY!
COME DOWN, ANGEL! DON'T FORCE ME TO FIRE!
OKAY--IF YOU WON'T SURRENDER, I'LL HAVE TO TRY TO WING YOU!
PTAK!
PTAK
IN MY CASE, THAT'S A GREAT CHOICE OF WORDS!
JUST THE SAME, I'M GLAD THE PROF HAD ME SPEND AN HOUR PRACTICING EVASION TACTICS THIS MORNING!
AS, BELOW...
SCATTER! HERE COME THE REST OF 'EM!
WE'LL FINISH OFF THE BEAST FIRST--THEN THE FUDGESICLE FREAK!
YOU BETTER BELIEVE IT!
BEAST! LOOK OUT!
WE'RE SORELY BESET BY FRIEND AND FOE ALIKE, ALAS!
THEN...
YOW! WHAT WAS THAT?
IT'S CYCLOPS! HE'S BACK!
WHOOOM!
10

CYKE! TALK ABOUT SIGHTS FOR SORE EYES! YOU SHOWED UP JUST IN TIME!

SO I SEE! BUT-- WE CAN TALK LATER!

LOOK! ONE OF THEM BLASTED A HOLE RIGHT THROUGH THE PAVEMENT--AND TWO OTHERS FELL THRU IT!

WITH YOUR USUAL PERSPICACITY, CYCLOPS, YOU'VE PROPERLY EVALUATED THE SITUATION! LET'S DEPART, INDEED!

RIGHT NOW, WE'D BETTER SPLIT! THAT CROWD'S STILL ANGRY!

THUNK!

WE LANDED ON A SUBWAY TRAIN!

I'VE BEEN RIDDEN OUTTA TOWN ON A RAIL BEFORE, BUT THIS IS RIDICULOUS!

SHUDDUP AND KEEP YER HEAD DOWN! WE'LL BE BACK!*

*AND YOU CAN BET WE'LL BE HERE TO MEET THEM! ---SMUG STAN.

ABOVE GROUND, THE BONA FIDE X-MEN MAKE A HURRIED EXIT...

IT'S GREAT TO SEE SOME ACTION AGAIN! BUT WHERE'VE YOU BEEN, SCOTTY-BOY?

THAT'S MY BUSINESS, ANGEL!

SAY--WHERE'S MARVEL GIRL?

SHE HAD TO STAY BEHIND--TO HELP THE PROFESSOR! WE'LL FILL YOU IN ON THE WAY!

WHILE, IN A HIDDEN LAB...

SO! THE ONE I SEEK MOST STILL CLOSETS HIMSELF IN SECRECY, EH?

BUT, LUCIFER KNOWS NOT THE MEANING OF DEFEAT! THERE ARE OTHER WAYS...

BUT THEN, ABRUPTLY...

AH! MY MENTO-WAVE RECEIVER INDICATES THAT PROFESSOR XAVIER HAS ALREADY PENETRATED MY MENTAL SCREEN!

HE CANNOT SUSPECT THAT I DESIRED HIM TO FIND ME--THAT, IN LOCATING ME, HE HAS NOW SEALED HIS OWN DOOM!

MOMENTS LATER, AT A CERTAIN POINT IN THE GREAT DESERT IN THE SOUTHWESTERN PORTION OF THE UNITED STATES, A STRANGE, OMINOUS DOME APPEARS FROM WITHIN THE VERY HEART OF A CRAGGY MESA...

...YET, NO EYES SEE AND NO VOICE REPORTS THIS AWESOME SIGHT-- ONE WHICH MAY WELL DETERMINE THE FATE OF THE EARTH ITSELF--!

AS THE OPALESCENT GASES THAT PREVENT ITS DETECTION FROM THE AIR FADE AWAY, AN AWESOME STRUCTURE HALTS ITS STRANGE, SILENT ASCENT! THEN, TWO MASSIVE PANELS PART--TO REVEAL A GIGANTIC *CANNON* THAT, ALMOST INSTANTLY, FIRES A BLAST OF *ENERGY* INTO THE ATMOSPHERE...

AND NOW, THE TIME HAS *COME!* ALTHOUGH I FAILED IN MY SCHEME TO LOCATE XAVIER--*HE* HAS FOUND *ME!* THAT WAS HIS FIRST MISTAKE IN DEALING WITH ME--AND IT SHALL BE HIS *LAST*, AS WELL!

NOW, MY POTENT BEAM WILL RIDE HIS OWN MENTAL WAVES BACK TO THEIR SOURCE-- BACK TO THE PROFESSOR HIMSELF! AND THEN, THE FIRST PART OF MY TASK WILL BE *COMPLETED!* THE WORLD WILL BE...*OURS.!!*

AT THAT SELFSAME INSTANT, A CONTINENT AWAY...

WITH THIS DEVICE, I HAVE MENTALLY PIN-POINTED OUR HIDDEN ANTAGONIST!

SO--IT IS HE! I SHOULD HAVE KNOWN!

PROFESSOR--WHO IS IT? CAN YOU TELL ME?

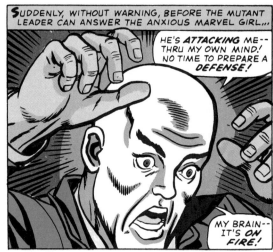

SUDDENLY, WITHOUT WARNING, BEFORE THE MUTANT LEADER CAN ANSWER THE ANXIOUS MARVEL GIRL...

HE'S ATTACKING ME-- THRU MY OWN MIND! NO TIME TO PREPARE A DEFENSE!

MY BRAIN-- IT'S ON FIRE!

THEN--SILENCE!

PROFESSOR--WHAT'S HAPPENED?

HE'S... SO RIGID, SO UNMOVING! IT'S ALMOST AS IF--

BUT NO! HE CAN'T BE DEAD! HE JUST CAN'T BE--!

I MUST CHECK-- TO SEE IF HIS HEART STILL BEATS!

THANK HEAVEN--HE'S ALIVE! AND YET, HIS HEARTBEAT IS SO SLOW-- HE MUST BE CONTINUING TO BREATHE BY SHEER MENTAL EFFORT! BUT-- HE CANNOT MOVE!

THAT IS... CORRECT, JEAN! YOU MUST USE MENTAL-WAVE AMPLIFIER-- AT ONCE!

IN MY MIND--I CAN READ HIS THOUGHTS! BUT, THEY'RE FAINT--DISTANT!

COMPLYING WITH PROFESSOR X'S URGENT COMMAND, JEAN ABRUPTLY DISCOVERS...

WHY--NOW YOUR THOUGHTS ARE COMING THRU MORE CLEARLY!

GOOD! THEN HEED MY WORDS--FOR I MAY HAVE LITTLE TIME!

WHAT DO YOU MEAN? WHO IS RESPONSIBLE FOR YOUR PLIGHT?

THIS IS THE WORK OF ONE WHOSE POWERS AND PURPOSE STAGGER THE MORTAL IMAGINATION--OF THE ONE I KNOW ONLY BY HIS EARTHLY NAME OF... LUCIFER!

LUCIFER! THEN-- HE HAS RETURNED!

YES--SO LISTEN CLOSELY TO THE TALE OF MY FIRST ENCOUNTER WITH HIM! LISTEN, FOR, THE FATE OF ALL HUMANITY HANGS IN THE BALANCE!

13

"SOME YEARS AGO, FASCINATED BY TALES I HAD HEARD OF A MYSTERIOUS WALLED CITY IN THE SHADOW OF THE HIMALAYAS, I JOURNEYED THRU THE RUGGED TERRAIN OF TIBET..."

THIS IS MY DESTINATION! I SEEM TO SENSE SOME OMINOUS, UNSEEN MENACE THAT LIES WITHIN--!

IT'S AS THOUGH MY ENTIRE LIFE, MY ULTIMATE DESTINY, WERE SOMEHOW BOUND UP BEHIND THOSE GRIM, GREY WALLS!

"AT THE GATE, MY SUSPICIONS WERE CONFIRMED..."

IT IS FORBIDDEN THAT ANY OUTSIDER MAY PASS THIS GATE! YET-- I BELIEVE YOU SHOULD BE ALLOWED ADMITTANCE!

THANK YOU! MY MISSION IS ONE OF PEACE, I ASSURE YOU!

THESE TWO ARE UNDER THE MENTAL DOMINATION OF ANOTHER'S BRAIN! I CAN FEEL IT!

"INSIDE THE CITY, I WAS AWARE OF SINISTER EYES FOCUSED UPON ME..."

THE THOUGHT-WAVES OF THESE PEOPLE-- THEY INDICATE ABJECT FEAR OF THE TYRANT WHO RULES THEM!

COME! IS THERE ONE WHO WOULD SPEAK TO A WAYFARER IN A STRANGE LAND?

SO! A VISITOR HAS COME! HE WILL BEAR CLOSE WATCHING!

I WILL SPEAK TO YOU, MY SON! WHAT DO YOU WISH TO KNOW?

I AM INTRIGUED BY YOUR GREAT WALLED CITY, AND I WISH AN AUDIENCE WITH ITS RULER!

NAY, BUT THAT IS IMPOSSIBLE! FOR, OUR MASTER DWELLS WITHIN YONDER CITADEL--AND EVEN WE ARE NEVER PERMITTED TO GAZE UPON HIM!

I CAN TELL HE SPEAKS THE TRUTH!

HOW LONG HAS THIS MAN BEEN YOUR OVERLORD?

I--I DO NOT KNOW, MY SON! IT IS AS IF-- TIME HAS CEASED TO EXIST FOR US --SINCE HIS COMING!

NOW, I MUST GO! I CAN SAY NO MORE!

AMAZING! MY SILENT PROBING REVEALS HIGHLY-COMPLICATED MACHINERY INSIDE THE TYRANT'S DOMICILE!

BUT HOW-- AND WHY??

I MUST PROBE FURTHER--LAY BARE THE SECRETS OF THESE DEVICES!

"EXERCISING MY MENTAL POWERS TO THE FULLEST EXTENT, I MADE AN INCREDIBLE DISCOVERY..."

THESE, THEN, ARE THE SOURCE OF THE TYRANT'S POWER!

BUT, THEY ARE MADE OF METALS NOT FOUND ON EARTH! THE ONE WHO HOLDS THIS CITY IN HIS SWAY--IS FROM ANOTHER WORLD!

14

EVIDENTLY, THE MACHINES ENABLE THE ALIEN TO CONTROL *SELECTED MINDS* AMONG THE POPULACE--AND THESE, IN TURN, KEEP THE *OTHER* CITIZENS IN LINE!

OBVIOUSLY, THERE IS MUCH MORE TO THIS SITUATION THAN THE MERE ENSLAVEMENT OF ONE LONE VILLAGE!

"HASTILY LOCATING SOME OF THE MORE REBEL-LIOUS ELEMENTS OF THE AREA, I OUTLINED A PLAN TO THEM...

...THEN, I CAN RENDER YOUR NAMELESS MASTER *HELPLESS*--IF *YOU* WILL HELP ME STORM HIS PALACE!

AY, THAT WILL WE DO! WE HAVE LONG AWAITED A *LEADER* IN OUR STRUGGLE AGAINST THAT UNSEEN FIEND!

THAT FOREIGN DEVIL MUST NOT LEAVE THIS DWELLING *ALIVE!*

"BUT, I HAD UNDERESTIMATED THE TRUE CUNNING AND POWER OF MY RELENTLESS, VIGILANT FOE...

"FOR, EVEN AFTER I HAD MENTALLY SCREENED MY COMRADES, HE TOOK CONTROL OF THE BRAIN OF *ONE* OF THEM, AND SO...

BY MEANS YOU WOULD NOT UNDER-STAND, I HAVE LOCATED A *TUNNEL* INTO THE CASTLE! ONCE INSIDE, WE WILL OVERTHROW ANY GUARDS --AND YOUR ANCIENT HOMELAND WILL BE *FREE* AGAIN!

FREE! DARE WE *HOPE* FOR SUCH A THING?

LONG AGO, WE WERE OUR OWN MASTERS! CAN SUCH A DAY DAWN ONCE MORE?

IT CAN-- IF YOU ACT *SWIFTLY!*

NOW--I STRIKE! *DEATH* TO ALL WHO WOULD REBEL!

"THE NEXT INSTANT..."

LOOK OUT! THAT CHANDELIER-- IT'S *FALLING--!*

LUCKILY, MY MUTANT BRAIN SENSED *TREACHERY* FROM SOMEONE IN THE ROOM--NOT A MOMENT TOO SOON!

HOLD! WHAT TRAITOR'S DEED IS *THIS?*

KWAM!

BY THE ETERNAL--!

THE *MASTER* --HE *KNOWS* OF OUR PLOT AGAINST HIM!

15

I HAVE THE VILLAIN! HE SHALL MENACE US *NO MORE!*

~UHHNN~--!

THE TYRANT MUST BE AWARE OF OUR PLANS! OUR ONLY CHANCE IS TO *ACT-- NOW!*

WE SHALL FOLLOW WHERE YOU LEAD, OUTSIDER!

THEN COME-- SWIFTLY! EVEN NOW, HE MAY BE PREPARING HIS *DEFENSES!*

"AS WE APPROACHED THE TUNNEL..."

THE FOOLS! DID THEY THINK ME *IGNORANT* OF THAT CORRIDOR BENEATH THIS ANCIENT CITADEL?

THE MEREST FLICK OF A SWITCH--AND IT SHALL BECOME THEIR *TOMB!*

THAT RUMBLING--! THE *WALLS* THEM- SELVES ARE CLOSING IN ON US!

NOTHING CAN STOP THEM! WE FOLLOWED THE STRANGER-- TO OUR *DOOM!*

NO--DON'T GIVE UP! KEEP STRUGGLING-- THERE IS *STILL* A WAY--!

RRRRRRRRRRRR

I MUST HOPE AND PRAY THAT MY MUTANT BRAIN CAN LOCATE THE MACHINERY THAT MOVES THESE WALLS WITHIN *MOMENTS!*

"FORTUNATELY, THE FATES WERE WITH ME--AND, FIFTEEN ANXIOUS SECONDS LATER..."

I'VE *FOUND* IT! ALREADY, AS I RIP THESE ESSENTIAL WIRES, THE WALLS BEGIN TO OPEN AGAIN!

BUT--WAIT! THAT HISSING SOUND BEHIND ME--!

A *BALL OF FIRE*--RUSHING TOWARDS US THRU THE TUNNEL! NO PLACE TO RUN--!

YET, THERE IS STILL A *CHANCE!*

16

WHILE PROBING THIS CHAMBER A MINUTE AGO, I DETECTED A *HATCH*, PLACED--*HERE*!

THE TOWNSPEOPLE ARE MOMENTARILY ENGULFED --BUT THE FIREBALL IS *EXTINGUISHED*!

SHOOSH!

OUR FOE HAS *FAILED* AGAIN!

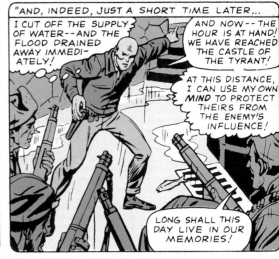

"AND, INDEED, JUST A SHORT TIME LATER...

I CUT OFF THE SUPPLY OF WATER--AND THE FLOOD DRAINED AWAY IMMEDIATELY!

AND NOW-- THE HOUR IS AT HAND! WE HAVE REACHED THE CASTLE OF THE TYRANT!

AT THIS DISTANCE, I CAN USE MY OWN *MIND* TO PROTECT THEIRS FROM THE ENEMY'S INFLUENCE!

LONG SHALL THIS DAY LIVE IN OUR MEMORIES!

"WHILE, IN ANOTHER SUBTERRANEAN SECTION OF THE PALACE..."

THE INTRUDER IS A FORMIDABLE OPPONENT! STILL, HE IS FORE-DOOMED TO *FAILURE* WHEN MATCHED AGAINST MY SUPERIOR MIGHT! NOW TO--

BEEP BEEP

--BUT WAIT -- THERE IS THE SIGNAL OF... *THE SUPREME ONE*!

AGENT ONE--OUR RELAY SYSTEMS RECORD THAT PART OF OUR EQUIPMENT ON EARTH IS *DESTROYED*! WHAT HAS HAPPENED?

AN UPRISING AMONG THE EARTHLINGS, SUPREME ONE! IT SHALL BE *CRUSHED*!

NO! TAKE NO RISKS THAT MIGHT PROVE FATAL TO OUR *CAUSE*!

YOU HAVE SPENT ENOUGH TIME IN *SECTOR "A"*! A NEW SANCTUARY HAS BEEN READIED IN *SECTOR "B"*! PROCEED THERE AT ONCE!

I HEAR-- AND OBEY, SUPREME ONE!

I SHALL *LET* THESE INSIGNIFICANT BEINGS OVERRUN THE CASTLE! BUT, THE FINAL VICTORY SHALL BE *OURS*!

"MEANWHILE, NOT FAR AWAY, I HAD PARTED FROM THE MAIN ATTACK FORCE...

THE PEOPLE HAVE TAKEN THE PALACE-- BUT THEIR FORMER TYRANT STILL ELUDES THEM!

IT IS FOR THE BEST! THEY COULD NEVER FATHOM THE TRUE NATURE OF ONE SO POWERFUL-- AND *ALIEN*!

STILL, *I* MUST FIND HIM-- CONFRONT HIM! FOR, I FEEL ALL LIFE ON *EARTH* MAY BE AT STAKE!

17

208

"THEN, ROUNDING A CORNER..."

SO! IT IS *YOU* WHO HAVE TYRANNIZED THIS CITY! WHO *ARE* YOU--AND WHERE ARE YOU *FROM*?

MY TRUE PURPOSE YOU SHALL *NEVER* KNOW --BUT, ON THIS PLANET I CALL MYSELF ...*LUCIFER!*

AND NOW--THAT NAME SHALL BE THE *FINAL* THING YOU HEAR! PREPARE TO DIE--FOR DARING TO OPPOSE THAT WHICH NO MORTAL CAN COMPREHEND!

THAT GREAT SLAB-- RELEASED FROM ABOVE AT THE TOUCH OF A SWITCH! I-- *CAN'T DODGE* --IN TIME!

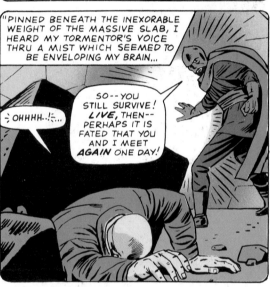

"PINNED BENEATH THE INEXORABLE WEIGHT OF THE MASSIVE SLAB, I HEARD MY TORMENTOR'S VOICE THRU A MIST WHICH SEEMED TO BE ENVELOPING MY BRAIN..."

OHHHH..!...

SO--YOU STILL SURVIVE! *LIVE*, THEN-- PERHAPS IT IS FATED THAT YOU AND I MEET *AGAIN* ONE DAY!

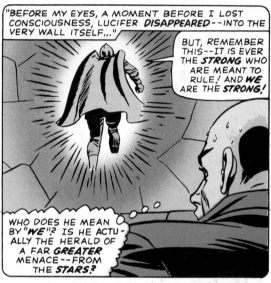

"BEFORE MY EYES, A MOMENT BEFORE I LOST CONSCIOUSNESS, LUCIFER *DISAPPEARED*--INTO THE VERY WALL ITSELF..."

BUT, REMEMBER THIS--IT IS EVER THE *STRONG* WHO ARE MEANT TO RULE! AND *WE* ARE THE *STRONG!*

WHO DOES HE MEAN BY *"WE"*? IS HE ACTU- ALLY THE HERALD OF A FAR *GREATER* MENACE--FROM THE *STARS*?

THEN, AS THE PARALYZED MENTAL MUTANT CONCLUDES HIS STARTLING NARRATION...

THEN-- *THAT* IS HOW YOU LOST THE USE OF YOUR LEGS YEARS AGO!

YES, JEAN! AND, IT IS YET *ANOTHER* REASON WHY I FOUNDED THE *X-MEN!*

FOR, I KNEW THAT ONE DAY MANKIND WOULD HAVE TO MEET THE RENEWED THREAT OF *LUCIFER!*

BUT, EVEN *XAVIER* DOES NOT FULLY REALIZE JUST HOW URGENT MANKIND'S PLIGHT TRULY *IS*! FOR, AT THIS VERY SECOND, BENEATH THE SOUTH- WESTERN DESERT...

IT IS DONE! I HAVE CONQUERED THE ONE EARTHLY MIND WHICH MIGHT HAVE DIS- COVERED MY INTENTIONS IN TIME TO *THWART* THEM!

AND NOW, THE TIME DRAWS NEAR, WHEN MY RACE SHALL FULFILL ITS MISSION--- ITS MAGNIFICENT *DESTINY!*

18

IN ASIA, I MANAGED TO EXTEND MY SWAY OVER AN ENTIRE CITY, AT *CLOSE RANGE!* BUT, MY EXPERIMENT WITH UNUS AND THE BLOB PROVES THAT *LONGER DISTANCES* ARE NOW POSSIBLE!

SOON, *NO NATION* SHALL ESCAPE THE TENTACLES OF OUR POWER! MANKIND SHALL EXIST ONLY TO SERVE *US!*

ALL IS IN READINESS! ONLY ONE STEP REMAINS --BUT THAT IS THE *GREATEST* ONE OF *ALL!*

AND SO...

SUPREME ONE, AFTER YEARS OF OBSERVATION, OF EXPERIMENTATION, AND OF WATCHFUL *WAITING*-- I CAN ANNOUNCE THAT--THE TIME HAS COME FOR *...DOMINUS!*

AT LAST! OUR RACE HAS WAITED LONG TO POSSESS THIS INCONSEQUENTIAL WORLD--FOR IT SHALL BE A STEPPING STONE TO GALAXIES AND UNIVERSES THAT CAN EASILY *DWARF* THE PALTRY *EARTH!*

THEREFORE, LET THE HUMANS AWAIT... *THE COMING OF DOMINUS!*

MEANWHILE, UNAWARE OF THE EARTH-SHATTERING EVENTS WHICH HAVE TRANSPIRED SINCE THEY LEFT WESTCHESTER, THE FUGITIVE X-MEN PREPARE TO RETURN TO THEIR UNIQUE SCHOOL....

IT'S SAFE TO VENTURE OUT NOW! IF NO ONE SEES MY *WHITE WINGS,* THE *REST* OF YOU ARE IN THE CLEAR!

BOY! I THOUGHT IT WAS *NEVER* GONNA GET DARK!

DON'T RELAX YOUR VIGILANCE, BOBBY!

UNDER THE CIRCUMSTANCES, CYCLOPS, THAT SEEMS A MOST *SUPERFLUOUS* PIECE OF ADVICE!

MAKING THEIR WAY BACK, THE FOUR MUTANTS DISCOVER...

MARVEL GIRL! WHAT HAPPENED TO THE *PROFESSOR?*

SCOTT, YOU'VE *RETURNED!* BUT, *TOO LATE!* HE WAS PARALYZED...BY *LUCIFER!*

LUCIFER? HE'S *RETURNED?!!*

WHAT ABOUT THE *PROF?* WILL HE PULL THRU?

I ...HOPE SO! HE'S GIVING ME DIRECTIONS FOR A *BEAM DISTORTER*-- FOR THE *BEAST* TO BUILD!

THEN START *RELAYING,* GIRL! AND DON'T STOP TO *BREATHE!*

FEVERISHLY, DESPERATELY, WITH MANUAL SKILLS FAR BEYOND THOSE OF MOST NON-MUTANTS, A WORRIED HANK McCOY LABORS AGAINST TIME ITSELF! AND, FINALLY...

HURRY, BEAST-- PLEASE HURRY!

THE PROFESSOR'S MENTAL MESSAGES ARE GETTING WEAKER-- ALMOST *INAUDIBLE!* IF YOU AREN'T FINISHED WITH THAT DISTORTER *SOON*--

I'M...*TRYING,* JEAN! IT'S A COMPLICATED PIECE OF MACHINERY, BUT I THINK...YES, THAT *DOES* IT!

I ONLY PRAY...THAT IT *WORKS!*

AS A TENSE SILENCE GRIPS THE X-MEN, THE DISTORTER-HELMET IS PLACED ON THEIR LEADER'S HEAD, AND, ANXIOUS SECONDS LATER...

LOOK! HE--HE'S STIRRING! IT'S *WORKING!*

HE'S GOING TO BE *ALL RIGHT!*

YES, I--THINK I WILL-- THANKS TO THE *BEAST* --AND *MARVEL GIRL!*

HE CAN *MOVE!* THE PARALYSIS IS *GONE!*

NOW, WE MUST *ACT!* THERE'S NOT A MOMENT TO LOSE!

THEN, AFTER A FAST BRIEFING---

HMM! THEN IT'S MANDATORY THAT WE *ENGAGE* LUCIFER, EH?

ANYTHING'S BETTER THAN WEARING *THIS* GADGET ANOTHER MINUTE!

QUIET, JEAN! LUCIFER ALMOST BEAT US *BEFORE!* IF HE'S STRONGER *NOW*--!

WHAT'S OUR PLAN OF *ATTACK,* PROFESSOR?

WE'LL FIX 'IM, BEASTIE!

WHILE UNDER THE INFLUENCE OF LUCIFER'S BEAM, I MANAGED TO PINPOINT ITS *SOURCE!*

OUR DESTINATION IS...THE *SOUTHWEST DESERT!*

AND SO...

AM I SLIDIN' THESE CRATES DOWN TOO *FAST* FOR YOU, JEAN?

NO, BOBBY--KEEP THEM COMING! HANK AND I CAN KEEP UP WITH YOU!

THE WAY SCOTT *SNAPPED* AT ME A WHILE AGO! HOW COULD I EVER HAVE THOUGHT HE MIGHT *CARE* FOR ME?

BEAST! YOU MAY START LOADING THE *PLANE,* NOW!

WITH ALL DELIBERATE ALACRITY, SIR!

MINUTES LATER, A SEEMINGLY SOLID WALL OF THE STATELY SCHOOL-BUILDING RISES--TO REVEAL A SLEEK PRIVATE JET, POISED MOMENTARILY BEFORE ROCKETING SKYWARD...

AS YOU KNOW, I PURCHASED THIS PLANE SEVERAL WEEKS AGO-- BUT OUR ENCOUNTERS WITH THE *SENTINELS* AND *MAGNETO* KEPT US TOO BUSY TO USE IT BEFORE!

IT'S BEEN ESPECIALLY FITTED FOR SHORT TAKE-OFFS AND LANDINGS!

YOU KNOW, BEAST, I CAN'T *WAIT* TO GET MY ICY MITTS ON LUCIFER! I DON'T *LIKE* HAVIN' PEOPLE THINK WE'RE *CROOKS!*

NOR DO I, MY FRIGID FRIEND! BUT, MORE THAN OUR *REPUTATIONS* ARE AT STAKE--IF I DEDUCE CORRECTLY!

YOU'RE RIGHT, HANK...

FOR, ALTHOUGH WE DO NOT KNOW THE PRECISE NATURE OF LUCIFER'S *MENACE* TO US...

...IT MAY WELL BE THAT *WE* SIX ARE THE EARTH'S SOLE HOPE FOR SURVIVAL!

NEXT ISSUE: THE STARTLING, SINISTER SECRET OF... *DOMINUS!*

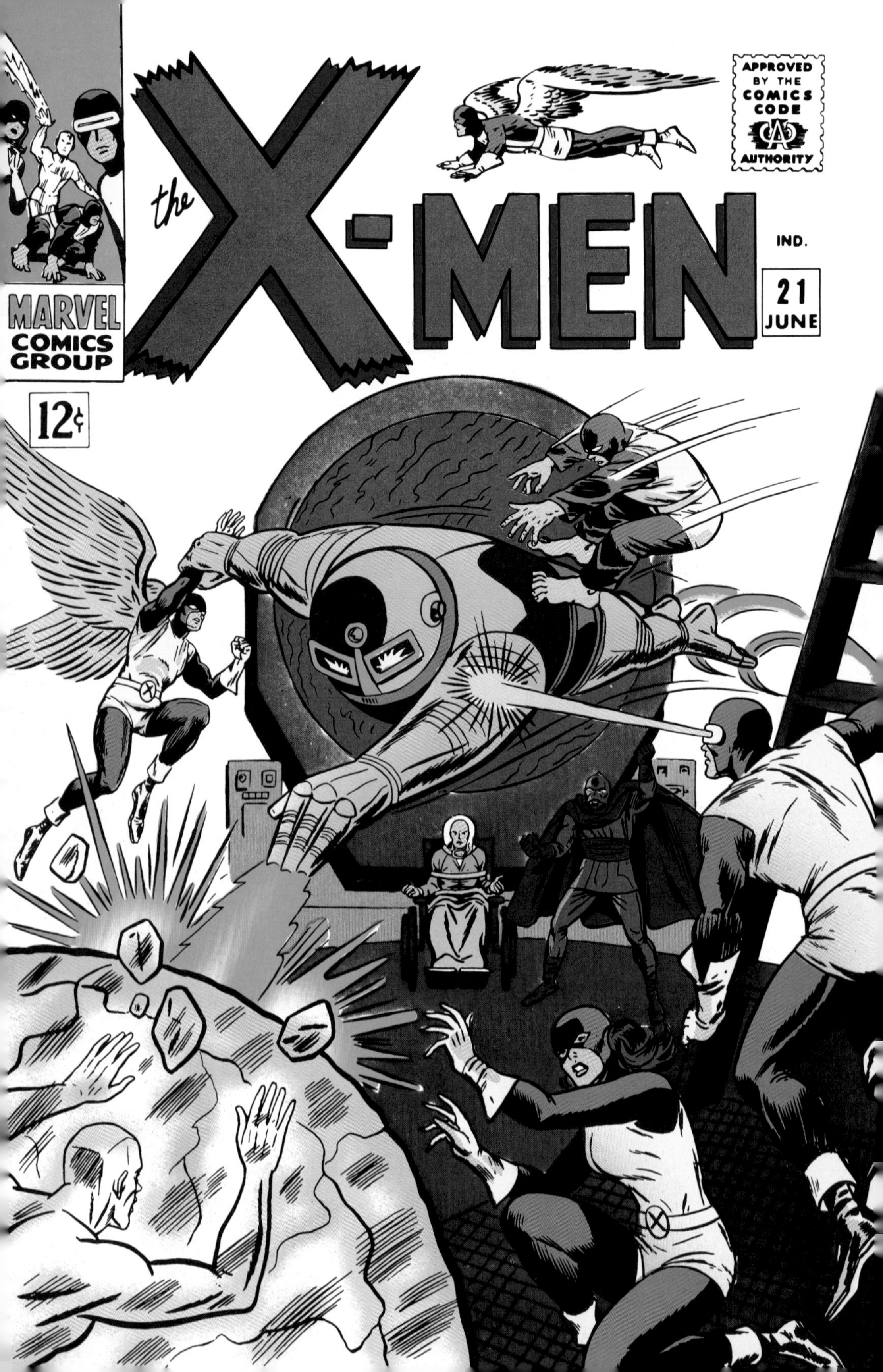
the X-MEN
MARVEL COMICS GROUP
12¢
IND.
21
JUNE
APPROVED BY THE COMICS CODE AUTHORITY

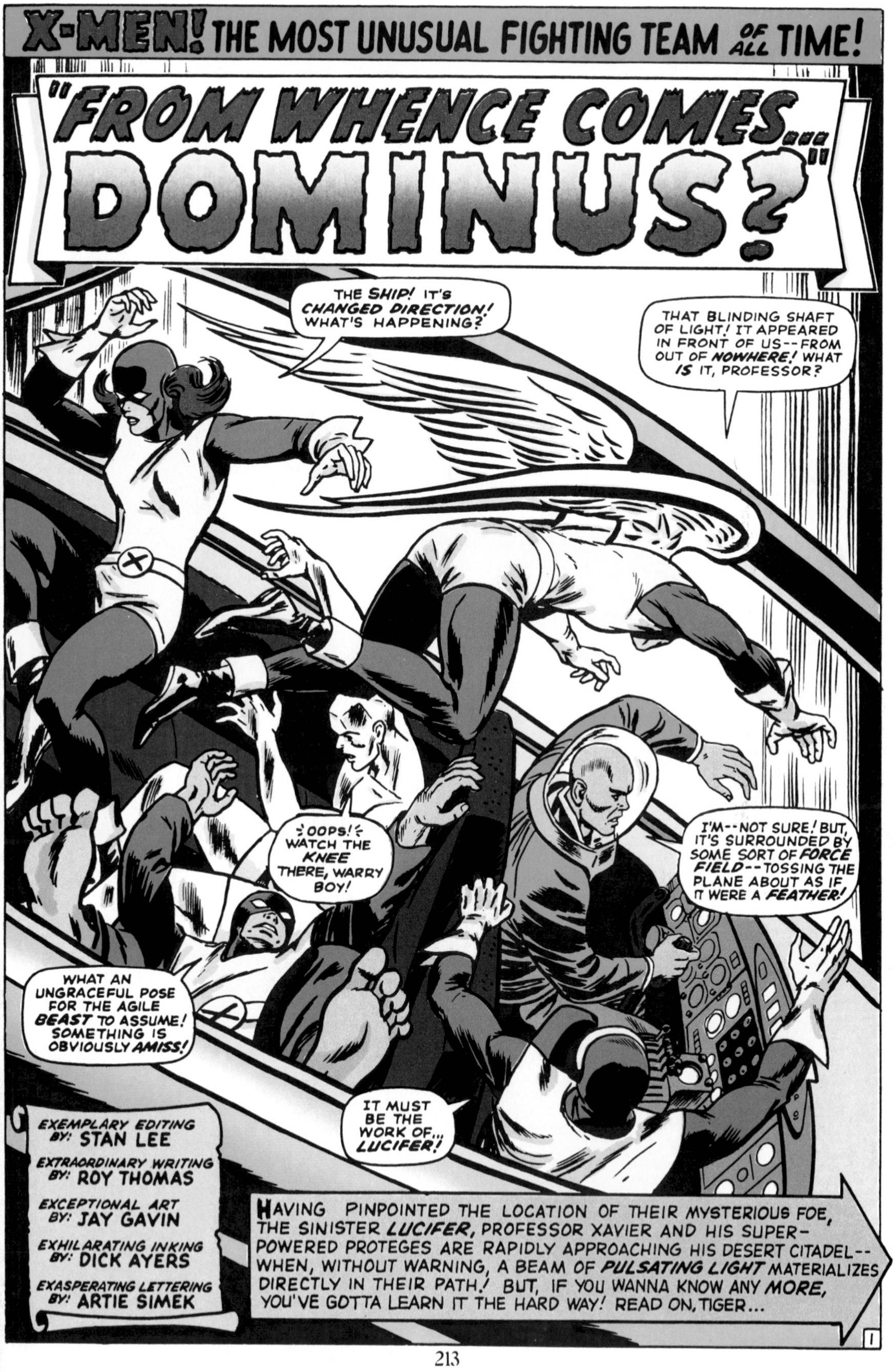
X-MEN! THE MOST UNUSUAL FIGHTING TEAM OF ALL TIME!
"FROM WHENCE COMES... DOMINUS?"
THE SHIP! IT'S CHANGED DIRECTION! WHAT'S HAPPENING?
THAT BLINDING SHAFT OF LIGHT! IT APPEARED IN FRONT OF US--FROM OUT OF NOWHERE! WHAT IS IT, PROFESSOR?
OOPS! WATCH THE KNEE THERE, WARRY BOY!
I'M--NOT SURE! BUT, IT'S SURROUNDED BY SOME SORT OF FORCE FIELD--TOSSING THE PLANE ABOUT AS IF IT WERE A FEATHER!
WHAT AN UNGRACEFUL POSE FOR THE AGILE BEAST TO ASSUME! SOMETHING IS OBVIOUSLY AMISS!
IT MUST BE THE WORK OF... LUCIFER!
EXEMPLARY EDITING BY: STAN LEE
EXTRAORDINARY WRITING BY: ROY THOMAS
EXCEPTIONAL ART BY: JAY GAVIN
EXHILARATING INKING BY: DICK AYERS
EXASPERATING LETTERING BY: ARTIE SIMEK
HAVING PINPOINTED THE LOCATION OF THEIR MYSTERIOUS FOE, THE SINISTER LUCIFER, PROFESSOR XAVIER AND HIS SUPER-POWERED PROTEGES ARE RAPIDLY APPROACHING HIS DESERT CITADEL--WHEN, WITHOUT WARNING, A BEAM OF PULSATING LIGHT MATERIALIZES DIRECTLY IN THEIR PATH! BUT, IF YOU WANNA KNOW ANY MORE, YOU'VE GOTTA LEARN IT THE HARD WAY! READ ON, TIGER...
1

THE NEXT MOMENT, AS THE PROFESSOR REGAINS CONTROL OF THE SMALL PRIVATE CRAFT, A NEW AND EVEN MORE STARTLING PHENOMENON GREETS THE EYES OF THE STUNNED MUTANTS...

LOOK! THAT BEAM SEEMS TO BE EMANATING FROM AN OPENING IN THE SKY ITSELF!

AND THAT'S NOT ALL! LOOK!

INSIDE THE SHAFT --MOVING AT INCREDIBLE SPEED-- SOME KIND OF MASSIVE SHAPES, STREAKING DOWN TOWARDS THAT BUTTE! WHAT CAN THEY BE?

BUT, NOT EVEN THE TRAINED MINDS OF THE EXTRAORDINARY X-MEN, UNDAUNTED BY THE DIREST OF THREATS, CAN HOPE TO FORESEE THE ULTIMATE, MIND-STAGGERING MENACE WHICH THESE OMINOUS FORMS PORTEND!

I HAVE NO IDEA OF THE EXACT NATURE OF THOSE SHAPES, BOBBY! BUT, THERE CAN BE NO DOUBT THAT THEY ARE RELATED TO THE THREAT WHICH THE EVIL LUCIFER POSES TO ALL MANKIND!

WHAT DO WE DO NOW, PROFESSOR? GO DOWN AND INVESTIGATE?

IN A MATTER OF MINUTES, ANGEL! BUT FIRST --DAWN IS BREAKING, AND I WANT TO OBSERVE THIS AREA BY SUNLIGHT BEFORE LANDING!

FOR, WE ARE NOW PREPARING TO ENGAGE THE ENEMY IN HIS OWN LAIR --AND IT IS ALWAYS THERE THAT HE IS MOST DANGEROUS!

MEANWHILE, NEARBY, OTHER EYES AS WELL HAVE WITNESSED THE AWESOME SIGHT!

THERE IT IS AGAIN-- THAT SAME LIGHT WE SAW LAST NIGHT!

SOMEHOW I HAD ME A HUNCH THAT WASN'T THE LAST WE'D SEE OF IT!

WHAT CAN IT BE, MR. MACK? I'VE NEVER SEEN ANYTHIN' LIKE IT BEFORE!

I DON'T KNOW, SMITH---BUT I SURE INTEND TO FIND OUT! C'MON, LET'S GO!

PORTER MACK DUDE RANCH

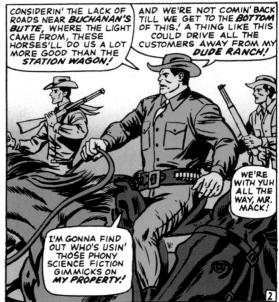

CONSIDERIN' THE LACK OF ROADS NEAR BUCHANAN'S BUTTE, WHERE THE LIGHT CAME FROM, THESE HORSES'LL DO US A LOT MORE GOOD THAN THE STATION WAGON!

AND WE'RE NOT COMIN' BACK TILL WE GET TO THE BOTTOM OF THIS! A THING LIKE THIS COULD DRIVE ALL THESE CUSTOMERS AWAY FROM MY DUDE RANCH!

I'M GONNA FIND OUT WHO'S USIN' THOSE PHONY SCIENCE FICTION GIMMICKS ON MY PROPERTY!

WE'RE WITH YUH ALL THE WAY, MR. MACK!

2

BUT, WHILE THE ANGRY DUDE RANCHER WORRIES ABOUT POSSIBLE LOSS OF BUSINESS, THE NEARBY X-MEN HAVE A FAR MORE *CRUCIAL* PROBLEM AT HAND...

THE SHAFT OF LIGHT--IT *VANISHED* JUST AS THE FIRST RAYS OF *DAWN* APPEARED! THERE'S JUST A WISP OF *SMOKE* COMING FROM THE TOP OF THAT BUTTE NOW!

THOSE ARE *OPALESCENT GASES,* JEAN! THEY ARE INTENDED, I SUSPECT, TO SHIELD SOMETHING *BENEATH* THEM FROM DETECTION FROM THE AIR!

THEREFORE, WE MUST DROP LOWER FOR A *CLOSER VIEW!*

Y'KNOW, I'M ALMOST BEGINNIN' TO THINK THAT OUR OLD BUDDY DOESN'T *WANT* US TO FIND HIM!

ON OCCASION, MY SNOWBOUND SIDEKICK, YOUR *FRIGIDITY* IS EQUALLED ONLY BY YOUR *PERSPICACITY!*

BUT, PROFESSOR, ARE YOU POSITIVE YOUR *BEAM-DISTORTER HELMET* WILL ADEQUATELY SHIELD YOU FROM POSSIBLE MENTAL ATTACK BY *LUCIFER?*

I MUST TAKE THAT *CHANCE,* HANK! LUCIFER MUST BE *STOPPED!*

PROFESSOR! I THINK I SEE OUR TICKET INTO LUCIFER'S HIDEOUT-- *DIRECTLY BELOW!*

YES, CYCLOPS --I THINK YOU'RE *RIGHT!*

I DON'T SEE ANYTHING *BELOW*-- EXCEPT A *RIVER!*

THEN...

I'LL SAY *THIS,* PROFESSOR! THIS NEW GO-BUGGY IS EVEN NIFTIER THAN MY *SPORTS CAR!*

BEASTIE BOY, DID YOU EVER NOTICE THE TINY SIGNS OF *MATERIALISM* IN WARREN'S CHARACTER?

BE KIND, LAD! BESIDES, YOU'RE BEGINNING TO SOUND LIKE *ME!*

JEAN--YOU'VE BEEN SO *SILENT!* IS ANYTHING WRONG?

WHY, NO-- OF COURSE NOT!

HE *NEVER* PAYS ANY ATTENTION TO ME--UNLESS HE THINKS THERE'S SOMETHING *WRONG!*

QUIET, EVERYONE! WE'RE LANDING NOW!

SUDDENLY...

YEESH! WHAT WAS *THAT?*

ERUPTING GEYSERS OF TREMENDOUS FORCE --AND *MAN-MADE,* I'M CERTAIN!

FOOSHHHH

FOOSHHH

IF EITHER OF THEM HAD STRUCK THE PLANE DIRECTLY, WE WOULD HAVE BEEN *DESTROYED!*

PRECISELY, ANGEL! AND IT'S THAT VERY *RIVER* WHICH, AS SCOTT OBSERVED, MAY HELP US SURPRISE OUR FOE!

NOTE HOW THE WATER BELOW FLOWS *TOWARDS* THE BUTTE--AND, NOT FAR FROM IT, DIS-APPEARS *UNDERGROUND!*

NOW I GET IT! HE'D NEED A BIG WATER SUPPLY LIKE THAT RIVER TO OPERATE THOSE *GEYSERS!*

CORRECT! AND SO, WE MAY BE ABLE TO TAKE HIM UNAWARES BY *FOLLOWING* THAT RIVER WHEN IT GOES UNDER GROUND--AND INTO THE VERY *CITADEL* OF LUCIFER!

AUTOMATIC PILOT *ON!* PREPARE FOR *HOVERCRAFT* LOWERING!

SECONDS LATER, ON A PLATEAU ABOVE THE TURBULENT RIVER...

FROM HERE ON, YOU WILL HAVE TO CARRY ON WITHOUT ME! HOWEVER, I'LL BE FOLLOWING YOUR EVERY MOVE BY *MENTAL TELE-PATHY!*

WE'LL TRY NOT TO LET YOU DOWN, SIR!

WE *MUST* CAPTURE LUCIFER --TO CLEAR OUR OWN NAMES!*

YES, WARREN! BUT, UNLESS I'M GREATLY *MISTAKEN,* THERE IS MUCH, MUCH *MORE* AT STAKE THAN MERELY THE REPUTATION OF THE *X-MEN!* SO-- BE *CAREFUL!*

I ASSURE YOU, SIR, ALL DUE CAUTION WILL BE EXERCISED!

WELL, BOBBY-- SHALL WE?

AFTER *YOU,* TWINKLE-TOES!

*LAST ISH, LUCIFER HAD *UNUS* AND THE *BLOB* FRAME OUR HAPLESS HEROES, REMEMBER? --FORGET-ME-NOT STAN!

3

WHILE YOU FOUR DESCEND, I'LL SCOUT AROUND *ABOVE!*

GANGWAY, ALL! THE *ICEMAN COMETH.*

MY *TELEKINETIC POWERS* WILL LOWER ME!

WATCH IT, *BEAST!* YOU MIGHT FALL AND *HURT* YOURSELF!

TO THINE OWN SELF BE *TRUE,* CYCLOPS!

YOU CLIMB DOWN *YOUR* WAY, AND I'LL SCRAMBLE DOWN *MINE!*

THEN, AS HE SWOOPS THROUGH THE CRISP MORNING AIR, THE HIGH-FLYING ANGEL SPIES...

OH OH! WHAT'S THIS? A *RECEPTION COMMITTEE* FROM *LUCIFER?*

AND YET--THEY DON'T LOOK LIKE THE TYPE OF GUYS THAT *HE'D* HANG AROUND WITH!

HEADS UP! IT'S ONE OF THE *X-MEN!*

I HEARD ON THE RADIO WHERE THEY'RE *WANTED,* BACK *EAST!*

GIVE 'IM A *BLAST!* MAYBE THERE'S A *REWARD!*

OH, *GREAT!* LOOKS LIKE IT'S OPEN SEASON ON *MUTANTS* AGAIN! I'D BETTER WARN THE *OTHERS!*

KRAK!

SCARE 'IM DOWN, YOU *FOOLS! HURRY!*

WE--*CAN'T,* BOSS! HE'S *TOO FAST!*

THE NEXT MOMENT, AS THE REWARD-HAPPY HORSEMEN ROUND A BEND IN THE CANYON...

IT'S THE *ANGEL*-- HE'S *WARNIN'* HIS PALS!

MARVEL GIRL! BEAST! LOOK OUT BEHIND YOU!

BUT HE'S *TOO LATE*--'CAUSE I'VE GOT THE *DROP* ON 'EM!

HANDS *UP,* YOU TWO!

BUT--WHO ARE *YOU?* AND WHY--?

THERE ARE TIMES, LADY, WHEN *QUESTIONS* HAD BEST BE PRECEDED BY *ACTION*--AND I THINK THIS IS JUST SUCH AN OCCASION!

I SUPPOSE YOU'RE RIGHT, BEAST! STILL, I WISH I KNEW WHAT WAS GOING ON!

THERE! THAT OUGHT TO KEEP *YOU* OUT OF MISCHIEF FOR A SECOND!

WH--? CAN'T *SEE!*

WHAT ARE THE *REST* OF YOU MISERABLE *COYOTES* DOIN'? *GRAB* 'EM! WHAT DO I *PAY* YOU FOR, ANYWAY?

SORRY, MISTER! YOUR MEN WOULD *LIKE* TO HELP YOU OUT, BUT THEY'VE GOT *OTHER THINGS* ON THEIR MINDS JUST NOW!

NOW, SUPPOSE THE WHOLE LOT OF YOU *CALM DOWN* FOR A SECOND, AND TELL US WHAT THIS IS ALL *ABOUT!*

FRAP!

DUCK! HE'S SPLATTERIN' *ROCKS* AT US!

4

NEXT, AS CYCLOPS TURNS HIS AWESOME RAY ON THE LEDGE ITSELF...

HELP! WE'RE FALLIN' INTO THE RIVER!

MAYBE WE'RE SAFER DOWN HERE!

WAIT! WHERE'RE YOU NO-GOODS GOIN'? COME BACK!

SORRY, MR. MACK, BUT WE GOT US SOME BUSINESS BACK IN TOWN!

SO--YER RUNNIN' OUT ON ME, EH? YER FIRED, THE WHOLE BUNCH'A YA!

THAT'S OKAY WITH US! AT LEAST, WE'RE STILL AROUND TO COLLECT UNEMPLOYMENT INSURANCE!

THEN, AS THE WATER-LOGGED WESTERNERS PULL THEMSELVES ASHORE...

LET 'EM GO! WHO NEEDS 'EM? I DIDN'T WIN THE BLUE VALLEY SHARP-SHOOTIN' CONTEST FOR NOTHIN'!

I'LL TAKE CARE'A THOSE BLASTED MUTIES BY MYSELF!

IN FACT, I THINK I'M ABOUT TO GET MY CHANCE RIGHT NOW!

WHAT A BREAK! THERE'S THE ONE CALLED ICEMAN--AND HE DOESN'T SEEM TO KNOW I'M HERE!

LOOKS LIKE YOU TOOK THE FIGHT OUT OF 'EM, CYKE! THEY'RE MOVIN' OUT!

I'LL JUST WING 'IM--AND FIND OUT WHAT THIS IS ALL ABOUT!

OH NO YOU DON'T, MISTER--!

THANKS, BUDDY--BUT WHY DIDN'T YOU LET ME HANDLE HIM?

LET'S JUST SAY I GOT TIRED OF EVERY-BODY AND HIS BROTHER TAKING POT-SHOTS AT US!

THE ANGEL! I FORGOT ABOUT HIM!

HERE'S THE LEADER OF OUR GUN-HAPPY PLAYMATES, ICEMAN! NOW, THE QUESTION IS-- WHAT DO WE DO WITH HIM?

I DEMAND YOU PUT ME DOWN, YOU CRIMINAL! I'M THE OWNER OF THIS LAND!

I DON'T KNOW WHAT YOU CROOKS ARE UP TO WITH THAT BEAM OF LIGHT OF YOURS, BUT YOU'LL NEVER GET AWAY WITH IT!

CROOKS, HUH? IT LOOKS LIKE NEWS OF THOSE NEW YORK ROBBERIES HAS SPREAD FAST!

WELL, WE CAN'T STOP TO EXPLAIN THINGS NOW! I'VE GOT AN IDEA--!

THERE! I'M SURE THE HORSE KNOWS THE WAY HOME-- AND, BY THE TIME YOU GET THERE, THE ICE WILL BE MELTED!

MEANWHILE, WE'LL BE TRYING TO SAVE YOUR SAND-COVERED SPREAD--AND MAYBE ALL OF MANKIND, TO BOOT!

HOW'LL I EVER EXPLAIN THIS TO THE BOYS BACK AT THE DUDE RANCH?

5

217

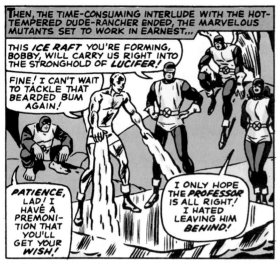

THEN, THE TIME-CONSUMING INTERLUDE WITH THE HOT-TEMPERED DUDE-RANCHER ENDED, THE MARVELOUS MUTANTS SET TO WORK IN EARNEST...

THIS *ICE RAFT* YOU'RE FORMING, BOBBY, WILL CARRY US RIGHT INTO THE STRONGHOLD OF *LUCIFER!*

FINE! I CAN'T WAIT TO *TACKLE* THAT BEARDED BUM AGAIN!

PATIENCE, LAD! I HAVE A PREMONITION THAT YOU'LL GET YOUR *WISH!*

I ONLY HOPE THE *PROFESSOR* IS ALL RIGHT! I HATED LEAVING HIM *BEHIND!*

OKAY, GROUP--IT'S *READY!* NOW TO RELAX AND LET THE *RIVER* DO THE REST!

HURRY, ALL OF YOU! WE'LL BE DRIFTING INTO THE *SWIFT CURRENT* IN A SECOND!

COMING, FEARLESS LEADER!

HMMM! SCARCELY MY CONCEPTION OF A *LUXURY CRUISER,* BUT THIS IS NO TIME TO BE *FASTIDIOUS!*

MOMENTS LATER, THE SURGING WATERS THEMSELVES BEAR THE COURAGEOUS X-MEN DOWNSTREAM...

YOU KNOW, I'D FEEL A WHOLE LOT *BETTER* ABOUT THIS WHOLE MISSION IF WE HAD SOME KIND OF IDEA ABOUT WHAT LUCIFER IS *UP* TO!

SO WOULD WE ALL, ANGEL! BUT, *WHATEVER* HIS SCHEME, WE ARE SWORN TO *COMBAT* IT!

FAR BE IT FROM THE HUMBLE *BEAST* TO INTERRUPT YOUR *RHETORICAL* REFLECTIONS, BUT WE SEEM TO BE APPROACHING THE ENTRANCE TO THE *UNDERGROUND* SEGMENT OF THE RIVER!

AND, AS THE DARK, FOREBODING WALLS OF A SUBTER-RANEAN CAVERN CLOSE MENACINGLY ABOUT THEM...

WHAT A *PLACE!* IF LUCIFER'S HIDEOUT *IS* AROUND HERE, I DON'T CARE MUCH FOR HIS *TASTE!*

YOU AND ME *BOTH,* BOBBY BOY!

AND I *CONCUR!* ONE ALMOST SUSPECTS THAT THE *CREATURE FROM THE BLACK LAGOON* IS HIS *INTERIOR DECORATOR!*

QUIET, EVERY-BODY! *LISTEN!* SOME STRANGE, MUFFLED *SOUND--*

IT SEEMS TO BE COMING FROM-- DIRECTLY *BENEATH* US!

BUT, BEFORE THE STARTLED TEEN-AGERS CAN ACT... *DISASTER!*

THE RAFT --IT'S *BREAKING UP!*

A MONSTROUS *WHIRLPOOL!* IT APPEARED *WITHOUT WARNING!*--PULLING US *DOWN!*

IT'S *LUCIFER!* HE KNOWS WE'RE HERE-- AND HE'S TRYING TO *DESTROY* US!

MOST SAGACIOUS DEDUCTION, MY FEATHERED FRIEND! THE MIND POSITIVELY *BOGGLES* AT YOUR PRODIGIOUS POWERS OF PERCEPTION!

TRY TO STAY *TOGETHER!* IT'S OUR ONLY *CHANCE!*

NOW, IF YOU'LL ADVISE US HOW TO *ESCAPE,* WE'LL ALL VOTE FOR YOU FOR *CLASS PRESIDENT!*

6

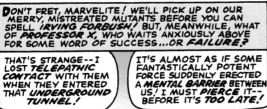

DON'T FRET, MARVELITE! WE'LL PICK UP ON OUR MERRY, MISTREATED MUTANTS BEFORE YOU CAN SPELL *IRVING FORBUSH!* BUT, MEANWHILE, WHAT OF *PROFESSOR X,* WHO WAITS ANXIOUSLY ABOVE FOR SOME WORD OF SUCCESS...OR *FAILURE?*

THAT'S STRANGE--I LOST *TELEPATHIC CONTACT* WITH THEM WHEN THEY ENTERED THAT *UNDERGROUND TUNNEL!*

IT'S ALMOST AS IF SOME FANTASTICALLY POTENT FORCE SUDDENLY ERECTED A *MENTAL BARRIER* BETWEEN US! I MUST *PIERCE* IT-- BEFORE IT'S *TOO LATE!*

THUS, COMPLETELY ABSORBED IN INTENSE CONCENTRATION, XAVIER FAILS TO DETECT TWO MASSIVE, INHUMAN FIGURES APPROACHING BEHIND HIM...

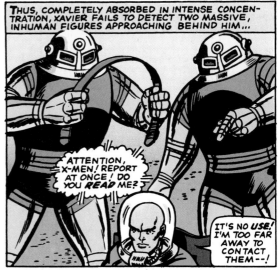

ATTENTION, X-MEN! REPORT AT ONCE! DO YOU *READ* ME?

IT'S NO *USE!* I'M TOO FAR AWAY TO CONTACT THEM--!

THE NEXT INSTANT...

ROBOTS! THEY'VE BOUND ME WITH SOME SORT OF *METAL BAND!* I CAN'T BREAK FREE--!

AND--THEY'RE IMMUNE TO MY MENTAL BLASTS! THEN--I'M *DEFENSELESS!*

SNAPP

OF COURSE! DID YOU HOPE TO CHALLENGE THE POWER OF *DOMINUS?*

COME, ROBOT *BETA!* WE SHALL BEAR THIS RELUCTANT PRIZE TO OUR MASTER!

IT SHALL BE DONE, ROBOT *ALPHA!*

PERHAPS THIS IS *BEST*--FOR ONLY IN THIS WAY COULD I GAIN ACCESS TO OUR FOE'S SANCTUM SANCTORUM!

BUT-- WHO IS *DOMINUS?*

FWOOOSH!

WE HAVE CAPTURED THE *FIRST* OF THE ONE GROUP WHICH MIGHT ENDANGER OUR PLANS! SOON, WE SHALL ENSNARE THE *OTHERS* AS WELL!

THEN, THEY ARE STILL *FREE!* PERHAPS THEY WILL BE ABLE TO FATHOM LUCIFER'S MASTER PLAN--AND STOP HIM, WHILE THERE IS STILL *TIME!*

FOR, WHILE THE BREATH OF LIFE REMAINS IN *ONE* X-MAN, LUCIFER WILL NEVER BE FREE TO PERPETRATE NEW EVIL!

BUT, BELOW, IN CAVERNS MEASURELESS TO MAN*, AN EXULTANT LUCIFER SEES THINGS QUITE *DIFFERENTLY*...

NOW, WITH MY MOST FORMIDABLE FOE A HELPLESS CAPTIVE, THERE REMAINS ONLY TO DISPOSE OF HIS MEDDLESOME TEENAGE ALLIES! THEN-- THE *VICTORY* IS *OURS!*

BUT FIRST, I MUST HASTEN TO THE MAIN CHAMBER TO GREET MY IMPLACABLE ENEMY--SO THAT I MAY FULLY *RELISH* MY LONG-AWAITED VICTORY!

*WHO SAYS THIS ISN'T THE MARVEL AGE OF QUALITY QUOTATIONS? --COLERIDGE-BUFF STAN.

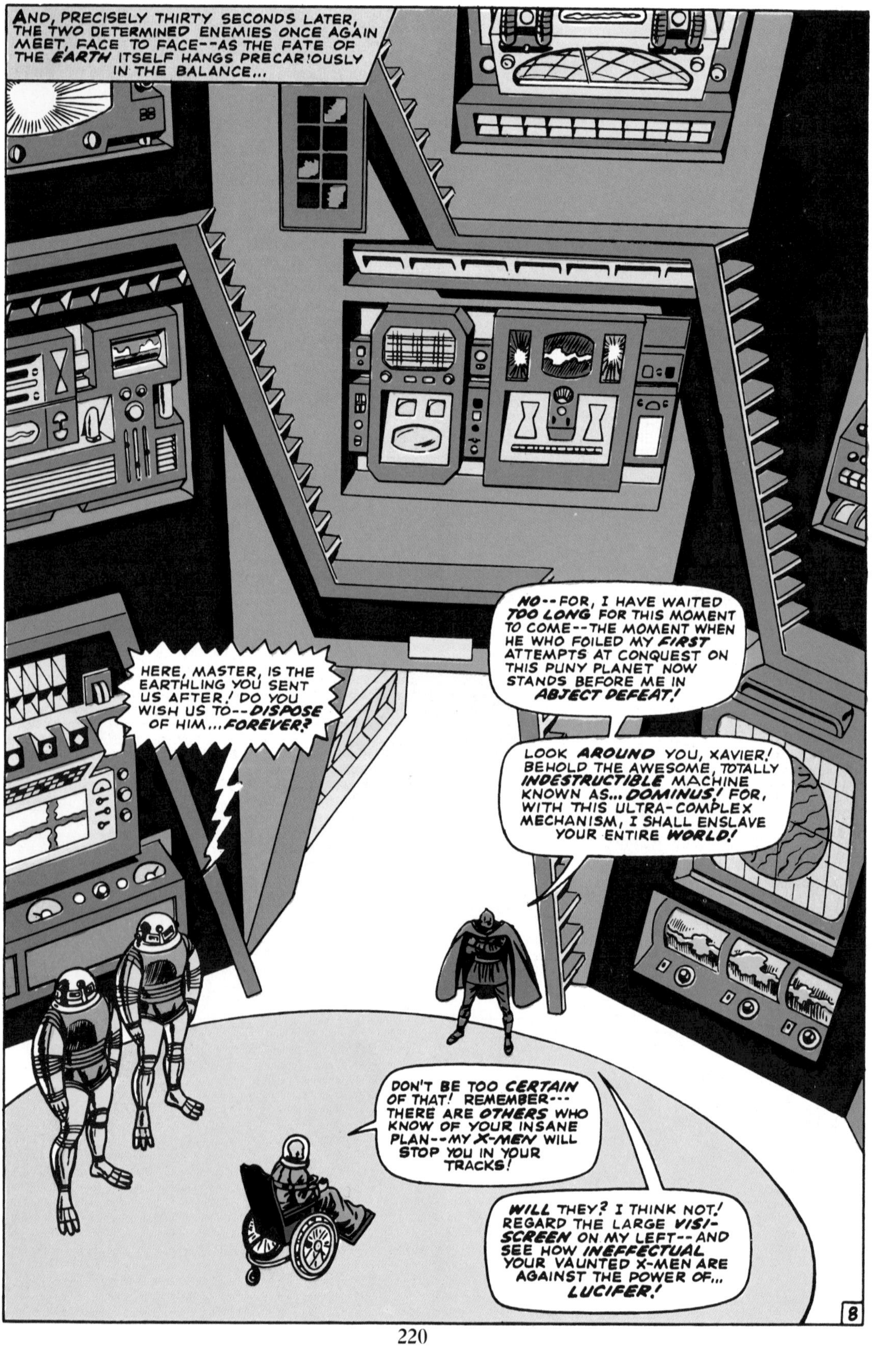
AND, PRECISELY THIRTY SECONDS LATER, THE TWO DETERMINED ENEMIES ONCE AGAIN MEET, FACE TO FACE--AS THE FATE OF THE EARTH ITSELF HANGS PRECARIOUSLY IN THE BALANCE...
HERE, MASTER, IS THE EARTHLING YOU SENT US AFTER! DO YOU WISH US TO--DISPOSE OF HIM...FOREVER?
NO--FOR, I HAVE WAITED TOO LONG FOR THIS MOMENT TO COME--THE MOMENT WHEN HE WHO FOILED MY FIRST ATTEMPTS AT CONQUEST ON THIS PUNY PLANET NOW STANDS BEFORE ME IN ABJECT DEFEAT!
LOOK AROUND YOU, XAVIER! BEHOLD THE AWESOME, TOTALLY INDESTRUCTIBLE MACHINE KNOWN AS...DOMINUS! FOR, WITH THIS ULTRA-COMPLEX MECHANISM, I SHALL ENSLAVE YOUR ENTIRE WORLD!
DON'T BE TOO CERTAIN OF THAT! REMEMBER--- THERE ARE OTHERS WHO KNOW OF YOUR INSANE PLAN--MY X-MEN WILL STOP YOU IN YOUR TRACKS!
WILL THEY? I THINK NOT! REGARD THE LARGE VISI-SCREEN ON MY LEFT--AND SEE HOW INEFFECTUAL YOUR VAUNTED X-MEN ARE AGAINST THE POWER OF... LUCIFER!
8

THEN, OBSERVING THE SCREEN INDICATED BY HIS GLOATING CAPTOR, THE PROFESSOR SEES...

I'M *SAFE!* LUCKILY, MY *WINGS* ENABLED ME TO BREAK THE WHIRLPOOL'S GRIP!

BUT--WHAT OF *MARVEL GIRL* AND THE REST? I CAN'T LET ANYTHING HAPPEN TO *THEM* --THEY'RE STILL DOWN BELOW!

THERE CAN BE ONLY *ONE* CHOICE FOR AN *X-MAN!* I MUST GO *BACK!*

NO MATTER *WHAT* DANGER LURKS BENEATH THESE SWIRLING WATERS, WE'LL FACE IT-- *TOGETHER!*

A SINGLE, MIND-RENDING SECOND THAT SEEMS AN ETERNITY--AND THEN...

MADE IT! I'M *UNDER* THE WHIRLPOOL--IN A HUGE *SUBTERRANEAN CAVERN!* FROM THE LOOKS OF ALL THESE *PIPES*, THIS MUST BE LUCIFER'S HEADQUARTERS!

AND--THERE'S *MARVEL GIRL* AND *CYCLOPS!*

HURRY, ANGEL! I--CAN'T HOLD ON--MUCH LONGER!

THERE YOU ARE--A LITTLE DAMP, BUT STILL INTACT! BUT, WHAT ABOUT *ICEMAN* AND THE *BEAST?*

THEY MUST'VE COME UP *ELSEWHERE* IN THIS CAVE! WE'VE GOT TO *FIND* THEM!

WAIT A MINUTE, *BOTH* OF YOU!

THERE'S SOME SORT OF *OPENING* RIGHT OVER THERE!

YEAH, I SEE IT, TOO! COULD IT BE THAT OUR MISSING BUDDIES GOT THERE *AHEAD* OF US? IT'S WORTH A *LOOK*-SEE, ANYWAY! C'MON, CYKE--I'LL GIVE YOU A *LIFT!*

I ONLY *PRAY* THAT NOTHING HAS *HAPPENED* TO THEM!

IF THEY'VE BEEN *HARMED,* JEAN, THERE'S NO POWER OF *EARTH* THAT WILL PROTECT LUCIFER FROM US!

HOWEVER, AS THE GRIM TRIO SET FOOT UPON THE UNDERGROUND LANDING...

IT'S A *TRAP!* SOME SORT OF *TRANSPARENT CAGE* IS CLOSING ABOUT US!

QUICK, MARVEL GIRL! USE YOUR *TELEKINETIC POWER* TO FORCE THE WALLS *BACK!*

I--*CAN'T!* THE FORCE BEHIND THEM IS *TOO GREAT!* WE'RE *CAUGHT!*

9

THEN, ABRUPTLY, OUR SCENE SWITCHES TO WHERE THE BULKY *HANK McCOY* PLOWS DESPERATELY THRU THE MURKY WATERS....

MY LUNGS ARE *BURSTING!* THE VORTEX OF THE WHIRLPOOL HURLED ME DOWN TO THE VERY *BOTTOM* OF THIS RIVER!

I MUST SURFACE *SOON*-- OR IT'S *BYE-BYE BEASTIE!*

A MOMENT LATER, THE ANTHROPOID X-MAN'S URGENT WISH IS GRANTED--OR *IS* IT?

-SPUTTER- MANY THANKS, FRIEND, FOR LENDING THE IMPERILED *BEAST* A HELPING HAND!

BUT-- *WHAT* A HAND! I STRONGLY SUSPECT I HAVE GONE FROM THE FRYING PAN INTO THE *BLAST FURNACE!*

HERE IS ONE OF THE REMAINING MUTANTS, ROBOT *GAMMA*--THE ONE KNOWN AS THE *BEAST!*

A MOST *UNGAINLY* SPECIMEN! BUT-- WHERE IS THE *OTHER* HUMAN STILL UNACCOUNTED FOR?

WHEREVER HE IS, YOU'LL NEVER LOCATE HIM!

AND, EVEN AS HANK STRUGGLES VAINLY TO FREE HIMSELF, THE *FIFTH* X-MAN ENTERS THE FRAY...

GOT TO HIT THAT OVER-SIZED GARBAGE PAIL WITH AN *ICY SURFBOARD* AT *FULL SPEED!*

OTHERWISE, THE BEAST AND I ARE *BOTH* IN HOT WATER!

I *DID* IT! THE IMPACT SENT THE ROBOT *SPRAWLING!*

BUT, WHAT ABOUT THE *OTHER* ONE?

KRAACK!

MANY THANKS, ROBERT! YOUR ARRIVAL WAS MOST PROPITIOUS, INDEED!

ALLOW *ME* TO ATTEND TO OUR OTHER CLANKING COMPEER, IF YOU WILL!

THE BIGGER THEY ARE, THE HARDER THEY *FALL*--IF YOU'LL FORGIVE THE CAPRICIOUS CLICHE!

-UHHH--!-

KLA—

I'LL TAKE YOUR *WORD* FOR IT! RIGHT NOW, LET'S MAKE OURSELVES *SCARCE*, PAL!

AS ALWAYS, LAD, OUR MINDS ARE *KINDRED SPIRITS!* LET'S RETREAT, INDEED!

10

LET'S **DEPART**, MR. DRAKE-BOY, WHILE THE DEPARTING'S **GOOD!**

THE NOBLE **BEAST** SHALL LEAD THE WAY!

I'M WITH **YOU**, MR. McCOY!

AND YET, IT ALMOST SEEMS AS IF OUR HAIRBREADTH ESCAPE WAS ACHIEVED **TOO EASILY--**

SUDDENLY...

A **METAL WALL--** DROPPING INTO PLACE!

LOOK, OUT! UHHNN--!

AND WE'RE ON A **COLLISION COURSE** WITH IT!

WHILE, IN THE VERY HEART OF LUCIFER'S SUBTERRANEAN STRONGHOLD...

OBSERVE, XAVIER, HOW **EASILY** I HAVE DISPOSED OF YOUR GROUP'S **THREAT** TO ME!

THUS SHALL YOUR ENTIRE **PLANET** FALL BEFORE THE MIGHT OF WE WHO TREAD THE **COSMOS** ITSELF!

THEN, IT'S **TRUE--**WHAT I ALWAYS **SENSED!**

LUCIFER IS AN **AGENT** OF SOME ALIEN, STAR-SPAWNED RACE!

STILL, THOUGH MY MIND CANNOT YET PIERCE THE **MENTAL SCREEN** WITH WHICH HE COMPLETELY SURROUNDS HIMSELF, PERHAPS I CAN **STILL** TRICK HIM INTO PROVIDING THE MEANS OF HIS OWN **DEFEAT!**

YOU **OVERESTIMATE** YOURSELF, LUCIFER! EARTH CANNOT BE CONQUERED BY A FEW GIMMICKS AND A HANDFUL OF ROBOTS!

SO--YOU WISH **FURTHER PROOF** OF OUR POWERS? THEN LISTEN-- WHILE I SPEAK OF **...DOMINUS!**

DOMINUS?

YES--FOR AGES NOW, MY RACE HAS PERFECTED IN **DOMINUS** A WEAPON OF INDESCRIBABLE POTENCY!

AND, THROUGH IT, THE ENTIRE **UNIVERSE** LIES WITHIN OUR REACH!

"EONS AGO, WE CREATED THE **ULTIMATE MACHINE--DOMINUS--**AS WELL AS THE COMPLEX ROBOTS NEEDED TO **OPERATE** IT...

11

"AND, WHILE YOUR *EARTH* WAS STILL A MASS OF FLOATING GASES, WE BEGAN TO EXTEND SWAY TO NEARBY WORLDS! ALWAYS THE PATTERN IS THE SAME..."

"WE ESTABLISH OUR HEAD-QUARTERS IN SECRET ON THE UNSUSPECTING PLANET, AND WHEN THE TIME IS RIPE--WE *STRIKE!*"

"SOON, YOUR WORLD--LIKE SO MANY BEFORE IT--SHALL BE BLANKETED BY RAYS DESIGNED TO TAKE AWAY THE *INDEPENDENT WILL* OF EVERYONE ON EARTH!"

IT WAS FOR THIS EXPRESS PURPOSE THAT THE IRRESISTIBLE MACHINE THAT WE CALL *DOMINUS*--AS WELL AS THE INDISPENSABLE ROBOTS THAT ALONE CAN *OPERATE* IT--WERE TELEPORTED TO EARTH THRU BEAMS OF IONIC LIGHT!

EVEN NOW, THE ROBOTS MAKE THE FINAL PREPARATIONS! SOON, YOU WILL WITNESS THE *END* OF MANKIND'S RULE ON EARTH!

YOU'RE *INSANE!* NO MERE *MACHINE* CAN POSSESS SUCH *AWESOME POWER!*

YOU STILL DO NOT BELIEVE? THEN, WATCH THIS SCREEN--AND SEE FOR *YOURSELF!*

"BEHOLD THE SCENE OF OUR *LAST* CONQUEST--A PLANET OF THE STAR *SIRIUS!* ONCE IT BOASTED A GREAT AND ADVANCED CIVILIZATION--NOW, ITS INHABITANTS SERVE US AS MERE *AUTOMATONS!*"

AND SO, WITH THAT ONCE-MIGHTY RACE NOW REDUCED TO SERVILE SLAVERY, *DOMINUS* HAS BEEN SENT *HERE!* SOON, YOUR PUNY SPHERE SHALL SHARE THE FATE OF COUNTLESS WORLDS *BEFORE* IT!

THUS IT SHALL *EVER* BE! FOR, IT IS OUR DESTINY TO *COMMAND!*

SO *THIS* IS THE *MAD* PLAN OF CONQUEST BEGUN A *DECADE* AGO--AND WHICH I HAVE ALWAYS KNOWN I WAS DESTINED TO *COMBAT!*

IF EVEN *HALF* OF WHAT HE SAYS IS *TRUE,* EARTH COULD BE IN THE GREATEST DANGER IT'S EVER KNOWN!

12

WHILE ELSEWHERE IN THE VAST UNDERGROUND COMPLEX...

IT'S NO USE--I CAN'T BREAK FREE! WHAT ABOUT *YOU*, SCOTT?

NEGATIVE! LOOKS AS IF LUCIFER HAS US RIGHT WHERE HE *WANTS* US!

MY WINGS ARE *USELESS* IN A SITUATION LIKE THIS-- BUT I MUST KEEP *TRYING!*

IF ONLY WE COULD RE-ESTABLISH MENTAL CONTACT WITH *PROFESSOR XAVIER!*

CYCLOPS, WHAT OF *ICEMAN* AND THE *BEAST?* WE HAVEN'T SEEN THEM SINCE WE WERE SEPARATED BY THAT MAN-MADE *WHIRLPOOL!*

WE CAN ONLY HOPE THAT THEY ARE STILL *FREE*--AND THAT SOMEHOW *THEY* WILL BE ABLE TO SMASH LUCIFER'S PLAN--WHATEVER IT MAY BE!

WAIT! SOMEONE'S APPROACHING-- *FAST!*

IT'S *BOBBY*--AND *HANK!* BUT, THEY'VE BEEN CAPTURED BY *GIANT ROBOTS!* WHAT ON EARTH--?

PUT THESE MORTALS INTO THE *COSMIC-CRYSTALLINE CUBE* WITH THE OTHERS!

HEAR THAT? MAYBE WE'LL GET OUR CHANCE *YET!*

CAREFUL, ANGEL! WAIT UNTIL THEY OPEN ONE SIDE OF OUR PRISON! THEN--

BUT, BEFORE THE X-MEN'S DEPUTY LEADER CAN FINISH...

-UHNNN!- WE'RE BEING HURLED *BACKWARDS!*

IT'S SOME SORT OF *INVISIBLE FORCE*--ACTIVATED AUTO-MATICALLY AS THE OPPOSITE SIDE OF THE CUBE OPENS!

WE SHOULD HAVE *KNOWN!* THEY'RE ONLY *TOYING* WITH US!

NOW TO--*HOLD!* WE ARE RECEIVING A MENTAL CALL FROM *LUCIFER!* HE DEMANDS OUR PRESENCE *AT ONCE!*

WE SHALL DEAL WITH THESE *LATER!*

THEY'RE TREATING US AS IF WE WERE MERE *CAGED ANIMALS*--TO BE DEALT WITH AT THEIR *LEISURE!*

PERHAPS THAT'S ALL WE *ARE*--TO *THEM!*

I ONLY HOPE THAT THE BEAST AND ICEMAN ARE ALL *RIGHT!* PERHAPS *TOGETHER* WE CAN MANAGE TO ESCAPE!

THEY SEEM TO BE UNHURT--ONLY *DAZED!* WHAT *HAPPENED* TO YOU TWO?

LOOK *ALIVE*, X-MEN! IT WOULD APPEAR WE'RE ABOUT TO GO ON A LITTLE *TRIP!*

I'M NOT *SURE,* BUT I FEEL LIKE THE *LINCOLN TUNNEL* COLLAPSED ON ME!

MY SENSATIONS *PRECISELY,* MY COLLOQUIAL COLLEAGUE!

13

225

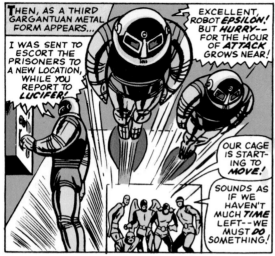

THEN, AS A THIRD GARGANTUAN METAL FORM APPEARS...

I WAS SENT TO ESCORT THE PRISONERS TO A NEW LOCATION, WHILE YOU REPORT TO *LUCIFER!*

EXCELLENT, ROBOT *EPSILON!* BUT *HURRY*-- FOR THE HOUR OF *ATTACK* GROWS NEAR!

OUR CAGE IS STARTING TO *MOVE!*

SOUNDS AS IF WE HAVEN'T MUCH *TIME* LEFT-- WE MUST *DO* SOMETHING!

JEANIE, GIRL, THE BEGINNINGS OF A *PLAN* ARE TAKING COGENT SHAPE IN MY CALCULATING CRANIUM!

COULD YOU PROJECT A MINISCULE AMOUNT OF TELEKINETIC ENERGY *THRU* OUR GLASS CAGE?

I THINK I SEE WHAT YOU HAVE IN MIND, HANK! I'LL... *TRY!*

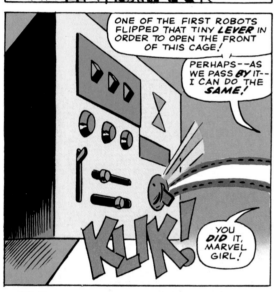

ONE OF THE FIRST ROBOTS FLIPPED THAT TINY *LEVER* IN ORDER TO OPEN THE FRONT OF THIS CAGE!

PERHAPS-- AS WE PASS *BY* IT-- I CAN DO THE *SAME!*

KLIK!

YOU *DID* IT, MARVEL GIRL!

AND, AS THE FRONT OF THE TRANSPARENT PRISON SILENTLY LOWERS...

I THINK I'VE LOCATED A *WEAK POINT* ON THE ROBOT'S BACK!

IF I'M WRONG-- WE'RE *DOOMED!*

ZAP!

GOOD OLD CYCLOPS -- ALWAYS THE VERY SOUL OF *OPTIMISM!*

YOU *GOT* HIM, SCOTT -- BUT WILL YOUR BLAST *STOP* HIM?

THE NEXT MOMENT, THE HIGH-FLYING ANGEL GETS HIS ANSWER, AS THE MONSTROUS CREATURE TOPPLES LIFELESSLY TO THE FLOOR...

HE'S DOWN FOR THE COUNT! YOU MUST HAVE *SHORT-CIRCUITED* HIM!

THIS IS NO TIME TO PAT OURSELVES ON THE BACK! WHO KNOWS HOW MANY *MORE* OF THESE THINGS ARE LURKING ABOUT?

ONE THING'S FOR SURE, CYKE-- A CHEERFUL CHARLIE YOU'RE *NOT!*

LISTEN! WE SEEM TO HAVE SOME SORT OF *ALARM!*

EEEEEE

JUST OUR LUCK! KNOCKING OUT THAT *TIN-CAN TERROR* MUST'VE DONE IT!

WHATEVER THE REASON -- WE'RE IN FOR IT *NOW!*

YOU'RE RIGHT-- AND I'VE A HUNCH THE *REST* OF THEM WON'T GIVE ME SUCH A CLEAN *SHOT* AT THEM!

EEEEEE

LET'S GO! THE BOUNDING *BEAST* SHALL LEAD THE WAY!

UNFORTUNATELY, THERE'S JUST ONE WAY WE *CAN* GO-- FORWARD, RIGHT INTO LUCIFER'S OWN *HEAD-QUARTERS!*

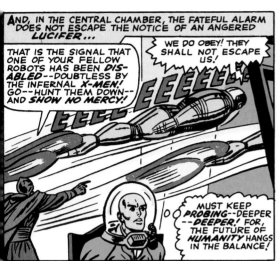

AND, IN THE CENTRAL CHAMBER, THE FATEFUL ALARM DOES NOT ESCAPE THE NOTICE OF AN ANGERED *LUCIFER*...

THAT IS THE SIGNAL THAT ONE OF YOUR *FELLOW* ROBOTS HAS BEEN *DISABLED*--DOUBTLESS BY THE INFERNAL *X-MEN!* GO--HUNT THEM DOWN-- AND *SHOW NO MERCY!*

WE DO OBEY! THEY SHALL NOT ESCAPE US!

MUST KEEP *PROBING*--DEEPER --*DEEPER!* FOR, THE FUTURE OF *HUMANITY* HANGS IN THE BALANCE!

SO, XAVIER--YOU PREFER TO PRETEND *INDIFFERENCE* TO THE FATE OF YOUR PRECIOUS MUTANTS!

THEN, KNOW *THIS*--I SHALL NO LONGER BE CONTENT MERELY TO *RECAPTURE* THEM!

THE X-MEN MUST BE *DESTROYED!*

MEANWHILE, FIVE GRIM FIGURES--TENSE BUT UNAFRAID IN THE MIDST OF MENACE--ARE APPROACHING EVER NEARER...

IT'S--*FANTASTIC!* WE SEEM TO BE WANDERING THRU *ENDLESS CORRIDORS* OF ULTRA-SCIENTIFIC MACHINERY!

ALL THAT'S MISSING IS *BORIS KARLOFF!*

HE MAY POP UP YET!

QUIET, EVERYBODY! TWO MORE *ROBOTS* --ZOOMING OUR WAY!

OUT OF SIGHT-- *QUICK!*

THEN, ALMOST BEFORE THE WARY X-MEN CAN TAKE COVER...

~WHEW!~ THOSE BABIES ARE TRAVELIN' LIKE THEY MEAN *BUSINESS!*

A MOST GRIEVOUS *UNDERSTATEMENT,* MISTER DRAKE!

WHEN DO WE STOP *HIDING*--AND START *FIGHTING?*

SOON, ANGEL-- BUT NOT *YET!*

RZOOOM

X-MEN! THIS IS *PROFESSOR XAVIER!* YOU MUST DO AS I DIRECT--WITHOUT *QUESTION!* WITHOUT *HESITATION!*

TELEPATHIC THOUGHTS-- FROM THE *PROF!*

GREAT! NOW WE'LL SEE SOME *ACTION!* WAIT'LL I GET MY HANDS ON *LUCIFER!*

WAIT! *LISTEN*-- THERE'S *MORE!*

UNDER NO CIRCUMSTANCES MUST YOU ATTEMPT TO DAMAGE THE *GIGANTIC MECHANICAL COMPLEX* WHICH IS CALLED... *DOMINUS!*

DOMINUS? SO *THAT'S* IT! THIS IMMENSE *MACHINE* ITSELF IS THE *DANGER* TO EARTH WE'RE PLEDGED TO DEFEAT, RATHER THAN THE *ROBOTS!*

CHECK, CYKE, OLD BOY! AND HERE'S A PASSAGE WHICH LOOKS LIKE IT LEADS TO THE VERY *HEART* OF THAT *MACHINE!* LET'S SCRAMBLE THRU IT AND DO SOME *TUBE-SMASHING,* WHILE WE'VE STILL GOT THE *CHANCE!*

NO, ANGEL--THAT'S JUST WHAT THE PROFESSOR SAID WE *MUSTN'T DO!* HE MUST HAVE SOME SORT OF *PLAN*--!

15

BUT, HOW DO WE KNOW THAT MENTAL COMMAND *WAS* FROM THE PROF? AFTER ALL, WE LEFT HIM ON THE *SURFACE!*

I DON'T KNOW ABOUT THE *REST* OF YOU, BUT *THIS* HIGH-FLYIN' BIRD IS GONNA HAVE A *LOOK* AT THE MENACE CALLED *DOMINUS!*

ANGEL! *WAIT!*

WARREN'S *RIGHT*, SCOTT! LUCIFER MIGHT BE SOMEHOW *DUPLICATING* THE PROFESSOR'S TELEPATHIC THOUGHTS!

ANYWAY, CYKE, WE CAN'T AFFORD TO TAKE THE *CHANCE!*

THEN, EMERGING IN THE VERY CENTER OF THE COLOSSAL SUBTERRANEAN COMPLEX, THE X-MEN SUDDENLY BEHOLD...

LUCIFER! AND *PROFESSOR X!*

THEN I WAS *RIGHT!* THE MESSAGES WERE *TRUE!*

BUT--*WERE* THEY, CYCLOPS? THE PROFESSOR'S SO STILL--SO *UNMOVING*--ALMOST AS IF HE'S UNDER LUCIFER'S *MENTAL DOMINATION!*

I MUST CONCUR, MY BIRD-LIKE BUDDY, THAT YOUR DIAGNOSIS SEEMS MOST *PROBABLE!*

THAT *MUST* BE IT! OTHERWISE, WHY WOULD HE JUST SIT THERE--STARING UNSEEINGLY AHEAD--INSTEAD OF CONTACTING US *AGAIN?*

THINK WHAT YOU *WILL*, FOOLS! NO MATTER WHAT ACTIONS YOU MAY TAKE, YOU ARE DOOMED TO *FAIL* AGAINST A SCIENCE THAT COMES FROM THE *STARS!*

DID YOU HEAR *THAT?* HE'S *GOTTA* BE REFERRING TO THIS MONSTROUS PIECE OF MACHINERY!

IT'S A *TRICK*, I TELL YOU! HE'S TRYING TO *CONFUSE* US--!

AND, IN YOUR CASE, HE *SUCCEEDED*, CHUM!

STILL, *WHAT ARE* WE GOING TO *DO?* TIME IS SO *SHORT!*

AND GETTING *SHORTER*, FEMALE! LOOK--OUR ALIEN ANTAGONIST IS SCURRYING FOR A *WEAPON!*

OH NO YOU DON'T, LUCIFER! I'LL USE YOUR OWN *CLOAK* TO STOP YOU!

CURSE YOU, MARVEL GIRL! MY *ROBOTS* WILL YET DESTROY YOU ALL!

MAYBE--AND MAYBE *NOT!* I'LL KEEP YOU SO TANGLED IN YOUR OWN CAPE THAT YOU WON'T BE ABLE TO *CALL* THEM!

AT THAT SAME INSTANT...

THAT *TEARS* IT! I'M RIPPING UP EVERYTHING I *CAN* BEFORE LUCIFER'S METALLIC ERRAND-BOYS SHOW UP!

NO--YOU *CAN'T!* THE PROFESSOR SAID THE RESULTS WOULD BE *DISASTROUS!*

BUT DISASTROUS FOR *WHO*--US, OR *LUCIFER?* SORRY, CYKE, BUT I'M WITH *ANGEL* THIS GO-ROUND!

ANGEL--COME *BACK!*

DON'T FORCE ME TO *STOP* YOU!

NO USE! HE WON'T LISTEN! THEN-- I HAVE NO *CHOICE*--!

THUS, BEFORE THE UNBELIEVING EYES OF HIS FELLOW X-MEN, THE DEPUTY LEADER *FIRES* ON THE FLYING FORM ABOVE...

--*UNHHNNN--!*

HE *DID* IT! CYCLOPS STOPPED THE ANGEL-- JUST BEFORE HE COULD REACH THOSE WIRES!

ZAK!

STUNNED --CAN'T FLY--!

I DON'T KNOW WHAT'S GOTTEN *INTO* CYCLOPS--

BUT, HERE'S WHERE I KNOCK IT *OUTTA* HIM!

OH! I CAN'T SLOW HIM *DOWN* FAST ENOUGH!

NEVER FEAR-- FOR THE *BEAST* IS HERE! BETWEEN THE *TWO* OF US, WE'LL BREAK HIS FALL!

AND, EVEN AS HANK McCOY LITHELY CATCHES THE PLUMMETING ANGEL, AN ANGRY *ICEMAN* HURLS HIS OWN FRIGID WEAPON--ONLY TO SEE...

THERE! MY *TELEKINETIC POWER* HAS DEFLECTED THAT CHUNK OF ICE!

THAP!

MARVEL GIRL! ARE YOU OUTTA YOUR *TREE?*

ARE YOU GONNA LET HIM GET AWAY WITH RAY-BEAMING THE *ANGEL?*

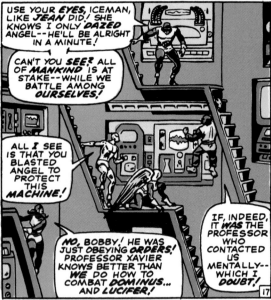

USE YOUR *EYES,* ICEMAN, LIKE *JEAN* DID! SHE KNOWS I ONLY *DAZED* ANGEL--HE'LL BE ALRIGHT IN A MINUTE!

CAN'T YOU *SEE?* ALL OF *MANKIND* IS AT STAKE--WHILE WE BATTLE AMONG *OURSELVES!*

ALL *I* SEE IS THAT YOU BLASTED ANGEL TO PROTECT THIS *MACHINE!*

NO, BOBBY! HE WAS JUST OBEYING *ORDERS!* PROFESSOR XAVIER KNOWS BETTER THAN *WE* DO HOW TO COMBAT *DOMINUS*... AND *LUCIFER!*

IF, INDEED, IT *WAS* THE PROFESSOR WHO CONTACTED US MENTALLY-- WHICH I *DOUBT!*

17

AND, FURTHERMORE, I--

WHAT'S THAT *SOUND* BEHIND ME?

BEAST! LOOK OUT! IT'S ONE OF THE *ROBOTS!*

I DIDN'T THINK IT WAS *SOUPY SALES!*

WHILE, BELOW, A MANIACAL LAUGH ARISES FROM THE THROAT OF THE FALLEN *LUCIFER*, FREE AT LAST OF MARVEL GIRL'S TELEKINETIC ATTACK...

GOOD! THE FIRST OF MY FIVE SURVIVING ROBOTS DIVES FOR THE KILL!

DESTROY THE MORTALS, ROBOT *DELTA*--AT ANY PRICE!

NOT *ONE* OF THE ACCURSED X-MEN MUST REMAIN *ALIVE!*

HOWEVER, EVEN BEFORE THE ANGERED ALIEN CAN FINISH...

SKRAK!

A NOBLE TRY, MY FRENZIED FRIEND--BUT IT'S OBVIOUS YOU DO NOT POSSESS THE AMAZING AGILITY OF NIMBLE *BEAST!*

HOLY SMOKE! THE ROBOT WAS COMPLETELY *DEMOLISHED*--AND THE MACHINE WAS *UNHARMED!*

BUT, I DON'T *UNDERSTAND!* WHY DID THE ROBOT ATTACK SO *RECKLESSLY* THAT IT WAS *DESTROYED?*

THAT'S *IT*--THE SECRET OF THE PROFESSOR'S TELEPATHIC *WARNING!* --

UH OH! SAVE IT FOR *LATER,* SCOTTY BOY! *HERE COMES ANOTHER ONE*--

--AND, IT'S HEADING STRAIGHT FOR *ANGEL!*

DUCK, WARREN!

I--CAN'T MOVE! MY WINGS-- STILL *NUMB!*

FIRST, THE HELPLESS ONE--AND THEN THE *OTHERS!*

THEN, AS TWO POWERFUL METAL HANDS REACH OUT FOR THE STRICKEN X-MAN...

ZIT!

THANKS, CYKE! YOU CAME THRU IN A *PINCH!*

THAT ALMOST MAKES ME FORGET THAT *YOU* MADE ME SUCH A VULNERABLE TARGET IN THE *FIRST* PLACE!

I--CAN'T EXPLAIN THAT *NOW,* WARREN! THAT INTENSE ENERGY-BLAST LEFT *ME* WEAK, ALSO!

YOU DON'T KNOW HOW SORRY I AM TO HEAR YOU *SAY* THAT, CYKE-- 'CAUSE HERE COME THE *REMAINING* THREE ROBOTS--MOVIN' *FAST!*

QUICKLY, BOBBY-- A *CURVED ICE SHIELD!* IT'S OUR *ONLY HOPE!*

HURRY, ANGEL!

RIGHT! EVERYBODY ON THIS PLATFORM-- *ON THE DOUBLE!*

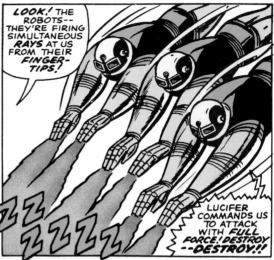

LOOK! THE ROBOTS-- THEY'RE FIRING SIMULTANEOUS *RAYS* AT US FROM THEIR *FINGER-TIPS!*

LUCIFER COMMANDS US TO ATTACK WITH *FULL FORCE! DESTROY--DESTROY!!*

THEN, ASTOUNDINGLY...

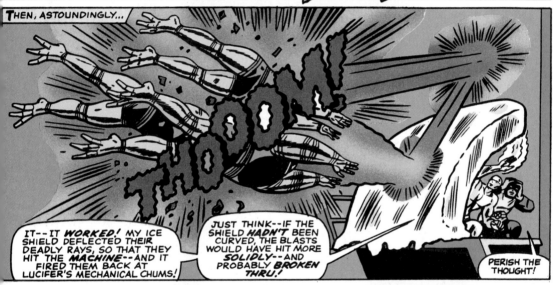

THOOOM!

IT--IT *WORKED!* MY ICE SHIELD DEFLECTED THEIR DEADLY RAYS, SO THAT THEY HIT THE *MACHINE--*AND IT FIRED THEM BACK AT LUCIFER'S MECHANICAL CHUMS!

JUST THINK--IF THE SHIELD *HADN'T* BEEN CURVED, THE BLASTS WOULD HAVE HIT MORE *SOLIDLY--*AND PROBABLY *BROKEN THRU!*

PERISH THE THOUGHT!

BELOW, FOR THE FIRST TIME SINCE THE CONFLICT BEGAN, PROFESSOR X SPEAKS...

YOUR ROBOTS ARE *FINISHED,* LUCIFER! YOUR SCHEME IS *ENDED!*

IT WAS *YOUR* DOING, XAVIER--YOU AND YOUR *ACCURSED X-MEN!* BUT, I SHALL YET LIVE TO HAVE MY *REVENGE!*

WAIT! THAT *NOISE--*THE *SUPREME ONE* CALLS!

BLEEP--BLEEP--BLEEP--BLEEP--

SLOWLY, HALTINGLY, LIKE A MAN IN A DREAM, THE DEFEATED ALIEN MOUNTS THE DAIS BEFORE A GIANT SCREEN...

AGENT ONE-- WHY HAVE THE ACTI-SIGNALS FROM THE ROBOTS *CEASED?*

IT IS BECAUSE --THEY HAVE BEEN *DEMOLISHED,* SUPREME ONE--BY AN *ADVANCED* BAND OF *EARTHLINGS!*

I HAVE NO EXCUSES-- I ONLY ASK FOR *MERCY* AT YOUR HANDS!

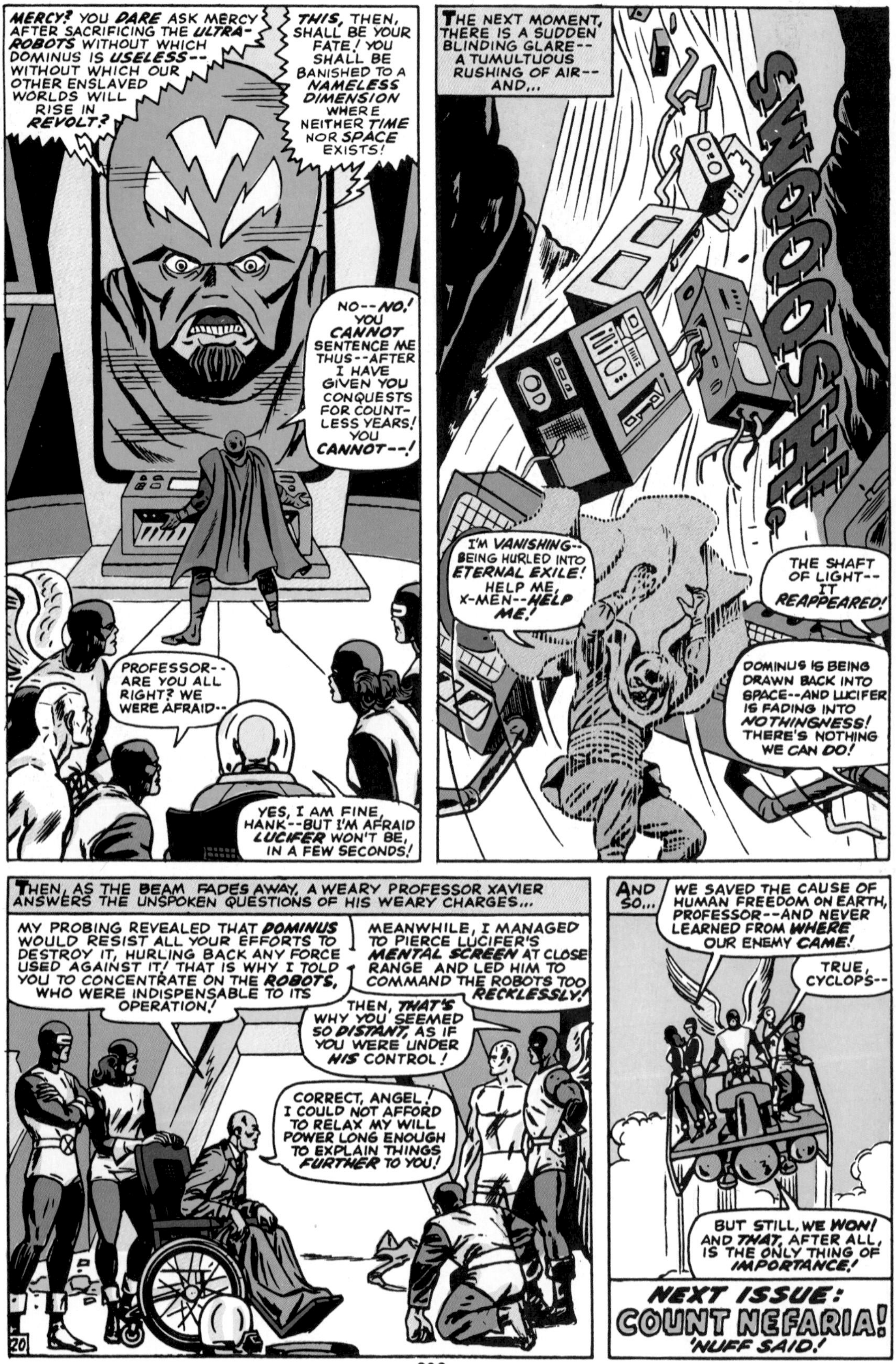
MERCY? YOU DARE ASK MERCY AFTER SACRIFICING THE ULTRA-ROBOTS WITHOUT WHICH DOMINUS IS USELESS-- WITHOUT WHICH OUR OTHER ENSLAVED WORLDS WILL RISE IN REVOLT?
THIS, THEN, SHALL BE YOUR FATE! YOU SHALL BE BANISHED TO A NAMELESS DIMENSION WHERE NEITHER TIME NOR SPACE EXISTS!
NO--NO! YOU CANNOT SENTENCE ME THUS--AFTER I HAVE GIVEN YOU CONQUESTS FOR COUNTLESS YEARS! YOU CANNOT--!
PROFESSOR--ARE YOU ALL RIGHT? WE WERE AFRAID--
YES, I AM FINE, HANK--BUT I'M AFRAID LUCIFER WON'T BE, IN A FEW SECONDS!
THE NEXT MOMENT, THERE IS A SUDDEN BLINDING GLARE--A TUMULTUOUS RUSHING OF AIR--AND...
SWOOSH!
I'M VANISHING--BEING HURLED INTO ETERNAL EXILE! HELP ME, X-MEN--HELP ME!
THE SHAFT OF LIGHT--IT REAPPEARED!
DOMINUS IS BEING DRAWN BACK INTO SPACE--AND LUCIFER IS FADING INTO NOTHINGNESS! THERE'S NOTHING WE CAN DO!
THEN, AS THE BEAM FADES AWAY, A WEARY PROFESSOR XAVIER ANSWERS THE UNSPOKEN QUESTIONS OF HIS WEARY CHARGES...
MY PROBING REVEALED THAT DOMINUS WOULD RESIST ALL YOUR EFFORTS TO DESTROY IT, HURLING BACK ANY FORCE USED AGAINST IT! THAT IS WHY I TOLD YOU TO CONCENTRATE ON THE ROBOTS, WHO WERE INDISPENSABLE TO ITS OPERATION!
MEANWHILE, I MANAGED TO PIERCE LUCIFER'S MENTAL SCREEN AT CLOSE RANGE AND LED HIM TO COMMAND THE ROBOTS TOO RECKLESSLY!
THEN, THAT'S WHY YOU SEEMED SO DISTANT, AS IF YOU WERE UNDER HIS CONTROL!
CORRECT, ANGEL! I COULD NOT AFFORD TO RELAX MY WILL POWER LONG ENOUGH TO EXPLAIN THINGS FURTHER TO YOU!
20
AND SO...
WE SAVED THE CAUSE OF HUMAN FREEDOM ON EARTH, PROFESSOR--AND NEVER LEARNED FROM WHERE OUR ENEMY CAME!
TRUE, CYCLOPS--
BUT STILL, WE WON! AND THAT, AFTER ALL, IS THE ONLY THING OF IMPORTANCE!
NEXT ISSUE:
COUNT NEFARIA!
'NUFF SAID!

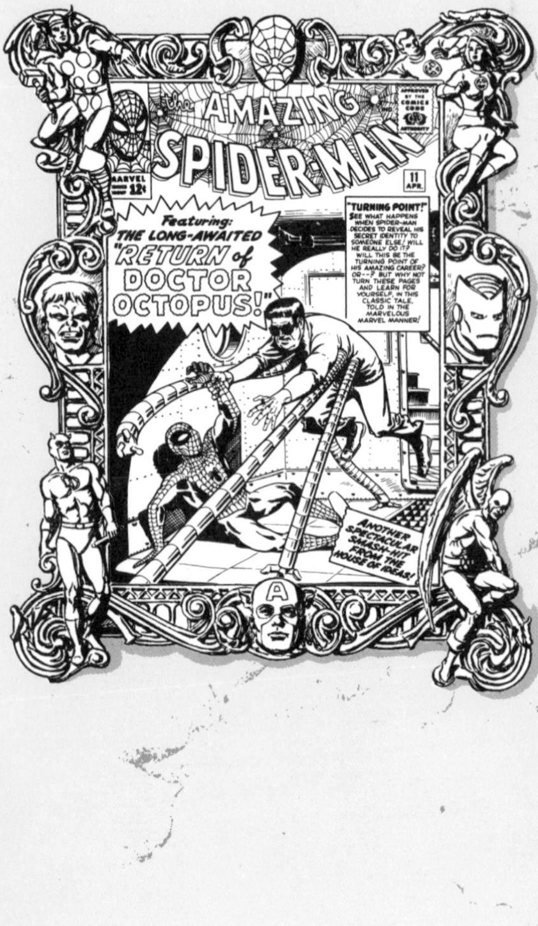
The AMAZING SPIDER-MAN
MARVEL
12¢
11 APR.
Featuring: THE LONG-AWAITED "RETURN of DOCTOR OCTOPUS!"
"TURNING POINT!" SEE WHAT HAPPENS WHEN SPIDER-MAN DECIDES TO REVEAL HIS SECRET IDENTITY TO SOMEONE ELSE! WILL HE REALLY DO IT? WILL THIS BE THE TURNING POINT OF HIS AMAZING CAREER? OR--? BUT WHY NOT TURN THESE PAGES AND LEARN FOR YOURSELF, IN THIS CLASSIC TALE, TOLD IN THE MARVELOUS MARVEL MANNER!
ANOTHER SPECTACULAR SMASH-HIT FROM THE HOUSE OF IDEAS!

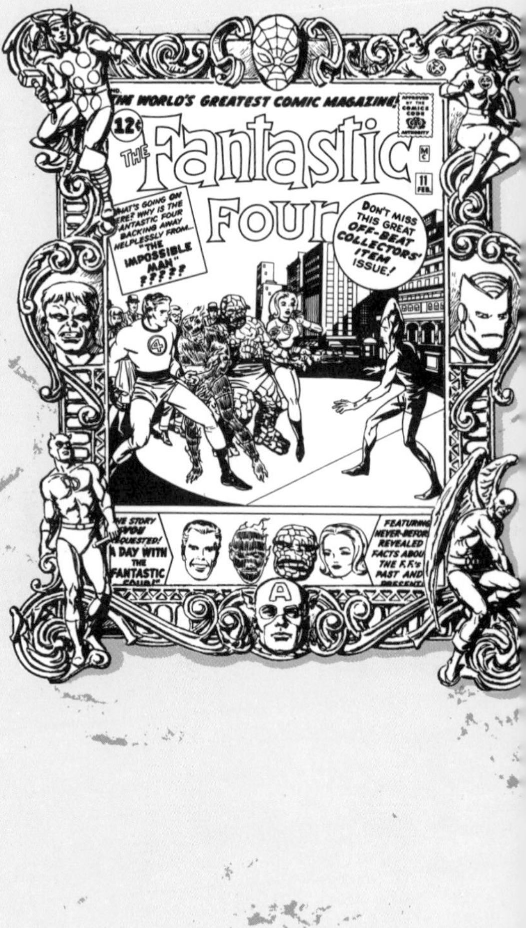
THE WORLD'S GREATEST COMIC MAGAZINE!
12¢
THE Fantastic Four
11 FEB.
"THE IMPOSSIBLE MAN" ?????
DON'T MISS THIS GREAT OFF-BEAT COLLECTORS' ITEM ISSUE!